D0151549

QIAOXIANG TIES

Studies from the
International Institute for Asian Studies

LEIDEN AND AMSTERDAM

PUBLISHED

HANI-ENGLISH, ENGLISH-HANI DICTIONARY
Paul W. Lewis and Bai Bibo

INDIA AND BEYOND
Edited by Dick van der Meij

DYNAMICS IN PACIFIC ASIA
Edited by Kurt W. Radtke, Joop A. Stam,
John Groenewegen, Leo M. van der Mey, Takuo Akiyama

NEW DEVELOPMENTS IN ASIAN STUDIES
Edited by Paul van der Velde and Alex McKay

A CONCISE HISTORY OF DUTCH MAURITIUS, 1598-1710
P.J. Moree

ASEM: A WINDOW OF OPPORTUNITY
Edited by Wim Stokhof and Paul van der Velde

ABIA SOUTH AND SOUTHEAST ASIAN
ART AND ARCHAEOLOGY INDEX
Edited by Karel R. van Kooij

QIAOXIANG TIES
Edited by Leo Douw, Cen Huang and Michael R. Godley

FORTHCOMING

NEW ASPECTS OF ASIAN STUDIES
Edited by Dick van der Meij

QIAOXIANG TIES

INTERDISCIPLINARY APPROACHES TO 'CULTURAL CAPITALISM' IN SOUTH CHINA

Edited by

LEO DOUW, CEN HUANG
AND MICHAEL R. GODLEY

KEGAN PAUL INTERNATIONAL
LONDON AND NEW YORK

in association with

INTERNATIONAL INSTITUTE FOR ASIAN STUDIES
LEIDEN AND AMSTERDAM

First published in 1999 by
Kegan Paul International
UK: P.O. Box 256, London WC1B 3SW, England
Tel: (0171) 580 5511 Fax: (0171) 436 0899
E-mail: books@keganpau.demon.co.uk
Internet: http://www.demon.co.uk/keganpaul/
USA: 562 West 113th Street, New York, NY, 10025, USA
Tel: (212) 666 1000 Fax: (212) 316 3100

Distributed by
John Wiley & Sons Ltd
Southern Cross Trading Estate
1 Oldlands Way, Bognor Regis
West Sussex, PO22 9SA, England
Tel: (01243) 779 777 Fax: (01243) 820 250

Columbia University Press
562 West 113th Street
New York, NY 10025, USA
Tel: (212) 666 1000 Fax: (212) 316 3100

© International Institute for Asian Studies 1999

Printed on Precision Fine acid-free paper
Printed in Great Britain
Jacket design by Jeremy Williams

ISBN 0-7103-0653-9

British Library Cataloguing in Publication Data
Qiaoxiang ties : interdisciplinary approaches to
'cultural capitalism' in South China. – (Studies from the
International Institute for Asian Studies, Leiden & Amsterdam)
1. Immigrants – China – Hong Kong – Social life and customs 2. Immigrants
– Taiwan – Social life and customs 3. Immigrants – Singapore – Social life
and customs 4. Chinese – Foreign countries – Social life and customs
5. Business networks – Social aspects – China 6. Social networks – Economic
aspects – China 7. Capitalism –China 8. National characteristics, Chinese
I. Douw, Leo II. Huang, Cen III. Godley, Michael R.
IV. International Institute for Asian Studies (Leiden, Netherlands)
306.3'42'0951
ISBN 0-7103-0653-9

Library of Congress Cataloging-in-Publication Data
A catalog record for this book is available
from the Library of Congress

ACKNOWLEDGEMENTS

This volume is a product of the research programme of the International Institute for Asian Studies, Leiden, entitled *International Social Organization in East and Southeast Asia: Qiaoxiang Ties during the Twentieth Century*. The programme will run from 1996-2000 (for a fuller description, please see the Appendix chapter). The book was prepared during a workshop at the International Convention of Asian Scholars, 25-8 June 1997, Noordwijker-hout, the Netherlands. The editors wish to acknowledge the enthusiastic and competent support of the IIAS staff during all the phases of the book's production. We are particularly grateful to Drs. Dick van der Meij for his unrestrained commitment in copy-editing the manuscript with the assistance of Rosemary Robson-McKillop BA (Hons.), and for the lay-out. We would like to thank the UvA-Kaartenmakers of the University of Amsterdam for compiling the map. Our gratitude also goes to the participants in the workshop whose presentations are not included in this volume, but who contributed positively to our discussions: Prof. Dai Yifeng, University of Xiamen, China; Prof. Josephine Smart, University of Calgary, Canada; and Prof. Zhang Yinglong, Jinan University, Guangzhou, China. We thank the Royal Netherlands Academy for the Arts and the Sciences (KNAW), and the Netherlands Organisation for Scientific Research (NWO) for subsidizing the travel fares of several participants to the workshop. Without the programme's funding provided by the IIAS, of course, nothing could have been achieved. We wish to express special thanks for IIAS's ample financial support to attract senior research fellows; this made possible, among other things, Michael Godley's decisive work on this book as a guest editor.

Leo M. Douw
Cen Huang
Michael R. Godley

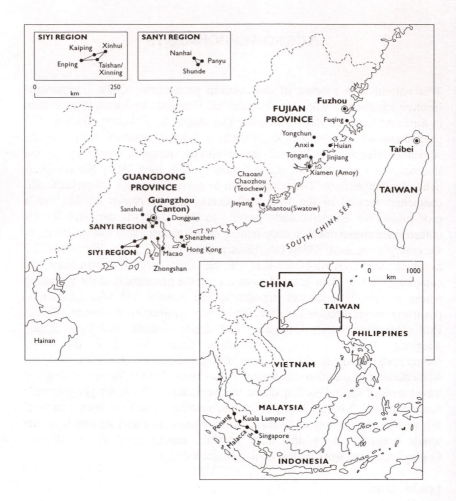

SIYI REGION

Kaiping · Xinhui
Enping · · Taishan/Xinning

SANYI REGION

Nanhai · Panyu
Shunde

0 ——— 250
km

FUJIAN PROVINCE

Fuzhou ⊙
Fuqing ·
Yongchun ·
Anxi · · Huian
Tongan · · Jinjiang
Xiamen (Amoy) ·

Taibei ⊙

TAIWAN

GUANGDONG PROVINCE

Guangzhou (Canton) ⊙
Sanshui ·
SANYI REGION
· Dongguan
· Shenzhen
Macao · · Hong Kong
SIYI REGION
Zhongshan

Chaoan/Chaozhou (Teochew)
Jieyang · · Shantou (Swatow)

SOUTH CHINA SEA

Hainan

0 ——— 1000
km

CHINA

TAIWAN

PHILIPPINES

VIETNAM

MALAYSIA

Penang ·
Malacca · · Kuala Lumpur
· Singapore

INDONESIA

CONTENTS

QIAOXIANG TIES:
'CULTURAL CAPITALISM' IN SOUTH CHINA

WANG GUNGWU

About sixty years ago, Professor Chen Da (Ta Ch'en) produced his pioneer work on Emigrant Communities in South China: A Study of Overseas Migration and Its Influence on Standards of Living and Social Change. By that time, Japanese scholars had also been publishing reports on the role that remittances sent by the Chinese in the Nanyang (Southeast Asia) were playing in the development of their home towns and villages in South China. Many other studies followed, including work done by scholars in the People's Republic of China after 1949, notably that by a group of young scholars under the leadership of Professor Lin Jinzhi of Xiamen (Amoy) University, who focused on industrial and commercial investments by overseas Chinese in Shanghai, Guangzhou, Fuzhou, Xiamen and other coastal cities.

Between 1949 and the 1980s, there were desultory studies produced from time to time that were designed to show that overseas Chinese capital, although in much smaller amounts than in the past, was still reaching Mao Zedong's China during the 1950s and early 1960s. But, with the Cultural Revolution of 1966-76, this source of funds for national and local development faded into insignificance. The question since the early 1980s is whether, following the success of Deng Xiaoping's economic reforms and the reopening of the Chinese mainland, that past involvement of overseas Chinese in China's modernization would be resumed and they would play the kind of role they had done before 1949. This has led to the larger question whether this resumption of their old ways is a function of the cultural factors at play in Chinese entrepreneurship.

The collection of essays in this volume represents a major research project that seeks systematically to explore this question. They are illuminating. They deserve to be carefully read by those who argue that so much has changed during the past fifty years that the overseas Chinese would not return to their traditional role, and by those who point to the fact that such Chinese are doing just that by restoring their contacts in well-established ways. What we have long needed are more specific examinations of the recent processes that have been established. Several papers bring out the point that, while mainland authorities have had to make use of their store of 'historical capital' to encourage the Chinese overseas to invest in their hometowns, many of the Chinese themselves use their 'historical capital', (the other side of the same coin?) to ease their way to successful investments.

The studies here highlight a major difference of approach between those who start from the aspirations of the Hong Kong and the Taiwan Chinese, as well as the Chinese overseas, and those who start from within China, from the sojourner-villages (*qiaoxiang*) themselves. From outside looking in, there are distinct differences between the application of Hong Kong capital and expertise and that of similar investments from Taiwan. And both Hong Kong and Taiwan entrepreneurs each bring with them distinct outlooks and experiences, and they also enjoy advantages when in mainland China that are different from those available to Chinese overseas who are foreign nationals living away on foreign soil. On the other hand, when studied from inside out, that is, from the point of view of the *qiaoxiang* kin groups and the officials responsible for their outside links, the differences among the three main types of external Chinese when they seek to reach back to their ancestral homes are far less important. These families and officials would be aware that they need to act differently towards each of the three types of Chinese, but when the deal is done and the investment sealed, the source of the funds would not really matter much to them.

The authors are aware of the subtleties in every *qiaoxiang* relationship and, when the essays are read with the attention they deserve, the rich textures and the several layers in the linkages extend our understanding of the current phenomenon much further than any other set of studies so far. There are many warnings not to oversimplify the issues, and not seek generalizations from incompatible outside data that have been juxtaposed by the *qiaoxiang* families and their respective local officials. These caveats add a degree of sophistication to the analyses presented here rarely seen in the flood of writings which the *qiaoxiang* phenomenon has aroused during the past decade. It gives me great pleasure to see this collection brought together and to note how it has been put into a larger perspective through the skilful introduction by Leo Douw, and how it is further helped by the impassioned plea for sensitivity in the concluding chapter by Michael Godley.

2

INTRODUCTION[1]

Leo Douw

'What ethnic Chinese from Hong Kong, Macao, and Taiwan did was to demonstrate to a skeptical world that *guanxi* connections through the same language and culture can make up for a lack in the rule of law and transparency in rules and regulations. People feel a natural empathy with those who share their physical attributes. This sense of closeness is reinforced when they also share culture and language. It makes for easy rapport and the trust that is the foundation of all business relations.' (Lee Kwan Yew, quoted in Ong and Nonini, 1997:181)

This book explores the claims, asserted by politicians in China and Southeast Asia, that cultural affinity facilitates business ventures into Mainland China launched by residents of Chinese descent in Hong Kong, Taiwan, and Southeast Asia. The economic boom which has occurred in South China over the past two decades seems to validate these claims in a highly conspicuous manner: the bulk of the foreign trade and investment in the coastal provinces of Guangdong and Fujian has come from ethnic Chinese residing abroad who have their roots in the area. The ethnic affinity required in Lee Kwan Yew's statement quoted above is obviously present, and in most cases linguistic affinity exists as well. But where does this leave the sharing of culture? At first glance the claim that cultural affinity does exist seems plausible. The business ventures of South Chinese descendants back into China can easily be represented as a return to their *Qiaoxiang*, a term understood to be translated as 'sojourner's village or hometown'. The cultivation of hometown ties is part and parcel of the Chinese culture of establishing *guanxi*, or relationships of mutual obligation between individuals, and is therefore also an inherent part of the social structure in which doing business in China is embedded at present. Moreover, ethnic Chinese communities abroad have usually preserved a distinctly Chinese cultural identity which is centred on the sharing of roots in the hometown. In looking at how the cultivation of *qiaoxiang* ties works in actual practice, our book, however, questions the plausibility of this apparent cultural affinity, even more so when the sharing of certain cultural traits is used as an explanation for business success and economic development. It is relevant to investigate from where these claims of cultural affinity originate, and to scrutinize their effects on society and politics. A few examples will be given to make these points clear to the reader.

QIAOXIANG TIES

The problems encountered by a brick factory in Yongchun, an economically backward county in Fujian province, is one example of what it means nowadays in China to cultivate ties with one's *qiaoxiang*. An interview with the managers of the factory, during a fieldwork trip in April 1997,[2] revealed that the quality of the local soil was not good enough for the competitive production of bricks, so that sales were low and the enterprise was being run at a loss. Despite this obvious drawback, it was asserted that the factory would not be closed down in the near future as it provided work to some fifty local workers, and, because Yongchun was his hometown, its Malaysian owner felt an obligation to the local community and administrators to keep the enterprise in production. The blow was cushioned because the owner had invested profitably in Fuzhou, the capital of Fujian province, and was therefore able to bear a loss in Yongchun (Interview 15 April 1997). This could lead to the conclusion that he used his hometown prestige and connections to facilitate opportunities for doing profitable business elsewhere in China. This type of relationship between the cultivation of hometown ties and business profits is not unusual. Quite the reverse in fact, in places like Yongchun, the cultivation of *qiaoxiang* ties often occurs at the intersection of the interests of the entrepreneurs and the ambitions of local officials. In the poorer districts in Guangdong and Fujian provinces, competition for foreign direct investment is fierce, and the hometown ties of overseas businessmen provide sufficient leverage to attract donations and funding for investment in public utilities and infrastructure. An enthusiastic local official in neighbouring Anxi county showed people around the rattan factory established by a Hong Kong hometown man, at the beginning of the 1980s, which served as a model for others to imitate. This official took pride in mentioning that the regulations on investment in his county easily out-competed those of nearby, economically advanced Xiamen, and were not very strict (Interview 17 April 1997). As if to illustrate this, he did not hesitate to order a soup at a banquet prepared from the local ant-eater, a species protected in China!

These examples illustrate that cultural sharing based on hometown ties implies more than just doing business alone. It also serves to connect business people to local officialdom, and therefore facilitates the negotiation of asymmetrical positions, in this case of economic versus political power. This also applies in settings other than those illustrated above. A shipping tycoon in Singapore, being a hometown man of Anxi county, is the president of the Singapore Ann Kway Huiguan (the Singapore Anxi Hometown Association), but his circle of acquaintances reaches into the very top echelons of the Beijing and Jakarta political establishments. His son is running businesses in Xiamen, in Fujian province, and how far his economic and political interests reach is anyone's guess. No doubt his world is much bigger than just Singapore and Anxi, and if he bothers about his hometown this would encompass the whole of China as much as it would Anxi. He himself emphasizes, that the capital which flows into China nowadays is international capital and cannot be fixed within the spatial dimensions covered by the hometown connection (Interview 3 April 1997). The cultural distinction implied in the use of the hometown or sojourner discourse obviously serves the interests involved in securing the entry of international, not only Chinese, capital into the economy of Mainland China.

There is another remark which should be made about cultural distinction as this is implied in the use of *qiaoxiang* ties. Apart from cementing co-operation, cultural distinction may also be used to articulate conflict among those who are supposed to share a culture. The Hongkongnese manager of a transnational enterprise in the Guangzhou Development Zone, for example, said in an interview that his approach to human resource management keeps to the middle road between the Taiwanese and Mainland styles. The same was averred by several of his colleagues in Malaysian-owned enterprises (Interviews 9-12 April 1997). The Taiwanese style was outspokenly unpopular at that time among managers with a mainland background, because it had allegedly taken on too much of a military garb. Taiwanese managers, in their turn, denigrated their workers' mentality, branding it typical of Mainland attitudes, namely, lax and undisciplined (see also Chan, 1998). The chapters in this book provide other examples which confirm that *qiaoxiang* ties and a shared Chinese identity do not imply a homogeneous cultural pattern, including automatic agreement on the handling of business and the management of enterprises. Instead, cultural idioms and discourses are used to articulate patterns of both co-operation and conflict, and people may play around, juggling the variety of identities that may be ascribed to them. Alan and Josephine Smart recount the experiences of the businessman Robert Chan whose ceramics company is established in Hong Kong but produces in the Special Economic Zone of Shenzhen, in Guangdong province, and sells mostly in North America. Depending on the situation, Robert uses one among the variety of identities which he has compiled in

5

the course of his life: Manchurian, overseas Chinese, Hong Kong Chinese, or dumb foreigner (from his Canadian citizenship) (Smart and Smart, 1998:117-18). These examples illustrate the insufficiency of an analysis which ascribes ethnic Chinese business success to the presence of cultural affinity. It would be truer to say that claims of cultural affinity are part of a more general discourse which starts from culture and identity as useful concepts for social analysis. Academic study should address multiple or hybrid identities at least as seriously as it does shared identities, and open up a perspective in which the emergence of culture-related discourses may be fruitfully linked to broader processes of social change. Cultural affinity is not the central issue in this inquiry; this is the *claim* that cultural affinity works to the benefit of business, the economy, and society.

CULTURAL CAPITALISM

The term cultural capitalism has been concocted by the editors in order to open up a problem that has attracted intense scholarly interest and controversy. Since the 1980s, the overriding emphasis in academic debate, on problems of culture and identity, if not race, brings up the question of how these recent uses of culture have been connected to the global spread of capitalism over the past few decades. In this case, does a peculiar Chinese-style capitalism exist? And if so, in how far does it contribute to economic development? (see also Brook and Luong, 1997; Hefner, 1998a; Redding, 1993). The issues involved have since long begun to transform classical overseas Chinese studies from a field of enquiry dominated by history into one which is visited just as frequently by anthropologists, political scientists, sociologists, and linguists (See Salmon, 1981). It is the purpose of our book to bring several of the relevant disciplines together in order to highlight the multiplicity of aspects which come into play in any attempt to understand how the cultivation of *qiaoxiang* ties works out in actual practice.

There are several challenges involved. The first is to understand what transnationalism is about. In this context, this term is generally understood to be the tendency for emigrant communities to unite on a common programme for action in order to build up multiple links with the mother country. The term 'transnation' is sometimes used in this sense, suggesting parallels with the nation and nationalism (Appadurai, 1991; Tölölyan, 1996; Basch et al., 1995; Smith and Guarnizo, 1998; Duara, 1997, 1998). Shared roots and claims of a shared culture provide the cement which binds the transnational communities together, and not only in the Chinese case. At the same time it is obvious that the concept of transnations encourages multiple or hybrid identities among its members. Transnationalism can only exist because of the participation of its members in societies and states which are separated by national borders. The term 'diaspora' has also changed its meaning somewhat in order to serve contemporary needs. Its use is no longer limited to being a catchword for migrants and refugees who have been forced to disperse because of the tragic loss of their mother country, but has now been reversed and taken on the meaning of an array of new opportunities for unity among the dispersed communities and their home basis (Tölölyan, 1996; Basch et al. 1995; Cohen, 1997; Reid, 1997: 36).

Anyone who attaches importance to economic development and cares about what diasporas or transnations might contribute to the wealth and well-being of future societies should also ask about the commitment of transnational constituencies to the public cause. In point of fact the new formations have been evaluated very differently. The pioneering work on the cultural politics of Chinese transnationalism by Aihwa Ong and Donald Nonini (1997) vilifies the present-day Chinese diaspora as 'ungrounded empires' ruled by big ethnic Chinese entrepreneurs in collusion with the political establishments of East and Southeast Asia, and presumably elsewhere, in the suppression of democratic claims and the sharing of business profits. Benedict Anderson has coined the term long-distance nationalism in order to pin down the loyalty 'without responsibility or accountability' (1992:11) of rich emigrant businessmen who support political movements in their home country. Other academics stress the inevitability of the existence of these new formations, and some of them would support the claims to their cultural cohesion made by politicians in the regions where they achieve a measure of success (Kahn, 1979; Redding, 1993; Wong, 1996). Most academic work suggests that new 'imagined communities' (Anderson, 1991) are emerging which live in a sometimes uneasy, but mostly dynamic interaction with the representatives of the established nation-states, and even critical reviews suggest that they might contain a potential for progressive social change. But no straightforward indicators for their transformative potential exist as yet. This is because it is not very clear how these formations interact with the national states which encompass them, how internally fragmented they are, and how far their influence in the wider emigrant communities reaches. All these issues have to do with the questions of cultural identity raised above: how does the existence of multiple or hybrid identity, so pertinent to the emergence of diasporas and transnations as defined here relate to common action for the common good by their membership? In order to answer these questions it should also be more clearly revealed under which conditions these formations could emerge at all, and subsequently attain a measure of success.

This is a second major challenge confronting those who study *qiaoxiang* ties and how their cultivation may be linked up with economic development. Cultural issues should be seen in the context of the stage at which present-day capitalism finds itself. Chinese transnationalism has its counterparts in the rest of the world, and has a history which dates back to the late nineteenth century. It cannot be studied satisfactorily in spatial and temporal isolation, a point which will be more closely argued in the next chapter. We have focused on how culture relates to the various aspects of business organization, in particular the extension of business organization across national borders: what is the role of hometown ties in establishing links among ethnic Chinese business communities outside China for the purpose of collective action? How does the Chinese bureaucracy play on hometown sentiments in order to attract foreign investment? Does cultural affinity play any role in the choice of locations for investment in Mainland China, or in the recruitment and management of labour? In answering these questions, what is being scrutinized is the cultural glue which causes the actors in transnational business to adhere together, not so much the broader question of how cultural discourses have come into being, and how they relate to economic development. Nevertheless, the materials presented in most of the chapters in our book do relate in many ways to these more encompassing questions; the chapters by Alan Smart and Michael Godley treat major aspects of them. For these reasons it is inevitable that this introduction pay attention to the spread of capitalism as a global process, with its roots in history, and how, in recent academic studies, this is being connected to the issue of cultural affinity.

The basic question to be addressed here is: is it necessary to distinguish between local varieties of capitalism on the basis of their cultural differences, in order to understand economic development? In other words: is there any use for the category of 'cultural capitalism', created by the editors, which sums up concepts in the academic literature such as Chinese capitalism, Chinese business networks, and Chinese diaspora capital? In addition to the argument which does attach a distinctive meaning to these concepts, at the risk of over-simplication I shall sketch its two major alternatives. The first of these is the argument which places primary importance on the market. The second is the one which emphasizes the role played by political power in economic development. Adopting the set-up of two outstanding summaries of the same topic (McVey, 1992; Biggart, 1997), I shall indicate the main uses but also the main problems of each of these arguments from our perspective, and how the contributions to our volume fit into the ongoing discussions.

The cultural argument maintains that the predominant norms and values of a society, and the concomitantly institutions based upon them, do have a decisive impact on economic development and the emergence of capitalism. Until the 1980s, it was generally believed by those adhering to this argument, that the so-called Third World societies were not capable of venturing into capitalist development, unless they changed to Western norms and values. After the Second World War, the US-based modernization school, elaborated on the writings of Max Weber and Emile Durkheim in their attempts to bear out this view. Thrift and diligence, and a measure of asceticism, were considered to be important values in stimulating the pursuit of wealth; individualism, personal trustworthiness and risk-taking, combined into competitive entrepreneurship were considered as crucial to the viability of free market institutions. Democratic political institutions embodied and protected these institutions, among which written contracts and private property were accorded a sacrosanct legal status. This view of modernization was replaced during the 1980s by other neo-Weberian approaches, but, during the 1990s have regained some of its previous high ground in academic discussions in the writings of Fukuyama (1992, 1995), Huntington (1996), and Landes (1998).

The late 1970s witnessed the rise of a different type of neo-Weberian approach. It was argued that non-Western societies possessed norms, values, and their concomitant institutions, which could serve as the functional equivalents to their Western counterparts, and make possible the development of capitalism. This opened the road for the acknowledgement that many paths towards modernity are viable (see also Alan Smart's chapter in this book). The functions of the Western norms and institutions mentioned above in the large-scale accumulation of capital were matched by the *chaebols* in Korea, the Japanese *keiretsu*, and the Chinese family. As Michael Godley argues in his essay, 'wealth-producing ideologies' of different types emerged which had effects similar to Max Weber's *innerweltliche Askese*. In this approach, the globalization of free market institutions is limited by the cultural constraints which each society forces upon them when they are adopted. Cultural distinction is, therefore, indispensable to the analysis of capitalist development.

The neo-Weberian approach is important because it pays due attention to the necessity to take account of norms and values in the organization of business life and, thereby, economic development. The contributions to our book by Hong Liu, Elizabeth Sinn, and Joseph Cheng and King-lun Ngok attest to the effectiveness of cultural appeals in the organization of Chinese business life and its global expansion. From our perspective the major drawback to this argument is that it may neglect the importance of interactions between actors from different cultural backgrounds in situations which are dynamic, as they are at the present day, exactly because markets mechanisms are being given more ample scope to work for the common good, and have begun to change social relationships. There are solid political reasons to be very cautious about cultural assertions of the Chineseness type, as Michael Godley warns in his contributions to this volume: reifications and essentializations which suggest too large a measure of durability, consistency, and homogeneity in cultural formations, may be conducive to a dangerous and violent 'clash of civilizations' in Huntington's sense. Below we shall consider how both the alternative explanations of economic development avoid or ignore these problems. Nevertheless, cultural explanations may have a use from the scientific point of view, when shared norms and values, which are supposed to be broadly shared in society by those theories, are considered as claims to cultural affinity, rather than entities which actually exist and how these claims are used by those who act upon them is examined. Among our contributors, Stephanie Chung makes it clear how important material interests were in the motives of the Siyi businessmen, during the early twentieth century, to act upon the appeals to their status as Chinese sojourners by the Qing Court and the Canton Government. Isabelle Thireau and Linshan Hua, and Khun Eng Kuah describe how cultural practice has helped to bring ethnic Chinese people from the vastly different societies of Hong Kong, Singapore and Mainland China together, and in doing so, facilitated business investment.

One major alternative to culture as the ultimate determinant of the economic order is the working of the free market, as this is enshrined in classical and neo-classical economics. The adherents to this school of thought believe that the free operation of market forces leads to optimal results for the largest number of people. In this approach, specific cultures may constrain or facilitate the free operation of market forces, but in both cases this is considered to be marginal to the analysis of the economic order. It is precisely this impersonal character of markets which makes them a useful, objective mechanism for rational economic decision-making by independent, profit-optimizing economic actors.

From this viewpoint, the global spread of free markets is the best guarantee of human progress, and is therefore the logical outcome of world history. The optimism about the potential for social progress which underlies free market thinking and its compelling logic have made it into an indispensable part of economic thought, if not its centrepiece. In this context, globalization, may be defined as the emergence, since the 1970s, of a new economic order, which comprises a global division of labour based on rapidly changing consumer demands and flexible production. This new order is helped by the strengthening and spreading of capitalism and free market institutions. Capital and labour are consciously set in motion in order to achieve optimal rates of economic growth. The importance of globalization in this sense for present-day economic life is obvious. Among our authors, Alan Smart, Isabelle Thireau, and David Schak underwrite the importance of rational market behaviour above, or alongside cultural factors, in the entrance of capital into new environments. However, the paramountcy of the market factor over the others, in economic development, is not so obvious. In a watershed article, Mark Granovetter has introduced the concept of embeddedness in order to argue that neither culture, in the sense of commonly shared norms and values, nor the top-down enforcement of rules and regulations can conjure up market behaviour and institutions as this was envisaged by neo-classical economists (1985). This is so because the latter conceive of economic actors as isolated individuals. If markets are to function properly, they must be embedded in social relations, such as business networks. This idea has exerted a definite influence on the study of Chinese business networks (see Hamilton, 1997, 1998; Hefner, 1998a, b), and on the thinking of Chinese economists. The ignorance of cultural factors, by the advocates of free market institutions, in determining economic choice, is matched by their ignorance of social and political factors.

The decisive impact of political power on the economic order is central to the argument of political economy approaches. Among these, we can make a distinction between those which allow culture a substantive role in the process of globalization; in this sense they resemble the cultural approaches, and those which conceive of culture as an instrument for the protection of material and political interests. Examples of the latter are the argument that cultural discourses such as Chineseness and Asian values justify harsh regimes of labour management (Chan, 1997), and the exploitation of family labour in the new order of flexible production (Dirlik, 1996). Cultural discourses are enacted by the parties which have an interest in maintaining this type of labour regimes, namely the entrepreneurs who run transnational enterprises, and the governments which facilitate their establishment. The substantivist answer is that the development of free markets may ultimately lead up to a society dominated by greed, selfishness, and appalling social inequity. Karl Polanyi is the founding father of the thought that 'capitalism' penetrates hitherto untouched and more harmonious societies, which have no choice but to react by asserting their own cultural identity, and creating a reactive culturalism (Mittelman, 1996b:232; Hefner, 1998b:8-11). China's visions of its own unique path to development, elucidated in Michael Godley's contribution below, may be taken as one variety of Polanyism, in as far as they consider capitalism as a creed alien to China's cultural heritage. The amorality of a marketplace working on impersonal principles, which dominates this vision, legitimates state action in curbing the influence of commodification processes and in this manner ascribes, from a perspective different from that followed in the neo-Weberian approaches, substantial meaning to social values and attitudes, or culture. This approach entails the alternative possibility, that globalization has an emancipatory function, namely for those groups which profit immediately from their enhanced position in the market (Mittelman, 1998b).

The main advantage of political economy approaches from our perspective is, that they articulate the active role of political actors, such as state governments, in the production of cultural discourses, and also in the regulation of the market. This point will be elaborated on below in the next chapter, on the production and functions of the Chinese sojourner discourse. In doing so, the chapter anticipates the findings of the other chapters, providing an additional context for them; the chapters by Isabelle Thireau and Linshan Hua, and Alan Smart have been an important inspiration for its argument. The chapter speculates on the role of culture as a facilitator of economic development, in the sense that it provides a language and rituals for the negotiation of new social and political relations. Cultural discourses apparently flower in those phases of the globalization process in which established social positions in the societies touched by it are being systematically and consciously undermined. Such a position acknowledges different positions within, and attitudes towards these discourses, depending on differences in power and function of those involved in them. Strong groups may impose the new rules of the game upon weak ones, strong states impose them upon weak states, but all have a certain space to negotiate on how to play. Maybe most importantly if one looks at the claims by the neo-Weberians and other modernizationists, this approach stresses the principal flexibility and changeability of culture, and questions the essentializations which go of necessity with claims of cultural affinity. It would also, by the way, make the question of whether transnationalism emanates 'from below' or 'from above' somewhat redundant (cf. Smith and Guarnizo, 1998): it is essential in this hypothesis that culture facilitates interactions between all involved actors, so that all have their part to play.

This touches on the question raised above of which role the social sciences may play in analysing Chinese transnationalism and how its imagery could be transmuted into an acceptable social doctrine. Exactly because it is generally assumed that the prevailing trend of globalization will continue for some time to come, the solution for latent social problems are sought in the political, moral, and ideological transformations of transnational organizations, polities, and constituencies. This is the reason that in a number of recent studies there is a sense of durability attached to the newly emerging transnations, and their discourses and imagery are being tested upon their democratic potential (Tölölyan, 1996; Ong and Nonini, 1997; Smith and Guarnizo, 1998). The central question here is, however, whether or not transnational connections as they exist at this moment would collapse, or be diffused, or indeed change progressively, when the growth potential of the ongoing globalization will have been fulfilled, or, as actually seems to be happening nowadays, erupts into a crisis. History has to be studied in order to answer the question. Talking about durability and change, history may provide examples of how earlier forms of transnationalism were affected by economic factors. This requires a careful consideration, of course, of the changes through which the global economy has passed, particularly since the successive industrial revolutions, beginning at the dawn of the nineteenth century, began to integrate the world economy in a way different to that in the earlier past. The revolution in the technology of communications which made the new imperialism of the late-nineteenth century possible, was very different from that which has been taking place since the 1970s. Nevertheless, taking history in a broad perspective, the long-term development has been towards increasing integration and the quickening of the pace of communications. Acknowledging this makes it more interesting to consider the setbacks in the long-term trend caused by economic crises, the World Economic Crisis of the 1930s foremost among them. The question of how long national states, particularly powerful ones, would be prepared to let globalization go its own way, and which answers the business elites which play such a dynamic role in transnational organization may provide to the irruption of crisis and disruption, has become relevant again.

The empirical study of *qiaoxiang* ties dynamics, therefore, should be concerned with the question of how transnations, or diasporic communities, come about, how they work on a day-to-day basis, and how they relate to the existing political formations which they are supposed to supplement, or, depending on the perspective taken, are in the process of transforming or replacing. The acquisition of a long-term perspective on their emergence is imperative, as is solid fieldwork on how people link up to them and use them for the advancement of their interests. The following chapter, which just as the present one has an introductory character, represents an attempt to look at transnationalism as a global, long-term phenomenon, and thereby place the Chinese case in a proper perspective.

In sum, our book as a whole contains elements of all the three approaches of economic development summarized above; several chapters analyse the uses of *qiaoxiang* ties as part of a cultural discourse which facilitates economic development. Even though the individual contributors may disagree with the approach of this problem area by Ong and Nonini (1997), our book accords most appositely with their programmatic statement, that:

'(T)he dynamic tension between the diversity of subjects, cultures, and identities, on the one hand, and the homogenizing ideologies of Chinese and cultural essences, on the other, holds the key to our understanding of identity-making in the new Asia. The synergy between flexible accumulation and mass markets has produced transnational publics in Asia in which essentializing symbols - of Chinese culture, capitalism, and other values - are absorbed, negotiated, deflected, mocked, or contested. ... Contemporary publics in Asia are not apolitical arenas but are thoroughly infused with the cultural politics of transnational capitalism. Identity formation is increasingly shaped by the struggles between dominant publics and counterpublics, heavily influenced by transnational markets, media, and capital.' (Ong and Nonini, 1997:329-30)

The findings in our book mostly pertain to the period before the onset of the present economic crisis in East and Southeast Asia; it may need a thorough reassessment within short. But the world has always changed quickly. Therefore, we maintain a good hope that the essays presented here will serve to further dynamize and develop the discussions on the acutely important issues summarized above.

THE BOOK; A MULTIDISCIPLINARY APPROACH

Our book intends to show the multiplicity of aspects of the discussions mentioned above by bringing research together from different academic disciplines. The most important disciplines represented here are anthropology, history, and political science. Aside from visiting the archives, our contributors have gone into the field to ask people how they use hometown ties for the advancement of their interests, or to ask about their actual work and business practice, and look whether hometown ties come up as an important factor at all.

There is a basic division between the chapters in the book following the second introductory chapter by Douw (on which was elaborated above), which is pertinent to the topics treated by them and to the disciplinary divide mentioned above. The first group of chapters, by Chung, Sinn, Liu, Cheng and Ngok, and Kuah, discusses the hometown or sojourner discourse as a relatively unproblematic fact, working towards the organization and profitable association of Chinese with different national backgrounds. In this group of chapters, the role of Chinese governments in the formation of the sojourner discourse is discussed as well as the role in that formation of voluntary associations in Hong Kong, Singapore, and Malaysia. *Stephanie*

Chung's essay elucidates the material interests which may be involved in engagement in a sojourner discourse. She provides a case study of the construction of hometown ties which may well serve as a microcosm of what is happening on a vast scale in different settings elsewhere in the world. During the first quarter of this century, the business people from the Siyi counties in Guangdong province, near Guangzhou, who had settled in Hong Kong after their sojourn in the United States, responded quickly to the appeal made by the Qing and Canton governments to their hometown sentiments in order to gain advantages over their competitors in Hong Kong. There are several telling features in this case. The outsider position of the *Siyi* people in Hong Kong is strikingly similar to the position of overseas Chinese in Southeast Asia, even though their competitors shared a Chinese culture with them. Also, the weakness of Sun Yat-sen's Canton government and the way in which the unscrupulous *Siyi* people made use of it in order to promote their interests in Guangzhou, Siyi and Hong Kong reveals the importance of the state's solvency should it decide to play the overseas Chinese card. The balance of power shifted decisively to the government's advantage when Chiang Kai-shek took over in 1928, inaugurating the collapse of the existing relationship. The case also illustrates what appears in many instances in the second part of the book that an explicitly shared culture even with one's fellow countrymen does not preclude basic misunderstandings about mutually agreed upon arrangements occurring.

Elizabeth Sinn shows how, during the 1930s and 1940s, multi-layered imagined communities were formed with Hong Kong as their spatial centre, and a hometown, Samshui in Guangdong province, as their cultural centre, which were effective in maintaining mutual bonds and bonds with China. The emphasis here lies on the socio-cultural aspects, even though at the same time it is undeniable that businessmen were the most aggressive organizers of this type of communities. They used a complex set of methods to give substance to the idea of a geographically widespread hometown community, by publishing *Qiaokan*, by vigorously soliciting donations, and by organizing funeral rites and thereby underpinning the value of filial piety. During the prewar period, the Chinese diaspora used its home basis to 'act global, and think local' (Schurmann, 1998). Although involvement in hometown affairs was substantial, even before the 1950s, there was a wider interest involving China as a whole.

Hong Liu can be said to enlarge upon this argument. Tracing the history of hometown associations in Singapore and Malaysia, he argues that a strong initiative prevailed among Southeast Asian business people to organize business and other ties with China, before as well as after the 1950s. The correspondence maintained with the hometown and donation

15

behaviour, served both to underpin and deepen the ties. Viewed from the Nanyang, the Chinese sojourner discourse was no one-way traffic from the various Chinese capitals, but was actively promoted from overseas. Just as in the case of the Samshui Huiguan, described by Sinn, before the 1950s the hometown-based associations among Singaporean and Malaysian business people seem to have identified more strongly with their hometowns than with other locations in China, whereas after that, the global context of business operation with China as one single important investment region emerged as more of a primary concern.

Joseph Cheng and *King-lun Ngok* provide an elaborate description of the apparatus erected over the past two decades by the PRC government for the conduct of economic diplomacy with ethnic Chinese business people residing abroad, and argue for generally positive judgements of its achievements; but this does not mean that some of its restraints are enviable. Even though the Chinese state is immeasurably stronger than was its predecessor in the case described by Stephanie Chung, the fact that most of its dealings are hidden behind the scenes harbours the danger of corruption.

Khun Eng Kuah's chapter brings us into the micro-dimensions of the sojourner discourse. She follows the reconstitution of a lineage with residence divided between Singapore and its hometown, Anxi county, in Fujian province. Kuah's description, based on anthropological fieldwork during the mid-1990s, reveals how ritual reconstitution of the lineage goes hand in hand with the establishment of new business in Anxi, but at the same time she argues that both processes are generated by different mixes of religious, emotional, moral, and material motives, entertained by different actors in the process. Sentimental and religious impetus was essential to get the project off the ground only to result, through implicated moral appeals, in material exchanges and, for Anxi, in economic development. The most articulate religious - emotional motive is nourished by the women involved, who execute the rituals; the outspoken material - instrumental motive is the province of officialdom. Because the various motives are relatively independent of one another, the result of the process may be quite contrary to what those involved would have expected or wanted, such as the revival of lineages in dealings with officials and social control. The essay supports the hypothesis that culture, in this case very much defined as ritual, serves to create space for the building of new relationships for mutual profit. It is noteworthy that the claim to cultural affinity comes from below in this case, even though it is gladly supported by the CCP cadres.

The second group of chapters, by Smart, Thireau and Hua, Huang, and

16

Schak, under which Kuah's essay may also be subsumed, looks how this type of actively constructed transnational links work in the everyday life of the officials, entrepreneurs and workers concerned. Here we enter the realm where the survival of material interests as a motive force for social and political organization can be studied, and the immediate relevance of 'culture' tested.

Alan Smart continues the preceding chapter in that he goes into the micro-relations involved in the Chinese sojourner discourse, but then, like those which follow, turns to transnational entrepreneurs and enterprise management, and to how the sojourner discourse worked in everyday practice during the early 1990s. That stage of development survives in many areas up to today, as regulations still do not cover most of the important business operations. In discussing the crucial issues of the establishment of relations with government officials and with labour, he maps out the opportunities and restraints created by such a situation, suggesting its necessity as a transitory stage and its terminality. The role of international rules of the game, collusive lying, trust as a result, rather than as a precondition, of negotiation, and cultural forms as a cover up of 'inequality among brothers'. Hometown ties are a way to circumvent kin obligations and promote patriotic images. From the tenet that 'cultural idioms' are productive because their ambiguity makes it possible to mobilize them in a variety of situations, particularly in fluctuating and uncertain ones, and use them (the idioms) interactively, the concept of trust, treated as a central form of social capital in recent academic literature, is scrutinized.

Isabelle Thireau and *Linshan Hua* continue much of Alan Smart's argument. They argue that social and political prerequisites determine the conditions under which ethnic Chinese capital enters China. Because they focus on the daily practice of business people, not on that of the performers of religious rituals, their chapter adds to the perspectives held by business people who are supposed, by the prevalent discourse, to make family relationships and *qiaoxiang* ties work in order to establish profitable business enterprises. It is argued, as Alan Smart does, that cultural sharing may help set up business in a situation for which no previous experience or jurisprudence exists, but that the employment of kin in factories and *qiaoxiang*-based diplomacy are skipped over as soon as a more predictable environment for business investment has been created. It is true, however, and significant that social investment of the 'traditional' type remains important for the establishment of a prospective investor's name among the local community and officialdom.

Cen Huang's essay looks into labour management issues in transnational firms in the Pearl River Delta Region. There is an odd paradox involved here because transnational investment of this type originates from business people who could be called migrants themselves and operate their firms with migrant labour. Nevertheless, many problems derive from the fact that labour contracts are almost invariably short-term, and even when they are not, the labourers usually do not attach themselves to one firm for a long term. Even though there is a tendency to describe labour conflicts in cultural terms, there is no need to emphasize cultural differences as the main source of conflict.

David Schak's essay in a sense extends Cen Huang's. Their arguments converge in the sense that cultural factors play no important role in the making of investment decisions and management practice. Culture in the sense of localized values, habits, and language is insignificant in comparison to material factors like geographical distance and mutual discrimination between mainlanders and Taiwanese because of social distance. (In fact, this may be taken to illustrate that culture IS important if defined as extra-economic behaviour which embeds economic behaviour and creates institutions which help to overcome contradictions between interest positions.)

Michael Godley concludes the book by looking back from a broad definition of *qiaoxiang* ties, as the relations with China of those abroad identifying as 'Chinese', in history, and forward into the future. As with the majority of chapters in the book, culture as such is not considered a decisive factor in economic development, but as an asset with enabling and restraining qualities. He asks how capitalism, as an idea, has been received in China over the past century, and how capitalism and development link up in Chinese thinking: are they compatible with Chinese culture? What was the role of Overseas Chinese as intermediaries in transmitting this idea? It is pointed out that a wealth-producing ideology is necessary to development, but that culture belongs to the sphere of politics and political ideology, not economic practice.

BIBLIOGRAPHY

Anderson, Benedict
1991   *Imagined Communities; Reflections on the Origins and Spread of Nationalism*. London: Verso
1992   *Long-distance Nationalism; World Capitalism and the Rise of Identity Politics*. Amsterdam: Centre for Asian Studies Amsterdam
Appadurai, Arjun
1991   'Global Ethnoscapes: Notes and Queries for a Transnational Anthropology', in: Richard G. Fox (ed.) *Recapturing Anthropology: Working in the Present*, Santa Fe: School of American

Research Press, pp. 191-210

Basch, Linda; Nina Glick Schiller and Cristina Szanton Blanc,
1995   'From Immigrant to Transmigrant: Theorizing Transnational Migration', *Anthropological Quarterly* 68(1), pp. 48-63

Biggart, Nicole Woolsey
1997   'Explaining Asian Economic Organization: Toward a Weberian Institutional Perspective', in: Hamilton, Gary; Marco Orrù and Nicole Woolsey Biggart (eds) *The Economic Organization of East Asian Capitalism*. Thousand Oaks, London, New Delhi: Sage Publications, pp. 3-32

Brook, Timothy and Hy V. Luong
1997   *Culture and Economy, the Shaping of Capitalism in East Asia*. Ann Arbor: The University of Michigan Press

Chan, Anita
1997   'Regimented Workers in China's Free Labor Market', *China Perspectives* 9, pp. 12-16
1998   (ed.) The Conditions of Chinese Workers in East Asian-Funded Enterprises, a special issue of the *Journal of Sociology and Anthropology* 30(4)

Cohen, A.
1997   *Global Diasporas: An Introduction*. London: UCL Press

Dirlik, Arif
1996   'Critical Reflections On "Chinese Capitalism" as Paradigm', in: Leo Douw and Peter Post (eds) *South China: State, Culture and Social Change during the Twentieth Century*. Amsterdam, Oxford, New York, Tokyo: KNAW, pp. 3-18

Duara, Prasenjit
1997   'Nationalists Among Transnationals: Overseas Chinese and the Idea of China, 1900-1911', in: Ong Aihwa and Donald M. Nonini (eds) *Ungrounded Empires, The Cultural Politics of Chinese Transnationalism*. New York, London: Routledge, pp. 39-60
1998   'Transnationalism in the Era of Nation-states: China, 1900-1945', *Development and Change* 29, pp. 647-70

Fukuyama, Francis
1992   *The End of History and The Last Man*. New York, Toronto, Oxford: The Free Press
1995   *Trust: The Social Virtues and the Creation of Prosperity*. New York, Toronto, Oxford: The Free Press

Granovetter, Mark
1985   'Economic Action and Social Structure: The problem of Embeddedness', *American Journal of Sociology* 91(3), pp. 481-510

Hamilton, Gary

1998   'Culture and Organization in Taiwan's Market Economy', in: Hefner, Robert (ed) *Market Cultures; Society and Morality in the New Asian Capitalisms*. Boulder (Col.): Westview Press, pp. 41-78

Hamilton, Gary; Marco Orrù and Nicole Woolsey Biggart

1997   *The Economic Organization of East Asian Capitalism*. Thousand Oaks. London, New Delhi: Sage Publications

Hefner, Robert

1998a   (ed.) *Market Cultures; Society and Morality in the New Asian Capitalisms*. Boulder (Col.): Westview Press

1998b   'Introduction: Society and Morality in the New Asian Capitalisms', in: Hefner, Robert (ed) *Market Cultures; Society and Morality in the New Asian Capitalisms*. Boulder (Col.): Westview Press, pp. 1-40

Huntington, Samuel P.

1996   *The Clash of Civilizations and the Remaking of World Order*. New York: Simon and Schuster

Kahn, Hermann

1979   *World Economic Development: 1979 and Beyond*. New York: Morrow Quill Paperbacks

Landes, David

1998   *The Wealth and Poverty of Nations; Why Some Are So Rich and Some So Poor*. London: Little, Brown and Company

McVey, Ruth (ed.)

1992   *Southeast Asian Capitalists*. Ithaca: Cornell University Press

Mittelman, James H. (ed.)

1996a   *Globalization: Critical Reflections*. Boulder, London: Lynne Rienner Publishers

1996b   'How Does Globalization Really Work?', in: Mittelman, James H. (ed) *Globalization: Critical Reflections*. Boulder, London: Lynne Rienner Publishers, pp. 205-28

Ong, Aihwa

1997   'Chinese Modernity: Narratives of Nation and of Capitalism', in: Ong Aihwa and Donald M. Nonini (eds) *Ungrounded Empires, the Cultural Politics of Modern Chinese Transnationalism*. New York, London: Routledge

Ong Aihwa and Donald M. Nonini (eds)

1997   *Ungrounded Empires, The Cultural Politics of Chinese Transnationalism*. New York, London: Routledge

Redding, S. Gordon,

1993   *The Spirit of Chinese Capitalism*. Berlin, New York: Walter de Gruyter

Reid, Anthony

1997   'Entrepreneurial Minorities, Nationalism, and the State', in: D.

Chirot and A. Reid (eds) *Essential Outsiders. Chinese and Jews in the Modern Transformation of Southeast Asia and Central Europe.* Seattle: University of Washington Press

Salmon, Claudine
1981 'The Contribution of the Chinese to the Development of Southeast Asia: A New Appraisal', *Journal of Southeast Asian Studies* 12(1), pp. 260-75

Schurmann, Franz
1998 'Chinese Overseas - Acting Global, Thinking Local - Seeking a Synthesis Between "Luodi Shenggen" and "Yeluo Guigen"', in: Zhuang Guotu (ed.) *Ethnic Chinese at the Turn of the Centuries.* Fuchou: Renmin chubanshe

Smart, Alan, and Josephine Smart
1998 'Transnational Social Networks and Negotiated Identities in Interactions Between Hong Kong and China', in: Michael Peter Smith and Luis Eduardo Guarnizo (eds) *Transnationalism from Below.* New Brunswick, London: Transaction Publishers, pp. 103-30.

Smith, Michael Peter and Luis Eduardo Guarnizo (eds)
1998 *Transnationalism from Below.* New Brunswick, London: Transaction Publishers

Tölölyan, Khachig
1996 'Rethinking Diaspora(s): Stateless Power in the Transnational Movement', *Diaspora* 5(1), pp. 3-36

Wong, Siu-lun
1996 'Chinese Entrepreneurship and Economic Development', in: Leo Douw and Peter Post (eds) *South China: State, Culture and Social Change during the Twentieth Century.* Amsterdam, Oxford, New York, Tokyo: KNAW, pp. 29-35

Notes

1. The author wishes to thank Arif Dirlik, Michael Godley, Cen Huang, David Ip, Hong Liu, and Henk Schulte Nordholt for their constructive comments on earlier drafts of his chapters; he remains solely responsible for the final text.
2. The data from the interviews mentioned below come from a fieldwork trip undertaken by the author and Cen Huang, during the period 1 April to 5 May, in Singapore, the People's Republic of China, Hong Kong, and Taiwan.

THE CHINESE SOJOURNER DISCOURSE

Leo Douw

This chapter speculates on the nature of present-day Chinese trans-nationalism. It elaborates on the suggestion made in the Introduction that assertions of cultural affinity are more important as an object of study than cultural affinity itself in explaining economic development (see above), and attempts to show that what is happening in China today is not unique, and fits into more general patterns of social change found all over the world. Looking from this vantage point, makes it easier to conceive of cultural idioms as belonging to a particular stage in the global spread of capitalism. The argument, even though it represents the personal vision of the present author, is intended to serve as another context for the chapters of the book.

INTRODUCTION

The Introduction suggested that transnationalism expands at times when capital and labour are set in motion in the world market, and national governments allow spaces to exist or grow where regulation is not very strict and free entre-preneurship is allowed to function. This advance in the globalization process profits from situations in which expatriate or foreign ethnic communities, or diasporas exist, whose loyalties are either not well established or may even be regarded as dubious, and where there are economic disparities between the home and the host countries. In any of these cases, identity politics play a role in creating transnational solidarity, mainly because of the lack of established institutions to deal with the newly created situations. These mechanisms allow transnational businessmen find themselves in a position which gives them the opportunity to negotiate between administrators and politicians at both (or multiple) ends of their transnational networks, a situation perhaps not very different from that of the European businessmen who, during the nineteenth century and earlier, transcended regional boundaries and helped create nations on the basis of shared culture and language. This creates new 'spaces' from which new economic and political constellations may emerge.

Therefore it is important to note under which conditions since the 1980s 'culture' has related to the spread of capitalism, replacing ideological discourses. By facilitating the negotiation of undetermined positions, mainly between business people and officials, it smoothes the way for the operation of capitalism and by its appeal to certain moral values it also constrains it. The fluidity of the negotiation process, essential in the initial phase of border-crossing, tends to turn towards the establishment of more predictable rules and arrangements, formal or informal. A Chinese economic community, in the sense of a 'Greater China', may take root regarding itself as discreet from the Western sphere in which in the longer run, the foreignness of the entrepreneurs will matter less, and sojourner discourses are no longer needed. But links with the rest of the world will also grow and intensify; mutual understanding remains imperative.

SOJOURNER DISCOURSES

The short excursion through some of the literature on non-Chinese 'transnations' which follows is intended to mark some of the general traits of these formations and their origins. In doing so, the importance of initiatives taken by national governments in the establishment of transnational solidarity and the uses of identity politics should become more clear. This may also serve to take away some of the magic and mystery surrounding the formation and operation of international Chinese business networks.

To begin with, the 'sojourner' discourses may be categorized as a special case of transnational idealism: they are different from other such idealisms, such as the European Idea or the concept of Asian Values. The contrasts may teach us about the specific character of the sojourners' transnationalism. One distinguishing trait is, of course, their appeal to a person's migratory state of life, which is lacking in the other examples. Migrants' myths, diasporic imageries, sojourners' discourses, they all appeal to the spiritual state in which migrants abroad are supposed to live. They imply a shared nostalgia, and a love of the faraway home community in which the migrants' families and friends have been left behind. The typical migrant is supposed to be a sojourner who is due to return to his hometown, in order to visit his kin and friends, establish a business, enjoy a pleasant old age, or, especially relevant to Chinese sojourners, be buried. (See for example Shami, 1998; on Chinese burials, see the contributions by Elizabeth Sinn and Khun Eng Kuah, below.) Such an appeal ignores divisions of class and gender, and is usually directed towards the successful migrant rather than the failed one. It connects people on the basis of shared roots and a shared culture which imply a certain achieved social status and morally enforceable duties. Nevertheless, these are never precisely circumscribed and can be subscribed to at will. The non-committal nature of sojourner discourses seems an important trait if their potential for progressive social change is a matter of consideration.

Another trait distinguishing sojourner-based transnationalism from other types is that it bridges the distance between countries with different levels of economic development. The sense of Utopia implied by sojourner discourses should not blind us to the possibly harsh realities of the material and political interests involved (Smith and Guarnizo, 1998). Migration and the possibility of the emergence of sojourner discourses specifically arise in situations where gross inequalities are a given: labour-sending countries like Pakistan, Indonesia, and the Philippines in Asia still suffer from economic underdevelopment, as do several countries of Southern Europe and the many Latin American countries which see their nationals move to the United States. Looking from the vantage point of the governments involved, the term transmigration has been coined in order to underline migration as an active process in which the governments of the sending countries have taken an overriding interest (Basch et al., 1995:48; 1997:7-8; 269-77; Smith and Guarnizo, 1998:9-10); this makes migration into something different in principle from being mere survival strategies taken by individual families and communities. When migration obtains on a certain momentum, the governments of the home countries may take an interest in their nationals abroad and no longer restrict their involvement with them to the granting of a visa. The corollary of transmigration is the deterritorialized nation. Governments may come to consider their constituencies abroad as part of the nation, even though no territorial claims are involved. The appeals to Chineseness in our field of enquiry are matched by those to Haitianness, Greekness, and Portugueseness elsewhere. (Basch, et al., 1995:52-3, 57; see also Duara, 1998:667-8.) A fast growing body of academic literature, treating the implications of large-scale migration, exists on Latino migrants. Many of the traits which characterize the Chinese case are to be found elsewhere. Remittances, business investment, and donations together constitute the material interest of developing countries in the maintenance of links with their migrants abroad (Smith and Guarnizo, 1998:8; Basch, et al., 1995:53). The remittance of migrants' money in some cases has become the major source of foreign exchange, as in El Salvador, and thereby has created a stimulus for emigration by itself. Local development projects may result from migrants' initiatives, as for example in Ticuani, a poor village in South Mexico, where donations were collected for the building of waterworks over a period of more than twenty years (Smith, 1998:196-7). This may result in the establishment of government departments specifically geared towards dealing with migrant communities abroad, the active organization of migrants' associations, and, if circumstances allow, the creation of sojourner discourses. In those cases, sojourning may quickly become a metaphor for materially supporting one's home country and imply that staying away is more profitable for those involved than a physical return. It may even give rise to a bias against returning (Basch, et al., 1997:127-9). The permitting of dual nationality has become commonplace among the migrant-sending countries of Latin America. El Salvador probably went farthest by providing its nationals abroad with legal assistance in 1994, in order to apply for political asylum in the United States (Mahler, 1998:70-1). It will be shown below that many of these situations have occurred in the Chinese case, particularly before 1949, and are happening again today.

Sojourners and their descendants abroad may take advantage of the state interest in them, or perhaps not. This creates a certain space for negotiation on the quid pro quo of their services and money. Even though governments have a capacity to play migrants off against one another, it nevertheless seems that the advantage is at least equally on the migrants' side. Links with the state may increase their status at home as much as abroad: the possibility of status-building at both ends of the migration chain provides another dynamic to sojourners' transnationalisms. The successful migrant often has better possibilities to show off in his home country than in the host society. His very status abroad as a foreign migrant may keep him down, a situation which may take a long time to erode, even when migration is successful. Voluntary associations, which just as in the Chinese case are often organized on a hometown basis, may assist in achieving higher status back home as much as in the host country. This, of course, usually builds on a previously achieved status which may involve not only a higher standard of living, but also a distinct lifestyle followed by the migrant families. Accordingly, governments may step in by asking prominent migrant entrepreneurs to perform diplomatic services abroad, bestowing honorary ambassadorships and other favours upon them, subsidizing hometown and home-state associations, and creating formal channels for communication with them and their constituencies (Smith and Guarnizo, 1998:8). This is a major source for the creation of multiple identities. Sojourners typically aspire to rising socially in both their host society and back home, both aspirations reinforcing each other. By supporting these aspirations for reasons of well-understood self-interest, governments compound the ongoing double (or multiple) integration processes. As has been argued above for the Chinese case (see Introduction), two or more-sided integration is characteristic of the transnational migrant rather than submission to one articulate, overarching discourse (Basch, et al., 1997:103-4; 248-51; 253-62; Goldring, 1998). This and the active involvement of national governments in the process corroborate the other point made above, on the case of Chineseness, that it is the interaction between multiple identity and assertions of cultural affinity which have to be studied, not cultural affinity in isolation.

These processes seem to build up more quickly nowadays, and certainly occur on a bigger scale than in the past. Formerly, migrants' identities started to shift with their departure from the home country. The resulting alienation, of necessity because of the much lessened possibility of contact with the home basis, created a bigger problem of reidentification the longer the sojourn lasted. Coupled with the foreigner status in the host country, with which identification is usually problematic, this gives reason to speak of double alienation as much as of double identification. In the past, nevertheless, the identification with the home country was easily lost, even when a distinct culture derivative from the home culture was maintained. In those cases, a protracted process of negotiation is obviously required at a time the links with the mother country are being restored or intensified. This factor may help explain why it took so long at the end of the nineteenth century, for the Chinese government to establish operative links with ethnic Chinese communities abroad. It may be different now but whether the post-colonial situation has produced a qualitative or only a quantitative change from the past is questionable. Mobilophones, faxes, e-mail, and air traffic have obviously changed transnational links to a large extent by ensuring the possibility of enduring contact with the home basis, making double and multiple identification easier. But there is no reason why this would have impaired the negotiation space of nationals abroad and their descendants in their relationship with their home government, all the more so since the structural causes underlying this type of transnationalism have survived, and may be supposed to play a bigger role because they have been made more visible by the same intensification of communication, namely the inequality between nations, and the ethnicization of migrants and their descendants abroad.

There is one more important point to be made before we conclude this section: in a world which sanctions the sovereignty of the nation-state, the institutionalization of transnational linkages is a problem of principle. It is no accident that these linkages are being taken care of by voluntary associations that are based externally, not on allegiance to political parties or national governments at home, but on cultural links with politically unthreatening hometowns, and with state organizations and departments in the home government which usually have no outspoken political profile. (Basch et al. 1995:56; Smith and Guarnizo, 1998:8; Goldring, 1998; Smith, 1998; Mahler, 1998). It is understood here as a matter of course that increased contacts with the mother country will usually involve a more articulate interest in political life. The problems of political loyalty which will more often than not arise from such an interest, however, are exactly the reason why sojourner discourses and weak institutionalization of this type of transnationalism are indispensable to governments. This is yet another angle from which it may be argued that cultural discourses are functional to the spread of capitalism. At the same time they underline why little hope can be held that transnations of this type will produce consistent and effective social doctrines, and undertake concomitant action.

This discussion suggests that the engenderment of sojourner discourses, in the past just as in the present, is conditioned by very similar circumstances: unequal levels of economic development between national states, the occurrence of transmigration, and the difficulty of integration into the host society. These circumstances are causally related, even though they may vary in importance between different situations in time and space. Again, this leads to posing the question of how important these variations are. Basch et al., for example, have characterized the complicated link between this type of transnationalism and present-day globalization as a new phenomenon (1997:23-4; see also Smith and Guarnizo, 1998). They argue that the colonial situation was replaced by another one in which newly-formed nations had to comply with the situation which worked towards the concentration of global economic activities in the three metropolises of London, Tokyo, and New York (cf. Sassen, 1991). This concentration caused poverty at home and brought about the flows of migration of which we are talking. At the same time, the ongoing crisis in the host countries could not provide the migrants with sufficient social status, even if they were successful, and contributed to their ethnicisation (Basch, et al., 1995:50). It is in line with this argument that Basch et al. emphasize that, in the colonial past, migrants thought mainly of building up a nation back home, free from colonial domination, whereas nowadays their feeling for community is two-sided (1995:52-3; 1997:23-4, 100-3). This argument, in the view of the author, is relevant to Chinese history as much as it is to Latin America. We should wonder whether the break, true though it may be, is so sharp that it is really crucial to understanding the formation of transnationalism. The question is whether or not very similar ambiguities were involved in the sojourner discourses under colonialism, and whether or not very similar circumstances brought them about.

The issue of continuity will come up again in the next section, which discusses the historical precedents of present-day Chinese transnationalism. It is most important to note here that the Chinese case is not completely unique, even if it may have begun earlier and may appear to be more successful nowadays than most others in generating economic development. Even though our book is limited to the Chinese case, it wishes to make a contribution to a social science approach which does more than articulate the uniqueness of the Chinese model.

A HISTORICAL PERSPECTIVE
ON THE CHINESE SOJOURNER DISCOURSE

The attention paid to the Chinese version of sojourner transnationalism has obviously been spurred on by the spectacular rise of foreign-Chinese trade and investment in South China over the past decade (Lever-Tracy et al., 1996:62-81; East Asia Analytical Unit, 1995:6). Careful comparative research should determine whether or not other diasporas have achieved similar results in their home countries. Even if they have, undoubtedly the Chinese case is an example of the successful implementation of 'politics of native roots'(Siu, 1993). The thorough integration of some of the most advanced districts in South China into the regional and global economy may even have reached a stage at which sojourner discourses have become superfluous; the officials involved in its implementation in South China may tell you that they are already looking for different tasks (Interviews, April 1997[1]). Therefore, South China's development over the 1990s is as much worthy of study for the impending demise as for the revival and expansion of sojourner transnationalism.

The conscious creation of an idiom that would enable the government of China and the ethnic Chinese merchants abroad to establish mutually profitable links took place in the last quarter of the nineteenth century. At that time, China's weakness in the international arena was exposed by the humiliating confrontations with the colonial powers, Japan foremost among them. At the same time, the steady growth of the colonial export economies in Southeast Asia required an increasing amount of Chinese coolie labour; this need for labour added to the flow of migrants who had begun to leave the Southern Chinese coastal provinces since the 1840s. The Qing state was forced to modernize its economy in order not to be colonized itself. It tried to join the international economy on a more equal footing, among other measures, by incorporating the Chinese migrant communities abroad into its cultural and political sphere, thus creating, in anachronistic terms, a Chinese 'transnation'. Below there will be a fuller discussion of how the Chinese state gradually established a sojourner discourse based on the assertion that *Huaqiao*, or 'Chinese sojourners', belonged to the Chinese culture and nation. The resulting discourse has served intermittently to obtain maximum profit from the ethnic link between China and its migrants and their descendants abroad. In view of what was said on the political aspects of transnationalism above, it is significant that open political identification with developments in China by ethnic Chinese abroad was not a striking feature of this link, even though it varied over time, reaching a high point during the 1930s and 1940s, and a low during the 1960s and 1970s.

Over the past century, the material interests that have connected China and its overseas communities are the major constant underscoring the viability and effectiveness of the Chinese sojourner discourse. The flow of remittances fluctuated severely over the period, but seldom failed to have an effect on the life-styles and material welfare of family members back home. On a wider scale they also supported China's balance of payments, and thereby provided a straightforward and natural stimulus for the national government to be concerned about its relations with its expatriates and their family members in China. The most crucial and contested link here is the extent to which ethnic Chinese and their descendants abroad were willing to invest directly in China's economy. This interest has been acknowledged by most Chinese governments since the late nineteenth century, aware that investment by expatriates could make up for the lack of capital and expertise suffered by China as long as its economy lagged behind internationally and was hampered by its isolation from the world market. Other than the remittance of money, investment depends not primarily on the presence of emigrants' family and friends back home, but on the share of profits to be derived from the investment, and on the trust that it can be made safely. In this respect, there appears to be a major difference between the past decade and the pre-war period, as will be shown later in this chapter. Nowadays, direct investment in productive enterprise is at a level so high that it comes near to making pre-war levels appear as insignificant.

China's lagging economic development is therefore an important factor conditioning its relationships with the ethnic Chinese abroad and their descendants, particularly the dynamic and successful entrepreneurs among them. The economic strength of the latter, combined with their relative freedom to place their investments where they wished, was their most important asset in dealing with successive Chinese governments. They could choose to emphasize their Chinese identity in as far as they were interested in building up economic links with China, and negotiate the conditions to be created by the Chinese state for it to secure their investment. Private economic gain was not the only factor that played a role in these negotiations. A stronger China was expected to enhance the status of the ethnic Chinese communities abroad, and could be expected to support their interests in confrontations with the colonial states, and subsequently, after decolonization, the national states in which they resided. This was important because for a long time their status as migrants or the descendants of migrants in those countries, rendered them liable to being politically suspect and consequently, vulnerable. The Chinese state could often play on this situation by appealing to the Chinese ancestry and identity of the ethnic Chinese and their descendants who resided abroad. After the 1950s, because migration to Southeast Asia was halted and the Chinese government adopted a single-nationality policy, the actual status of sojourner applied to a decreasing number of ethnic Chinese abroad, and claims to cultural affinity were more cautiously worded than they had been before that time. Prior to the 1950s, the Chinese state provokingly claimed *ius sanguinis* for all migrants from China and their descendants which made them, in the Chinese view, citizens of the Chinese state. The prospect of a strong China seems to have been the most important asset of the successive Chinese governments in appealing to their constituencies abroad, even though after the 1950s this was found to be an increasingly more difficult card to play. Its willingness to and indeed capability of creating a stable environment for foreign trade and investment has fluctuated over time and must be considered to have been a liability most of the time, up until at least the 1980s.

Culture provided the language in which the terms of negotiation could be conveniently couched: immediate engagement in political strife 'at home' was nearly always dangerous, and, after the 1950s, also no longer acceptable to the government of the People's Republic of China. In looking at the longer-term development of Chinese transnationalism, as said, open political engagement and activity was limited, and reached a high point during the 1930s and 1940s, when China suffered from crisis and war and was evident also in the somewhat eccentric Philippine case where ethnic Chinese remained citizens of the Republic of China until after 1975, and continued to be divided along Chinese, not Philippine, political lines until in the 1980s (See, 1998; Carino, 1998; Tan, 1981.). Otherwise, assertions of cultural affinity helped create an environment in which the natural alienation from China among the ethnic Chinese communities abroad could be softened, and concrete deals and transactions could be negotiated. The large-scale emigration from China during the colonial period was helpful in bridging the gap. Continuing links among the communities abroad and China during the period after migration halted completely have helped in starting up the re-entrance of capital into China since the 1980s. But it should be noted, as was also suggested in the Introduction, that differences abounded. One fundamental point is that Chinese migrant communities, just as those existing elsewhere, have always been very diverse in their class and gender composition, in the measure of their assimilation into the host society, and in their loyalty to the home country (for a recent overview, see Skinner, 1996) Another important marker is that being born and having grown up in China by itself during the same period was not the only factor determining allegiances to Chinese governments, the hometown, or even one's own family. Recent emigrants could alienate themselves quickly from their home situation and their sense of Chineseness (Chen Ta, 1940; Duara, 1997:51; 1998:662), whereas fourth generation emigrants could rediscover their Chinese roots and develop strong loyalties with political groupings in China (Purcell, 1965:447). After decolonization, the framework of international relations within which Chinese governments appealed to the sojourner sentiments of Chinese overseas communities may be very different from that in the past, and recent migrants may be fewer in number, but the diversity itself among ethnic Chinese and their involved interests in establishing links with China may not differ very much. Therefore, the issue of negotiating identity and material interest, which determines much of the practice, if not the content, of the sojourner discourse has remained crucial. It has remained imperative to know who generated the discourse, who responded to it, and why they did.

During both the initiating and the revival phases of the Chinese sojourner discourse, elaborate and protracted negotiation were needed to regularize and routinize the 'return' to China of foreign Chinese business people. The virtually unhampered expansion of global capitalism, partly facilitated by China's opening-up, in both situations has gone hand in hand with an increasingly cultural discourse, supported by academic writings. In the eyes of this author, it is an interesting phenomenon that several of the most important treatises on Asian society which have emphasized the importance of cultural difference were published in the 1900s, at the time when the Chinese sojourner discourse began to make headway.[2]

A quick look at the history of the Chinese sojourner discourse will serve to elaborate these points.

Creation: 1883-1909
Nowadays PRC historians claim that the full-blown cultivation of hometown ties was in place in the 1870s, in the sense not only of maintaining trade relations and sending remittances to one's family, but also of donating money to communautarian purposes (Fang, 1998). At that time, however, an official attitude towards Chinese emigrants which considered emigration high treason and therefore a capital crime lingered on. It took a good thirty years before the Chinese government had capitalized on these informal ties and created substantial links with the overseas Chinese communities on the basis of a shared Chinese culture and nation. The officially sponsored alienation meant that regaining a measure of allegiance among overseas migrants was a protracted and complicated process in which mutual reconnoitring and negotiation were required before shared interests could be established. Of course the colonial situation under which Chinese nationalism was suspect and was usually considered inimical to the established regimes, must be added.

The new, internationally-directed sojourner discourse could be built on ancient practice. For a long time hometown links both within China and abroad hometown served as a basis for association among merchants (Goodman, 1995; Yen, 1986). From the late 1870s, the Chinese government took a number of initiatives to enlist the support of ethnic Chinese business people. It established a consulate in Singapore (1877) and made the sale of honorific titles among wealthy merchants abroad easier (Yen, 1970). During that time, the official attitude towards emigrants had already begun to change. The actual situation made the law which strictly prohibited emigration up to 1859 an anachronism since mass emigration from South China had started during the 1840s. In 1859, the law was relaxed and the road was free for a change of attitude among Qing officialdom towards the Chinese abroad and their gradual de-criminalization. An important step was taken in 1883, when the probably casual use of the term *Huaqiao* (Chinese Sojourner) by the diplomat Huang Zunxian was followed by the official use in the Sino-French Treaty of 1885, of the term *Qiaoju*, literally 'sojourning residents', as a designation for all decent ethnic Chinese living in Vietnam (Wang, 1981a:122; Zhuang, 1989:343-50). It is significant, that the latter term implied not only the right to official protection of those whom it designated, but also the possibility, or even probability, that the sojourn abroad would not be temporary, but lasting (Wang, 1981a). This reflects the official interest in the transmigrants' position rather than the general migrant's dream of returning home after having become rich. This also made it possible to include the majority among the Chinese abroad who had not been born in China and whose ancestry abroad often encompassed more than one generation. In 1893, the court was successfully petitioned and lifted the already superannuated ban on emigration overseas.

The decade after 1898 was crucial to the formation of the *Huaqiao* discourse. Undoubtedly the weakening of dynastic power was a vital cause. War indemnities had been imposed on China in 1895 after its defeat in the First Sino-Japanese War. These were added to in 1900 in the wake of the Boxer Uprising. The Treaty of Shimonoseki, which signalled the rise of Japan as a regional colonial power, acknowledged the need to protect Japanese citizens in China as well as Chinese citizens in Japan. Immediately after the Sino-Japanese War, in official parlance the term *Huaqiao* began to include all overseas Chinese and even, particularly because of the journalistic activity of Liang Qichao, imbued the imagined *Huaqiao* with the qualities of colonists. The Chinese overseas should not only be protected as Chinese nationals, but also as Chinese colonists, namely as counterparts of the European colonists who had been so much more successful abroad by dint of their being protected by their home governments (Wang, 1981a, b). This gave the Chinese sojourner discourse a sharper political edge. China should maintain colonial ambitions of its own, and on those terms compete with Western and Japanese colonialism.

Despite the apparent inclusion of all people of Chinese descent in the *Huaqiao* concept, emissaries from the Chinese government and, after 1898, reformists like Liang Qichao and Kang Youwei addressed only the wealthier strata among the business communities overseas. It would be until 1903 before the appeal was broadened somewhat, and began to impact on the lower strata

(Wang, 1981, a, b; Duara, 1997, 1998). The reason for this was Sun Yat-sen's rather sudden success in Southeast Asia. Several circumstances which were related to the expansion of the colonial states in Southeast Asia contributed to that success. In the first place, around the turn of the century there was an acceleration in the migration of Chinese coolie labour for the expanding colonial economies. This high tide of emigration would last until the 1930s. This complicated the social structures of the various Chinese communities in Southeast Asia. A more articulate division along class lines in the areas in which large Chinese enterprises dominated the local economies, for example in Malaya emerged. Also, smaller enterprises began to be established by talented new immigrants with commoner origins. The social divisions must have often coincided with the divide between the established economic elites of older Chinese origin, largely integrated into native society even though in many cases in a process of re-sinification, and the newly arrived *totoks*, who had relatives back home in China for whom they were responsible (Skinner, 1996; Dobbin, 1996). Certainly, the protection extended by the Qing government to the Chinese emigrants meant that many men had their wives join them, and there was a vast increase in the rate of females overseas (this again confirms that already by the time the permanent character of Chinese sojourning must have been implied in the term *Huaqiao*: the bringing in of wives meant the establishment of families abroad, which made a return home less probable). In the second place, the process of state formation going on in Southeast Asia meant that the Chinese establishment lost much of its political influence, and became more oriented towards strictly economic business enterprise (Dobbin, 1996:164-90). This was mainly because of the abolition of the revenue and opium farms in the Dutch and British colonies, which took place in 1900 and 1909 respectively. This may have added to the competition among Chinese business people of different social origins in Southeast Asia.

Both changes took place during the time when republican *Huaqiao* rhetoric was being added to the existing state and reformist propaganda. This created a situation in which every Chinese living abroad could, in principle, be mobilized on the basis of his Chinese descent. One other example of China's increased presence was the establishment of Chinese Chambers of Commerce in Southeast Asia during the 1900s, on the initiative of the Chinese government and all formally falling under the Chinese law of 1904 (Yen, 1985). Being Chinese became more important, not least because of the emergent local nationalisms in Southeast Asia, and consequently the sensitivity towards the sojourner discourse increased, even among those who had long since forgotten about their Chinese ancestry. Despite the vast differences between the ways the various Southeast Asian countries worked out these new contradictions, there was an upsurge in associational life everywhere. In the

Philippines, all *Tongxianghui* still existing in the 1930s had been established since 1908 (Zhuang, 1996:172-3). In Hong Kong the formation of regional associations accelerated around 1910 (Sinn, 1997:377), and in Singapore similar developments took place. (Ng, 1992:475-9) Most of this was inspired by the need to keep communications with the hometown working, and therefore these were highly localized and concerned with the whole spectrum of economic, social, and political life. At the same time, just as the recently established Chinese Chambers of Commerce did, they supported the business transactions and the fostering of contacts with the bureaucracy in China on a Chinese ethnic basis.

In 1909, the final step was taken by the Qing government when it proclaimed its Nationality Law, in which the possibility of Chinese citizenship was claimed for any person of Chinese descent, on the basis of the *ius sanguinis*. The Law was emphatically directed against the claims of the colonial governments in Southeast Asia, particularly the Dutch government in the Netherlands East Indies, that they would offer legal protection to their ethnic Chinese subjects (Wang, 1981a; Yen, 1986). When the Qing fell in 1911, a solid basis had already been laid for the full development of the first phase of the Chinese sojourner discourse. The paradigm of the permanently sojourning colonist, well-protected by his home government and willing to reciprocate that protection by political loyalty and economic support, had grown into an inescapable discourse for those involved in the establishment of transnational linkages between China and the people of Chinese descent abroad. This leaves the fundamental question of how far this established the terms of negotiation on mutual involvement, or the involvement itself.

High tide: 1909-55
Between the 1910s and the 1930s, the *Huaqiao* discourse may be said to have reached its apogee, in the sense that it was effective in generating economic support and political loyalty among the Chinese overseas. Loyalty to the *qiaoxiang* became an important value upon which social connections could be built, among Chinese abroad. Nationalist activity in Southeast Asia continued and was instrumental in keeping Chinese culture and language alive, and, coalescing with factors internal to the situation in Southeast Asia, engendered a process of re-sinification (Coppel, 1996). The practical side of this was that people of Chinese descent could aspire to making careers in China and had a material interest in not becoming too alienated from their home country. It is interesting to note, as was mentioned above, that even among third and fourth generation Chinese descendants, the sojourner mentality could achieve the status of a lively ideal, and sometimes produced the sincere wish to return to China (Purcell, 1965:447). Anti-colonial activity remained a vital concern for the colonial authorities, and reached a high point after 1926, at the time of the

Kuomintang power take-over. Others, however, began to resent even the obligations to their families and integrated into the societies of their host countries (Chen, 1940).

Most of the support during this period was economic. Certainly, no vast support in the sense of big investment in large-scale modernization projects, which Nationalist pamphleteers may have hoped to attract, ever resulted. Only two or three per cent of the total flow of remittances was used for productive investment, the remainder was private family income, often consisting of business profits (Remer, 1933:178-9). In actual fact, the capacity of the South Chinese economy to absorb productive investment was very low at the time. Much of the money sent went into real estate or was invested in Shanghai. Nevertheless, there was an upsurge in donations. Pertinently, much investment was in the modern sector of the economy, and in many cases definitely initiated a measure of modernization. And at least, the vast increase in the flow of remittances during this period helped to keep up China's balance of trade (Douw, 1995:117-23).

The *Huaqiao* discourse was confirmed in 1929, when the *ius sanguinis* became part of the Kuomintang Nationality Law. During the period from the 1930s until the early 1960s, it would be true to say that the discourse worked in a political rather than an economic sense. The flow of remittances was often interrupted by the course of political events. There were upsurges in the flows of remittances and donations, the latter in particular, during the war years. The World Economic Crisis led to the return of large numbers of emigrants, for whom the Kuomintang government had to show its concern. Conversely, as was mentioned above, China's predicament provoked more of an open commitment to its cause than had been the case in the previous decades. The chapters by Hong Liu and Elizabeth Sinn in this volume show that the internationalization of ethnic Chinese associational life was very intense during this period, and remained so during the war years.

Avoidance: 1955-80.
A crucial break in the development of the sojourner discourse came in the mid-1950s, when the government of the People's Republic of China relinquished its right to address Chinese descendants abroad as its citizens, and urged them to choose between the nationality of their countries of residence and citizenship of the People's Republic of China. The *ius sanguinis* was replaced by the *ius soli*. The Kuomintang government in Taiwan kept to the old usage, a step which was of some consequence to the political divisions among ethnic Chinese abroad, particularly in the Philippines. Indubitably the change of attitude on the Mainland had to do with the decolonization of Southeast Asia. There was a political need to eliminate the idea of a Chinese Fifth Column, and both the necessity and indeed the possibility to use the Chinese overseas as an anti-

colonial force had declined. The old *Huaqiao* rhetoric had become politically undesirable, even dangerous, and for that reason was avoided. This has remained so up to the present day.

Nevertheless, the old constellation of mutual interests had remained largely intact. The PRC government was as interested in attracting remittances, donations, and investment from abroad as its predecessors had been, and therefore tried its best to accommodate Overseas Chinese Kin (*Qiaojuan*) and Returned Overseas Chinese (*Guiqiao*). It also did not completely disavow the role of protector of Chinese overseas assumed by its predecessors: the evacuation of Indonesian Chinese, around 1960, and the adoption of Vietnamese Chinese, during the late 1970s are examples of this sense of responsibility (Godley, 1989; Suryadinata, 1996).

From the late 1950s, this constellation of mutual interest began to be undermined and then destroyed by the emergence of radical politics. It became politically disadvantageous to be connected with Chinese overseas and, during the Cultural Revolution, a cause for discrimination and even persecution. Emigration and the remittance of money drew to a standstill, only to recover gradually when China re-entered the community of nations, in the course of the 1970s. By that time, the criminalization of Chinese overseas entrepreneurs as capitalists had gone so far, and the trajectories along which China and the countries of Southeast Asia had developed had diverged so much, that a protracted process of negotiation had again become necessary, before a measure of routine in the relations between China and the ethnic Chinese abroad could be achieved. The restoration of the Chinese sojourner discourse, from the late 1970s, served this purpose. The negotiation of identity and material interest started again, in a process comparable to that which had led to the creation of this discourse around the turn of the century. How similar both processes were would depend on which factors are emphasized in considering the process. The virtual absence of recent Chinese sojourners in Southeast Asia, the implementation of single-nationality policies, and, consequently, the participation of the ethnic Chinese in Southeast Asian societies makes the situation of the past two decades very different from that in the early twentieth century. At the same time, the political fact of a Chinese government that claims cultural affinity with an imagined ethnic Chinese diaspora abroad cannot be ignored, nor can those of politicians and businessmen who underwrite these claims, and act upon them. China's position as a capital-scarce, labour-rich country, as opposed to the Southeast Asian ethnic Chinese 'diaspora' as basically materially by and large successful, but politically vulnerable business and trading minorities, had not changed as much as might have been desired; this set the stage for the revival of the earlier 'transnation'.

GLOBALIZATION AND THE CHINESE SOJOURNER DISCOURSE

It can be plausibly argued that globalization, in the sense of the liberalization of world markets, was stimulated most by the developed countries, the USA first among them, and that the emergence of the export economies elsewhere was a reaction to that initiative. The PRC case fits this picture. China's isolation came to an end around the time the USA actively began to revise its position in the world around 1970. Diplomatic relations were normalized first between China and the USA's closest allies in the region, Japan and the Philippines. Around the mid-1970s, the principle of single nationality gained more widespread currency among the ethnic Chinese in Southeast Asia. This created the political, legal, and diplomatic conditions for a gradual restoration of the sojourner discourse, phase two, and for the revitalization of international Chinese associational life on the basis of Chinese ethnicity. By affirming the principle of single nationality introduced in 1955, the Nationality Law of 1980 signalled another major shift on the route towards the reconstitution of the Chinese sojourner discourse. *Qiaoxiang* regained their status as bureaucratically circumscribed entities, a move which in fact recognized their importance to international economic development. Around the same time, the PRC government set up Special Economic Zones (SEZs) for the specific purpose of attracting overseas Chinese investment. Cultural and linguistic affinity was supposed to provide a direction for the new policies. The SEZs in Fujian province faced Taiwan, those in Guangdong province were situated opposite Hong Kong, which simultaneously was the gateway to Southeast Asian capital. During this period, the regionally based voluntary associations among ethnic Chinese proliferated as one vehicle for international communications, including on the Chinese market. At the same time, the CCP underwent a process of revamping its pejorative ideological approach of the ethnic Chinese abroad, and set out actively to stimulate ethnic Chinese investment by breathing new life into the old fabric of *qiaoxiang* relations. Donations were stimulated for all kinds of public uses, infrastructure, schools, libraries, not to mention temples and ancestral halls. Politics in the PRC had to adjust to these newly introduced social forms, because they were still suspected of being feudal remnants. Clan associations in fact are still forbidden. But it is clear that a vast semi-official apparatus was built up in order to negotiate the conditions under which transnational linkages could be established. This is described in great detail by Cheng and Ngok, below (see also Huang, 1994). The return to the hometown once again provided the paradigm in which Chinese officialdom and foreign entrepreneurship of Chinese ancestry could unite for the pursuit of the common interest.

It was only in the late 1980s, when Taiwan allowed direct investment in the PRC by its citizens and the basic conditions for an economically united

'Greater China' were fulfilled, that transnational organizations could be fully realized. During the early 1990s, diplomatic relations between the PRC and the remaining countries in East and Southeast Asia were restored. Until that time, the hometown associations (*qiaoxianghui*) had convened their membership in Singapore or Hong Kong. Afterwards, conventions could be held in the hometowns in China themselves. Moreover, PRC politicians began to attend those meetings publicly. The upsurge in associational activity, more fully described in Hong Liu's chapter in this book (see also, Liu, 1998), was borne along by an unprecedented upsurge in direct investment from Hong Kong, Taiwan, and Southeast Asia.

This again poses the question of how important culture is for economic development. The answer suggested by the essays in our book is that however vigorously claims to a shared cultural heritage are being expressed, their effectiveness may be limited in time, space, and social impact. In other words, again, no analysis of cultural discourses is complete without an answer to the question of from whom they emanate and who responds to them, and why. The findings in our book contribute to providing that answer. Several of its chapters, as was mentioned in the Introduction, emphasize the successes achieved by the use of the Chinese sojourner discourse, engendered in particular from Beijing, Singapore, and Hong Kong, and that of its precursors in the first half of the twentieth century (the chapters by Sinn, Liu, and Cheng and Ngok). Its restrictions, however, are demonstrated equally cogently, in several of the other chapters. Stephanie Chung's contribution makes it clear that weak governments may be hijacked by ruthless transnational business groups, which use their double identities and legal statuses to advance their own material interests single-mindedly. The contributions by Cen Huang and David Schak also suggest the importance of material interests and factors external to cultural affinity which determine investment decisions and management policies in transnational enterprises. The chapters by Alan Smart, and Isabelle Thireau and Linshan Hua disclose yet another perspective on the constraints by which the participants in cultural discourses are bound. The predominantly local, personal, and particularistic character of these discourses may trap the entrepreneurs and officials involved in undesired situations from which no easy escape is possible, and eventually may lead to losses in business ventures. This makes relevant the question of whether the call for diasporic idealism, as implied in Tölölyan (1996), Ong and Nonini (1997), Smith and Guarnizo (1998), and others, is not overstretching the issue in view of the structure and *raison d'être* of the type of transnations discussed here. Firstly, they are very lightly institutionalized, as was already noticed above. In the Chinese case, it is possible to point to the vast bureaucratic apparatus sitting on Overseas Chinese affairs. But in actual fact, this is an apparatus which keeps a political low profile on purpose. Similarly, any association between ethnic

Chinese abroad is voluntary, personal and informal. There are several very good reasons why this situation exists. (One reason is the stage of the globalization process, in which these socio-political formations have emerged: exactly at times when it is systematically unclear which deals could be made, and how profits should be distributed between the enterprises, the shareholders, the governments and the workers. Personal acquaintance and the assertion of social and cultural closeness may be a help in creating negotiation space for the settlement of precisely these issues. The politics of native roots seem to provide for these needs, because of their singularly emotional appeal and their lack of ideological articulation, especially at a time when governments allow free markets and capitalism to develop without a clear vision of where that might lead to. The handling of sojourner discourses then becomes part of a larger political game which can give rise to uncontrollable tensions, as is clear from the abundance of ethnic violence in our time. This seems another factor which may explain the inarticulateness of cultural discourses, as well as the political low-profile character of the related organizations just mentioned. This is not to say that diasporic utopias could never contribute to the formation of social ideals; rather that anyone who fully acknowledges the temporary and transitory character of migrant discourses should doubt whether anything stable in the ideological realm could ever result from them.

The most important issue at stake is, how to look at cultural claims as a possibility for creating negotiation space in otherwise unregulated situations, such as those created by globalization processes: it may transpire that sojourner discourses are only really powerful at a stage of economic development in which large disparities between nations coexist with materially successful but socially unsatisfactory migration abroad. Several years ago, popular attitudes in Taiwan turned against Taiwanese emigrants who had until then been welcomed as beneficiaries of the economy. This case shows how the achievement of economic integration may re-alienate emigrants from their home country, and even result in serious tensions. More importantly, the self-defeating tendency which may be inherent in the sojourner discourse is indicative of the tensions with which it is fraught and which determine the terms of negotiation, of material as well as mental, identity-related interests, between the administrators and business people who engage in it. The officials engaged in the implementation of overseas Chinese policies in the economically advanced regions of Guangdong province, mentioned above, who say that they have begun to look for different tasks, are a case in point. It would seem that a certain degree of routinization of procedures and of economic equity, if not social integration, make an appeal to ethnic specificity redundant. This would mean that diasporic idealism is built on very loose sand.

CONCLUDING REMARKS

The restoration of the Chinese sojourner discourse, during the 1980s and 1990s, was undoubtedly part of the globalization process which has been defined above (Introduction). This began in the early 1970s, when the Bretton Woods system collapsed, along with changes in the structure of the US economy which stimulated the rise of export-oriented industrialization in Third World countries. The rise of the East Asian NICs played an essential part in the process. Despite the fact that there were precedents for the industrialization of Third World countries, particularly in Latin America, the rise of the NICs not only brought vast changes to these countries themselves, but also gave a completely new turn to the debates on Third World economic development. The spectacular growth achieved by South Korea, Taiwan, Hong Kong, and Singapore, in the wake of the post-war growth of Japan, questioned the foundations of post-war development theory, and began to ask afresh how the free play of market forces in the world economy was related to state development policies, institutional and political change, and cultural factors for the achievement of economic growth. The entry into China by business people of Chinese descent during the 1980s and 1990s has no doubt contributed to the rise of East and Southeast Asia in global economics and power relationships, and, as noted above, has become the major factor in the increase of foreign investment in and trade with China. Expansion into China was an extension of the transnationalization of business pursued by ethnic Chinese since the 1970s, which had contributed so greatly to the rise of the NICs. The ways in which these business communities deal with the present economic crisis is equally important for the status of the region in the world. The completely new evaluation of Chinese culture and its potential for engendering economic development that has resulted from this has thoroughly changed the landscape of development studies.

This leaves unanswered the question, of in which cases economic development is achieved, and in which it is not. The ongoing economic crisis is doing more than putting the Asian growth regimes to the test, it challenges the theories based upon their recent successes. The wide range of scientific inquiry encompassed in this book proves that overseas Chinese studies is no longer a corner dominated by history in the wider flow of Southeast Asian studies, but a field in which every social science participates in order to grasp the pace and quality of change of our world. The tensions between sojourner discourses, including the organizations based upon it, and the national states, which allow the sojourners space to manoeuvre, and the requirements of social equity and stability, which may conflict with a fast pace of change, may all surface when growth slows down or comes to a halt, however temporarily, and result in less negotiation space and a more rigid social stratification. There may be a return to discourses based on class, or perhaps more materially-oriented uses of cultural discourses. A similar effect might be reached by the routinization of transnational procedures, such as trade and investment regulations. But then, China is vast, and development will be unequal for a long time to come.

BIBLIOGRAPHY

Basch, Linda; Nina Glick Schiller and Cristina Szanton Blanc
1995   'From Immigrant to Transmigrant: Theorizing Transnational Migration', *Anthropological Quarterly* 68(1), pp. 48-63
1997   *Nations Unbound; Transnational Projects, Postcolonial Predicaments and Deterritorialized Nation-states*. Amsterdam: Overseas Publishers Association
Carino, Theresa
1998   'Philippine-China Relations and the Philippine Chinese', in: Zhuang Guotu (ed.) *Ethnic Chinese at the Turn of the Centuries*. Fuchou: Renmin chubanshe, pp. 173-95
Chen, Ta
1940   *Emigrant Communities in South China: A Study of Overseas Emigration and its Influence on Standards of Living and Social Change*. New York: AMS, (repr. 1978 New York: Institute of Pacific Relations)
Coppel, Charles A.
1996   'Peranakan Construction of Chinese Customs in late Colonial Java', in: Leo Douw and Peter Post (eds) *South China: State, Culture and Social Change during the Twentieth Century*. Amsterdam, Oxford, New York, Tokyo: KNAW, pp. 119-31
Dobbin, Christine
1996   *Asian Entrepreneurial Minorities, Conjoint Communities in the Making of the World-economy, 1570-1940*. Richmond: Curzon Press
Douw, L.M.
1995   'Overseas Chinese Entrepreneurship and the Chinese State: The Case of South China, 1900-1949', in: R.A. Brown (ed.) *Chinese Business Entreprise in Asia*. London, New York: Routledge, pp. 115-36
Duara, Prasenjit
1997   'Nationalists Among Transnationals: Overseas Chinese and the Idea of China, 1900-1911', in: Ong Aihwa and Donald M. Nonini (eds) *Ungrounded Empires, The Cultural Politics of Chinese Transnationalism*. New York, London: Routledge, pp. 39-60
1998   'Transnationalism in the Era of Nation-states: China, 1900-1945', *Development and Change* 29, pp. 647-70

East Asia Analytical Unit
1995   *Overseas Chinese Business Networks in Asia*. Department of Foreign
        Affairs and Trade, Australia
Fang, Xiongpu
1998   '*Zhongguo Qiaoxiangde Xingcheng yu Fazhan* (The Establishment
        and Development of the Chinese Hometown Villages)', paper
        presented at the International Conference for *Qiaoxiang* Studies,
        Jinjiang, Fujian province, 28-31 October 1998
Godley, Michael
1989   'The Sojourners: Returned Overseas Chinese in the People's Republic
        of China', *Pacific Affairs* 62(3), pp. 330-52
Goldring, Luin
1998   'The Power of Status in Transnational Social Fields', in: Michael
        Peter Smith and Luis Eduardo Guarnizo (eds) *Transnationalism from
        Below*. New Brunswick, London: Transaction Publishers, pp. 165-95
Goodman, Bryna
1995   *Native Place, City, and Nation*. Berkeley, Los Angeles, London:
        University of California Press
Huang, Songqu
1994   '*Lun Huaqiao Huaren yu Qiaoxiangde Guanxi ji Qi Xin Bianhua* (A
        discussion of the New Transformations of the Relationship Between
        Ethnic Chinese Overseas and Sojourner Villages)', in: Guangdong
        Huaqiao Huaren Yanjiuhui, *Huaqiao yu Huaren* (Ethnic Chinese
        Abroad) 5, pp. 70-5
Lever-Tracy, Constance; David Ip and Noel Tracy
1996   *The Chinese Diaspora and Mainland China: An Emerging Synergy*.
        New York: St. Martin's Press Inc.
Liu, Hong
1998   'Old Linkages, New Networks: The Globalization of Overseas
        Chinese Voluntary Associations and Its Implications', *The China
        Quarterly* 155, pp. 582-609
Mahler, Sarah J.
1998   'Theoretical and Empirical Contributions: Towards a Research
        Agenda for Transnationalism', in: Michael Peter Smith and Luis
        Eduardo Guarnizo (eds) *Transnationalism from Below*. New
        Brunswick, London: Transaction Publishers, pp. 64-100
Ng, Wing Chung
1992   'Urban Chinese Social Organization: Some Unexplored Aspects in
        Huiguan Development in Singapore, 1900-1941', *Modern Asian
        Studies* 26(3), pp. 469-94
Ong, Aihwa, and Donald Nonini

1997   *Ungrounded Empires; the Cultural Politics of Modern Chinese Transnationalism*. New York, London: Routledge

Purcell, Victor
1965   *The Chinese in Southeast Asia*. London, Kuala Lumpur, Hong Kong: Oxford University Press

Remer, C.F.
1933   *Foreign Investments in China*. New York: Macmillan Company

Sassen, Saskia
1991   *The Global City; New York, London, Tokyo*. Princeton (NJ): Princeton University Press

See, Teresita Ang
1998   'The Ethnic Chinese as Filipino's in the 21st Century', in: Zhuang Guotu (ed.) *Ethnic Chinese at the Turn of the Centuries*. Fuchou: Renmin chubanshe, pp. 122-72

Shami, Seteney
1998   'Circassian Encounters: The Self as Other and the Production of the Homeland in the North Caucasus', *Development and Change* 29, pp. 617-46

Sinn, Elizabeth
1997   'Xin Xi Guxiang: A Study of Regional Associations as a Bonding Mechanism in the Chinese Diaspora. The Hong Kong Experience', *Modern Asian Studies* 31(2), pp. 375-97

Siu, Helen
1993   'Cultural Identity and the Politics of Difference in South China', *Daedalus* 122(2), pp. 19-45.

Skinner, G. William
1996   'Creolized Chinese Societies in Southeast Asia', in: Anthony Reid (ed.) *Sojourners and Settlers; Histories of Southeast Asia and the Chinese*. Sydney: George Allen & Unwin

Smith, Robert C.
1998   'Transnational Localities: Community, Technology and the Politics of Membership within the Context of Mexico and U.S. Migration', in: Michael Peter Smith and Luis Eduardo Guarnizo (eds) *Transnationalism from Below*. New Brunswick, London: Transaction Publishers, pp. 196-241

Smith, Michael Peter and Luis Eduardo Guarnizo
1998   'The Locations of transnationalism', in: Michael Peter Smith and Luis Eduardo Guarnizo (eds) *Transnationalism from Below*. New Brunswick, London: Transaction Publishers, pp. 3-34

Smith, Michael Peter and Luis Eduardo Guarnizo (eds)
1998   *Transnationalism from Below*. New Brunswick, London: Transaction Publishers

Suryadinata, Leo

1996   'China's policy towards the ethnic Chinese in Southeast Asia. Continuity and Change', in: Leo Douw and Peter Post (eds) *South China: State, Culture and Social Change during the Twentieth Century.* Amsterdam, Oxford, New York, Tokyo: KNAW, pp. 103-13

Tan, Antonio S.

1981   'The Philippine Chinese Response to the Sino-Japanese Conflict, 1931-1941', *Journal of Southeast Asian Studies* 12(1), pp. 207-24

Tölölyan, Khachig

1996   'Rethinking Diaspora(s): Stateless Power in the Transnational Movement', *Diaspora* 5(1), pp. 3-36

Wang, Gungwu

1981a   'A Note on the Origins of Hua-ch'iao', in: Wang Gungwu, *Community and Nation: Essays on Southeast Asia and the Chinese.* Sydney: George Allen & Unwin, pp. 118-28

1981b   'Southeast Asian Hua-ch'iao in Chinese History-writing', *Journal of Southeast Asian Studies* 12(1), pp. 1-15

Yen, Ch'ing-hwang

1970   'Ch'ing Sale of Honours and the Chinese Leadership of Singapore and Malaysia 1877-1912', *Journal of Southeast Asian Studies* 1, pp. 20-32

1985   'Ch'ing China and the Singapore Chinese Chamber of Commerce, 1906-1911', in: Leo Suryadinata (ed.) *Southeast Asian Chinese and China: The Politico-economic Dimension.* Singapore: Times Academic Press

1986   *A Social History of the Chinese in Singapore and Malaysia, 1800-1911.* Singapore: Oxford University Press

Zhuang, Guotu

1989   *Zhongguo Fengjian Zhengfude Huaqiao Zhengce* (The Overseas Chinese Policies of China's Feudal Government). Xiamen: Xiamen daxue chubanshe.

1996   'The social impact on their hometown of Jinjiang emigrants' activities during the 1930s', in: Leo Douw and Peter Post (eds) *South China: State, Culture and Social Change during the Twentieth Century.* Amsterdam, Oxford, New York, Tokyo: KNAW, pp. 169-83

Notes

1. Cf. Introduction, note 2.
2. Here are meant the writings by Weber, Sombart and Simmel, see Dobbin (1996:4-10).

MOBILIZATION POLITICS:
THE CASE OF SIYI BUSINESSMEN IN HONG KONG, 1890-1928

STEPHANIE PO-YIN CHUNG

The very term *huaqiao* is primarily a political construct, which was
transplanted to 'overseas Chinese' communities, where residents inspired by
the notion of 'commercial war' and the Qing Government's 'rights recovery
movement', formed chambers of commerce to advance the economic
interests of the homeland, and their native districts in particular. Although
considerable work has now been done on the rebuilding of *qiaoxiang* ties, it
is important to remember that the 'construction of ethnicity', like the
'invention of tradition', is always situational: easily manipulated by the
participants for varying, and sometimes quite different, purposes (Ranger
and Hobsbawn, 1983:1-14). This chapter accepts that 'mobilization politics'
is a major theme in modern Chinese history and agrees with other
contributors that the Chinese residing abroad have been important targets.
But by looking into the experience of Siyi migrants in Hong Kong earlier
this century, the following pages will also illustrate how *huaqiao* identity
has interacted with changing political and economic realities, whilst always
serving the self-interest of the parties involved.

INTRODUCTION

Contemporary interest in transnational business networks evokes a crucial
topic in modern Chinese history: namely the making of new political
traditions (see Harrison, 1996). In Imperial China, overseas Chinese were
long referred to by the government as *Fanhe* (Zhuang, 1989). Traditionally,
governments had adopted an intimidating, punitive policy toward subjects
who went abroad. The first of these can be traced back to the Ming
dynasty. *Fanhe* were regarded as 'dissenters abandoning their ancestral
graveyard and mother homeland'. In principle, they were regarded as

Tianchao qimin (dissenters abandoned by the Heavenly Kingdom) and were forbidden to return to China. Such policies were inherited by the Manchu regime. The attitude toward *Fanhe* was reaffirmed in 1806 when a Qing law was passed prohibiting, in principle, any Chinese person from moving. However, after the forced opening of China in 1841, the Qing Government gradually recognized that global market forces were encroaching upon China.

The abolition of slavery in Britain (1807), Portugal (1815), USA (1875), and Spain (1920), highlighted a severe shortage of labour in the world market. In 1859, the Chinese subjects were formally allowed to leave China, as a 'Bureau for Worker Recruitment' was established in Canton (Guangzhou) with government approval. After a power struggle between a 'hard liners' clique' and a 'Western-minded clique' in Peking, a *Tsungli Yamen* was established in 1860 under the patronage of Prince Kung (Wright, 1957). In 1866, this new 'foreign affairs office' reached an agreement with the British and French and proclaimed a 22-clause 'Recruitment Guideline for the Export of Chinese Labourers'. From 1848 to 1874, more than 500,000 Chinese had left China for Nanyang, the USA, and South Africa. In 1868, a Chinese Consulate was established in the USA. In 1876, the Qing Court conducted a thorough survey on overseas Chinese living in Nanyang. In 1877 and 1879, Chinese Consulates were established in Britain and in Russia respectively. The above measures indicated a major change in the Qing Government's policy toward overseas Chinese.

The idea of *huaqiao* was closely related to the development of a new governing mentality in China. The term was coined in the 1880s. It can be found in a petition from Zheng Guanying to Li Hung-chang in 1883. In this petition, Zheng suggested to Li that the China Navigation Company (established under Li's patronage as part of the 'Western affairs movements') should make the effort to build up closer networks with the *huaqiao* in Nanyang. The idea was later transplanted to Japan and the term *Huaqiao Xuexiao* (Overseas Chinese School) was coined by the Chinese settlers in Yokohama. In the 1890s, with the slogans of 'right-recovery movement' and 'commercial war',[1] the Qing Government appealed to overseas Chinese for support to 'recover' railways and mines from foreign capital. In 1899, the Qing Government openly declared that they regarded *huaqiao* as 'patriotic overseas Chinese'. This new policy was reinforced by measures introduced in the name of the Late Qing reforms. China's first law on chambers of commerce was introduced in 1904. The law led to a proliferation of regional chambers of commerce in different parts of China. The law, significantly, also applied to the overseas Chinese communities. The policy led to a redefinition of the relationship between the Peking

46

government and the overseas Chinese (Rankin, 1986). After 1905, such new ideas as *huashang* (Chinese merchants), *huaren* (Chinese people), *huagong* (Chinese labour), and *huamin* (Chinese people) gained even further in popularity. More significantly, China's first law on nationality promulgated in 1909 declared that 'persons with Chinese blood', whatever their place of residence, were entitled to be considered Chinese nationals. An academy was also established in Nanjing in 1911 to recruit students from among the returned overseas Chinese. This was the same year that a *Qiaowubu* (Bureau of Overseas Chinese Affairs) was set up by the Qing Court, along with a registration system for all the Chinese living abroad (Campell, 1923; FitzGerald, 1972). All these measures were intended to strengthen ties with the diaspora.

The collapse of the dynasty only accelerated the above changes. Its demise, followed by the emerging North-South divide between Canton and Peking from 1911 to 1928 and, subsequently, the power struggle between the KMT (*Guomindang*) and the Chinese Communist Party (CCP), helped highlight the importance of 'mass mobilization' in twentieth century Chinese politics. The overseas Chinese were regarded by different political authorities as a major target for these mobilizations. Other than the chambers of commerce, the establishment of trade unions and surname associations was encouraged by different regional political authorities in China. In 1914, the Peking government (under Yuan Shikai) introduced an Overseas Chinese Protection Law. In 1923, the Canton government (under Sun Yat-sen) established a separate *Qiaowu weiyuanhui* (Committee on Overseas Chinese Affairs). In 1926, under this *weiyuanhui,* the KMT established an Education Department aimed at supervising the quality of education provided by the *Huaqiao Xuexiao* (Overseas Chinese schools) which had been set up in many Chinese communities. From the 1930s, the CCP and the KMT both endeavoured to build up their own networks with the overseas Chinese. To achieve these aims, new laws were introduced; new government departments were established. Both the KMT and the CCP were competing for recognition and financial support from ethnic Chinese living abroad. The official mentality, as indicated by the above changes, had undergone a dramatic transformation; to outflank their political competitors, they had to mobilize the support from the 'overseas Chinese'.

SIYI SETTLERS AS *HUAQIAO*

The construction of the *huaqiao* idea had much to do with efforts of both the concept's 'creators' and its 'users'. Other than the initiatives of the government, the overseas Chinese had also made enormous efforts to reshape the idea. While paying lip-service loyalty to the central governments, the overseas Chinese developed an agenda of their own. The Siyi men's experience serves as a very revealing example.

The 'Siyi *huaqiao*' were of humble origin. By the late nineteenth century, Siyi county was regarded by the Cantonese as one of the poorest and as a 'non-Cantonese' area of Guangdong. The Siyi region is one of the most mountainous areas in Guangdong, so fertile land was limited. The Siyi dialect was regarded by the Sanyi people (Nanhai, Panyu, and Shunde) as 'corrupted Cantonese'. By the 1920s, the Siyi area had experienced a rapid 'upward mobility' in status: Siyi county was known to be a patriotic *qiaoxiang* and Xinning was named a 'model county' by Sun Yat-sen's Canton government. The inferiority of the Siyi men's social status helps, in part, to explain why they were so eager to identify themselves as 'progressive *huaqiao*', supported the late Qing reforms, and financed the new government after 1911. The 'upward mobility' of the Siyi men is quite relevant to their access to overseas networks. With the forced opening of China, demands for manpower in the world market led to an outflow of Cantonese labourers to Europe and America. In Guangdong, Xiangshan county and the so-called Siyi (literally, Enping, Kaiping, Xinning, and Xinhui counties) region were the major *qiaoxiang* where the greatest number of overseas migrants originated. A scarcity of arable land, as well as their proximity to Hong Kong and Macao, made Siyi and Xiangshan counties ready sources of low-cost labour. In 1848, the discovery of gold in California also increased the outflow of labourers to the USA. Because the cost of passage to America was very high, the majority of these voyages were financed by a middleman, known as 'coolie agents' in Hong Kong. Many others also migrated to Hawaii and Australia (Chung, 1998; see also Zheng and Cheng, 1992; Woon, 1984). California was the most popular destination, however.

In 1849, there were about 700 Chinese settlers in California. In 1851, this figure had increased to 12,000, and many of them were railway-builders. In 1886, a large number of the labourers working on California farms were Chinese. Before 1878, there were no Chinese consuls and diplomatic officials in the USA, so Chinese migrants tended to organize themselves into clusters of organizations. For a long period of time, no centralized leadership emerged among these Chinese settlers. Social differences among these Chinese settlers were very strong. These social cleavages can be illustrated by the rise and decline of the Chinese associations in the US. In California, for example, a Sanyi Huiguan and a Siyi Huiguan were formed in 1851. The former was organized by Cantonese from Nanhai, Panyu, and Shunde counties; the latter was organized by Cantonese from Xinhui, Xinning, Enping, and Kaiping counties. The Sanyi region, constituting a major part of the Cantonese provincial capital, was the centre of the silk industry in Guangdong. Because of the contrasting poverty of the Siyi region, the social divide between Sanyi and Siyi people was clear from the very beginning. Other differences among settlers from the four counties were very strong too. For example, in 1854, people from Xinning (one of the four counties) withdrew from the Siyi Huiguan and formed themselves into a Ninyang Huiguan. In 1862, members of the Siyi Huiguan who bore the family name Yee formed themselves into a Hehe Huiguan. The Siyi Huiguan also changed its name to Gangzhou Huiguan. Disputes among members of different clans and districts were common. In 1854, there was a 'Weaverville War' between the Siyi men and the Xiangshan men. In 1856, fighting broke out between the Sanyi men and the Hakkas. By the 1860s, the above six associations decided to make a compromise and formed themselves into an united organization, known as the 'Chinese Six Companies'. Its members acted as judges and money-lenders. It also made rules on currency, weights, measures, and market prices. The 'Six Companies' set restrictions on the movements of Chinese immigrants. When the Chinese labourers reached San Francisco, they had to register with the 'Six Companies'. When they planned to return to China, the labourers had to inform the 'Six Companies' too. They could purchase ship tickets only after the 'Six Companies' had made sure that all their debts had been settled (Hoexter, 1976; Hong, 1955).

The history of the Siyi settlers had entered a new chapter by the 1880s, when Washington adopted exclusion policies toward Chinese immigrants. In protest, many returned to China. While some went back to their native counties, a considerable number decided to reside in Hong Kong which they thought would provide better business opportunities. Living in Hong Kong, many of them used the territory's advantageous location to establish trading firms engaged in selling Chinese goods to the overseas Chinese communities in the US (Chung, 1998). These firms, known as the 'Golden Mountain Houses' ('golden mountain' referring to California), also involved themselves in the remittance business between South China and the American Chinese communities. With these resources, Siyi native banks started to challenge the established Shunde clique, and became the most influential clique of native banks in South China. Beginning in the 1890s, Siyi was regarded as one of the wealthiest regions in Guangdong because of its overseas remittance networks. Before finding out more about these Siyi migrants, let us first take a look at the social setting they encountered in Hong Kong.

THE SIYI COMMUNITY IN HONG KONG

The overwhelmingly-Chinese population of Hong Kong was built up by waves of immigrants from South China. Each time China was in political turmoil, there was a drastic population increase in Hong Kong. The idea of 'Hong Kong people', however, did not yet exist. The Chinese population of Hong Kong was transient in nature. Many of them thought that they would just stay in Hong Kong temporarily and would return to China after having saved an adequate amount of money. They therefore maintained very close connections with their ancestral home. The majority paid regular visits to their home villages and worshipped their ancestors there. Almost all of them believed that they should die in their home village. If this hope could not be fulfilled, their bodies and coffins should be transported back to China and buried near to their ancestral temples. As a consequence, familial and geographical networks played very important roles in organizing these 'sojourners' into a community. Temples, guilds, hometown associations, common-surname organizations and charitable institutions had constituted the core of their communal activities. It is no surprise that, by the 1870s, the most influential leaders of Hong Kong's Chinese community were the directors of the Tung Wah Hospital (Sinn, 1989).

The returned Siyi migrants who came to reside in Hong Kong in the 1880s, immediately found that they were regarded by the established Chinese leadership as 'outsiders'. The Siyi men were a marginal group compared to the indigenous communities. Hardly any of them were appointed into the Tung Wah directorate, a channel through which the Hong Kong Government hand-picked its Chinese legislative councilors (British-recognized local leaders). The British rulers likewise categorized them as inferior and uneducated people, as will be shown below (p. 10). Thus, as an isolated social group, the Siyi men were forced to build up their own web of networks. In 1900, the Siyi men were the core donors for the first Chinese Young Men's Christian Association in Hong Kong. The most prominent of these donors were Li Yu-tang and Yang Xian (Xianggang Qingnianhui (ed.) , 1901; see also Tan, 1958:297-327; Feng Shaoshan [ed.], 1991:187). It should be noted that many of these self-styled Chinese Christians, despite their belief, did not abandon their practices of ancestor worship.

When, in the late-1890s, the Qing Government appealed to the Chinese merchants, including those residing overseas, to give financial support for what it called a 'commercial war' against foreign goods and concessions, the marginalized Siyi men in Hong Kong quite readily identified themselves as *huaqiao*. Utilizing the new commercial codes, the Siyi men in Hong Kong formed themselves into capital syndicates to invest in China. For example, a *Siyi Steamship Company* and a *Xinning Railway Company* was formed in 1904 and 1906, respectively (Yen Ching-hwang, 1982; Zheng Dehua and Cheng Luxi, 1992). In 1904, Li Yu-tang and Yang Xian also organized a Society to Oppose the United States Exclusion Treaty Against Chinese Laborers. They initiated a large-scale boycott against American goods in South China as a protest of the renewal of the United States Exclusion Treaty (Chan Lau, 1991:67-8).

MOBILIZING *HUAQIAO*

In Imperial China, merchants had always adopted tactics of advancing their social status through the purchase of official titles (often 'donating' a large sum of money to the government). The official title, qualifying the merchant to address government officials as colleagues, would also entitle the merchant to petition directly to the officials. Proximity to the core of political authority was, even then, a significant asset for business endeavours. The cultivation of patronage networks was a safety net for merchants investing in China, which lacked an adequate institutional framework. Before 1904, China did not have such concepts as company law, limited liability, stock exchange, or capital market. Instead, the cultivation of personal networks, along familial, ethnic or geographical lines, was extremely important to secure personal and business protection. Familial and geographical connections turned out to be very convenient channels through which money, networks, social protection, and political patronage could be obtained. Ancestral temples and regional associations were two of the most important institutions for these networking activities (Faure, 1996; see also W. Chan, 1995).

In the first decade of this century, a new element was injected into Chinese politics. In 1902, the Qing Court, recognizing the need to reorganize central-provincial relations, introduced measures to institutionalize power divisions. In 1904, the Qing Court helped redefine how élite status was to be achieved when the Imperial Examination was abolished and further raised the status of merchants with the establishment of the first chamber of commerce. According to the new regulations, regional chambers of commerce were sanctioned by the Peking Government as its local agents to maintain communication between government and merchants, and to provide protection to local businessmen. The chambers provided new avenues for merchants' upward mobility. As a result, Chinese regional chambers of commerce (*shanghui*) were set up in large numbers both inside and outside China (Chung, 1998). This was all part of a 'mobilization' effort to attract regional merchants for political and economic support.

From 1905 onward, employing the slogan 'rights recovery', the Qing Government began to recover railway concessions given to foreign investors. The overseas Chinese community was regarded by the Qing Court as a major source for tapping the needed capital. A railway company was set up with this capital in 1906 and the railway was 100 per cent privately owned. While many of the shares were subscribed to by overseas Chinese, some of the largest shareholders were found amongst overseas returned merchants in Hong Kong. They included Li Yu-tang and his Siyi associates (Chan, 1991:90-1; Rhoads, *China's Republican Revolution*, pp. 31-3, 62-3, 92-4).

Traditionally, if merchants intended to advance their social status and to build up networks with government officials, the easiest solution would be the purchase of an official title from the central government. In 1904, however, the Imperial Examination was abolished. By doing so, the Qing Court had reshaped the ways in which élite status was to be defined in China. Also in the same year, China's first law on chambers of commerce was introduced. The central government explicitly sanctioned regional chambers of commerce with the expressed function of providing protection to merchants and allowing them to present opinions to officials.[2] Because of these measures, regional chambers of commerce *(shanghui)* were set up in great numbers. As of 1909 in Hong Kong, the first regional chamber of commerce was the *Siyi Shanggong Gongsi Zonghui* (the Siyi Chamber of Commerce). In early 1910, equipped with the slogan of 'commercial war', the *Siyi* Chamber of Commerce also petitioned the Peking government through the Commissioner of Industrial Promotion *(quanyedao)* for approval to develop a new port in China.[3] They asked to be granted land in south China for the development of a modern trading port which would compete with Portuguese Macao and British Hong Kong. A joint-stock syndicate, with 580,000 silver taels in capital, was proposed by and subscribed to through the Siyi Chambers of Commerce. With the approval of the Qing Government, the Siyi men initiated a large-scale port-market development scheme in Siyi.[4]

We learn from the above that the Qing Court, after repeated military defeats, had adopted 'mobilization tactics' from the 1890s onwards. The tactics intended to appeal to local merchants for political and economic support. Chinese living in Hong Kong were included in the Qing officials' political agenda. The Hong Kong Siyi men, given their 'marginal status' (against the established Chinese community) in the colony, were more than willing to seize this golden opportunity to advance their political and economic status in China. Understandably, they immediately identified themselves as 'patriotic *huaqiao*'.

POLITICAL INFLUENCE IN SOUTH CHINA

The above state-*huaqiao* relationship, however, underwent a drastic change in the 1910s. In 1911, the Qing Government announced the nationalization of all private railways in the provinces. This immediately evoked severe opposition among railway shareholders in different provinces, who formed themselves into different railway protection societies and announced their opposition to any infringement upon provincial interests by the Peking Government. Confrontations accumulated, and when a military mutiny broke out in Wuhan, armed uprisings also broke out in different parts of China. The chambers of commerce and the Railway Protection Societies in the southern provinces took the opportunity to declare their provinces independent from the Peking Government.[5] In the South, the Chairman of the Guangdong Railway Protection Society was Li Yu-tang, the chairman of the Siyi Chamber of Commerce in Hong Kong.[6]

As *huaqiao* living in Hong Kong, the Siyi men had Hong Kong as their safe haven. They could retreat easily to Hong Kong when they felt insecure in China. In 1911, because of the severe suppression by the Governor-General in Canton, Li Yu-tang moved the Guangdong Railway Protection Society back to Hong Kong and handled Canton affairs in 'remote control'. In November, Guangdong became the eleventh province in China to declare itself independent.[7] At a meeting held on the premises of the Siyi Chamber of Commerce in Hong Kong, Hu Hanmin, known to be a close follower of Sun Yat-sen, was elected as the Governor-General of the newly established Canton Revolutionary Government. Backed up by the Siyi 'thirty-man subscription team' (*sanshiren chouxiangtuan*), this new Governor-General went to Canton on the day following the meeting. Upon his arrival in Guangzhou, Li Yu-tang was appointed Provincial Treasurer of Guangdong. Li Yu-tang's son, his two brothers and his son-in-law also held posts in the Canton Government. The thirty-man subscription team was renamed the 'Subscription Bureau in Hong Kong' (*zhugang chouxiangju*). Yang Xian was appointed director of this bureau, which was located in Hong Kong. Its members were issued with appointment charters to collect subscriptions from among overseas Chinese on behalf of the Canton Revolutionary Government.[8]

As *huaqiao* living in Hong Kong, the Siyi men also regarded Hong Kong as a safe haven for their economic investments in China. They could register their businesses in Hong Kong but operated their businesses in China. As British companies, Siyi businesses in China enjoyed diplomatic and legal protection given by the government of Hong Kong. In late 1911, for example, Li Yu-tang and members of the Subscription Bureau formed the Bank of Canton in Guangdong but registered it as a British company in

Hong Kong. As Li later explained, the move was intended 'to put the project [of financing the Canton government] on a business basis by establishing a bank of Hong Kong under the Companies Ordinance, [and] to operate in aid of the rehabilitation of the Canton Note Currency'.[9] One of the most difficult problems facing the new government was finance, especially the provision of military expenses for the various people's armies stationed in Canton after 1911. Li Yu-tang, as the Provincial Treasurer, returned to Hong Kong immediately following his appointment and raised a loan of HK$408,000 within a few days (*Huazi ribao*, 24 June 1913; Tan, *Zhongguo Xinhai geming huiyilu*, pp. 289-90). The Subscription Bureau in Hong Kong sought to raise a loan of HK$5 million from overseas Chinese, including HK$1 million in the colony (*Huazi ribao*, 17, 18 November 1911. Tan, *Zhongguo Xinhai geming huiyilu*, pp. 290-307).

In Hong Kong, the only threat the Siyi men had to deal with was the disapproval of the colonial governor. Alarmed by the close connection between the Siyi men and the Canton Government, the Governor of Hong Kong sent a long report to the Colonial Office in 1912. He was alarmed by what he saw as the poor accounting practices of the Guangdong Treasury, which came under the control of Li Yu-tang:

'[It] has been managed very badly. It was practically emptied ... The Chinese community of Hong Kong supplied between $2,000,000 and 53,000,000 - all spent (or embezzled) without any account having been kept. Following this the pernicious device was resorted to of issuing notes without any reserve to back them up.' (*Huazi ribao*, 17, 18 November 1911. Tan, *Zhongguo Xinhai geming huiyilu*, pp. 290-307.)

A worrying fact to the Governor was that Canton's depreciating currency was circulating in Hong Kong. The Governor explained that 'the circulation [of Canton currency] was maintained here [in Hong Kong] in spite of its general unpopularity ... not only by official pressure from Canton but also by means of intimidation practised by so-called patriotic associations and by the influential persons who were financially interested.' (CO 129/392, May to Harcourt, 4 October 1912.) The Governor was pointing his finger at Li Yu-tang.

The Governor recorded that a Society of Chinese Abroad for the Promotion of Patriotic Subscriptions was formed in Hong Kong, and intimidated the Chinese chambers of commerce and guilds into accepting the depreciating Canton currency at its full face value (CO 129/392, May to Harcourt, 4 October 1912). The Chinese press in Hong Kong recorded that Li Yu-tang and the Siyi Chamber of Commerce in Hong Kong were organizing a Society of Overseas Chinese for the Promotion of Patriotic

Subscriptions. In early October, at a meeting with all the major chambers of commerce in Hong Kong, the Society 'resolved' that Canton's currency would be accepted in the colony at its face value and that the chambers would draw up a scale of fines to be imposed for any breach of this requirement (*Xunhuan ribao* (Universal Circulating Herald), 5, 9, 10 October 1912). The governor, in response to the Siyi men's activities, published a 'notice of caution,' in the Government Gazette drawing public attention to the Bank Notes Ordinance of 1895, banning the circulation of any currency without the sanction of a Secretary of State signified through the Governor (*Hong Kong Government Gazette*, No. 314, 12 October 1912).

Immediately following the notice's publication, a tramway boycott broke out in Hong Kong. The Hong Kong Tramway Company, following the government's instruction, enforced the policy of accepting Hong Kong currency as the only medium of paying fares. A boycott initiated by the Chinese against the Tramway Company followed (Jung-fang Tsai, *Hong Kong in Chinese History*, pp. 270-87). The Governor reported to the Colonial Office that the Siyi men were behind the boycott, and that they carried out large-scale intimidation measures in Hong Kong forbidding Chinese from using the tramway. Concerning the Siyi Chamber of Commerce, the Governor commented, with contempt, that:

> 'This association is composed originally of returned California and Australian coolie and artisan emigrants, who though they could often talk fair English, could not write their own names in any language ... for the most part [of it] are men of little or no education.' (CO 129/399, May to Harcourt, 16 January 1913)

The Governor directed his resentment to Li Yu-tang and his associates. Amidst the tramway boycott, a Boycott Prevention Ordinance was introduced into Hong Kong in late 1912 (Chan, *China, Britain and Hong Kong*, pp. 112-13). The Governor also wrote an eleven-page letter to the Colonial Office in January 1913. The caption of the letter was '*Sze Yap* Association [the Siyi Chamber]'. The Governor started with the observation that the Siyi men had 'principally ruled Canton' since 1911:

> 'It was through the *Sze Yap* Association [Siyi Chamber of Commerce] that money and men were procured from Hong Kong for the revolution in Canton. When Canton was handed over to the revolutionary party, Li Yuktong [Li Yu-tang] was made the Provincial Treasurer and almost all the important positions under the new Provincial Government were given to *Sze Yap* [Siyi] men ... [The Chamber] was the right hand of the

Canton Government. It constituted its intelligence department, commissariat and financial agency.' (CO 129/399, May to Harcourt, 22 January 1913. See also Chan, *China, Britain and Hong Kong*, p. 115)

The colonial governor's words might be somewhat exaggerated, but the Siyi men did play a very important part in financing the new Canton Government. In 1911 and 1912, Li Yu-tang had transmitted at least three loans to the amounts of HK$260,000, HK$1,700,000 and HK$4,030,000 to the Canton Government.[10] The colonial governor suggested that these activities to finance the Canton Government had the particular aim of lining Li Yu-tang's own pocket. In the same letter, the Governor claimed that:

'[Li Yu-tang] went to Canton a poor man, held office as Provincial Treasurer for a few months and returned to Hong Kong with many hundreds of thousands of dollars. He [has] since invested over $100,000 [Hong Kong dollars] in Hong Kong in land alone.'[11]

Contemporary materials and the memoirs of a Cantonese revolutionary confirm that before 1911 Li Yu-tang's 'Golden Mountain House' business was on the brink of bankruptcy, but that he became the 'Insurance King' of south China by the 1910.[12] By the 1920s, Li was the chief promoter of at least 12 banks and insurance and mortgages businesses in South China. The rapid growth of Li Yu-tang's wealth after 1911 might be related to Canton politics in several ways. The following serves to underline this point. Firstly, the Siyi men's loans to the Canton Government returned very high profits. In 1913, Yang Xian, the Director of the Subscription Bureau in Hong Kong, recalled that:

'[The uprising] ... was a success without the casualty of a single soldier ... [because] I and my associates requested Governor-General Hu [Hanmin] for a charter to raise loans in Hong Kong and collected within half a day, the sum of over 400,000 [Hong Kong dollars] and had it transported to Canton immediately ... Originally, it was scheduled that 2 dollars would be repaid for each dollar loaned, but I proposed that 1.5 dollars be repaid for each dollar loaned.' (*Huazi ribao*, 24 June 1913)

The recollection of Yang Xian is confirmed by an advertisement in the Hong Kong Chinese press in November 1911. All six subscription offices in Hong Kong were business firms owned by Siyi or Xiangshan returned migrants. An interest rate of 50 per cent was promised (*Huazi ribao*, 18 November 1911).

Secondly, in order to sustain the Canton Revolutionary Government, a large amount of currency was forced into circulation both inside and outside Guangdong.[13] As early as 1912, the colonial governor had observed that Li Yu-tang had gained a great deal from his role as the Provincial Treasurer:

'In addition to the authorized issue of $16,000,000 [in Canton currency] ... Li Yuk-tang made an issue of $55,000,000 for his own benefit ... He left Hong Kong a poor man but has, since his return, invested very largely in the Colony and is now reported to be a rich man ... his methods as Master of the Mint and of the Currency and the Note Redemption Departments are ... open to the gravest suspicion.' (CO 129/391, 'Political Situation in Canton', 23 July 1912)

We learn from the above records that the Siyi men had gained a huge monetary return by claiming themselves as 'Patriotic *huaqiao*', as well as by financing the Canton Government. Sun Yat-sen's regime in Canton had a structural problem. Sun had to organize a government with no income from taxes and no control over the armies. Before 1924, when the Whampoa Academy was set up with Soviet support, Sun had to rely on the fragile loyalty of troops from Guangxi and Yunnan. To prevent the armies from mutiny, Sun had to provide proper 'maintenance expenses' for the troops (*China Weekly Review*, 25 August, 8 September 1923; Cheng, 1993:140-5). As a result, he turned to *huaqiao* for loans and donations, which explains, in part, why he always referred to the *huaqiao* as the 'mother of the Revolution'. The Siyi men's close association with Sun Yat-sen's revolutionary party was apparently an asset for their business endeavours: during the 1910s and the 1920s, Li Yu-tang's business empire was at its summit. The formula worked well for Li, as least until 1924, when the Soviet influence began (Chung, *Chinese Business Groups in Hong Kong*).

DOING BUSINESS WITH SOUTH CHINA

Being a *huaqiao* group in Hong Kong, the Siyi men could adjust fairly easily to their degree of involvement in Guangdong politics. As *huaqiao* living in Hong Kong, the Siyi men also regarded the territory as a safe haven for their business investments in China. The Siyi men's controversial political activities, and their connections with the Canton Revolutionary Government, turned out to be very significant assets for their business endeavours. British law guaranteed that the Siyi men could (like other merchants in Hong Kong) register their firms as British business companies. So, they registered their businesses in Hong Kong and operated them in South China. As foreign-registered companies, these Siyi firms could enjoy legal protection guaranteed by the British law although this did not diminish the importance of personal networks. Quite a number of the shareholders were Siyi *huaqiao* living in Siyi, Hong Kong, Nanyang, and the US. Familial and ethnic networks can also easily be found among the shareholders (Chung, 1998).

It is not accidental that many of these registered firms owned by the Siyi *huaqiao* were engaged in mortgage, brokering, insurance and banking businesses. Their connection with the Canton Government actually gave them advantages to invest in these businesses. In late 1911, for example, Li Yu-tang and other Siyi leaders founded a Bank of Canton in Canton. Remarkably, they registered the Bank in Hong Kong. Li stated that they regarded the task of rehabilitating the Canton paper currency as a business project and they also intended 'to put the project on a business basis by establishing a bank of Hong Kong under the Companies Ordinance.' (CO 129/391, May to Harcourt, 16 August 1912). By lending to the Canton Government, the Siyi men enjoyed an interest rate of 50 per cent as a return. To sustain the Canton Revolutionary Government, a large amount of currency was forced into circulation both in Guangdong and Hong Kong (Ou, 1933:9-10; Chen and Yu, 1991, pp. 57-9). Siyi men had gained a huge monetary return by claiming themselves as 'patriotic *huaqiao*'. In 1923, for instance, a Guangzhou Registration Bureau for Government Properties and a Guangzhou Government Property Clearance Office were set up in Guangzhou with government approval. Both institutions were under the control of the Siyi men. The Bureau was responsible for the registration of immovable properties in Guangzhou city. All properties controlled by lineage, temple, and guild were confiscated as 'public properties' until land deeds issued by the government were produced (Chung, 1998. See also *Guangzhou shizheng gongbao, yijiu'ersan*, 1924). The Clearance Office was responsible for organizing auctions for the above confiscated properties. The British recorded in 1923 that because of these auctions, Canton had an 'outburst of speculation in real estate' (CO 129/480, Enclosure, 9 May 1923). The *China Weekly Review* also noticed in 1923 that the boom in 'lands and shares was the most outstanding feature' of the year (*China Weekly Review*, 7 February 1924). Amidst this boom, some of the auctioned properties could be purchased, through personal networks, with a much lower price. The Siyi men, remarkably, benefited from these speculations. The memoirs of a government official in Canton recorded that there was a proliferation of investment and mortgage companies in Canton in the 1920s. He remarked that quite a number of these companies were set up by those Siyi men who had close connections with the Canton Government (Chung, 1998; see also *Shenbao*, 16 October 1923, *China Weekly Review*, 8 and 29 March 1924).

The legal protection provided by Hong Kong, combined with their political connections to the Canton Government, placed Siyi businessmen in a privileged position: permitting them to lend to the government, to issue currency, and to speculate on Guangdong real estate. There is no question that Li's business empire was closely related to his close association with Sun Yat-sen. This formula worked well for Li, as least until 1924, the year the Soviet aids arrived to Canton. But the point here is the way that *huaqiao* status gave Siyi businessmen the legitimacy they needed to interfere in neighbouring Guangdong.

COMPETITION BETWEEN OVERSEAS CHINESE

The Hong Kong Governor felt threatened upon finding that the Siyi men's political and economic influence was expanding in South China. He made vain attempts to contain the Siyi men's activities. The Society Ordinance of 1911, for example, had done very little to stop the Siyi men from exerting political influence in Guangdong. The ordinance, aimed at controlling the 'criminal and political activities' of the 'commerce and trade unions' in the colony, compelled all societies there to register under government auspices. Those associations, whose activities appeared to be 'calculated to excite tumult or disorder in China', would be declared unlawful (*Ordinance of Hong Kong*, 1911, Hong Kong 1911). The ordinance was aimed at the Siyi Chamber of Commerce.

The Siyi Chamber of Commerce was banned in the colony in 1917 (*Hong Kong Administrative Report*, 1917:C13). The British authorities believed that the organization was the 'black hand' behind the political turmoil in Guangdong, and that its chairman was one of the most dangerous Chinese in South China. But, despite official proscription, the Siyi men had not lost their influence in Hong Kong. Their Chamber could be banned, but the Siyi men could maintain their power in a different way. They could, for example, adjust their sense of identity, and set up other associations in Hong Kong. In 1916, one year before the banning of the Siyi Chamber, a Wuyi General Chamber of Industry and Commerce (*Wuyi Gongshang Zonghui*) was established in Hong Kong. Core members of this new association, other than the settlers from Heshan were none other than those Siyi leaders active in Guangdong politics. Two separate associations organized by the surnames of Yee and Chan were also established in Hong Kong by the old members of the Siyi Chamber. Ethnic identity was very flexible indeed. It could be adjusted fairly easily by 'users' in different political and social contexts. The Hong Kong Governor, finding no reliable legislative measures to control the Siyi activists, turned to other *huaqiao* groups in Hong Kong for assistance.

He found ready allies because the dominance of the Siyi *huaqiao* in Guangdong politics had also alarmed non-Siyi Chinese groups in the colony who were, themselves, intent on diminishing Siyi dominance over Cantonese business and politics. The method they adopted was none other than claiming themselves as '*huaqiao*' and forming themselves into similar regional chambers of commerce. As a consequence, we witness the number of *huaqiao* associations in Hong Kong increasing, from two in 1909 to sixteen in 1913 (Sinn, 1990:178-9). All these new Chinese associations placed a heavy emphasis on their *huaqiao* identity. Although many of these non-Siyi leaders had received an English education, and some of them were Eurasians, they chose to present their Chineseness by performing annual sacrifices to Confucius and establishing a 'Confucian Church' in the colony (Chung, 1998; see also *Xianggang shangye jiaotong renming lu*, 1914; *Anglo-Chinese Directory*, 1922). The ambiguity of *huaqiao* identity can be further illustrated by the following example.

The story dates back to 1919, when Canton was undergoing a series of urban redevelopment programmes. In that year, the Siyi Chamber of Commerce in Hong Kong liaised with their counterpart in the Siyi counties to purchase three pieces of public land in China. These properties were previously a *yamen* and a prison. To encourage Siyi Chinese to invest, all subscribers were entitled to install their ancestors' spiritual tablets in an 'ancestral temple' which was to be built upon one of the sites. The number and the size of 'ancestral tablets' were, not surprisingly, determined in proportion to the amount of each subscribers' contribution. In light of the political instability in Canton, the land deeds were kept by the Siyi *huaqiao* residing in Hong Kong. In 1931, great confusion arose over the nature of the collaboration when the Hong Kong group voted to sell the properties. The native group in Siyi, however, insisted on retaining the properties for charitable purposes (as an ancestral hall). The point of conflict was that although the native association in Siyi regarded the collaboration as an indivisible ancestral trust, the Siyi Chambers of Commerce in Hong Kong announced that the collaboration was actually a 'joint-stock company' and they were entitled to sell the land with their majority shares (*Taishan Gonghui Yuekan* (Monthly publication of the Taishan Chamber of Commerce) (Canton, 1933), pp. 17-19, 24-30). To these Hong Kong merchants, ethnic and *huaqiao* identity was an asset in business investment.

The timing of this conflict (that is, in 1931) is not accidental. After the death of Sun Yat-sen in 1925, and after the nominal unification of China in 1928, the core of the KMT leadership had gradually shifted to Shanghai. The new KMT leader, Chiang Kai-shek had gathered under his wings a new alliance of chambers of commerce based in Shanghai. The most prominent of these merchant leader was T.V. Soong. Without a strong patron (like Sun Yat-sen), the leadership of the Siyi Chamber under Li Yu-tang gradually disintegrated. Different cliques of Siyi men emerged in South China. Without a strong leader like Li Yu-tang, the Siyi Chamber in Canton was competing with the Siyi Chamber in Hong Kong for government recognition (and control over common property). The most symbolic of these struggles occurred in 1936 when the Bank of Canton was facing severe financial difficulties. T.V. Soong, with Chiang Kai-shek's support, had announced his plan to take over the Bank. The manager of the Bank, himself a Siyi man, had appealed to the Siyi fellowmen for financial support to save the Bank. The different Siyi cliques, however, decided to have the Bank dissolved. The incident symbolized a formal collapse of the Siyi men's business empire in South China.

CONCLUDING REMARKS

The coining of the idea of *huaqiao* has much to do with a new governing ideology developed in modern China. This ideology can be symbolized by a major shift in government mentality - from the idea of 'mandate' to the ideas of 'reform' and 'revolution'. This shift gave rise to the politics of 'political mobilization'. Chinese governments believed that in order to outflank their political competitors, the 'overseas Chinese', like other Chinese under their rule, had to be mobilized under government control. By saying this, I am not suggesting that the political and economic behaviour of all overseas Chinese was determined by governmental policies in China. The process of redefining the power relationship between the emperor and his subjects (or 'government and citizens') is a constant negotiation between the ruler and the ruled. We have learnt from the history of the Siyi Chamber how 'mobilization politics' developed and operated in modern China. The idea of *huaqiao* was first coined by the Qing Government, but the usage of the idea was subjected to manipulation by the concept's 'users'. *Huaqiao* and ethnic identity, after all, is situational. It was (and still is) a significant asset for business and political investment in China.

Beginning in 1911, the 'mobilization politics' set off by the Qing Government, for example, had turned against the Central Government. In the 1920s, the fall of the Siyi men's business empire in South China had a lot to do with new developments in the national politics of China - when the KMT nominally united China and gained control of the *huaqiao* construct. Before China was nominally unified again by the KMT in 1928, the overseas Chinese adapted the idea of '*huaqiao*' to their own needs. For Chinese living overseas, the idea of *huaqiao* not only satisfied their affective needs, the idea justified their participation in China's political development. With official justification and protection, the self-styled *huaqiao* could advance their political and economic status in the home county, in China, and in the overseas communities within which they lived.

BIBLIOGRAPHY

Anonymous
1922   *Liugong Zhubo xingshu* (An Account of the Activities of the Venerable Liu Zhubo). Hong Kong
1948   *Xianggang Siyi shanggong zongju guangfu tekan* (Special publication of the Siyi Chamber of Commerce on the Recovery of Hong Kong). Hong Kong
Campell, P.C.
1923   *Chinese Coolie Immigration to Countries within the British Empire.* London: Oxford University Press
Chan Lau Kit-ching
1991   *China, Britain and Hong Kong 1895-1945.* Hong Kong: The Chinese University Press
Chan, W.K.K.
1995   'The Origins and Early Years of the Wing On Company Group in Australia, Fiji, Hong Kong and Shanghai: Organization and Strategy of a New Enterprise', in: Raj Brown (ed.) *Chinese Business Enterprises in Asia.* London: Routledge
Chen Datong and Chen Wenyuan
1914   *Bainian shangye* (One Hundred Years of Commerce). Hong Kong
Chen Fulin and Yu Yanguang (eds)
1991   *Liao Zhongkai nianpu* (A Chronological Biography of Liao Zhongkai). Hunan: Hunan chubanshe
Cheng Tiangu
1993   *Cheng Tiangu huiyilu* (The Reminiscences of Cheng Tiangu). Taibei: Longmeng
Chung, S.P.Y.
1998   *Chinese Business Groups in Hong Kong and Political Change in South China.* London: Macmillan and New York: St. Martin's Press
Faure, D.
1996   'The Lineage as Business Company: Patronage Versus Law in the Development of Chinese Business', in: Raj Brown (ed.) *Chinese Business Enterprises, Critical Perspectives,* Vol. 1. London: Routledge

Feng Shaoshan (ed.)
1991   *Guangdong jinxiandai renwu cidan* (A Biographical Dictionary of Guangdong in the Modern and Contemporary Eras). Guangzhou: Guangdong keji chubanshe

Feng Ziyou
1953   *Geming yishi, 1946-47* (Reminiscences of the Revolution). Taibei: Shangwu

Fincher, J.
1958   'Political Provincialism and the National Revolution', in: M. Wright (ed.) *The Chinese Revolution*

FitzGerald, S.F.
1972   *China and the Overseas Chinese*. London: Cambridge University Press

Harrison, H.
1996   'State Ceremonies and Political Symbolism in China, 1911-1929'. Unpublished D.Phil. thesis, University of Oxford

Hoexter, C.K.
1976   *From Canton to California: The Epic of Chinese Immigration*. New York: Four Winds Press, 1976

Hong, Y.C.
1955   *A Brief History of the Chinese American Citizens Alliance*. San Franciso: Chinese American Citizens Alliance

Lin Jinzhi
1989   *Jindai Huaqiao tuozi guonei qiyi shiziliao xuanji, Guangdong quan* (The investment of the Overseas Chinese in Modern China, Guangdong). Fujian: Fujian Renmin chubanshe

Orth, J.V.
1991   *Combination and Conspiracy, A Legal History of Trade Unionism, 1721-1906*. Oxford: Clarendon Press

Ou Jiluan
1933   *Guangdong zibishi* (A history of paper currency in Guangdong). Canton: Zhongshan daxue jingji tiaochazu

Quan Hansheng
1960   'Tielu guoyua wenti yu Xinhai geming' (The railroad nationalization question and the 1911 Revolution), *Zhongguo jindaishi zongkan* 1

Rankin, M.B.
1986   *Elite Activism and Political Transformation in China, Zheijiang Province, 1865-1911*. Stanford: Stanford University Press

Ranger, T. and E. Hobsbawn (eds)
1983   *The Invention of Tradition*. Cambridge: Cambridge University Press

Rhoads, Edward J.M.
1975   *China's Republican Revolution: The Case of Kwangtung, 1895-1913*. Cambridge, Mass: Harvard University Press
Scalapino, Robert A. and Yu, George T.
1985   *Modern China and its Revolutionary Process*. Berkeley: University of California Press
Sinn, E.
1989   *Power and Charity, The Early History of the Tung Wah Hospital, Hong Kong*. Hong Kong: Oxford University Press
1990   'A History of Regional Association in Pre-war Hong Kong', in: E. Sinn (ed.) *Between East and West, Aspects of Social and Political Development in Hong Kong*. Hong Kong: Centre of Asian Studies, University of Hong Kong
Tan Yongnian,
1958   *Zhongguo Xinhai geming huiyilu* (Reminiscences of the 1911 Revolution). Hong Kong: Rongqiao
Tsai, Jung-fang
1993   *Hong Kong in Chinese History*. New York: Columbia University Press
Wang Er-min
1977   '*Shangzhan guannian yu zhongshang sixiang*' (The Concept of Commercial War and the Mercantilist Ideology), in: Wang Er-min (ed.) *Zhongguo jindai sixiang shilun* (A Discussion of Modern Chinese Intellectual History). Taibei: Huashi
Woo Sing Lim,
1937   *The Prominent Chinese in Hong Kong*. Hong Kong: Five Continents Book Company
Woon Y.F.
1984   'An Emigrant Community (*chiao-hsiang*) in the Ssu-yi Area, South China 1885-1949: A Study of Social Change', *Modern Asia Studies*, 18(2), pp. 273-306
Wright, M.
1957   *The Last Stand of Chinese Conservatism: The Tung Chih Restoration, 1862-1874*. Stanford: Stanford University Press
1968   *The Chinese Revolution, the first phase, 1900-1913*. New Haven: Yale University Press.
Xianggang Qingnianhui (ed.)
1901   *Qingnianhui shiye gailue* (A history of the Young Men's Association). Hong Kong
Yen Ching-hwang
1982   'The Overseas Chinese and Late Ch'ing Economic Modernization', *Modern Asian Studies* 16(2)

Zheng Dehua and Cheng Luxi
1992   *Xinning tielu yu Taishan qiaoxiang* (The Xinning Railway and the
        Overseas Chinese community in Taishan). Guangzhou: Zhongshan
        daxue
Zhuang Guotu
1989   *Zhongguo fengjiao zhengfu de Huaqiaozhengce* (The Overseas
        Chinese Policy of China's Feudal Government). Xiamen: Xiamen
        Daxue Chubenshe
Zhu Ying
1990   '*Qingmo shanghui di chengli yu guanshang guanxi di fazhan* (The
        Establishment of the Chambers of Commerce and the Development
        of the Relationship between Merchants and Officials in the Late
        Qing), *Shehui kexue zhanxian* 2

Notes

1. For a discussion of the notion of 'commercial war' see Wang Er-min,
   1977, pp. 233-380.
2. Zhu Ying, '*Qingmo shanghui di chengli yu guanshang guanxi di fazhan*'
   The establishment of the chambers of commerce and the development of
   the relationship between merchants and officials in the late Qing), in
   Shehui kexue zhanxian, No. 2 (1990), pp. 67-73.
3. On a discussion of the notion of 'commercial war', see Wang Er-min,
   '*Shangzhan guannian yu zhongshang sixiang*' (The concept of
   commercial war and the mercantilist ideology), in: Wang Er-min,
   Zhongguo jindai sixiang shilun (A discussion of modern Chinese
   intellectual history) (Taibei: Huashi, 1977), pp. 233-380.
4. *Guangdong Guangzhuo shangfou zhangcheng* (Regulation of the port-
   market development scheme in Gangzhou) (Canton, 1910).
5. For a general description of the crisis, see Scalapino, Robert A. and Yu,
   George T., *Modern China and its Revolutionary Process*, pp. 301-8. On
   railway and provincialism, see Quan Hansheng '*Tielu guohua wenti yu
   xinhai geming*' (The railroad nationalization question and the 1911
   Revolution), *Zhongguo jindaishi zongkan*, No. 1, (1960), pp. 209-71;
   John Fincher, 'Political Provincialism and the National Revolution', in
   Mary Wright (ed.), *The Chinese Revolution*, pp. 185-226.
6. Tan, *Zhonggo Xinhai geming huiyilu*, pp. 305-11.
7. Rhoads, *China's Republican Revolution*, pp. 135-52, For an account of
   the Guangdong merchant community in these political developments, see
   Qiu Jie, '*Guangdong shangren yu Xinhai geming*' (The merchants of
   Canton and the 1911 Revolution), *Jinian Xinhai geming qishi zhounian
   xueshu taolunhui lunwenji* (Guangzhou, 1981), Vol. 1, pp. 362-96.

8. Tan, *Zhougguo Xinhai geming huiyilu*, pp. 308-10. A general description of the Chamber's activities in the 1911 Revolution can also be found in *Xianggang Siyi shanggong zongju guangfu tekan* (Special publication of the Siyi Chamber of Commerce on the recovery of Hong Kong), Hong Kong 1948, pp. 1-2. For the history of Hu Hanmin, see Boorman and Howard, (eds), *Biographical Dictionary* 2, pp. 159-66. See also Hu Hanmin, *Zizhuan* (Autobiography), in *Geming wenxian*, Vol. 3, (Taibei: Zhongyang wenwu), pp. 372-422.

9. This statement was recorded by the Registrar-General of Hong Kong in his interview with Li Yu-tang in 1912. See CO 129/391, May to Harcourt, 16 August 1912.

10. Que jue, '*Guangdong zhengfu chuqi di caizheng zhuanguang*' (The financial situation of the early Guangdong government), in: Zhongguo renmin zhengzi xieshang huiyi weiyuanhui (ed.), *Jinian Xinhai Geming qishi zhounain shiliao quanji*, pp. 201-7.

11. Same as 7.

12. The following materials record that Li was on the brink of bankruptcy by 1911 and was known to be the 'Insurance King' in the 1910s and 1920s. Feng Ziyuo *Geming yishi 1946-47* (Reminiscences of the Revolution), Reprint. Taibei: Shangwu, 1953. pp. 193-201; *Guangdong jinxiandai rewu cidian*, p. 187; *Chuanji wenxue* 38:1 (January 1976), pp. 144-5; Woo Sing Lim, *The Prominent Chinese in Hong Kong*, pp. 7-8 of the supplement; Chen Fulin and Yu Yanguang (eds), *Liao Zhongkai ninpu* (A Chronological Biography of Liao Zhongkai) (Hunan: Hunan chubanshe, 1991), pp. 57-9.

13. According to Ou Jiluan, a sum of 13 million in Canton currency was issued in 1913. The face value of this unsecured currency immediately depreciated by 30 per cent. See his *Guangdong zibishi* (A history of paper currency in Guangdong) (Canton: Zhongshan daxue jingji tiaochazu, 1933), pp. 9-10. A corroborating account can be found in Chen Fulin and Yu Yanguang (eds), *Liao Zhongkai nianpu* (A Chronological Biography of Liao Zhongkai) (Hunan. Hunan chubanshe, 1991), pp. 57-9. Liao was the vice-treasury of Guangdong under Li Yu-tang in early 1912.

COHESION AND FRAGMENTATION:
A COUNTY-LEVEL PERSPECTIVE ON
CHINESE TRANSNATIONALISM
IN THE 1940S[1]

ELIZABETH SINN

The Chinese diaspora - a result of the dispersal of Chinese people outside of China[2] - is characterized by tension between the forces of cohesion and of fragmentation. In this chapter, I propose that, to evaluate and define the nature of these tensions, it is instructive to examine the phenomenon at a micro-level. The diaspora is a complex combination of many sub-groups - even individuals - often interacting and juxtaposed with each other in untidy ways. The sub-groups may be variously classified: by family, place of common origin, locality overseas, occupation, social class, etc. The following pages focus on one sub-group, natives from the Guangdong county of Sanshui, and examine the bonding mechanisms - in particular, the way *tongxianghui* (same-native-place associations) accentuate and perpetuate a sense of Sanshui identity transnationally. While the power of regionalism among Chinese migrant communities, both inside and outside of China, has been studied, its dynamism still remains to be fully explored.[3]

INTRODUCTION

In Hong Kong, which occupied a pivotal position in the global network of Chinese overseas, the history of Sanshui *tongxiang* (also meaning, in another context, persons belonging to the same native place) organizations from the late nineteenth century to 1949 demonstrates the dynamic and multi-directional nature of socio-economic relationships. *Tongxiang* sentiments were, in fact, complex: with different contents and means of expression under different circumstances and in different times. For analytical purposes, we may simplify by saying that the *tongxianghui* interacted with Sanshui people within three distinct arenas. The first was within Hong Kong itself, where it cared for *tongxiang* by providing them material and spiritual security. The second arena encompassed interactions between Sanshui sojourners in Hong Kong and the home-county. Here, it enabled the sojourner to maintain ties with the home-county, and in the process, it also became the mechanism by which the home-county could reach out to its native sons (see, especially, Sinn, 1997a:375-97). Maintaining *qiaoxiang* (localities in China from which emigrants originate, and thus, the native place of sojourners) ties was a major concern. The above two arenas of interaction have been studied elsewhere. In this paper I will emphasize a third arena, in which the *tongxianghui* served, ideally at least, as the nerve centre for communication with Sanshui natives everywhere, regardless of their physical location. I will analyse the *tongxianghui*'s efforts at addressing and cultivating the consciousness of a Sanshui community - an identity stemming from one place, the Chinese county of Sanshui, but transcending this place's territorial confines - and at materially integrating Sanshui natives in localities in China and overseas. This purposeful creation of a 'global' Sanshui consciousness had both integrative and fragmenting effects within the larger Chinese world.

SANSHUI AS A *QIAOXIANG*[4]

The Sanshui case is used to illustrate one type of *qiaoxiang* tie, which, with its emphasis on inter-locality integration, contributed to the solidarity within certain sectors of the Chinese diaspora. It is difficult to ascertain when the first migrants left Sanshui, but evidently people began emigrating in the second half of the nineteenth century and, between the beginning of the twentieth century and the 1930s, emigration was very active. It was estimated that by about 1937 there were 20,000 Sanshui natives in Singapore, 10,000 in Vietnam, 300 in Malacca, 180 in Kuala Lumpur, 100 in Ipoh, 150 in the Philippines, 300 in America and 60,000 in other places altogether, presumably including Hong Kong (*Sanshui Xianzhi*, 1995:1289). It is worth noting that women were also migrating from Sanshui in considerable numbers, and in Singapore they became so prominent as earth-carriers on construction sites that 'Sham-shui women' became almost a generic term for women labourers. In Chinese, these women were known as 'red headcloth' (*hong toujin*) because of the special headgear they wore (Chiang, 1994:238-63 and *Sanshi Xianzhi*, pp. 1298-300). As in the case of emigrants from other parts of China, Sanshui natives formed *tongxiang* organizations in their host localities. Earlier organizations included the

Sanshui Huiguan established in Singapore in 1884, the Sanshui Gongsi in Penang in 1885, and the Sanshui Huiguan in Malacca in 1919.

Originally founded in the 1880s, the first Sanshui organization in Hong Kong was the Dunshantang, and significantly, in light of the third arena of interaction discussed above, the occasion giving Sanshui natives the opportunity to express their Sanshui identity was the need to build a grave for the unclaimed bones of Sanshui natives repatriated from Southeast Asia. (In fact, from the 1860s to the 1880s, a number of *tongxiang* groups in Hong Kong were also formed as a result of having to build 'communal graves' for co-regionals repatriated from abroad, thus stimulating the trend of *tongxianghui* formation.) This shows that Sanshui natives had, since the nineteenth century, identified not only with those residing in the home-county, nor only with those in Hong Kong, but with those in other localities as well.

The Sanshui Natives Association (SNA), founded in 1912 as the 'Commercial and Industrial Association of Natives of Sam Shui Resident in Hong Kong', and successor to the *Dunshantang*, played an important role in maintaining linkages within this perceived extended community of Sanshui natives. Its functions included keeping *tongxiang* in various localities informed about each others' conditions, and encouraging and being actively involved in the formation of Sanshui *tongxianghui* in other localities. From the very beginning, the SNA played an important role as a high-profile point of contact for *tongxiang* in Hong Kong, the home village and abroad. It should be emphasized that, besides the Sanshui *Tongxianghui*, other Chinese voluntary associations in Hong Kong, which was the main gateway to South China and an international centre of migration, shipping, communications remittances and other forms of capital flow, were also able to play that pivotal role for a variety of transnational Chinese groups.[5] Hong Kong often formed the node through which the multi-directional bonding process extended (Sinn, 1998:105-7).

THE NATURE OF THE LEADERSHIP

Up to 1950, the SNA in Hong Kong played a major role in the multi-directional/inter-locality integration of fellow-regionals in different areas of activities including organizing inter-locality activities such as fund-raising and the repatriation of human remains and maintaining friendships and contact with *tongxiang* in other localities through personal and institutional connections. Most symbolically, it performed this bonding role through the publication of a newsletter targeted at fellow-regionals in Sanshui, Hong Kong and other localities on the Chinese Mainland and overseas. Fund-raising, a major activity conducted by the SNA, included the raising of money for disaster relief in the native place, for investment or for charitable or social purposes from among the *tongxiang* in various localities. Such operations involved large-scale organization in logistics, publicity and currency arrangements which associations in Hong Kong were best-placed to provide. In 1938, for instance, when South China was invaded by the Japanese, the SNA organized the Sanshui Natives Relief Society (*Sanshui yiqiao chaozhen hui*) to mobilize support from Singapore, and other Southeast Asian localities to raise funds to relieve war suffering in Sanshui. The funds were distributed among the different districts within Sanshui according to the severity of the damage.[6]

Another way to connect sojourning *tongxiang* around the world with the home village was by providing services to *tongxiang* who had died abroad. As noted above, it was precisely the need to provide burial for unclaimed remains of Sanshui natives who had died in Nanyang that had led to the foundation of the Dunshantang in the first place. It is well-known that Chinese people cherish a proper burial and emigrants in the nineteenth and early twentieth centuries further cherished the idea of being buried in the native place. Great efforts were made to repatriate human remains, so that even if a sojourner failed to return to die in his home village, which would have been considered ideal, at least his remains could be returned for interment or re-interment. This was the ultimate meaning of 'returning to one's roots'.

With Hong Kong occupying a pivotal position in the global network of Chinese overseas, many voluntary associations in Hong Kong performed this service on a grand scale.[7] The multi-directional and multi-level pattern of Chinese migration is also most clearly reflected in this operation as well. For example, in 1948, a first shipment for the year of 1,400 sets of bones of sojourners was organized by the Guangzhou-Zhaoxing Association in Vietnam for repatriation to China. Among these, 63 boxes were bones of Sanshui natives; a few months later, a second shipment with 160 boxes of Sanshui natives' bones followed. Each time, the Vietnam Sanshui *Tongxianghui* in Cholon assisted in the operation. It issued lists of the names of the deceased, the names of their *xiang* and the number of the bone-boxes destined for Sanshui, and the list was also publicized in the *Sanshui Xunkan*, published in Hong Kong.[8] Sanshui *Tongxiang* in Guangzhou and the various *xianggongsuo* (village government offices) were urged to help in the operation (*Xunkan* no. 40 [15.5.49]:2). It was an operation that required co-ordination on many levels and in many directions. One may well imagine that before the bone-boxes reached Cholon, it demanded the collaboration of many groups in many localities in various parts of Vietnam to make the operation possible. After leaving

Cholon, Hong Kong and Guangzhou, the bones still had to be handled by different groups in different *xiang* in Sanshui before they reached their final resting place. If one multiplies this one operation by the many sets of Chinese bones which had been returned over the decades from different continents to the hundreds of native places in China, one gets an idea of the scale of the operations as well as the density of inter-locality co-operation among *tongxiang* of different levels (Sinn, 1997b:230-52).

Apart from raising funds for the native place or for repatriating bones, another primary function of *tongxianghui* was '*lianluo xiangqing*' (promoting affection among *tongxiang* through keeping in touch) by keeping them informed of each other's activities, and helping each other in a number of ways. Communication by post or by word of mouth was an important means to maintain these ties. Where there were formal *tongxiang* associations, inter-*tongxianghui* relations were formally and closely maintained. For example, in 1925, when the Guangzhou *tongxianghui* was formed, representatives were sent from the SNA to establish communications (*JJT*, p. 52). Again, when the Hanoi *tongxianghui* was founded in 1947, it issued a letter to *tongxianghui* 'in different localities', naming specifically those in Hong Kong, Guangzhou, Chanjiang, Peru, Cholon, Singapore and Malacca, seeking advice from them and expressing the hope to forge unity to benefit county and country (*Xunkan* no. 21 [1.9.47]:3). We can even detect a demonstrative effect - one group of *tongxiang* in one locality might be stimulated or encouraged to form a *tongxianghui* through contact with a sister association in another locality. It was claimed that Sanshui natives in Chanjiang (Guangzhouwan), for example, set up their own body after they became aware that *tongxianghui* existed in Guangzhou, Hong Kong and Southeast Asia (*Xunkan* no. 13 [30.11.46]:1). It is also interesting to note that in the case of Sanshui, *tongxianghui/huiguan* outside of China were formed earlier than those inside China. Inter-locality relations were also sustained through mutual visits by members of *tongxianghui* of different localities. Usually a Sanshui individual who happened to be visiting Hong Kong, for instance, would drop by at the Hong Kong association to be received with due hospitality and to exchange information with its members.

It is worth noting that the first 'official' visit by a representative to *tongxiang* overseas was made in January, 1948. He Jirui, sent by the Guangzhou and Hong Kong associations, made a two-month visit to the *tongxiang* organizations in Malacca, where new premises were being opened, as well as to Singapore, Kuala Lumpur, Ipoh, Penang, Siam and Vietnam.[9] This kind of visit was naturally aimed at promoting the sense of unity among Sanshui organizations. In fact, in what might appear to us a surprising move, he also suggested that the individual *huiguan* on the

British Malay Peninsula should form themselves into a Federation of Malaya Sanshui *tongxianghui*. His suggestion met with warm response and preparations were afoot for the formation of such a body.[10]

THE NATURE OF IDENTITY

As we examine the activities of the Sanshui organizations, a number of old questions come to mind. To what extent was the consciousness of a community of Sanshui natives living in different localities spontaneous or mobilized, self-initiated or manipulated, primordial, imagined or contrived? Or was there a mixture of these elements, mutually-reinforcing and also sometimes conflicting?[11] No attempt will be made here to answer these questions definitively, but they will guide the investigation in this study.

Sanshui Leaders as a Social Elite
To analyse the forces of cohesiveness in Sanshui migration, we may begin by discussing the agents who mobilized, manipulated and reinforced *tongxiang* sentiments and then by examining their newsletter, the *Sanshui Xunkan*, which was designed as a mechanism for building solidarity among Sanshui people.

The active members and leaders of the SNA up to 1950 were mainly shopkeepers and small-to-medium merchants in Hong Kong, with no particular identifiable ideological bias. Like most leaders of such voluntary associations, they were self-appointed, civic minded and status seeking. By providing services to their *tongxiang*, and sometimes also to other groups in Hong Kong, they acted as a social elite. We may assume that the extension of their service nexus beyond Hong Kong to other localities was a strategy to enhance their elite status. In spreading their service and reputation back home to Sanshui, they rose in status in the home-county and became better placed for influencing events there; we may even say that, metaphorically, some fulfilled the high ideal of *'yijin huanxiang'* (returning to the homeland in full glory) in this way. By widening their services to 'constituencies' beyond Hong Kong and Sanshui, they further attained inter-locality and transnational recognition. The wide range of their activities had great emotional and material ramifications, strengthening the position of individual *tongxianghui* members in many types of networks. Rallying migrants in other localities behind themselves also gave the Hong Kong Sanshui leaders more leverage when dealing with the local Sanshui authorities.

The Sanshui Xunkan

The most symbolic effort at creating unity among Sanshui sojourners was the publication of the *Sanshui Xunkan*. First appearing in 1946, the newsletter was issued fairly regularly until 1950. From the start, it was targeted at a transnational readership - at readers among Sanshui natives in the home county, Hong Kong and other localities on the Mainland and overseas. Its mission, to create unity among Sanshui natives, was spelt out in the inaugural editorial: 'This is time for building the nation. It is also a time of great hardship. Whether it is the family, the *xiang*, the county or the nation, there is need for unity, and for the pooling of ideas and energy in order to pursue development. Thus, the question is how the Hong Kong association can mobilize the many *tongxiang* in Hong Kong as well as in other localities to press ahead with affairs in the home county.' (*Xunkan* no. 1 [5.5.46]:1) All aspects of the county needed to be improved, the editorial went on to say, and if one county could not progress properly, it would obstruct the progress of the entire nation.

Obviously, while emphasizing nation building, the *Xunkan* also highlighted *xian* (county) building and solidarity among Sanshui natives around the world. Its key function was '*lianluo xiangqing*'.[12] In practice, the *Xunkan* provided a mechanism for Sanshui natives to exchange news among themselves, to keep in touch with each other, to discuss matters concerning the home county and co-operate in the effort to construct the county. Though the nation came into this declaration of intent - and rhetoric about the nation appeared often afterwards as well - it will be seen from the content of subsequent issues that it was really the county of Sanshui that was the genuine focus of interest. In this respect, the newsletter may be seen as an attempt to create a one-county-centred world in a transnational context - an exercise of unity in groundlessness.[13]

It should be noted that *qiaokan* were, by the 1940s, a fairly common form of literature published by various groups targeted at fellow-regionals. The first, the *Xinning Zazhi*, was published in 1909, and its role in enhancing ties between sojourners and the native place is amply analysed by Madeline Hsu (Hsu, 1998). I would suggest that further systematic study of *qiaokan*, showing how different groups at different times, using different rhetorics and strategies, attempted to maintain inter-locality linkages, will provide a broader view of multi-directional networking and thus shed light on the nature of the Chinese diaspora in new ways.

In Sanshui itself, during the Sino-Japanese war, a weekly, the *Sanshui Zhoukan*, was being operated under very difficult conditions from Pukang (*Xunkan* no. 2 [15.5.46]:1). Even at the same time that the SNA in Hong Kong was publishing its *Xunkan*, two other Sanshui newsletters were being published. One was published in Guangzhou, called the *Yijiang Xunkan*, and the other, the *Sanshui Zhoubao* (Sanshui Weekly) was published at Xi'nan, the county capital after the Pacific war. Obviously, each organization ran its own show, but they were not mutually exclusive. There was much overlapping in content since they reprinted some of each other's articles and also extracted information from each other. Some writers also contributed to all three papers.[14]

Such proliferation of *qiaokan* from one county alone reflects the intensity and density of the multi-directional linkage and the high demand for information. Nor was the *Sanshui Xunkan* the SNA's first efforts at publishing a newsletter. An earlier effort had been made in the spring of 1940 to organize a monthly journal, the *Sanshui Yuekan*. However, only six issues appeared between June 1940 and November 1941. A month later, in December, war broke out in Hong Kong itself.

The *Sanshui Xunkan* first appeared in May 1946, just months after the war ended. A newsletter to be published every ten days was planned, since it was believed that a *xunkan* would be able to disseminate news more effectively than a monthly. However, it was not long before this frequency was abandoned; and after Issue no. 8, it became irregular, sometimes taking more than a month before the next issue appeared. The last issue, no. 46, appeared on 10 May 1950, half a year after the liberation, when the editor admitted it was no longer easy to report on conditions in Sanshui. In response to the many *tongxiang* in Hong Kong and overseas writing in to make enquiries about the native place, the editor apologized for being unable to obtain further information (*Xunkan* no. 46 [10.5.50]:4).

The distribution pattern of the *Xunkan* mirrors the transnational network of Sanshui migrants. Besides being distributed free to Sanshui natives in Hong Kong, the newsletter was also sent to the different villages in Sanshui - to government offices, *xianggongsuo*, schools, shops and other public places where people could obtain copies free. In these places, the paper was posted for the public to read. In addition, it was sent to Sanshui *tongxianghui* in different cities in China, including Guangzhou and Shanghai. The overseas dimension was equally important, as the *Xunkan* was sent to Singapore, Vietnam, Siam, Malacca, Ipoh and other places and even as far afield as Peru and Panama.[15] It was claimed that some 3,000 copies of each issue were distributed (*JJT*, p. 59). Apart from institutions, the *Xunkan* was also posted to specific individuals who asked for it (*Xunkan* no. 38 [20.2.49]:1).

The newsletter was financed by donations from directors and ordinary members of the SNA. It carried advertisements as well, and the presence of advertisements advertising for companies overseas and for goods for the overseas market is another sign that a geographically dispersed readership was anticipated.[16] It is also interesting to note that some donations from overseas *tongxiang* were made specifically toward financing the newsletter in Hong Kong, which may be taken as further indication that the newsletter was not only read, but also appreciated, abroad.[17]

The timing of the *Xunkan's* appearance is significant. During the war years 1937-45, intense nationalism was aroused among Chinese overseas, and *tongxiang* organizations in many parts of the world were instrumental in mobilizing support for war relief on the Chinese Mainland. After the war, nationalism continued to be promoted as nation-building became the chief rallying cry in China. It is therefore not surprising that the *Xunkan* called for the unity of all Chinese. What IS striking is that it also appealed for county-level unity. Was promoting a Sanshui identity a strategy to build nationalism? Was the *Xunkan*, while paying lip-service to nationalism, really seeking to foster regional identity? Or was it possible, in different times and different contexts, for it to pursue both goals, despite the potential tensions and contradictions involved?

THE CONTENTS OF THE *SANSHUI XUNKAN*

While the *Sanshui Xunkan* symbolizes the effort to maintain multi-directional links, it is also useful as a source of information on how those links were actually maintained and the substance of the networks. The contents of the periodical reflect partly the kinds of concerns sojourners had regarding the native place, or at least, the concerns that the editor of the *Xunkan* expected the sojourners to have, and partly the kinds of information and views that various parties, including officials and residents in Sanshui and the leaders of the SNA in Hong Kong, wished to publicize.

General Information about Sanshui

The main focus of the newsletter was on general conditions - political, social, economic - in Sanshui. Such information came from various sources, official as well as unofficial. Situated at the confluence of three rivers, the county of Sanshui, which literally means three rivers, was constantly subject to alternate drought and flooding. Many of the reports were naturally on drought and flood conditions (*Xunkan* no. 1 [5.5.46]:1), with detail descriptions of the sufferings, irrigation projects, conditions of embankments etc.[18] In addition, in these early post-war years, reports were frequently made on war damages. The conditions of crops and harvest and crop prices also featured from time to time. For the traveller, there was information on transportation, health requirements and so on (*Xunkan* no. 2 [15.5.46]:1-2).

Another important type of information was related to the redrawing of boundaries which resulted from the reorganization of administrative districts. Up to 1946, the whole county had been divided into 46 *xiang*, but after that, the number was reduced to 23, necessitating large-scale remapping and change in the administrative structure (*Xunkan* no. 1 [5.5.46]:1). Changes of personnel in the administration and the work of various levels of government within the county were reported, sometimes by reprinting official reports, and sometimes by reports made by reporters and commentators. There was much coverage on law and order and on court rulings; official corruption and other social evils were frequently exposed (*Xunkan* no. 10 [27.8.46]:2).

From 1947, when China introduced constitutional reforms, the *Xunkan* paid great attention to the various levels of elections - national, provincial and county - with the greatest enthusiasm displayed where county participation in these elections was involved. The campaigning of Sanshui representatives became a contentious issue in the newsletter.[19] Most of the discussions on the constitutional framework focused on the county and *xiang* levels rather than the national. It seems also that partly because of the need to elect representatives to the county assembly, sub-county level activities were stimulated. For example, natives of Tongshu *xiang* residing in Guangzhou organized a meeting to discuss and put forward a *xiang* representative (*Xunkan*, no. 33 [15.9.48]:1). The rivalry between candidates and cliques gave rise to heated discussion (*Xunkan*, no. 33 [15.9.48]:2). Other squabbles were also reflected as the *xiang* elections drew near. There were even some theoretical writings on ideas of democracy and problems in the present situation (*Xunkan* no. 34 [15.10.48]:2 and no. 35 [15.11.48]:1). Significantly, after the county assembly was formed, the proceedings of its meetings appeared in the *Xunkan*, providing a blow-by-blow account of the debate (*Xunkan*, no. 35 [15.11.48]:1-2). Such reporting would naturally give the sojourner-reader a sense of immediacy regarding conditions back home.

Many Voices

The newsletter emphasized its own neutrality. Since it was not affiliated to any party, it claimed that its position was unbiased and that it was willing to publish the writings submitted by different sides - as long as their accounts were true. Its aim to be just was described in the most colourful terms: 'We hold a transcendental position (*chaoran gongzheng de lichang*). Like the god Apollo, we stand tall like a mountain and unashamed before heaven and earth.'[20] It, therefore, carried conflicting impressions of the situation in Sanshui. Nor did it only paint a rosy picture in order to attract investments or donations, but also exposed social, economic and other problems, reflecting the deep concerns for the county shared by residents and sojourners alike. At least, it reflected the desire to engage Sanshui sojourners in a discussion of the problems of the native place, and to focus their minds on a Sanshui-centred world.

One problem that caused constant complaints was the prevalence of gambling and drugs in the county. The *Xunkan* printed official communiques emphasizing the government's determination to fight these social evils. It also printed ordinary people's appeals to government to take the matter seriously (*Xunkan* no. 4 ['first third of June, 47']:1). Different authors sent in comments on what they regarded as the root cause of the evils and made suggestions on how they could be eradicated.[21] Moreover, a lively debate ensued. Yet another issue of grave concern was education, which was widely regarded as backward. There was constant demand for the reconstruction of schools which had been severely damaged during the war years, and for improvement.[22] Harsh and arbitrary taxation was a constant bone of contention,[23] and from 1948, great anger was vented against the forcible drafting of men into the army.[24]

Appealing to Tongxiang

It would seem that much of the writing in the *Xunkan*, whether reports of disasters in the county or the backwardness of the schools or protests against government, was not published for the mere sake of supplying information. Clearly there was an eagerness to appeal to *tongxiang* abroad for a variety of purposes.

One objective, of course, was to encourage sojourners to make donations to the native place. What is especially relevant for us here is the way the fund-raising was operated. We see that, often, when a disaster struck, an appeal would first appear in the *Xunkan*, urging the *tongxianghui* of different localities on behalf of the native place to do their part. The response of the various *tongxianghui* would then be reported, giving details of the activities they undertook to raise the funds while listing the amounts raised and names of donors. It is important to note that this was not only an effective means of recording the effort of each organization, or a way of rewarding their contribution in a worthwhile cause by broadcasting it, or even of creating some friendly competition by showing what others had given, but above all, this means of publicizing the efforts of sojourners must also have added to the sense of unity and common purpose among them. Moreover, through these activities, the inter-locality links became manifest.

Apart from being called upon to make donations for charitable or community purposes, sojourners were also called upon to make investments in the native place.[25] One example was the Lubao-Xi'nan road planned in 1946. A prospectus published in the form of a 'Letter to *tongxiang*' addressed to fellow-villagers in Hong Kong, the mainland and overseas, stressed that a good transportation system was the key to other improvements in Sanshui, and urged that 'Such an effort to bring benefit to the native place (*zaofu sangzi*) is too urgent to allow delay.' The original plan was to raise a capital of N$50m, divided into 5,000 shares at N$10,000 per share. Sanshui people in Hong Kong and Guangzhou took the lead in calling for subscribers. Later, because of the instability of the National currency, the Hong Kong dollar was substituted as the denominator for subscriptions (*Xunkan* no.14 [1.1.47]:3). Suggestions for an extension of the road and further subscription followed (*Xunkan* no. 35 [15.11.48]:1). Apart from transportation, there was also an appeal for overseas Chinese capital to be invested in agriculture in Sanshui (*Xunkan* no. 26 [5.2.48]:2). Generally, however, appeals for investments were rather low-key in comparison with appeals for donations and other kinds of demonstration of solidarity.

It is useful to note that the *Xunkan* also had other motives for reaching out to sojourning *tongxiang*. It was a forum for debate, and behind the conflicting comments and protests about problems at home was the belief that the *tongxiang* in different localities had the ability and the leverage - based partly on their remittances, donations and investments - to set things right in the home county and make things happen. As one of the correspondents wrote, 'Talking about construction in the county, if we expect the local residents to push it themselves, it would be very difficult, and yet it is also a question of whether the authorities would improve the villages. It appears to the author that it would be easier if the *tongxianghui* provide the drive.' Fortunately, he added, there were *tongxianghui* in different localities, and though he felt that some associations might not realize the urgency of the task at the moment,[26] he was clearly using the publication to drive home this message to them. From the many protests published in the newsletter and also editorials appealing to the government for action, it was obvious that sojourning *tongxiang* had a vital role to play as pressure groups as well as arbiters between the *laobaixing* (the ordinary people) and the powers that be.

Inter-Locality Communications

Another important component part of the *Xunkan* was information on *tongxiang* in various localities. Besides coverage of the SNA'S activities there were frequent reports on the activities of other Sanshui *tongxianghui* as well. Reports were often made when a new organization was being formed, and we have noted how, in the case of the Hanoi *tongxianghui*, it sent an open letter to *tongxianghui* in various localities seeking their advice and support, and the letter was printed (*Xunkan* no. 18 [5.5.46]:4). The opening of the new premises of an organization was another subject of interest; for instance, much attention was paid to the *huiguan* in Malacca when its new premises were opened (*Xunkan* no. 27 [14.3.48]:3). The establishment of a Sanshui free school in Singapore, the performance of the spring sacrifice by the Kuala Lumpur *huiguan* (*Xunkan* no. 40 [15.5.49]:2), and a visit paid by the Guangzhou *tongxianghui* to the home village (*Xunkan* no. 17 [5.4.47]:1) were also considered worthy of reporting. While the cynical may say that most of the coverage focused on the fund-raising activities of *tongxianghui* for Sanshui, there was genuine interest in the conditions of Sanshui *tongxiang* abroad - what was going on among them (*Xunkan* no. 6 ['last third of June, 4']:1) - as well as concern for their wellbeing. In 1946, for instance, when hostilities broke out between the French and the Vietnamese in Haiphong, a letter of consolation was sent by the SNA to Sanshui natives in that city (*Xunkan* no. 14 [1.1.47]:3). Of course in many other practical ways, such as the repatriation of bones earlier mentioned, co-operation among *tongxianghui* in different localities was indispensable.

Inter-locality co-operation was imperative also for locating lost family members, relatives and friends, which, with the dislocation of war, was a specially common problem during this period. The *Xunkan* ran a column, sometimes entitled '*Dai zhuan jiashu*' (redirecting letters from home) and sometimes '*Yiwu tongxun*' (free correspondence service), inviting fellow-regionals to write in to seek such assistance. Letters came from many directions; some were from *tongxiang* abroad trying to reach their relatives at home, or were written by persons in Sanshui seeking friends and relatives outside the county. Readers were invited to write to their families, with the *tongxianghui* undertaking to forward the letters however difficult the task. Such letters were published in the *Xunkan* and also copied and sent to the various *xianggongsuo*. The directors and ordinary member of the SNA would also try to help the correspondents forward their letters through other channels. Outgoing letters came from Sanshui and other Chinese localities, for example, Nanhai and Liuzhou (*Xunkan* no. 24 [1.12.47]:3) or from abroad, mainly Southeast Asia. Frequently, when a relative was located, a letter of thanks would be sent to the *Xunkan* and published.[27] It appears that the SNA was fairly successful in this task.[28]

Inter-locality caring is also reflected in the donations made, not only to the *guxiang* (the native place), but among the *tongxianghui* themselves. When the Malacca *huiguan* purchased its new premises, contributions were received from *tongxiang* in other localities including Singapore, Ipoh and Kuala Lumpur.[29] This may be seen in the annual report of the Malacca *huiguan* reprinted in the *Xunkan*. The reprinting of the entire annual report over two issues of the periodical itself demonstrates how closely the *tongxianghui* kept tabs on each other's activities, and reveals the sense of obligation among them. We have already noted that the operation of the *Sanshui Xunkan* was partially supported by donations from *tongxiang* in different localities as well.

Pulling at Heart Strings

Apart from the contents noted above, we should also note two other features, the language used and the self-promotion of the SNA members. One is justified to characterize the overall style of writing in the *Xunkan* as melodramatic and sentimental and designed to pull at the sojourners' heart strings. Reports on disasters were couched in emotive - sometimes even hysterical - terms to stress the hardship and despondence faced by those at home. For instance, a report from Singapore reads:

'Since our fellow-regionals residing in Perak received the SNA's appeal for donations of relief funds, and learnt about the cruel trampling by enemies in the last few years and the great changes in the land as farmhouses are turned into rubbles and natural disasters fall one after another. The land is swarming with the sorrow of those fleeing from disaster everywhere.' (*Xunkan* no. 2 [15.5.46]:1)

Another good example of sensationalism is the headline used for a report on a drought which reads:

'Tragic! Drought! The farms are all bare and wells are being drilled at the bottom of ponds. The land is swarming with the sorrow of those fleeing from disaster everywhere and victims await immediate relief.' (*Xunkan* no. 1 [5.5.46]:1)

Complaints against officials and social evils were full of raw anger. These were no doubt aimed at moving the sojourner and prompting him to action. Another way of maintaining a sentimental relationship was through the many writings about the local customs, landmarks, and other objects of symbolic significance such as local gazetteers,[30] schools, village gods and temples, not to mention gossip. The sojourners' emotional and cultural attachments to the native place were thus enhanced and renewed, if not reinvented.

Self-Promotion by Sanshui leaders

As importantly, the newsletter enriches our understanding of the agents who cultivated and perpetuated transnational *tongxiang* ties. It consistently paid tribute to the SNA's committee members, publishing full lists of names of donors and amounts they donated and the activities they organized for the welfare of *tongxiang*. In particular the short biographies of active SNA members published periodically betray how it served as an instrument of status enhancement and self-aggrandizement. For instance, from issue no. 3 onwards, there was a series entitled '*Yiren lueshu*' (brief descriptions of county-fellows). According to the editor, it was necessary to have such a series because since the Association had been founded some thirty years ago, it had been the hard work of the earlier founders and those who followed in their footsteps which had enabled the continuation of this difficult enterprise. Their contributions, therefore, should not be forgotten. A typical entry follows:

> 'The Association's Adviser: Tang Chengpu. Mr Tang, 61, is a native of Nan Bao'an village. Coming to Hong Kong before the Republican period, he first worked in a medicine shop, and later in a grocery and then import/export firm. After some years, he organized and operated the Defeng Peru traders' firm, and has been doing so for the past 20 years. Experienced in business, he is quiet and dependable. When he was young he was very hardworking and eager to learn. His ambition is to promote education and without exception, he supports young men in their quest for advancement. The author has himself benefited from his instructions and enjoyed his teaching like the warm spring wind. Mr Tang is swift in action, and he is always energetic in any activity pertaining to fellow-regionals. He claims that his principle in life is to say few words but take much action, not to seek honour but hope to commit few errors.' (*Xunkan* no. 3 ['last third of May, 46']:3)

Since it was unlikely that many of the SNA leaders, who were mainly small merchants and shopkeepers, would ever get their names into provincial-level or national-level press of any kind, the *Xunkan*, which was local and yet international, provided the ideal vehicle for far-reaching self-advertisement for them. Moreover, apart from self-advertisement, the SNA leaders also paid tribute to the leaders of Sanshui *tongxianghui* in different localities, thus elevating the status of their counterparts as well. One can imagine such function was reciprocal so that the relationship among the leaders of various associations was symbiotic and mutually-reinforcing.

CONCLUDING REMARKS

Up to 1950 at least, Chinese emigrants abroad operated on many levels, negotiating between national, provincial, prefectural, county and sub-county identities and positioning themselves as the situation required. At different times too, different forces moulded migrant identity, sometimes distancing Chinese migrant communities from each other, and sometimes alienating migrants from the native place. The case of the SNA allows us to examine how a group of identity-shaping agents operated to maintain *qiaoxiang* ties, and the main mechanism they used in the process. The *Xunkan* reflects the paradox that regionalism was both a centripetal and centrifugal force. It could be an obstacle to national unity just as it could contribute to the national cause as well (See Fincher, 1968 and Goodman, 1995). When nation-region interrelations are extended to the Chinese beyond China, the picture becomes even more complex. Clearly the Sanshui *Xunkan* wished to emphasize that 'being Sanshui' was complementary to 'being Chinese'. But by attempting to concentrate the Sanshui migrants' minds and hearts narrowly on Sanshui county, and also materially, by appealing for their support in terms of donations, investments and so on, it inevitably pitted the county as a focus of allegiance against the nation, a more abstract entity, as a whole.

Regionalism played an integrative role in the Chinese diaspora in a particular way. In the case of Sanshui, by uniting migrants on a *tongxiang* basis, creating a transnational community among them and binding this community to the home-county - even though less directly to the nation, and even though possibly alienating non-Sanshui natives - regionalism made the Chinese diaspora more cohesive, through a series of 'mini-diasporas', as it were, and these were in turn interlinked and interlocked with each other in complex ways.

The Sanshui case thus suggests how ambiguous and constantly shifting the interrelations between national and regional sentiments could be among Chinese in the diaspora. The identities of sojourners were shaped by a range of different forces, both spatial and temporal. From the standpoint of China as a whole, some of these forces were integrative in nature, mutually reinforcing and complementary in impact, while others were disintegrative, competing, and at cross purposes with one another. A clearer recognition of the dynamic - and also untidy - configuration of these different kinds of forces will help us achieve a more accurate and nuanced understanding of the processes by which identities in the Chinese diaspora were shaped over time.

BIBLIOGRAPHY

Anderson, B.
1983   *Imagined Communities: Reflections on the Origin and Spread of Nationalism*. London: Verso, 1991

Chiang, C.
1994 'Female Migrants in Singapore: Towards a Strategy of Pragmatism and Coping', in: M. Jaschok and S. Meirs (eds) *Women and Chinese Patriarchy: Submission, Servitude and Escape.* London: Zed Books and Hong Kong: Hong Kong University Press
Chirot, D. and A. Reid (eds)
1997 *Essential Outsiders. Chinese and Jews in the Modern Transformation of Southeast Asia and Central Europe.* Seattle: University of Washington Press
Cohen, R.
1997 *Global Diasporas: An Introduction.* London: UCL Press
Dou Jiliang
1942 *Tongxiang zuzhi zhi yanjiu* (The Study of Regional Institutions). Chongqing
Dusenbery, V.A.
1997 'Diasporic Imagings and the Conditions of Possibilities: Sikhs and the State in Southeast Asia', *Sojourn* 12(2)
Fincher, J.
1968 'Political Provincialism and the National Revolution', in: M.C. Wright (ed.) *China in Revolution: The First Phase 1900-1913.* New Haven and London: Yale University Press
Goodman, B.
1995 *Native Place, City, and the Nation: Regional Networks and Identities in Shanghai, 1853-1937.* Berkeley, Los Angeles, London: University of California Press
Ho Ping-ti
1966 *Zhongguo huiguan shilun* ('An Historical Survey of Landsmanns-haften in China'). Taibei
Hsu, M.
1998 'Redefining the Meaning of "Home": American Taishanese and their Transformation from Workers to Settlers Overseas, 1849-1989', unpublished paper presented at the International Conference on the Ethnic Chinese' Manila, 26-8 November
Kuhn, P.
1998 'Is there a History of the Overseas Chinese?'. Unpublished paper presented at the Association for Asian Studies Annual Meeting
Ma Mung, Emmanuel
1998 'Groundlessness and Utopia: The Chinese Diaspora and Territory', in: E. Sinn (ed.) *The Last Half Century of Chinese Overseas.* Hong Kong: Hong Kong University Press
Reid, A.

1997   'Entrepreneurial Minorities, Nationalism, and the State', in: D.
        Chirot and A. Reid (eds) *Essential Outsiders. Chinese and Jews in
        the Modern Transformation of Southeast Asia and Central Europe*.
        Seattle: University of Washington Press
Sanshui xian difangzhi bianzuan weiyuanhui (ed.)
1995   *Sanshui Xianzhi* (Local Gazetteer of Sanshui County). Guangzhou:
        Guangdong renmin chubanshe
Sinn, E.
1989   *Power and Charity: The Early History of the Tung Wah Hospital,
        Hong Kong*. Hong Kong: Oxford University Press
1990   'A History of Regional Associations in Pre-War Hong Kong' in: E.
        Sinn (ed.) *Between East and West: Aspects of Social and Political
        Development in Hong Kong*. Hong Kong: Centre of Asian Studies,
        University of Hong Kong
1997a   '*Xinxi guxiang*: A Study of Regional Associations as a Bonding
        Mechanism in the Chinese Diaspora. The Hong Kong Experience',
        Modern Asian Studies 31(2)
1997b   'Philanthropy and the Business World' in: Wang Gungwu and
        Wong Siu-lun (eds) *Dynamic Hong Kong: Business and Culture*.
        Hong Kong: Centre of Asian Studies, University of Hong Kong
1998   'Hong Kong's Role in the Relationship between China and the
        Overseas Chinese', in: L. Pan (ed.) *Encyclopaedia of the Chinese
        Overseas*. Singapore: Archipelago Press and Landmark Books
Wang Gungwu
1993   'The Chinese Diaspora and the Development of China'.
        Unpublished paper presented at the Asia Society, Hong Kong in
        December

Notes

1 The author is grateful to the Japan Foundation for funding parts of the research on this paper. She is also grateful to Professor Paul A. Cohen for his comments on earlier drafts, as she is to members of the panel at the ICAS meeting for their feedback.
2 The use of the term 'Chinese diaspora' has been much disputed. Some critics object to its use because of its origin in the Greek Bible, with its Jewish messianic implication that the diaspora would one day be regathered to the motherland. Others wonder if the diversity of the Chinese, coming from such diverse regions in China and ending up in widely different localities overseas, and so subject to different migration experiences, share enough sense of unity to be encompassed by such an overall term (for example, Kuhn, 1998). Moreover it is also viewed as

problematic to include in the 'Chinese diaspora' people who are second, third or more-generation descendants of Chinese migrants, who have become assimilated to the culture of the host country and adopted its citizenship, and whose own identity as 'Chinese' is hazy. However, scholars who are aware of the debate and the limitations of the word continue to use it for want of a better term. (Wang Gungwu, 1993 but see also E. Ma Mung, 1998, pp. 35-47). In one of the latest books on migrant groups Anthony Reid chooses to use the term diaspora in Abner Cohen's modern sense, defining it as 'a nation of socially interdependent, but spatially dispersed communities' (D. Chirot and A. Reid, 1997, eds, p. 36) But also consult R. Cohen, 1997 for attempts to redefine 'diaspora' in order to make it more widely applicable. I have also benefited from discussions with Ng Wing-chung on this subject.

3. The two classic works on *tongxiang* associations remain Dou Jiliang, 1942 and Ho Ping-ti, 1996. See also: Sinn, 1990 and 1997a, and Goodman, 1995.

4. It is claimed that by the 1990s, about two-thirds of Sanshui people reside outside of the native county (inclusive of those in Hong Kong and Macao), making it a '*qiaoxiang*'. See *Sanshu xianzhi*, 1995 p. 1289 and table, p. 12.

5. One important example was the Tung Wah Hospital. See Sinn, 1989.

6. *Lu Gang Sanshui Tongxianghui jinxi jinian tekan* (The 50th anniversary of Sam Shui Natives Association Hong Kong - hereafter cited as *JJT*). Hong Kong, p. 54.

7. For early examples, see *JJT*, p. 53; for 1934, see p. 54.

8. *Xunkan* no. 31 (15.7.48), p. 2. Organized by the *Guangzhao Yizi yunsong xianqiao guzhi huiji zonghui*.

9. *Xunkan* no. 26 (5.2.48), p. 1; for more reports on his visit, see no. 27 (14.3.48), p. 3.

10. *Xunkan* no. 31 (15.7.48), p. 1; see also Lu Benliang, '*Yiren yingyou zhi renshi*', *Xunkan* no. 1 (5.5.46), p. 4.

11. Benedict Anderson's *Imagined Communities,* first published in 1983 remains the classic treatment of community consciousness formation. A work more pertinent to diasporic communities is V. Dusenbery, 1997.

12. Lu Jingrong, '*Lianluo xiangqing fazhan huiwu*' (Maintaining affection among *tongxiang* and developing the work of the association), *JJT*, p. 41.

13. For the idea of groundlessness in the diaspora, see Ma Mung, 1998.

14. Huang Wenhan '*Weilu xiubi*' (casual writings from the Wei lodge), *JJT*, p. 47.

15. '*Qing ben Gang ji ge di tongxiang quanzhu ben kan yinshuafei shu*' (An invitation to tongxiang in Hong Kong and all other localities to support the publication costs of this newsletter), *Xunkan* no. 7 ('first third of July', 46), p. 3.

16. *Xunkan* no. 32 (15.8.48), p. 4. Another indication is the advertisements of services overseas, e.g. the Malacca Printing Company.
17. For list of donors from Siam and Tonkin and Hanoi, see *Xunkan* no. 12 (30.10.46), p. 3; for Kuala Lumpur, see no. 31 (15.7.48), p. 3. There are also lists from Vietnam, Malacca and Perak.
18. *Xunkan* no. 20 (1.8.47) is devoted to the description of the floods; followed by a description of collapsed embankments in no. 21 (1.9.47), p. 2.
19. (*Xunkan* no. 23 (1.11.47):1, 2, 4; no. 25 (5.1.46):3; no. 28 (8.4.48):3; no. 32 (15.8.48):2.
20. '*Benkan yi zhounian*' (On the first anniversary of this newsletter), *Xunkan* no. 18 (5.5.47), p. 1.
21. *Xunkan* no. 5 ('second third of June, 47'), p. 1. '*Zhi you yi tiao lu*' (There is only one road to take), no. 4, ('first third of June, 46'), p. 4; '*Siqu suoying*' (A description of the Fourth District), no. 11 (30.9.46), p. 2.
22. *Xunkan* no. 6 ('last third of June, 46'), p. 4; no. 9 (5.8.46), p. 1; no. 19 (10.6.47), p. 4.
23. *Xunkan* no. 2 (15.5.46), p. 1; no. 6 ('last third of June'), p. 1; no. 13 (30.11.46), p. 1.
24. *Xunkan* no. 29 (10.5.48), pp. 1-3 and no. 30 (15.6.48) p. 1.
25. One of the most famous early enterprises funded by overseas Chinese was the Xinning (Taishan) Railway completed in 1920.
26. Lu Benliang, '*Dui tongxianghui zhi guanjian*' (Views on the *tongxianghui*), *Xunkan* no. 5 ('second third of June, 46'), p. 3.
27. For a letter from a person in Siam seeking someone in Peru, see *Xunkan* no. 11 (30.9.46), p. 2. Most of the requests came from Southeast Asia, especially Vietnam and Siam.
28. See in particular thank you letters reprinted in *Xunkan* no. 17 (5.4.47), p. 3 and no. 24 (1.12.47), p. 3.
29. *Xunkan* no. 41 (20.6.49) p.3 and continued in no. 42 (15.7.49), p. 3.
30. '*Ben xian juxing choushe xiuzhiguan huiyi*' (Meeting on the organization of the gazetteer compilation office in our county), *Xunkan* no. 9 (5.8.46). p. 4.

BRIDGES ACROSS THE SEA:
CHINESE SOCIAL ORGANIZATIONS IN SOUTHEAST ASIA AND THE LINKS WITH *QIAOXIANG*, 1900-49[1]

HONG LIU

Over the past two decades or so, with the implementation of China's open-door policy and massive scale of economic reforms, the Chinese diaspora have invested a substantial amount of capital in their ancestral hometowns. Accompanying this global revival and expansion of *qiaoxiang* ties, the social and cultural interactions between the Chinese overseas and their kinfolk in China have also been significantly bolstered. As a result, greater scholarly attention is being directed to their relationship.[2] This chapter addresses some of the issues pertaining to the historical precedent of organized Chinese transnationalism. By employing a Nanyang-centred perspective, it attempts to answer the following three questions. First, how did Chinese social organizations in Southeast Asia establish institutional links with *qiaoxiang*? Second, what kinds of connections did they build in constructing and, then, sustaining the ties discussed in this book? Third, how could those historical patterns of linkages be compared with the developments after 1949? With respect to modern Chinese transnationalism, what contemporary ramifications and theoretical implications can be drawn from this historical legacy?

INTRODUCTION

The current surge of both commercial and scholarly interests in *qiaoxiang* is by no means a new phenomenon. After the turn of the twentieth century, physical and cognitive connections constituted one of the foremost strategies for the Chinese diaspora in engaging in the activities of gaining political influence, economic expansion, social regeneration, and cultural imagination. While the causes and development of these linkages have been carefully documented and studied (Chen, 1937; Lin, 1988; Hicks, 1993), the focus of the existing literature has been on efforts such as investments, remittance, and charitable projects undertaken by 'overseas Chinese' as individuals. The significant role of social organizations in constituting and maintaining a variety of institutional linkages between Southeast Asia's Chinese communities and villages in South China has largely escaped scholarly scrutiny, thus impeding a more thorough understanding of the dynamics and patterns of modern Chinese transnationalism. In terms of geographical coverage and time frame, this chapter is mainly concerned with the activities of Chinese social organizations in British Malaya (Singapore in particular) during the first half of the century. While the bodies discussed here do not include the entire spectrum of Chinese associations existing in Nanyang, they are representative of overseas Chinese adaptive social organizations in terms of their origins, historical evolution, and functions (see for example, Wickberg, 1994; Hicks, 1995). For an overview of developments after 1949, this chapter uses examples from Singapore as well as other Southeast Asian countries.

The data are predominately drawn from the archival collections of major Chinese social organizations in Singapore, especially minutes of management committee meetings and correspondence between them and their counterparts in the *qiaoxiang*. Only recently declassified, these materials have not been systematically exploited before and they may shed some new light on the issues under discussion. This chapter also makes use of special publications of Chinese associations and contemporary journalist accounts.

INSTITUTIONAL FOUNDATIONS

With the formation of sizeable Chinese communities in Southeast Asia at the turn of the twentieth century, three major types of social organizations, which had emerged a few decades earlier, became increasingly indispensable for the social and economic life of immigrants, especially those of the first and second generations. The first was territorial associations or *huiguan*, which were based on the principle of same locality; the second was clan or surname associations, organized according to the principle of real/fictive kinship; and the third was trade or guild associations, representing those engaging in the same kind of trade or economic activities. This section will briefly examine the functions of the first and third types of Chinese associations, which were more active in constructing and promoting *qiaoxiang* ties.

Regional Associations and their Influences
What were the functions of regional associations? While it is true, as has

88

been commonly suggested, that the major functions of Chinese associations were to provide social and educational welfare support for fellow-regionals, their commercial role should not be overlooked. For one thing, as a result of long-developed and widespread *bang* (dialect-based politico-socio-economic grouping) structure and trade specialization, regional/dialect groupings were intimately and extensively linked with specific types of commercial activities (Cheng, 1985; Suyama, 1962). Moreover, many regional associations were established for the purpose of promoting business networks among their fellow members both within and without the national boundaries. As the 1910 inaugurating statement of the Singapore Fuqing Association put it: 'Our association aims specifically at networking business and promoting fellow-countymen feelings' (Fuqing Association, 1980:360). Partly as a reflection of this commercial agenda, many regional associations were structurally organized to include individual members, commercial and firm members, and group members (Fuqing Association, 1980:47; Nan'an Association 1986; Cheng, 1985:45).

In addition to these social, cultural, and commercial functions, regional associations played an indispensable role in linking the Chinese diaspora communities with their hometowns. As will be detailed later, this linkage served the interests of both individuals and institutions. Take the example of the Singapore Anxi Association's activities during the first month of 1940, which included holding wedding ceremonies for five couples, providing 200 certificates for those returning to China, arbitrating seven disputes among the members, and forwarding twenty letters to the Anxi municipal government (Anxi Association Minutes of Meetings, hereafter, MM, Feb. 3, 1940). This is just an indication of how extensive regional associations were being utilized to establish/renew *qiaoxiang* contacts.

Because of their multiple functions, regional associations, which numbered more than fifty by the end of the 1930s (Fu, 1939:162; Guan, 1940:944), commanded substantial influences among the Chinese communities in Singapore. As a rule, their leaders were important business and community leaders. Tan Kah Kee (Chen Jiageng), for example served as the chairman of the powerful Fujian Provincial Association (Hokkien Huay Kuan) for more than 20 years, while the Chaozhou Association (Teochew Poit Ip Huay Kuan) was founded in 1929 and headed by the prominent entrepreneur Lim Nee-soon. The membership was fairly large. For instance, the Singapore Fuzhou Association had more than 1,000 members, while the Hainan Association claimed more than 5,000 members at the end of the 1930s (Fu, 1940:938-9). Regional associations were also a major medium through which the Kuomintang (*Guomindang*) government contacted the local Chinese communities. In fact, local Chinese were required to provide supporting materials from a *huiguan* before they could obtain any official certification from the Chinese embassy (Jinjiang Association MM, July 1, 1947).

Trade Associations and the Chinese Chamber of Commerce

Throughout the first half of the twentieth century, trade associations and commercial guilds were mushrooming in Singapore, reflecting the rapid commercial growth of this strategically located entrepôt (Ng, 1992). While those associations did not have direct connections with *qiaoxiang*, they nevertheless established and maintained some indirect links with the hometowns. This partly derived from the fact that many trade guilds were formed by merchants from the same locality and this fellowmen-feeling underlined these business associations. In Singapore there were four different textile trade associations during the first half of the twentieth century, and they represented the interests of four different dialect/regional groups (Cheng, 1985:37). Through this indirect linkage, trade associations were also involved in the construction of *qiaoxiang* ties.

The single most important Chinese social organization in Singapore during the period under discussion was the Singapore Chinese Chamber of Commerce (SCCC). Established in 1906, it was one of the first such organizations formed outside of China. From the very beginning the Chamber intended to exert influences on both business and social arenas in the Chinese communities within and without Singapore. According to Yen Ching-hwang, during its early years, the Chamber was used by the Qing government as a vehicle for political control and for exploiting the economic potentials of overseas Chinese, and through this process, it became 'the leading economic and social institution in the local Chinese community' (Yen, 1995:149-50). Later, under the Republic, SCCC took on a variety of functions, ranging from taking care of social welfare and education, serving as the Chinese government's representative, to leading anti-Japanese activities. The major source of SCCC's influence derived from the sheer power of its leadership. The Chamber's management committee was composed of leaders from each Chinese *bang*, and nearly all of the Chinese community leaders from various *bang* in Singapore were presidents or council members of the Chamber at one time or another. This structure lent credit to its claim as the representative of the Chinese community as a whole, though the Hokkiens were the strongest in the SCCC leadership.[3]

Unlike *huiguan* or *huiguan*-cum-trade associations, the SCCC did not directly represent a particular regional group, hence, it did not aim at promoting specific *qiaoxiang* ties. Its organized linkages were rather diverse, working mainly with concerned official agencies in Beijing as well as the General Chamber of Commerce in Beijing and Shanghai. However, because the great majority of the Chamber leadership was born in China (Fujian and Guangdong in particular), they were naturally concerned about developments in their hometowns and might use their influence for the advancement of this localistic concern. This endeavour was reinforced by the fact that the SCCC was regarded as an official organization representing the interests of Chinese not only in Singapore, but also, to a significant extent, maritime Southeast Asia. From time to time, the Chinese national governments (Qing and Republican) transmitted their official instructions to overseas Chinese through the institutional channel of the SCCC (Liu, 1997, 1998a).

In short, in colonial Singapore Chinese social organizations took on a dual role: vertically, they articulated and represented the interests of specific locality, clan, and trade and acted as a linkage between the colonial state and Chinese communities at large; horizontally, Chinese associations served as a nexus connecting various similar associations in Southeast Asia, and more importantly, with *qiaoxiang*. The functions of Chinese associations, which often extended beyond the national boundaries, were wide-ranging, from providing social services to forming business networks. The need of both Chinese national and *qiaoxiang* governments to approach the overseas Chinese communities through the intermediary of these associations reinforced their essential position as the principal and indispensable channel of communication between Southeast Asian Chinese and their hometowns. It is exactly because of these reasons that Chinese social organizations in Southeast Asia were being constructed as a key institutional foundation in building and sustaining the bridges across the sea, reaching a diverse spectrum of Chinese on both sides of the South China Sea.

HISTORICAL PATTERNS

By employing the examples from Singapore, I have pinpointed the institutional foundation of the linkages between Southeast Asian Chinese communities and *qiaoxiang*. Let us now take a closer look at how this foundation was being lifted institutionally to become a bridge crossing the South China Sea, connecting the Chinese diaspora with their hometowns. There were various types of organized channels that served two different interests and constituencies. More specifically, there emerged five patterns of bridging Chinese social organizations with *qiaoxiang* during the first half of the twentieth century: namely, applying political leverage, engaging in economic construction, building social relief and protection mechanisms, providing systemic guarantee/enforcement for business trust, and promoting the revival of Chinese tradition and culture.

Political Leveraging

Throughout the period under consideration, overseas Chinese social organizations constituted an important source of external influence upon local politics in *qiaoxiang*. This influence was mainly collectively built upon the existence of a large number of Chinese immigrants living in Southeast Asia and the significant economic benefits they brought back in the forms of remittance, investment, and charitable contributions. In the meantime, the fact that a number of local Chinese community leaders were enlisted to the Chinese national government reinforced the leveraging power of such agencies located outside of China. Lim Keng Lian, president of the Singapore Anxi Association, was invited to serve as the vice chairman of China's Overseas Chinese Affairs Commission in 1947 (Anxi Association MM, July 12, 1947). Because of the combination of economic resources, political influence, and social standing, Chinese social organizations were used as an apparatus to apply political leverage and push certain political changes in *qiaoxiang*.

Within the realm of political leveraging, there emerged two sub-patterns: the push for reform of certain broad-based policies; and more frequently, the call to implement specific local-oriented policies. While most activities of political leveraging were applied directly to the village governments, some were carried out through circuitous channels of influence. The pressures and suggestions first went through the higher authorities above *qiaoxiang*, such as the provincial and national governments, which were then being exerted upon the *qiaoxiang* authorities.

The case of Taishan (Guangdong) represents the first sub-pattern of political influence. In August 1947 representatives from various Taishan associations in Malaya met in Singapore and formed the Pan-Malaya Federation of Taishan Associations. The meeting was concluded with a highly politicized statement: 'In the past the county of Taishan was not well governed. Since we have a united organization [the Pan-Malaya Federation] now, we must keep a watchful eye over the county government, implement reform policies and make local politics clean' (Taishan Association, 1948:2).

Most of the political measures taken by overseas Chinese social organizations fell within the second pattern and were more specific in their demands, aiming at improving the local policy environments. In 1930, the Singapore Chaozhou Association appealed to the Ministry of Railways and the Guangdong provincial government, opposing the refinancing plan for the construction of Chaozhou-Shantou railway. In 1934, together with other Chaozhou-affiliated associations in Singapore and Malaya, the Association worked with the SCCC in urging the Guangdong provincial authorities to 'completely overhaul and improve the financial system in Shantou' (Chaozhou Association, 1979:298, 398).

During the above-mentioned two-day meeting of the Pan-Malaya Federation of Taishan Associations, a total of 23 resolutions was passed, 16 of them were directly concerned with the hometown and/or its ties with overseas Chinese communities. Among these, five were about the needs and means to exert political influence in Taishan. Resolution 15, for instance, put forth various methods of 'promoting local autonomy, implementing a democratic system, and electing overseas Chinese representatives into the County Council'. Resolution 17 urged the Guangdong provincial government to 'eliminate local corruption', while Resolution 23 appealed to the Administrative *Yuan* and the Guangdong Government to allow Taishan to enjoy a higher degree of self-governance (Taishan Association, 1948:2, 6-9).

In a similar vein, at the request of the Malacca Tongan Association, the Singapore Tongan Association in 1929 lent its support to the nomination of two candidates for local political posts in Tongan, even though its leadership felt that it did not have legitimate jurisdiction for such an endorsement (Tongan Association MM, Oct. 20, 1929). During the 1930s, the Singapore Chaoan Association sent letters to various agencies of the Guangdong government, urging them to take measures to stop local village heads from collecting labour levies from relatives of overseas Chinese (Chaoan Association, 1962:132).

Those activities of applying political leverage through the agency of associations were manifestations of two important developments with respect to the Nanyang Chinese communities. In the first place, it was a clear indication that the great majority of them still regarded themselves as first and foremost Chinese citizens. A reading of various associations' minutes of meetings reveals unmistakably that their paramount concerns were those issues dealing with *qiaoxiang*, while local (Southeast Asia) affairs seldom appeared to be the chief considerations. This sojourner mentality led to the Chinese diaspora's heightened interests in the political vicissitudes of the *qiaoxiang*, prompting them to link both emotionally and physically with hometown affairs. Second, the sheer volume and continuous flow of political leveraging from overseas Chinese organizations indicated that various levels of the governments in China, from the central to the local *qiaoxiang* ones, were receptive of the influence from the outside. Although it is difficult to ascertain how effective this political impact actually was, the very fact that political pressures from Chinese associations in Southeast Asia were continuously and constantly coming in may be seen as a sign that they perhaps reached certain intended goals.

Economic Construction

The second major pattern of linkages between overseas Chinese social organizations and *qiaoxiang* was economic. The comparative economic strength of the Chinese diaspora communities made them an ideal target of the *qiaoxiang* governments in courting financial contributions, and Chinese social organizations served as a focal point and institutional nexus for various parties to pursue this agenda. This broad function of economic construction can be further divided into three sub-categories: Chinese associations constituted simultaneously as a forum to propagate official 'fund-raising' messages, as a means to accumulate actual capital for economic development, and as the agency to represent mainland companies.

Because of their considerable influence, organizational capacities, and broad membership base, associations were an indispensable stop for visiting Chinese officials, from the central and local *qiaoxiang* governments alike. The records of the Singapore Anxi Association reveal that a large number of visiting officials pleaded for financial support to *qiaoxiang* in particular and China in general. And their plea was formulated with a mixture of official nationalism and parochial sentiments. In arguing the need to obtain local Chinese communities' financial contributions, a visiting official from the Anxi county government stated in 1929 that 'without the assistance of overseas Chinese [originated from Anxi], it would be impossible to carry out any economic construction' (Anxi Association MM, Oct. 19, 1929). Based upon similar premises, the Vice Minister of the Ministry of Overseas Affairs urged Anxi Association members to set aside some of their business profit for 'investment in China as an indication of supporting the nation' (Anxi Association MM, Oct. 20, 1946). Addressing the same Association, the consul of the Chinese embassy emphasized that overseas Chinese had a long tradition of supporting China, which earned them the honour of 'Mother of the Revolution', and that it was their moral obligation to help the motherland (Anxi Association MM, Oct. 20, 1946).

Partly inspired by this combined power of broad-based nationalism and localistic loyalty, Chinese social organizations were actively involved in the efforts to raise funds for economic construction in the hometown. In the 1947 Pan-Malaya Federation of Taishan Associations meeting, more than a quarter of the resolutions were concerned with the promotion of Taishan's economy. Resolution 5, for instance, suggested that overseas Chinese resources should be tapped for local economic development and that the county government should formulate detailed plans in urging overseas Taishanese to form corporations in order to invest in their hometown (Taishan Association, 1948:8-9). More concrete efforts of fund-raising were undertaken through the channel of associations. For example, both the Fujian Economic Development Holdings Company and Huian Fishing

Company were successful in raising funds by using the Singapore Huian Association as an effective venue (Huian Association MM, Nov. 24, 1946; Jan. 26, 1947). With the expectation of raising 50 million *yuan*, representatives of the Anxi Bus Company were pleasantly surprised that their first meeting in the Singapore Anxi Association received overwhelming response, and that 35 million was collected in that meeting alone. The Association also sent delegates back to Anxi to participate in the general meeting of the Company's stockholders (Anxi Association MM, June 29, Aug. 2, 1947). The formation of the All-Malaya Federation of Nan'an Associations was specifically for the purpose of 'undertaking economic construction in the hometown, mobilizing financial resources from overseas, and sending delegates back home (for the building of the Yihai Highway)' (Nan'an Association, 1986:42).

Sometimes these economic construction efforts acquired social ramifications as well. Throughout the first half of the 1930s, one of the major agendas of the Singapore Tongan Association was to build a prison in the hometown. In a management committee meeting, its chairman stated that the prison in Tongan had been run down and as a result, those people who had not been tried were put together with the criminals, which made him 'feel very uncomfortable'. 'Although it is the responsibility of the county government,' he continued, 'it may take ten to twenty years for them to complete such a project.' And he concluded that the construction of the prison was better to be financed by the Tonganese overseas. His suggestion was warmly received and the participants of the meeting contributed S$25,000 on the spot. With this sound beginning, the new prison was completed in the following year (Tongan Association MM, Aug. 18, Dec. 16, 1934; Oct. 20, 1935).

Chinese associations also served as agencies for companies in *qiaoxiang* or elsewhere. In 1949 Hong Kong's Jiyou Bank provided the Singapore Tongan Association with detailed information concerning its clientele and marketing strategies, asking the Association's help in courting for the business of those fellow-regionals (Tongan Association MM, May 7, 1949). The Singapore Chinese Chamber of Commerce was the agent for 16 major Chinese companies, including the Chinese Commercial Bank, Sin-Thai Shipping Company, and the Bank of China, some of which were located in *qiaoxiang* and/or had substantial business dealings with them (Liu, 1998a). Thus, overseas Chinese associations were used by both their leaders and the *qiaoxiang* authorities to reach a broad social and geographical spectrum of the Chinese diaspora to raise capital for the hometowns' economic development. Together with individual investments and remittance, this collective effort played an indispensable part in accumulating a diverse range of financial resources for building the *qiaoxiang* economy.

Social Relief and Protection

As the most important social mechanism within the overseas Chinese communities, associations were constantly approached by the immigrants not only for various social and welfare services in their adopted land, but also for issues dealing with the *qiaoxiang* ties. In the process of articulating, representing, and materializing the interests of those Chinese from the common localities, kinship, and dialect groups, associations played the role of organizer, protector, and arbitrator in the social arena. Throughout the first half of the twentieth century, there were numerous cases in which overseas Chinese associations raised funds for their respective hometowns. Two major sub-patterns are visible. The first was local-oriented relief programmes and the second was geared toward the accomplishment of broader national goals.

The first half of the twentieth century witnessed a series of natural disasters in South China and one of the first places/organizations that the victims in *qiaoxiang* turned to for help were Chinese social organizations overseas. For example, in a 1920s meeting of the Singapore Chaozhou Association, S$10,500 was collected for the purpose of rebuilding a dike in Chaozhou that had been damaged by a recent flood (Chaozhou Association, 1979:223). The Anxi government wrote to the Singapore Anxi Association in 1939, requesting its help in raising relief funds and the latter collected S$15,000 in the first management committee meeting (Anxi Association MM, Feb. 28, 1939; April 14, 1940). In 1946, acting upon Tan Kah Kee's suggestion, the Singapore Tongan Association started building a hospital in Tongan (Tongan Association MM, June 2, 1946).

The second pattern of social relief activities stretched the *qiaoxiang* ties to the nationalist cause. The Chinese diaspora's support of the mainland's anti-Japanese movement was a case in point.[4] It was concerned with not only the fate of hometowns, but also China's survival as a nation-state. Associations such as *huiguan* played a key role in the tremendous fund-raising efforts of the Nanyang Chinese. Take the example of the Singapore Chayang Association. With the escalation of Japan's invasion of China, the Association stepped up its fund-raising drive. In January 1939, for the purpose of responding to the visit of government special envoys to Singapore, the Association put out an announcement in the local Chinese newspaper. In addition to raising funds for the national anti-Japanese activities, the Committee to Save the Hometown was subsequently founded. The Association also co-ordinated with its counterparts in other parts of British Malaya and established the Nanyang Foundation with an initial capital of S$100,000 (*Nanyang Siang Pau*, Jan. 9, 1939; June 30 & July 10, 1940). This is just one of the numerous cases when Chinese associations worked collectively in helping both the hometown and the nation. In this process, locality and nation were integrated and nationalist concerns gradually transcended parochial sentiments.

Throughout the first half of the twentieth century, the day-to-day management of *qiaoxiang*-related issues most frequently concerned the protection of social and financial interests of overseas Chinese in their hometowns. This task occupied a significant place in the associations' overall dealings with China. They were also involved in providing protection of property rights and acting as mediators in disputes. Property disputes back in China frequently occurred to the disadvantage of many Chinese overseas, who felt that a collective mechanism was needed to represent and protect their interests, and associations assumed such a role. Two resolutions formulated during the 1947 Pan-Malaya Federation of Taishan Associations meeting thereby urged the National Commission of Overseas Chinese Affairs, the Guangdong Provincial Government, and the Taishan County Government to take stern actions in dealing with the violation of overseas Chinese property rights (Taishan Association, 1948:4-5). In 1946, a member of the Singapore Huian Association requested it to arbitrate with the Huian County Government in the fight to get back his property that had been occupied illegally (Huian Association MM, July 7, 1946). Two years later representatives of a Tongan village wrote to the Singapore Tongan Association, relating the quarrel of their village with a neighbouring village that had been going on for over a few hundred years and asking the Association's mediation. After lengthy discussions in the management committee meetings, it was decided that the Association should step in. And it subsequently sent out four official letters, two to the disputing parties, one to a prominent local community leader, and one to the local government (Tongan Association MM, July 17, 1948).

Guardian of Business Trust

As mentioned earlier, overseas Chinese social organizations served as an important institutional foundation for establishing and maintaining business networks both in the national and regional contexts. This business networking inevitably had something to do with the formulation of trust both as a concept and as a practice. It has been convincingly established that one of the enduring features of Chinese business practices is trust (*xinyong*), which helps reduce transactional costs (the search for trading partners, costs of contract negotiation and enforcement, etc.) (Mackie, 1992; Tong and Yong, 1998). 'While monetary capital is limited, the capital of trust is boundless', a SCCC publication declares. 'If a businessman does not abide by business ethic [which is the foundation of trust], he is just like committing suicide' (SCCC, 1931:20). The question is, then, how to forge and sustain business trust, both personally and institutionally?

While it has been correctly pointed out that traditional Chinese values - Confucian ethic in particular - have been instrumental in the formation of business trust, the cultural element is more like 'software', or what Douglass North calls 'informal constraints' (conventions and codes of behaviours).[5] Its effective operation requires a set of compatible 'hardware', or 'formal constraints' (institutions). Defined as 'any constraint humans devise to shape their interactions', institutions 'reduce uncertainty by providing a structure to everyday life'. As such, 'the institutional framework plays a major role in the performance of an economy' (North, 1990:25, 69). This institutional hardware and formal constraints were, and continue to be, important in the colonial and postcolonial societies, where the legal infrastructure has been inadequate and the lack of long-term agreements and the non-existence of secure property rights has led to high transaction costs. In any event, for pre-1945 Southeast Asian Chinese business communities, whose commercial activities had been traditionally transnational and cross-regional, the attaining and retaining of a formal and familiar (ethnic-based) institutional framework would be essential. Because both the colonial and Chinese governments did not care much about the internal affairs of Chinese communities, the Chinese diaspora had to devise their own formal constraints to shape their business interactions. As the most well-organized and adequately financed institutions with a long-standing history, reputable leadership, and regional networking, associations became the indispensable structures to be reckoned with. In addition to formulating and sustaining social ethic that underlay business conducts, social organizations served as an important third party enforcement mechanism for business trust.

The Singapore Jinjiang Association, for example, recorded the cases when its members sought its institutional help in retrieving debts (Jinjiang Association MM, June 7, 1946). In 1948, the Anxi Association in Penang engaged in a concerted action with its Singapore counterpart in dealing with an embezzlement case of a former manager at the Anxi Bus Company, in which the overseas Anxi fellows had invested a substantial amount of money (Anxi Association MM, April 10, 1948). As a result of its tremendous influence and multi-*qiaoxiang* representations, the Singapore Chinese Chamber of Commerce (SCCC), was unquestionably the key regional institution in serving both as the guardian of trust and the enforcement mechanism against trust abuse. For instance, in 1931, the Chamber acting on behalf of its member, Lim Dinmao, requested the court in Amoy to 'reclaim the S$90,000 debt' owed by a former manager of Lim's branch in Amoy (SCCC, 1931:6). In the meantime, a series of correspondence (about ten letters between SCCC and various organizations in *qiaoxiang*) provides another interesting case showing how SCCC went through a number of localities and worked with different organizations in punishing the abuse of trust. The case involved two business firms in Singapore, whose money was embezzled in late 1930 by Tay Zinan, a businessman in Kluang (Malaya). Upon receiving complaints from the two owners, the Chamber first appealed directly to Tay. But he took the money and ran away, returning to his hometown in Jieyang (Guangdong). Starting from December 1930 the case was formally filed with SCCC, which then communicated with the two firms in Singapore, the Shantou Chamber of Commerce (which had commercial judicial control over Jieyang), the Municipal government of Jieyang County, and the Court of Jieyang County. In addition to supplying information such as Tay's whereabouts in China, the Chamber also suggested appropriate ways of dealing with this case. By April 1931 Tay was finally arrested and charged by the Court in Jieyang (see for details Liu, 1998a).

The above examples indicate clearly that overseas Chinese social organizations served as a central protection and enforcement mechanism for the business communities. Their well-established institutional linkages within the region of Southeast Asia and with the relevant organizations in *qiaoxiang* significantly facilitated this function. The existence of dense social/locality/kinship networks of interaction, in turn, helped reduce the costs of transacting, thus playing a major part in the development of economic ties between Southeast Asian Chinese and their hometowns. Seen from a theoretical perspective, Chinese associations assumed the role somewhat similar to the institutions such as courts, which constitute one of the three central components of 'the social system' that is essential to the proper working of the economic system.[6]

Cultural Impact
The role of Chinese associations in constructing *qiaoxiang* ties extended to the cultural arena, affecting the process of cultural change both within the Chinese communities of Southeast Asia and in China.[7] The former activities were mainly carried out through the dissemination of *qiaoxiang*-related information as a means to strengthening the real/fictive ties with the hometown; and the latter were primarily undertaken through the promotion of traditional Chinese culture and values.

Although distanced by the vast sea, the majority of Chinese (with the exception of the Straits-born and English-educated) in Malaya prior to 1949 remained sentimentally attached to their hometowns; the 'sojourning mentality' was a prevailing mood of the time. One way of maintaining such sentimental ties with *qiaoxiang* and the relatives there was through associations, which served as a transit place for disseminating information concerning hometowns. For example, county-level newspapers were subscribed and circulated, in part through the agency of *huiguan*. The internal publication of the Singapore Fuzhou Association was specifically designed to publish news about China in general and Fuzhou in particular (Huian Association MM, July 7, 1946; Fuzhou Association MM, May 21, 1946).

Overseas Chinese social organizations were also keen in promoting Chinese tradition in *qiaoxiang* through various means such as financing selected village schools. In 1947, the Pan-Malaya Federation of Taishan Associations passed a resolution entitled, 'Improving education in Taishan, uplifting cultural standards, and creating sound morals'. Complaining that students in Taishan did not study hard enough and that teachers were not willing to work hard to improve the education standard, the resolution formulated six specific measures to combat 'this deteriorating tendency'. They included such strategies as sending inspectors from overseas Taishan associations back to check the progress, providing financial rewards to good teachers, and urging the county government take steps to improve conduct at schools. These measures, moreover, were to receive unflinching support from overseas Taishan associations. A related resolution appealed the county government to 'order everyone to lead a simple lifestyle and to nurture good morals'. It claimed that most people in Taishan lived beyond their means and that gambling and robbery were rampant. And it was the responsibility of the county government to take necessary steps to end these decadent habits (Taishan Association, 1948:6-8). In a management committee meeting, the Singapore Huian Association raised 3.5 million *yuan* to support the founding and maintaining of a junior high school in Huian (Huian Association MM, Nov. 24, 1946). Although it is unclear as to whether or not the Association was directly involved in the daily management of this school, it was possible that the influence of its leadership, including its value systems, was at least indirectly felt.

Summing up, during the first half of the twentieth century, Chinese organizations in British Malaya established and maintained a diverse range of patterns in maintaining ties with South China. Politically, they constituted an institutional basis for applying influence upon *qiaoxiang*, either by directly appealing to the local governments, or indirectly through the provincial and/or national governments. In the economic sphere, Chinese associations served as a major venue through which investment plans were formulated and funds collected to support village construction. Socially, Chinese organizations provided essential assistance in an effort to protect the interests of their members. In the realm of business, they acted as a central mechanism to supply both formal and informal constraints to the working of business trust within the Chinese communities. Culturally, these associations formulated and reinforced the real/imaginary attachments to *qiaoxiang* by disseminating information pertaining to the hometown and by hosting visiting delegations. Their intention to uphold traditional culture was partly supplemented by the efforts to (re)establish 'sound' morals in their respective hometowns through the selective use of financial resources for school funding.

CHANGE AND CONTINUITY: THE AFTERMATH OF 1949

With the founding of the People's Republic of China (PRC) in 1949, the ties established and sustained by overseas Chinese organizations underwent fundamental transformation, both in terms of the substance of the linkages and the format of the exchange. Two periods are discernible. The first, from 1949 to 1980, witnesses a dramatic decline in the extent of physical contact and the virtual suspension of most channels of communication; the second period, from 1980 until the present, is characterized by the global revival of *qiaoxiang* connections, and this global surge has been partly led by overseas Chinese organizations, particularly those in Southeast Asia.

The Disruption of the Qiaoxiang *Ties*

The years after 1949 saw a series of substantial changes that would reshape the nature and characteristics of Chinese communities in Southeast Asia and their relationship with *qiaoxiang*. For one thing, with the founding of communist China, its socialist transformation policies, including the stern policy toward the land-owning class (to which the relatives of some overseas Chinese belonged), significantly alienated the Chinese diaspora communities. More importantly, with the establishment of new nation-states in Southeast Asia and the subsequent formulation of assimilative and/or discriminatory policies toward the Chinese, the sojourning mentality that had characterized the Chinese communities was gradually replaced by a local-oriented identity (Wang Gungwu, 1991; Suryadinata, 1997). Collectively, the altered environments on both sides of the South China Sea led to some important changes with respect to Chinese associations' links with *qiaoxiang*. Although the bridges did not entirely break down, they were severely damaged.

In the first place, the political leveraging role was reduced to a minimum. Overseas Chinese organizations ceased to be a force affecting either local or national political processes on the mainland. In contrast to the pre-1949 period, when associations frequently attempted to influence certain political agendas in *qiaoxiang*, there were only isolated examples of such efforts, and they were confined to specific policy issues. For instance, the Singapore Chaoan Association in 1950 telegraphed the Chamber of Commerce in Shantou, urging it to take measures to prepare for the imminent famine. In the same year the Association suggested the local county government to make some adjustments on remittance rates (Chaoan Association 1962:132).

The economic construction endeavours were also halted. In 1951 the Anxi Bus Company, which had drawn large enthusiastic backing among the overseas Anxiese prior to 1949, invited the Singapore Anxi Association to invest in the company and to send delegates to participate in the general meeting of shareholders in Anxi. The management committee meeting in Singapore revealed that 'no one is interested in this invitation and no delegates are to be dispatched' (Anxi Association MM, Feb. 25, 1951). The effort to build roads in the hometown by the Pan-Malaya Federation of Nan'an Associations was entirely stopped after the Communist take-over (Nan'an Association 1986:38).

The social relief role of Chinese associations in *qiaoxiang* likewise ceased. An official message issued in 1951 by the Singapore Tongan Association, which had been in the forefront of helping the hometown, was a clear signal of such a changing orientation. After a lengthy discussion on the Association's past contributions to the hospital in Tongan, the management committee decided that 'such contributions should absolutely be stopped'. 'Our Association aims at networking fellow countymen feelings and advancing business interests', the official resolution continued. 'In the future, we should pay greater attention to local [Singapore] social welfare, such as supporting the Foundation of Preventing Tuberculosis' (Tongan Association MM, June 29, 1951).

In the cultural arena, *qiaoxiang* ties were similarly disrupted. Before 1941, the great majority of Chinese associations were concerned about promoting their own Chinese (sub)ethnic cultures. By the end of the 1940s, there was a gradual shift of focus, and they came to realize that they ought to pay equal attention to both local (Southeast Asian) and Chinese cultures (see for example, Puning Association, 1949:45). After the 1950s, however, organized and public activities to celebrate cultural affinities with China were significantly reduced, and most associations were more interested in promoting local affairs, such as celebrating Singapore's self-governance in 1959.

It is clear that the years between 1949 and 1980 saw the reverse of the extensive interactions between Chinese organizations and *qiaoxiang* that had been going on during the previous four decades. Such a disruption was in large part due to the rapidly changing external environments in both China and Southeast Asia. The need to survive in a new and much harsher condition within the framework of new (indigenous) nation-states forced Chinese associations to be more adaptive and fully localized in their political and cultural orientations. However, because the disruption was

102

mainly precipitated by a hostile external environment, the internal structures of the overseas Chinese associations and their old connections with *qiaoxiang* were mostly preserved. This was to lay an institutional basis for the regional and global revival of *qiaoxiang* ties in the closing two decades of the twentieth century.

The Global Revival of Qiaoxiang *Ties since 1980*

Since the early 1980s there have been increasing signs and activities of the revival of the relationships. This revival stems from a variety of internal and external factors. For one thing, the growing importance of global capitalism and the remarkable economic growth in Southeast Asia (at least until 1997) have fundamentally reshaped the Asian-Pacific scene, in which ethnic Chinese have been one of the major players. New policies of the PRC central government and local *qiaoxiang* authorities in attracting foreign capital, especially that of Chinese descent, have provided further opportunities to reconnect the missing ties between the Chinese diaspora communities and their ancestral hometowns. Moreover, by the 1980s, the identity dilemma that had long beset the Chinese overseas had largely been resolved, with the permanent adoption of local (Southeast Asian) identities. This new environment provides a framework within which the linkages with *qiaoxiang* were to be re-established, but under different premises. Politically, as citizens of the new Southeast Asian nation-states, the Chinese diaspora engage their ties with the ancestral hometowns with little or no political baggage. Culturally, because the majority of them was born in Southeast Asia and brought up in an environment that has not been friendly to Chinese culture and education, they approach *qiaoxiang* with significantly less emotional attachment.

The global revival of *qiaoxiang* ties is manifested in at least two aspects. In the first place, the investments by the Chinese diaspora in their hometowns, Fujian and Guangdong in particular, grew dramatically. In 1994 alone, the diaspora-dominated inflow of foreign money contributed to 8 per cent of China's capital investment, up from 3.6 per cent in 1985. Foreign-affiliated ventures produced nearly 20 per cent of the economy's total industrial output and nearly 30 per cent of total exports in 1994. China's amazing development boom, economists agree, could not have taken place without the diaspora. Chinese from Hong Kong, Taiwan, and Southeast Asia account for 80 per cent of all foreign investment in China, which is concentrated heavily in South China (Biers, 1995; Liu, 1998b).

Secondly, the social linkages between overseas Chinese communities and *qiaoxiang* have also been re-established and expanded. The mushrooming of Chinese associations' worldwide gatherings, as well as the increasing tendency to hold such meetings in *qiaoxiang*, is another clear indication of the reviving ties. For example, more than 4,000 Teochews worldwide gathered in Shantou in November 1997. Regional associations of Fuzhou, Jinjiang, Anxi, Tongan, Nan'an, to name just a few, have all held regular international conventions in their respective hometowns (see Liu, 1998b for detailed examples).

The current global revival of *qiaoxiang* ties, within which Chinese organizations from Southeast Asia play a dynamic leading role, bears both continuity and discontinuity with the historical patterns that had existed prior to 1949. For one thing, they have been similarly guided by the principles of locality and kinship and driven by the need to expand social, cultural and business networks beyond the national boundaries, including in *qiaoxiang*. Their major domain of influence continues to be in the realm of economic reconstruction, particularly in infrastructure, socially charitable projects (such as building schools and hospitals), and cultural regeneration (shaping subethnic identities) (Liu 1998b).

There are, however, at least two structural differences. First, unlike overseas Chinese social organizations' pre-1980 practices, which established links with *qiaoxiang* mainly through bilateral relations, the current global revival of *qiaoxiang* ties has been characterized by a greater degree of multi-locality involvement. For example, the International Jinjiang Federation was formed in May 1997 and is composed of member associations from Asia, Europe, North America, Australia, and South Africa. It was evolved from the Union of Jinjiang Societies in Asia formed in 1990 with members in Singapore, Malaysia, Indonesia, Macao, the Philippines, Taiwan, and mainland China. Together they have been involved in the concerted efforts to undertake social and economic projects in Jinjiang (Sinn, 1997). International bodies of this kind are in turn marked by a significant degree of institutionalization, with specifically-designated agencies to carry out the international missions, and with ideological justifications to legitimate this new pattern of organized Chinese transnationalism.

Secondly, as a result of the expanded international stage and multi-layer involvement, the benefits brought out by Chinese organizations' efforts have been more remarkable and wide-ranging. Take the example of Anxi county. According to official statistics, during the 18 months' period since the First Anxi World Convention in 1992, more than 3,000 overseas Anxiese visited their hometown for tourism and economic activities. They spent 49.5 million *yuan* (US$5.7 million) in charitable projects (such as hospitals and schools) and set up 51 factories worth of 92.4 million *yuan* (US$10.7 million), with additional capital of US$64.8 million being put in Anxi. Compared with the period prior to the Convention, the number of new factories nearly doubled, while the amounts of overseas Anxiese's investment increased by 4.6 times. In the meantime, the total output of the county's enterprises in 1997 has increased 10 times over five years earlier (*Anxi Xiangxu* [*Hometown News from Anxi*], April 6, 1994).

In brief, the post-1949 era has seen both continuity and discontinuity of the historical patterns of bridging *qiaoxiang* ties that had existed during the first half of the twentieth century. This changing pattern is a clear testimony that organized forms of Chinese modern transnationalism have been conditioned by two fundamental factors. Externally, they are subject to the shifting environments in both Southeast Asia and China; internally, their revival and expansion are determined by the strength of their organizational structure, leadership, and membership. It is precisely because of this reason that those associations which were historically active (such as Anxi and Tongan) have been more successful in recovering from the low tide of the years between 1950 and 1980 and have skilfully capitalized the new wave of globalization to expand their hometown connections.

(RE)CONSTRUCTING TRANSNATIONAL TIES: THE ROLE OF CHINESE ASSOCIATIONS

This survey of the role of overseas Chinese social organizations in the making and sustaining of *qiaoxiang* ties throughout the twentieth century shows that a Nanyang-centred perspective does provide some different insights as to the dynamism and patterns of modern Chinese transnationalism. The Nanyang pattern, for example, has been largely instigated and led by organized societal forces, with the supplement of individual efforts. The dynamism from *qiaoxiang*, on the other hand, seems to have been primarily a state/local government sponsored project with strong ideological underpinning, and its intention has been to politically and culturally domesticate the Chinese diaspora and to mobilize economic resources for China's development (see for example, Duara, 1997). The convergence of these two types of dynamisms - from Nanyang Chinese social organizations, whose concern was to provide various aids to their hometowns, and from the *qiaoxiang* governments, whose purpose was to utilize overseas Chinese through the agency of their associations - led to the formation, development, and expansion of organized *qiaoxiang* ties during the first half of the twentieth century. Between 1950 and 1980, when both sides of the South China Sea felt no such need and impetus to continue this strategic alliance, or were prevented from engaging in such connections, the structural bridge was closed and the traffic halted. Since 1980, the changing environment of global capitalism and the abundant opportunities which emerged with China's economic reform provide significant incentives for the Chinese diaspora to renew, reclaim, and reaffirm their long-standing ties with the ancestral hometowns.

This case study of overseas Chinese associations' crucial role in the making and sustaining of the *qiaoxiang* ties highlights some of the major themes that are centrally concerned with the patterns of modern Chinese transnationalism. Three issues seem to be particularly relevant in this connection: the cultural dimension of Chinese transnationalism; the integration of parochial loyalty and trans-locality sentiments; and the convergence of vertical representations and horizontal linkages. In the first place, the transnationalizing activities of ethnic Chinese, including that led and engaged by associations, have been fundamentally based upon a familiar cultural tradition. The extensive communications between Southeast Asian Chinese communities and *qiaoxiang* extended into the economic, political, social and cultural spheres, but as this essay has demonstrated, the core of these interactions lay in sustained cultural linkages that transcended the national boundaries. The significance of this cultural dimension can be discerned from two angles. For one, overseas Chinese association itself has been an extension and symbol of Chinese culture in the sense that it embodies some of the basic principles of Chinese culture and tradition, such as Confucianism and the Chinese lineage. Moreover, one of the two major reasons for the establishment of Chinese associations overseas has been the intention to uphold Chinese culture in the adopted land (see Cheng, 1988). Secondly, and more importantly, the cultural affinity, such as commonality in race, (real/fictive) kinship, locality, and languages, serves as a strong bond linking the associations with *qiaoxiang*, both institutionally and individually. This cultural affinity survived during the harsh years between 1950 and 1980, partly through the shift of the associations' focuses from politicized, nationalistic Chinese culture to de-politicized, local-oriented subethnic cultures. In this new form of cultural representation, commonality in locality and sub-language links with *qiaoxiang* has been emphasized while cultural connections with China as a nation-state are being downplayed. Because of this partial survival of (sub)cultural affinity, the linkages with *qiaoxiang* were rebuilt with considerable easiness.

The transnationalization of *qiaoxiang* ties is, therefore, a reworking of Chinese (sub)culture(s) that have survived and expanded under different environments in China and Southeast Asia. Because of their close association with Chinese culture (both institutionally and spiritually) and long-standing historical role, social organizations in Southeast Asia have constantly been revitalized and (re)constructed as a key foundation for the building of *qiaoxiang* ties throughout the twentieth century.

Secondly, Chinese association has served as a focal point in integrating parochial loyalty with nationalistic sentiments during the first half of the twentieth century. As we have shown, the diverse patterns of bridging *qiaoxiang* ties were geared predominantly toward the locality, but they were sometimes linked explicitly with larger national causes, such as during the anti-Japanese movement in the second half of the 1930s. It was mainly through this integration of local and national concerns that Chinese identities were to become more diverse and flexible, incorporating not only local sentiments, but also increasingly nationalistic and cosmopolitan ideals. While associations, particularly those founded upon the locality principle, were oriented toward the affairs specifically concerned with the hometowns, there was an increasing tendency during the first half of the twentieth century to link localistic agendas with broader nationalist issues. This was not only a product of the rising tide of nationalism among Chinese overseas since the turn of the twentieth century, it was also a consequence of the deliberate intentions of the Chinese nationalists/officials from the mainland to instill overseas Chinese with a sense of nation-state and nationalist pride (Duara, 1997). Moreover, the associations' own strategies of using provincial/national authorities as a viable venue in affecting *qiaoxiang* agendas further bolstered the integration between local interests and national concerns. As a result, Chinese associations in Southeast Asia gradually transcended their original localistic focuses and demonstrated a marked interest in trans-locality affairs. This was most evident in the anti-Japanese war during the 1930s, when saving the nation had an immediate bearing upon the efforts to help the hometown. This integration of local/national sentiments has become a defining characteristic of association leadership in the post-World War II era, who have exerted simultaneous influences upon both the local and national scenes in China.

Last but not least, Chinese association has constituted an essential nexus of vertical representations and horizontal linkages in the articulation of *qiaoxiang* ties. Compared with individual-based *qiaoxiang* linkage, association has been more effective in reaching broader constituencies both within and without the (Southeast Asian) national boundaries. Vertically, these associations represent a diverse range of regional and sectional interests, which bolster their claim as the spokesperson for a large segment among the Chinese communities. Horizontally, they have had long-established close relationship with counterparts in the region of Southeast Asia. As the paragraphs above have demonstrated, this horizontal linkage allowed them to undertake some concerted actions in affecting the local social and political processes in *qiaoxiang*.

CONCLUDING REMARKS

In retrospect, the organized transnationalizing practice of the Chinese diaspora during the first half of the twentieth century set a historical precedent to the present-day global revival of *qiaoxiang* ties. Like its predecessor, the current upsurge of linkages is based upon, and sustained by, the (sub)cultural affinity, real/fictive imaginary links with the hometown, and the strategic manoeuvre from the mainland. Alongside with this parochial tie, national and regional agendas also play a part in cementing the bridges across the sea. The fuller spin of globalizing forces, moreover, has provided additional concrete in supporting those bridges linking Southeast Asian Chinese communities and *qiaoxiang* during the closing years of the twentieth century, a trend that will be likely to continue well beyond the turn of the millennium.

BIBLIOGRAPHY

1) Minutes of Meetings (MM)

Hin Ann Huay Kuan	Minutes of meetings, 1945-83
Sam Kiang Huay Kwan	Minutes of meetings, 1948-73
Singapore Ann Kway Association (Anxi Association)	Minutes of meetings, 1929-71
Singapore Foochow Association (Fuzhou Association)	Minutes of meetings, 1945-57
Singapore Hokkien Huay Kuan	Minutes of meetings, 1950-64
Singapore Hui Ann Association (Huian Association)	Minutes of meetings, 1925-75
Singapore Poon Yue Association	Minutes of meetings, 1946-61
Singapore Tung Ann District Guild (Tongan Association)	Minutes of meetings, 1929-64

2) Special Publications of Chinese Associations

Chaoan Association
1962 *The 25th Year Commemorative Publication of Singapore Chaoan Association.* Singapore: Chaoan Association
Chaozhou Association
1979 *The 50th Year Commemorative Publication of Singapore Teochew Poit Ip Huay Kuan.* Singapore: Chaozhou Association

Fuqing Association
1980   *The 70th Year Commemorative Publication of Singapore Futsing Association (1910-1980)*. Singapore: Fuqing Association
Nan'an Association
1986   *Lam Ann Association 60th Anniversary*. Singapore: Nan'an Association
Puning Association
1949   *Singapore Pulin Association's 8th Anniversary*. Singapore: Pulin Association
Singapore Chinese Chamber of Commerce (SCCC)
1931   *Singapore Chinese Chamber of Commerce Special Commemorative Publication*. Singapore: Singapore Chinese Chamber of Commerce (SCCC)
Taishan Association
1948   *Bulletin of the Federation of Taishan Association of Malaya (Inaugural Issue)*. Singapore: Taishan Association

3) Secondary Works

Akashi, Yoji
1970   *The Nanyang Chinese National Salvation Movement, 1937-1941*. Kansas: Center for East Asian Studies, the University of Kansas
Biers, Dan
1995   'Staying the Course: Mainland Upsets Don't Faze Overseas Chinese Investors', *Asian Wall Street Journal*, 19 July 1995, p. 11
Chen Da
1937   *Southeast Asian Chinese and Societies of Fujian and Guangdong*. Changsha: Sanwu yishuguan
Cheng Lim Keak
1985   *Social Change and the Chinese in Singapore*. Singapore: Singapore University Press
Douw, Leo and P. Post. (eds)
1996   *South China: State, Culture and Social Change during the twentieth Century*. Amsterdam: Royal Netherlands Academy of Arts and Sciences
Duara, Prasenjit
1997   'Transnationalism and the Predicament of Sovereignty: China, 1900-1945', *American Historical Review*, 102(4), pp. 1030-51
Fu Wumun (ed.)
1939   *The Nanyang Siang Pau Year Book*. Singapore: Nanyang Siang Pau
Godley, Michael
1981   'The Treaty Port Connection: An Essay', *Journal of Southeast*

Asian Studies, 12(1), pp. 248-59

Guan Chupu (ed.)

1940   *Ten Years of Sinchew Jit Poh*. Singapore: Sinchew Jit Poh

Hicks, George (ed.)

1993   *Overseas Chinese Remittances from Southeast Asia, 1910-1940*. Singapore: Select Books

1995   *Chinese Organisations in Southeast Asia in the 1930s*. Singapore: Select Books

Lin Jinzhi

1988   *An Outline of Overseas Chinese Investment in Domestic Enterprises in Modern Times*. Xiamen: Xiamen University Press

Liu, Hong

1997   'The Singapore Chinese Chamber of Commerce and Industry and Singapore-Malaysian Economic Interactions: A Case Study of Regional Interdependence', paper presented at the International Conference 'Chinese Populations in Contemporary Southeast Asian Societies: Regional Interdependence and International Influence', University of Illinois at Urbana-Champaign, March 10-12

1998a   'Think Locally, Act Regionally: the Singapore Chinese Chamber of Commerce and Industry as an Institutional Nexus of Chinese Business Networks in Asia', paper presented at the international workshop *Asian Business Networks*, jointly organized by Tokyo University and the National University of Singapore, March 31-April 2

1998b   'Old Linkages, New Networks: The Globalization of Overseas Chinese Voluntary Associations and Its Implications', *The China Quarterly* 155, pp. 582-609

2000   'Globalization, Institutionalization and the Social Foundation of Chinese Business Networks', in: Henry Yeung and Chris Olds (eds) *The Globalization of Chinese Business Firms*. London: Macmillan

Mackie, Jamie

1992   'Overseas Chinese Entrepreneurship', *Asian-Pacific Economic Literature* 6, pp. 41-64

Ng, Wing Chung

1992   'Urban Chinese Social Organization: Some Unexplored Aspects in *Huiguan* Development in Singapore, 1900-1941', *Modern Asian Studies* 26(3), pp. 469-94

North, Douglass

1990   *Institutions, Institutional Change and Economic Performance*. Cambridge: Cambridge University Press

Ong, Aihwa & Donald Nonini (eds)

1997   *Ungrounded Empires: The Cultural Politics of Modern Chinese Transnationalism*. New York: Routledge

See Chinben

1988   'Chinese Organizations and Ethnic Identity in the Philippines', in: Jennifer Cushman and Wang Gungwu (eds) *Changing Identities of the Southeast Asian Chinese since World War II*. Hong Kong: Hong Kong University Press, pp. 319-34

Sinn, Elizabeth

1997   '*Xin Xi Guxiang*: A Study of Regional Associations as a Bonding Mechanism in the Chinese Diaspora. The Hong Kong Experience', *Modern Asian Studies* 31(2), pp. 375-97

Suryadinata, Leo (ed.)

1997   *Ethnic Chinese as Southeast Asians*. Singapore: Institute of Southeast Asian Studies

Suyama, Taku

1962   'Pang Societies and the Economy of Chinese Immigrants in Southeast Asia', in: K.G. Tregonning (ed.) *Papers on Malayan History*. Singapore: Journal of Southeast Asian History, pp. 193-213

Swedberg, Richard

1990   *Economics and Sociology: Redefining their Boundaries: Conversations with Economists and Sociologists*. Princeton: Princeton University Press

Tong Chee Kiong and Yong Pit Kee

1998   'Guanxi Bases, Xinyong and Chinese Business Networks', *British Journal of Sociology* 49(1), pp. 75-96

Wang Gungwu

1991   *China and the Chinese Overseas*. Singapore: Federal Publications

Wickberg, Edgar

1994   'Overseas Chinese Adaptive Organizations, Past and Present', in: Ronald Skeldon (ed.) *Reluctant Exiles? Migration from Hong Kong and the New Overseas Chinese*. Hong Kong: Hong Kong University Press, pp. 68-84

Yen Ching-hwang

1995   'Ch'ing China and the Singapore Chinese Chamber of Commerce, 1906-1911', in: Leo Suryadinata (ed.) *Southeast Asia and China: The Politico-Economic Dimension*. Singapore: Times Academic Press, pp. 133-60

1998   'The Overseas Chinese and the Second Sino-Japanese War, 1937-1945', *Journal of South Seas Society* 52, pp. 150-60

Yong, C.F.

1992   *Chinese Leadership and Power in Colonial Singapore*. Singapore: Times Academic Press

Notes

1. I would like to thank Leo Douw, Michael Godley, and Elizabeth Sinn for their constructive comments on the earlier drafts of this chapter and to Ms Guo Huifen for her capable research assistance. Part of the research for this chapter was underwritten by a research grant from the National University of Singapore (RP970008) for which I am grateful.
2. See for example, Douw and Post, 1996; Ong and Nonini, 1997; Liu, 1998b. *'Qiaoxiang'* refers to the ancestral hometowns of the Chinese overseas, located principally in the provinces of Fujian and Guangdong.
3. For a detailed discussion of pre-World War II leadership structure within the Singapore Chinese community, see Yong, 1992.
4. For a general discussion about the role of overseas Chinese in the anti-Japanese movement, see Akashi, 1970 and Yen, 1998.
5. North, 1990, p. 4. Kenneth Arrow also argues that '[f]or there to be trust, there has to be a social structure which is based on motives different from immediate opportunism'. See Swedberg, 1990, p. 137. (I am indebted to Professor Kunio Yoshihara for bringing my attention to the important theoretical insights articulated by North and Arrow, both of whom are Noble Prize-winning economists.) For a more detailed theoretical discussion on the relationship between institutionalization, trust, and the social foundation of Chinese business networks, see Liu, 2000.
6. According to Arrow, all three elements of the social system are needed for the economic system to work: 'the element of communication, such as codes, symbols, and understanding; the element of shared social norms, which is the reasonable expectation that the norms will be followed even if it would be profitable not to follow them at least in the short run; and thirdly, the existing institutions for enforcement, which themselves operate outside the market system and are needed for enforcement purpose'. See Swedberg, 1990, pp. 139-40.
7. This role can be seen within a broader dimension of modernization efforts undertaken by overseas Chinese since the turn of the twentieth century. See Godley, 1981 for a fuller discussion.

GOVERNMENT POLICY IN THE REFORM ERA: INTERACTIONS BETWEEN ORGANS RESPONSIBLE FOR OVERSEAS CHINESE AND *QIAOXIANG* COMMUNITIES

JOSEPH Y.S. CHENG AND KING-LUN NGOK

Support from the ethnic Chinese diaspora, including the residents of Taiwan, Hong Kong and Macao, has been an important factor in the success of China's economic reforms after 1978 (see, for example, S. Stewart, 1995). Not only were 'overseas Chinese' amongst the pioneer investors, but they have also constituted a major source of capital in the reform era. Since 1978, more than 80 per cent of foreign investments in China have come from Hong Kong, Macao, Taiwan and the Chinese in Southeast Asia (Liu Yingjie, 1997:33). In the 1980s, the investments were mainly from Hong Kong and Macao but, because of greatly improved relations between the People's Republic and Southeast Asian countries, along with the further opening of China, businessmen (especially leaders of major business groups) abandoned their previously-cautious attitude. Many have now invested in the areas their ancestors originally came from (R.N. Clough, 1995:236). Besides the obvious improvements in the political environment, the tremendous efforts of organs responsible for overseas Chinese affairs (ORFOCA) at various levels in China has been another significant factor in attracting diaspora investments. Having adopted a policy intentionally designed to advance the country's development, they have taken advantage of the expanding contacts with communities abroad and, engaging in a form of 'economic diplomacy', actively encouraged ethnic Chinese to return to their 'motherland' to visit and, whilst there, to discuss the feasibility of capital investments, including the setting up of factories.

INTRODUCTION

'Overseas Chinese' is an ill-defined term, but it has been used loosely in China and outside China, and among officials, academics, journalists and ordinary people. The overseas Chinese as an economic culture has attracted considerable attention in the past two decades in proportion to their increasing economic influence, especially in Southeast Asia (see Redding, 1993; Wang 1991; and Lin Tien-way 1991). In September 1980, the third session of the Fifth National People's Congress (NPC) formally approved the Nationality Law of the People's Republic of China (PRC), which clearly stipulates that it 'does not recognize PRC citizens to have dual nationality'. The Nationality Law further stipulates that when a PRC citizen residing in a foreign country voluntarily accedes to or acquires foreign citizenship, he or she will automatically forfeit his or her PRC citizenship. From a legal point of view, foreign citizens of Chinese descent should not be categorized as *huaqiao*, which refers to Chinese living in foreign countries who retain their PRC citizenship. Regarding the former, they should simply be identified as ethnic Chinese (*huaren*); so they are American Chinese if they are US citizens, Indonesian Chinese if they are Indonesian citizens, etc. Foreign citizens of Chinese descent who subsequently acquire PRC citizenship but who continue to reside in foreign countries are *huaqiao*. There is a gray area remaining though; Chinese living in foreign countries who hold Taiwan passports and those who hold no passports are probably categorized as *huaqiao* as well, though they are subject to different treatment from those holding PRC passports upon entry into China. People of Chinese descent in Hong Kong before 1997, in Macao before 1999 and in Taiwan have always been regarded as compatriots because Hong Kong, Macao and Taiwan are considered parts of China by the PRC government. Wang Gungwu, a renowned authority on the subject has suggested abandonment of the concepts of *huaqiao* and *huaren*, as these two terms are no longer appropriate. Overseas Chinese who have acquired US citizenship, for example, are simply US citizens of Chinese descent.[1] However in this chapter, 'overseas Chinese' must still be taken to include anyone living in a foreign country (including Hong Kong before its return to China), with or without PRC citizenship since official government investment statistics make no distinction between *huaqiao* and *huaren*. It should, nevertheless, be noted that, according to one 1985 estimate, more than 85 per cent of the broadly-defined overseas Chinese category had already taken up foreign citizenship.

The authors will first introduce the major hometowns of overseas Chinese and the functions carried out by China's organs responsible for overseas Chinese affairs.[2] They will then present a macro-analysis of the relationship between the hometowns of overseas Chinese and the overseas Chinese communities abroad. This will be followed by a more focused analysis of how *qiaoxiang* attempt to attract overseas Chinese visitors and investment, using Xinhui in Guangdong and Jinjiang in Fujian as examples.

Finally, an assessment will be made on the interaction patterns between *qiaoxiang* and Chinese living overseas.

IMPORTANT HOME VILLAGES

The term *qiaoxiang* usually refers to communities where many overseas Chinese originated and where their family members may still reside; hence *qiaoxiang,* by definition, maintain considerable overseas connections (Fang Xiongpu and Xie Chengjia (eds), 1993:309). Basically, the *qiaoxiang* label depends on the number of overseas Chinese, returned overseas Chinese and family members of overseas Chinese who can claim a relationship. At present, excluding Taiwan, Hong Kong and Macao, there are about 30 million overseas Chinese residing in over 100 countries and regions (Fang Xiongpu and Xie Chengjia (eds), 1993:4). According to the Kuomintang (*Guomindang*) government in Taipei, at the end of 1997, overseas *huaqiao* and *huaren* amounted to 33.24 million, with 81 per cent of them in Asia and 14.2 per cent in the Americas (*Shijie Ribao* [a Chinese newspaper in Bangkok] 9 April 1998). Most of the overseas Chinese originated from the coastal provinces of Guangdong and Fujian, Guangxi (an autonomous region), Hainan, Shandong, Zhejiang and the interior province of Yunnan. These provinces include China's major *qiaoxiang*, but Guangdong and Fujian are the most significant and had been able to attract considerable overseas Chinese investments even before 1949 (Lin Jinzhi and Zhuang Weiji, 1985 and 1989).

In 1996, Guangdong estimated that 14.72 million overseas Chinese originated from the province, residing mainly in Southeast Asia and North America; and it claims to be the largest 'hometown' province in China. Residents in Taiwan, Hong Kong and Macao who originated from Guangdong numbered about 6.18 million. There were more than 0.25 million returned overseas Chinese and 7.57 million family members of overseas Chinese in Guangdong; and those with family members in Taiwan, Hong Kong and Macao amounted to 7.05 million (Zhongguo Qiaolian, 1996:73). Important *qiaoxiang* areas in Guangdong are Huaxian, Panyu, and Zengcheng in Guangzhou; Baoan in Shenzhen; Zhuhai Special Economic Zone; Zhongshan City; Shunde, Nanhai and Sanshui in Foshan; Taishan, Kaiping, Enping, Xinhui and Heshan in Jiangmen; Zhanjiang City; Qingyuan City; Chenghai and Chaoyang in Shantou; Puning and Jiedong in Jieyang; Meixian, Dabu, Fengshun and Jiaoling in Meizhou; Huiyang and Huidong in Huizhou; Gaoyao and Sihui in Zhaoqing; Chaozhou City and Dongguan City.

Fujian claimed (also according to 1996 estimates) that over 8 million overseas Chinese originated from the province, spreading over one hundred countries and regions, with 90 per cent living in Southeast Asia, mainly in Indonesia, Malaysia, the Philippines, Singapore and Thailand. Compatriots in Hong Kong and Macao originating from Fujian numbered more than 0.8 million, while returned overseas Chinese and family members of overseas Chinese amounted to over 8 million. About 80 per cent of the population in Taiwan originated from Fujian; and 12,000 of them had returned to settle in the province (Zhongguo Qiaolian, 1996:74). The major *qiaoxiang* areas include: Quanzhou, Jinjiang, Shishi, Huian, Yongchun, Anxi, Xiamen, Tongan, Zhangzhou, Longhai, Nanjing, Zhaoan, Dongshan, Fuzhou, Fuqing, Minhou, Changle, Lianjiang, Putian, Xianyou, Longyan, Yongding, Gutian and Pingnan.

ORGANS RESPONSIBLE FOR OVERSEAS CHINESE AFFAIRS

The ORFOCA include the Party and state bodies as well as mass organizations with responsibilities for overseas Chinese, returned overseas Chinese and family members of overseas Chinese. Ever since its establishment, the PRC has placed considerable emphasis on overseas Chinese affairs (see S. FitzGerald, 1972). On 19 October 1949, the Central People's Government established an Overseas Chinese Affairs Commission. In 1954, it became the Overseas Chinese Affairs Commission of the PRC, although it was subsequently abolished in June 1970 at the height of the Cultural Revolution. Its responsibilities were transferred to the State Council's Office of Overseas Chinese Affairs, created in January 1978. Like other ministries, it has a number of bureaus and offices and is responsible for policy-making in the field of overseas Chinese affairs. With the exception of Tibet, every provincial unit has an Office of Overseas Chinese Affairs under the provincial government; and there are over 1,400 organs responsible for overseas Chinese affairs at the county level and above (Fang Xiongpu and Xie Chengjia (eds), 1993:338).

The State Council's Office of Overseas Chinese Affairs is an administrative organ in the central government. Both the NPC and the Chinese People's Political Consultative Conference (CPPCC) have their respective Overseas Chinese Committees, reflecting the priority attached to overseas Chinese affairs in the legislature and the country's top advisory body. The NPC's Overseas Chinese Committee assumes responsibilities for legislation and monitoring the work of the government in implementing the statutes concerned in the field of overseas Chinese affairs. It also plays a role in diplomatic activities related to overseas Chinese work. The CPPCC's Overseas Chinese Committee mainly serves in liaising with overseas Chinese communities but also conducts research and surveys, discusses related legislation and policies, and supervises government work in the area.

In 1956, the All-China Federation of Returned Overseas Chinese was established as a unit of the CPPCC. It works to promote the legitimate rights of returned overseas Chinese, family members of overseas Chinese and overseas Chinese, develops contacts with overseas Chinese communities at the people-to-people level, and cultivates economic and cultural exchanges with overseas Chinese. Again, with the exception of Tibet, the Federation has its organizations in all provincial units. In 1994, the Federation had more than 2,700 organs at the county level and above; and it had over 8,000 affiliated mass organizations at various levels (*Guangdong Qiaobao*, 18 June 1994).

The China Overseas Exchange Association, established in 1992, is an organization affiliated to the State Council's Office of Overseas Chinese Affairs. The Association aims to assist the Office of Overseas Chinese Affairs in the capacity of a mass organization, or a non-governmental organization (NGO) in international exchanges. Hence it engages in liaising with overseas Chinese communities and their organizations, strengthening ties of friendship, and promoting exchanges and co-operation. Its establishment reflected the Chinese authorities' awareness that overseas Chinese felt uncomfortable being treated as *huaqiao*, and they sought due recognition as foreign citizens of Chinese descent. Many provincial units, especially *qiaoxiang* provinces, also established their Overseas Exchange Associations affiliated with their Offices of Overseas Chinese Affairs. Moreover, the China Travel Service and foreign branches are also committed to help the Offices of Overseas Chinese Affairs at various levels in promoting contacts and exchanges.

As the two most important *qiaoxiang* provinces, Guangdong and Fujian have a comprehensive framework of ORFOCA. In provincial, prefectural city, and county/county-level city governments, Offices of Overseas Chinese Affairs have been set up. The Office of Overseas Chinese Affairs of the Guangdong provincial government was established in 1980; its predecessor was the Overseas Chinese Affairs Commission created in 1950. The Fujian counterpart of the latter was set up in the same year; but its Office of Overseas Chinese Affairs was established in 1978. In July 1992, Overseas Exchange Associations were established in both provinces, as affiliates to the respective Offices of Overseas Chinese Affairs; and the exercise was repeated down to the county level. Guangdong and Fujian also have their Federations of Returned Overseas Chinese founded in 1958 and 1959 respectively. In the mid-1990s, Guangdong claimed to have more than 2,560 Federations and affiliated organizations at various sub-provincial levels, while Fujian had 429 Federations at various sub-provincial levels (Zhongguo Qiaolian, 1996:73-4). The two provincial People's Congresses both have an Overseas Chinese Committee, and the two provincial people's political consultative conferences have their respective Overseas Chinese Work Groups. The Guangdong Provincial People's Political Consultative Conference even set up a Guangdong Overseas Friendship Association (Guangdong *Haiwai Lianyihui*) in 1987.

MAINTAINING TIES WITH FAMOUS PERSONS

The ORFOCA of Guangdong and Fujian pay special attention to successful people originating from their respective provinces. These are leaders in the industrial, commercial and financial sectors in the countries/regions where they live, as well as leading professionals and academics. Some become leaders of the overseas Chinese *qiaoxiang* associations with considerable prestige and mobilization power. The ORFOCA obviously plan to use their contacts and friendly ties with notable people in mobilization networks.

From the early 1990s, various levels of Offices of Overseas Chinese Affairs in Guangdong have sent officials every year to visit famous persons in relevant overseas communities in order to introduce to them developments in the province, and to solicit their comments and advice. The provincial Office of Overseas Chinese Affairs also uses government funds every year to invite leaders of overseas Guangdong communities to visit the province, and they are usually well received by the provincial leaders. In making these invitations, the provincial ORFOCA carefully collect data on the development plans of major business groups controlled by overseas Guangdong communities, and the people invited are considered potential investors in Guangdong. During their visits, arrangements are made to expose them to investment opportunities and to initiate investment negotiations. For example, in 1995, the provincial office of Overseas Chinese Affairs paid for the visits of more than 30 groups (275 people) of entrepreneurs to examine and discuss investment opportunities in the province. The office facilitated the conclusion of 11 projects totaling 930 million *yuan* (*Guangdong Nianjian* Editorial Committee, 1996:675).

Table I Annual Invitations to Overseas Chinese Community Leaders and Famous Persons from Guangdong on Government Expenditure, 1990-6

Year	No. of Persons	No. of Countries/Regions Involved
1990	415	17
1991	391	20
1992	460	18
1993	367	15
1994	/	/
1995	611 350	17 20
1996		

Source: Guangdong *Nianjian* Editorial Committee (ed.), *Guangdong Nianjian* (Guangdong Yearbook) (Guangzhou: Guangdong Nianjianshe), 1991-7 issues.

Apparently, Guangdong ORFOCA's efforts to link up with famous overseas persons originating from the province brought handsome results. In 1993, the provincial Office of Overseas Chinese Affairs assisted the conclusion of fourteen investment projects amounting to US$380 million. In 1994, the Office facilitated the signing of nine investment projects valued at over 10 billion *yuan* (*Guangdong Qiaobao*, 8 December 1995). From 1991 to 1994, Offices of Overseas Chinese Affairs at various levels in Guangdong invited 4,091 experts in science and technology to visit Guangdong; and the provincial Office invited 59 such individuals to engage in academic exchanges with their counterparts in the province (*Guangdong Qiaobao*, 8 December 1995).

In liaison with famous overseas persons originating from the province, the Guangdong Overseas Exchange Association has played a significant role. In fact, some honorary chairmen and advisors of the organization were similarly recruited themselves. After the Association's establishment in July 1992, it claimed in just two years to have established close contacts with over 20 countries in Southeast Asia and North America, over 30 overseas Chinese *qiaoxiang* associations, and over 150 famous overseas persons originating from Guangdong (*Guangdong Nianjian* Editorial Committee, 1994:601). Such liaison work is mainly aimed at attracting overseas Chinese investments. For example, the Association concentrated on the important overseas Chinese *qiaoxiang* associations in Malaysia in 1995. The Malaysian Federation of Chaozhou (Teochew) Associations (*Chaozhou Gonghui Lianhehui*) is the highest organ of overseas Chaozhou *qiaoxiang* associations in Malaysia. The Malaysian Federation of Chinese Associations (*Zhonghua Dahuitang Lianhehui*) established in 1991 is the highest organ of overseas Chinese *qiaoxiang* associations in Malaysia, involving the major overseas Chinese businessmen and community leaders in all thirteen states of Malaysia. In 1995, the Guangdong Overseas Exchange Association succeeded in inviting business delegations from the two Malaysian federations to visit Guangdong to study business opportunities and engage in cultural exchanges (*Guangdong Qiaobao*, 13 October 1995 and 14 November 1995).

The Guangdong Overseas Friendship Association under the provincial people's political consultative conference is responsible for approaching famous overseas persons originating from Guangdong within the framework of 'united front' work. In the early 1990s, for example, the Association helped to settle the real estate inheritance for the families of Li Hanhun, Zhang Fakui and Aw Boon Haw (Hu Wenhu) (*Guangdong Qiaobao*, 26 July 1995). Li and Zhang were famous Kuomintang generals before 1949; Aw was a famous overseas Chinese entrepreneur in Malaysia and Singapore.

Similarly, Offices of Overseas Chinese Affairs at every level in Fujian also concentrate on famous overseas persons originating from the province. Every year they invite some of them to visit Fujian, and the visitors are well received by the provincial leaders. In 1993, for example, the latter received 20 batches of visitors totalling 344 (*Fujian Jingji Nianjian* Editorial Committee, 1994:66). In 1995, the provincial Office of Overseas Chinese Affairs received 323 overseas Chinese visitors, and 87 of them met the provincial leadership (*Fujian Nianjian* Editorial Committee, 1996:106).

In the early 1990s, the Office of Overseas Chinese Affairs of Yongding county approached Sally Aw, the daughter of Aw Boon Haw. After the Second World War, Aw Boon Haw encouraged the overseas Fujian communities in Southeast Asia to invest in the economic construction of the province. In March 1993, Sally Aw returned to her hometown to visit her ancestors' tombs. In September 1994, she was invited to officiate at the inauguration ceremony of the Aw Boon Haw Memorial Hall. In return for the honour, Sally Aw donated five million *yuan* as the first instalment in support of the Aw Boon Haw Foundation established at the same time; she also decided that incomes from her real estate in Fuzhou, Xiamen, Guangzhou and Shantou would go to the Foundation (*Fujian Nianjian* Editorial Committee, 1995:73). Sally Aw's case is interesting because in the first place, the ORFOCA usually want to honour overseas Chinese leaders who have contributed to the development of their hometowns so as to create a demonstration effect to encourage followers. Secondly, Sally Aw heads a media empire in Hong Kong which, among other businesses, controls two newspapers, *The Hong Kong Standard* and the *Sing Tao Daily News*. At least until the mid-1980s, her media empire had adopted a pro-

Kuomintang stand. Hence, the winning over of Sally Aw attracted considerable publicity.

In March-April 1993, the Fujian Office of Overseas Chinese Affairs concentrated on the reception of a delegation from the Philippines General Federation of Chinese Entrepreneurs (*Huashanglian Zonghui*). The General Federation was set up in 1954, and is the largest overseas Chinese *qiaoxiang* association in the Philippines. It has a membership of 150 *qiaoxiang* associations and about half a million individual members, with the vast majority of them originating from southern Fujian. The General Federation is the lobbying group for Filipino Chinese interests, and engages in direct consultation with the Government of the Philippines. Hence the delegation was prominently received by the provincial Party secretary, Jia Qinglin, and other provincial leaders. It visited Fuqing, Quanzhou, Jinjiang and Xiamen, and concluded a number of letters of intent on investment projects (*Fujian Nianjian* Editorial Committee, 1995:73).

In October 1994, the Fujian Office of Overseas Chinese Affairs received the president of the Lee Foundation in Singapore, Lee Chengyi. His father, Lee Guangqian, was a well-known overseas Chinese entrepreneur in Singapore; and his grandfather, Tan Kah Kee (Chen Jiageng), was probably the most-famous overseas Chinese leader in the People's Republic of China. This was Lee's first visit to his hometown, Meishan town in Nanan city; and during his visit, he attended a number of ceremonies for projects funded by his donations amounting to over 35.6 million *yuan* (*Fujian Nianjian* Editorial Committee, 1995:73).

Informal interviews of Guangdong officials from its ORFOCA and overseas Chinese businessmen who had visited their hometowns in Guangdong on trips organized by the Guangdong ORFOCA reveal the following pattern. Apparently the targets are first identified by the ORFOCA offering the formal invitations. The ORFOCA probably has a long list and a short list, the former is for general reference based on long-term careful gathering of information, and the later is associated with an annual plan, or an action programme with a defined time horizon. Considerable efforts are involved in studying the background of the target famous overseas persons, and the research concentrates on details, which may be of use at a later stage. Such detailed information may range from the target's daily habits, diet, networks of relatives, friends and business associates in his country of residence as well as those in his hometown, life history, values, etc. An initial assessment is probably made on how difficult it will be to approach the target and win his trust. The ORFOCA then maps out a strategy to contact the target and gradually persuade him to accept an invitation to visit his hometown. It is usually important to make use of the target's networks of ties and secure his confidence through someone he trusts. It is important to understand the target's values so that the appropriate incentives will be offered. Of course, the Communist Party of China has a tradition and ample expertise in this area. Imagine how a Kuomintang general or senior official was won over in the civil war years; the skills and standard operating procedures should not be too different in winning over famous overseas persons. The major difference today is that considerable corruption exists. So the official of the ORFOCA may assist the targeted businessman to invest in his hometown, and in return expects a gift or even a bribe. At the same time, the targeted businessman may also offer gifts or bribes to the officials of the ORFOCA contacting him to facilitate his business venture in his hometown. Sometimes gifts and bribes are offered simply to ensure that the donations will fulfil the designated purposes.

Many overseas Chinese businessmen are impressed by the efforts made to make their visits rewarding and the VIP treatment accorded them by the local officials. They are often surprised by the detailed information their host ORFOCA have of them; some of them, however, feel uncomfortable. A vast majority of the visitors feel an obligation to do something for their hometowns in return for the hospitality they have received, and the minimum they can offer is a donation. This explains the success of China's ORFOCA and the importance attached to their work in the *qiaoxiang* provinces.

In organizing delegations to visit China, the ORFOCA concerned believe it is important to identify the overseas Chinese *qiaoxiang* associations which enjoy the trust of the respective overseas Chinese communities and which have the organizational competence and mobilization power to assume the responsibility of organizing the delegations desired by the ORFOCA. The next step is to identify the responsible persons of the associations who can make decisions and who are sympathetic to the cause of the ORFOCA. If those who can make decisions are not sympathetic, then the ORFOCA will have to work on the sympathetic leaders and urge them to persuade those who wield power in the *qiaoxiang* associations. In the last resort, the ORFOCA might need to cultivate another, less known, *qiaoxiang* body.

Skilful officials take care to foster a competitive atmosphere so that their invitations become an honour to be sought after. This type of work obviously requires great patience. Sometimes because of an over-eagerness to achieve results, the weaknesses of inadequate preparatory work are revealed. Follow-up work is considered very important. ORFOCA take pride in maintaining close contacts with famous overseas persons and *qiaoxiang* associations for decades. In line with the usual practices of united front work, major reviews are held at all levels of ORFOCA at fixed intervals; and often an assessment is made after a major operation. Model cases are identified to serve as reference materials for officials involved in overseas Chinese affairs.

In recent years, evaluation of the work of ORFOCA at the local level tends to be on a competitive basis. Leaders of local governments usually urge their ORFOCA to do better than their counterparts in other counties, cities and provinces. The criteria for evaluation are often reduced to quantitative indicators, especially amounts of donations received and investments secured. Such criteria exert pressure on the officials concerned to achieve results quickly, thus giving their visitors the impression that ORFOCA are mainly after their money.

ORGANIZING ACTIVITIES TO PROMOTE TIES

Kinship ties and feelings for the hometown are the basis of *qiaoxiang*'s relations with overseas Chinese. How to maintain and promote these ties and feelings has been the fundamental task of ORFOCA. Since the 1980s, the ORFOCA of Guangdong and Fujian have been organizing many activities to cultivate overseas Chinese's feelings for China and for their roots in China. These activities may be divided into four broad categories: a) using the occasions of traditional festivals such as the Chinese New Year, the *Yuanxiao* Festival (the first full moon of the lunar year), the Mid-Autumn Festival, etc.; b) using the celebration activities during National Day, the changing of the status of a county to a county-level city, etc.; c) exploiting the traditional festival activities with strong local characteristics; and d) developing modern themes such as summer camps, winter camps, and so on.

The ORFOCA usually invite overseas Chinese to visit their hometowns during the Chinese New Year, the *Yuanxiao* Festival and the Mid-Autumn Festival. These three festivals are traditional occasions for family reunions and for overseas visitors to return home. Many *qiaoxiang* organize special activities to attract overseas Chinese visitors during these festivals; and the *Yuanxiao* Festival in Chaozhou, the Chinese New Year in Shantou, the Mid-Autumn Festival in Dabu in Guangdong, the Chinese New Year garden parties in Fuzhou, and the *Yuanxiao* Festival in Quanzhou in Fujian with its handicraft market and cultural/arts activities are among the more attractive.

National Day naturally is another good occasion. In view of the rapid economic development in Guangdong and Fujian in the past two decades, many counties have become county-level cities; and these are again perceived as important occasions to invite overseas Chinese guests to enhance their pride for their hometowns and to introduce to them the achievements and future plans of their hometowns. Such occasions offer good opportunities for attracting overseas Chinese investments. When Xinhui became a county-level city, when Dongguan became a prefectural city, and when Longhai and Jinjiang in Fujian became county-level cities, they all fully exploited the occasion. Similarly, the four special economic zones, Shenzhen, Zhuhai, Shantou and Xiamen, all held large-scale celebrations during their tenth anniversaries.

Traditional festivals with local characteristics obviously have their attraction. Examples are: the kite festival in Yangjiang, the lychee festival in Shenzhen, Maoming and Dongguan, the puppet festival in Quanzhou, the camellia festival in Longyan, the lychee festival and *longyan* (a fruit) festival in Putian, the tangerine festival in Yongchun, the daffodil festival in Zhangzhou, and the tourist festival for the ancient *Hakka* architecture in Yongding.

The ORFOCA in Guangdong and Fujian are now turning their attention to the younger generations of overseas Chinese. They are aware that the famous overseas persons and leaders of overseas Chinese *qiaoxiang* associations they have been cultivating are getting old. Summer camps, winter camps and various activities for overseas Chinese youth reflect this trend.[3] Since 1993, the Guangdong Office of Overseas Chinese Affairs, the Guangdong Overseas Exchange Association and the Guangdong Youth's Federation have been organizing annual Guangdong Overseas Chinese Youth Carnivals (*Lianhuanjie*). The overseas guests are joined by some young people in Guangzhou, and they together enjoy programmes with an emphasis on Chinese national characteristics including visits to scenic spots, schools and enterprises. The ORFOCA hope to strengthen the younger generations of overseas Chinese feelings for China and their hometowns through these activities. They also target the successors to important overseas Chinese businessmen and leaders of overseas Chinese *qiaoxiang* associations.

Table II Participation in Guangdong Overseas Chinese Youth Carnivals, 1993-5

Year	No. of Overseas Participants	No. of Countries/Regions Involved
1993	240	8
1994	200	10
1995	300	7

Source: Guangdong *Nianjian* Editorial Committee, *Guangdong Nianjian* (Guangdong Yearbook) (Guangzhou: Guangdong Nianjianshe), 1994-6 issues.

As expected, the operation of ORFOCA has its problems as well. In the 1990s, the obvious difficulty is the lack of co-ordination and excessive competition among various levels of local government. The latter has often resulted in famous overseas persons and overseas Chinese business leaders receiving too many invitations and requests for donations. They naturally do not have a good impression of the ORFOCA and can hardly treat their invitations as honours. To some extent, this excessive competition is similar to that in attracting foreign investment, with local governments undercutting each other by offering better conditions to foreign investors.

Many of the activities organized by ORFOCA gradually become repetitive. It demands great efforts to maintain the attraction of annual traditional festivals, for example, particularly when keen competition exists in neighbouring counties and cities. Sometimes visitors find it difficult to accept that while lots of money are spent on extravagant functions, especially banquets, yet at the same time, local officials appeal to them for contributions to the economic construction of their hometowns. Occasionally lavish entertainment can be counter-productive. The obvious phenomena of corruption in China have sometimes dampened the enthusiasm of overseas Chinese too, though this is usually not a problem for investors who consider it part of the investment environment in developing countries.

Many overseas Chinese businessmen would like to make a clear distinction between charitable contributions to their hometowns and genuine economic investments. They may be willing to make some donations, but they want to make their business decisions on purely 'business' grounds. They sometimes find the propositions made by ORFOCA officials confusing and disturbing when these officials ask them to invest in projects which are unacceptable from a business point of view as contributions to their hometowns. At the same time, a vast majority of overseas Chinese businessmen have a limit on their donations, and they find the follow-up work of ORFOCA burdensome. As officials of ORFOCA are eager to secure donations and investments, they tend to categorize overseas Chinese visitors in terms of their wealth. Naturally this causes resentment among those who are less well off. This phenomenon is perhaps most conspicuous in ORFOCA's frequent courting of the alumni associations of prestigious universities in China.

PUBLICATIONS FOR THE OVERSEAS CHINESE

Major ORFOCA regularly produce publications for overseas Chinese, with an emphasis on the developments in their *qiaoxiang*. These are an effective means of communication, and they are sometimes known as 'collective family letters'. The majority do not have a fixed publication schedule, and they tend to focus on local events and issues with a strong folksy character. They normally try to avoid the image of official publications and adopt a low political profile, so that they may be acceptable to overseas Chinese readers over a broad political spectrum. The ORFOCA in Guangdong and Fujian produce almost 190 publications, with a total annual overseas circulation of over two million copies.

Basically such publications are free of charge and even the postage is paid by the ORFOCA. The latter believe that the publications can reach all socio-economic strata of overseas Chinese communities, and serve a useful function in promoting kinship ties and *qiaoxiang* ties. In view of the high expectations, work conferences are held among the publications for overseas Chinese in Guangdong and Fujian respectively, to exchange experiences and to give credit to outstanding publications. Besides the publications mentioned above, the ORFOCA in Guangdong and Fujian also produce picture books, pictures/photos and videotapes for overseas Chinese *qiaoxiang* associations and individuals.

Table III Guangdong's Publications for Overseas Chinese, 1991-5*

Year	No. of Publications	Circulation (10,000 copies)
1991	133	> 138
1992	138	> 120
1993	140	> 140
1994	144	> 100
1995	145	> 100
1996	145	> 150

* Including the *Guangdong Qiaobao* (Guangdong Overseas Chinese News) published by the Guangdong Office of Overseas Chinese Affairs.

Source: Guangdong *Nianjian* Editorial Committee, *Guangdong Nianjian* (Guangdong Yearbook) (Guangzhou: Guangdong *Nianjianshe*), 1992-7 issues. No concrete figures are provided for the respective circulations of 1994 and 1995.

Table IV Fujian's Publications for Overseas Chinese, 1990-3*

Year	No. of Publications	Circulation (10,000 copies)
1990	26	39
1991	25	42
1992	34	64
1993	43	135
1994	50	141

* Including the *Fujian Qiaobao* (Fujian Overseaas Chinese News) published by the Fujian Office of Overseas Chinese Affairs.

Source: Fujian *Jingji Nianjian* Editorial Committee, *Fujian Jingji Nianjian* (Fujian Economic Yearbook) (Fuzhou: Fujian Renmin Chubanshe), 1991-4 issues; Fujian *Nianjian* Editorial Committee, *Fujian Nianjian 1995* (Fujian Yearbook 1995) (Fuzhou: Fujian *Renmin Chubanshe*, 1995).

THE CASE OF XINHUI, GUANGDONG

Xinhui is a famous *qiaoxiang* in Guangdong. Together with Taishan, Kaiping, Enping and Heshan, the five counties or county-level cities are known as 'Wuyi'. Xinhui has an area of 1,679 sq.km. with a population of 0.88 million. But overseas Chinese originating from Xinhui amount to over 0.67 million spreading over fifty countries and regions, hence the saying: 'There is a Xinhui inside China; there is another Xinhui outside China.' (Kong Qingrong and Liang Shan (eds), 1994:101)

ORFOCA in Xinhui obviously seek to mobilize overseas Chinese originating from Xinhui to contribute to economic development. These organs include: the United Front Work Department of the city Party committee, the Office of Overseas Chinese Affairs of the city government, the Federation of Returned Overseas Chinese, the People's Association for Friendship with Foreign Countries, the Overseas Friendship Association, etc. Besides these specialized organs, mass organizations such as trade unions, youth's federations, women's federations and departments of culture, education, propaganda, civil affairs, foreign trade, customs, etc. all participate in overseas Chinese work. Hence the network for overseas Chinese affairs is extremely broad in Xinhui (Kong Qingrong and Liang Shan (eds), 1994:138).

It has to be admitted that the personnel of such organizations overlap to a great extent. Typically, most of the key members of the United Front Work Department serve at the county people's political consultative conference; and they may at the same time work as leaders of the mass organizations, especially the Overseas Friendship Association. Key members of the Office of Overseas Chinese Affairs also overlap with those of the United Front Work Department; and the senior members of both usually assume important positions or advisory roles in the mass organizations upon retirement.

As early as the 1950s, Xinhui's ORFOCA began to contact overseas Chinese as well as compatriots from Hong Kong and Macao originating from Xinhui and encourage them to return to their hometown for visits and to participate in its economic construction. In the reform era since 1978, the ORFOCA have combined overseas Chinese work and economic construction and have developed much experience in 'economic diplomacy'.

Overseas Chinese originating from Xinhui often establish clansmen's associations and kinship organizations (*tongxianghui* and *zongqinhui*), i.e., *qiaoxiang* associations, among themselves, and these are important targets of the ORFOCA. Since the late 1970s, the Xinhui government as well as its town and township governments, together with their ORFOCA, send delegations overseas every year, especially to Southeast Asia, Hong Kong and Macao. They go as official government delegations, or as informal groups from mass organizations (NGOs), or as economic entities investigating business opportunities. When the overseas clansmen's associations and kinship organizations celebrate their anniversaries, hold inauguration ceremonies for their new office-bearers, etc., the Xinhui government and its ORFOCA will send congratulatory telegrams or even send delegations to attend. Their efforts have been rewarded by the fact that leaders of overseas clansmen's associations, kinship organizations and trade associations have gradually established good relations with the Xinhui government and often organize delegations to visit their hometowns, seek to identify their roots there, and explore investment opportunities (Kong Qingrong and Liang Shan (eds), 1994:111).

The Xinhui government and its ORFOCA also send delegations to take part in the spring festival activities of overseas Xinhui *qiaoxiang* associations, organize various types of business conferences and symposiums with overseas Xinhui trade associations, and arrange Cantonese operas, singing and dancing troupes, sports teams, dragon boat teams and various artists groups to visit the overseas Xinhui communities.

Naturally the Xinhui government and its ORFOCA attempt to attract leaders and famous persons of overseas Xinhui communities to visit their hometown. For example, Xinhui's change of status from a county to a county-level city in 1992 presented a good occasion for strengthening contacts with overseas Xinhui communities. Xinhui leaders visited Hong Kong and organized a grand reception for important overseas guests (Kong

Qingrong and Liang Shan (eds), 1994:112). Similarly, the founding of the Xinhui City People's Association for Friendship with Foreign Countries in April 1992 offered another opportunity to establish and renew overseas contacts. Various activities with local characteristics are organized for the same purpose; they include the lychee festival, the *hechong* (a local insect which is considered a delicacy) festival, the mandarins and oranges festival, the dragon-boat races, etc.

Publications by the ORFOCA are regarded as effective channels of communication; and many have appeared after 1978. At present, there are almost twenty such publications with the endorsement of the provincial authorities, with a total annual circulation of about 100,000 (Kong Qingrong and Liang Shan (eds), 1994:114).

Overseas Chinese originating from Xinhui have become a significant source of donations for philanthropic and infrastructural projects such as hospitals, clinics, schools, roads, bridges, etc.; and the Xinhui authorities have been trying their best to show their appreciation. Grand ceremonies are usually organized upon the projects' completion to give recognition to the donors, and very often buildings are named after them. Statues of famous overseas Xinhui persons have been erected, including those of Chen Jinglun, Feng Pingshan and Huang Kejing (Kong Qingrong and Liang Shan (eds), 1994:116). Those who have made substantial contributions to Xinhui's economic construction are granted the titles of 'honorary citizen' or 'Prize for Contributions to the Promotion of Xinhui' (*Guangdong Nianjian*, 1993:628).

Xinhui's ORFOCA have been successful in establishing and consolidating the city's ties with its overseas Chinese communities and enhancing the latter's attachment to their hometown as well as their contribution to its development. According to Xinhui's Office of Overseas Chinese Affairs, from 1979-93, overseas Xinhui communities, including those in Hong Kong, Macao and Taiwan made donations to establish 446 primary and secondary schools, built or expanded 77 hospitals, and constructed 135 bridges, 645 km. of roads, 20 buildings, 98 kindergardens and child-care centres, 102 old people's homes, 254 water supply projects and 32 cultural facilities, amounting to a total value of over HK$800 million. They had also invested in 580 enterprises, involving a sum of about US$760 million (Kong Qingrong and Liang Shan (eds.), 1994:56).

THE CASE OF JINJIANG, FUJIAN

Jinjiang is situated along the south-eastern coast of Fujian and is a major *qiaoxiang* of the province. It has an area of 649 sq.km., and was formerly a county under the prefectural city of Quanzhou. In 1992, it changed its status to a county-level city because of its rapid economic development in the past decade.

Jinjiang has poor soil. Historically many people from Jinjiang emigrated, and so there are many overseas Chinese originating from Jinjiang. The city claims to have three million people inside and outside China, with 2.14 million residing overseas, including Hong Kong, Macao and Taiwan. The bulk of overseas Chinese originating from Jinjiang are in Southeast Asia, mainly in the Philippines, Indonesia, Malaysia and Singapore (*Huaren Jingji Nianjian* Editorial Committee, 1995:165).

Before the economic reforms began in 1978, Jinjiang was notorious for being a 'sweet potatoes county', meaning that it was poor and the people had to rely on sweet potatoes as the staple food. Since 1978, the Jinjiang leadership has accorded priority to overseas Chinese work, and attempted to attract overseas Chinese originating from Jinjiang to participate in economic construction in the hometown. The success of this strategy has been reflected by the fact that Jinjiang is now the most advanced region in Fujian, and for many years it has been included in the top one hundred counties (and county-level cities) in China in terms of comprehensive economic strength (Lin Jinzhi (ed.), 1993:531). It cannot be denied that overseas Jinjiang communities have played an important role in Jinjiang's economic development in the economic reform era.

Jinjiang's ORFOCA have developed many forms and channels of contacts with the overseas Jinjiang communities in view of the urgent need to attract their investments. Besides the normal institutional framework, the Jinjiang authorities created a *Qiaoxiang* Construction Commission headed by the leaders of the city Party committee and the city government; further, a Leadership Group on Overseas Chinese Donations for Welfare Facilities involving the leaders of the city Party Committee, the city government and the Office of Overseas Chinese Affairs was established to elicit donations.

The strategy of Jinjiang's ORFOCA emphasizes the targeting of organizations among overseas Jinjiang communities and the exploitation of various kinds of celebration activities. Overseas Jinjiang communities in Hong Kong, Macao and Southeast Asia seem to be well organized, and their *qiaoxiang* associations include: the Hong Kong Jinjiang Clansmen's Association (*Tongxianghui*, established in 1985); the Macao Jinjiang Clansmen's Association (*Tongxianghui*, established in 1987); the Singapore Jinjiang Clansmen's Association (*Huiguan*, established in 1918); the Malaysian Jinjiang Clansmen's General Association (*Tongxiang Zonghui*); the Philippines Jinjiang Clansmen's General Association (*Tongxiang Zonghui*, established in 1993) and the Asian Federation of Jinjiang Associations (*Shetuan Lianhehui*, established in 1990). Moreover, a World

Jinjiang People Friendship Conference is also held periodically.

These overseas Jinjiang *qiaoxiang* associations have proved to be an asset for the overseas Chinese work and economic diplomacy of Jinjiang's ORFOCA. The latter have been trying to attract overseas Chinese investments mainly through such overseas Jinjiang *qiaoxiang* associations. Since the early 1990s, Jinjiang's ORFOCA, especially the Office of Overseas Chinese Affairs and the Federation of Returned Overseas Chinese, have been actively visiting the overseas Jinjiang *qiaoxiang* associations and the famous overseas business leaders originating from Jinjiang to promote friendship, to introduce to them the developments in Jinjiang and to invite them to visit Jinjiang to participate in various celebration activities. Jinjiang party and government leaders also take part in the activities of the overseas Jinjiang community organizations. For example, in 1992, they formed a delegation to attend the fifth anniversary celebration of the Macao Jinjiang Clansmen's Association (*Fujian Jingji Nianjian,* 1993:107). In 1993, the Office of Overseas Chinese Affairs and other ORFOCA sent a delegation to attend the eighth anniversary celebration of the Hong Kong Jinjiang Clansmen's Association, the inauguration ceremony of the Philippines Jinjiang Clansmen's General Association, the First World Jinjiang People Friendship Conference, the third anniversary celebration of the Asian Federation of Jinjiang Associations, and the seventy-fifth anniversary celebration of the Singapore Jinjiang Clansmen's Association. At the same time, the Jinjiang city government and its ORFOCA actively encourage the overseas Jinjiang *qiaoxiang* associations to form delegations to visit their hometown (*Fujian Jingji Nianjian,* 1994:66, 70). In 1995, Jinjiang's ORFOCA and their provincial counterparts jointly invited the Philippines and the Malaysian Jinjiang Clansmen's General Associations to visit Fujian (*Fujian Nianjian,* 1996:108).

The Jinjiang city government and its ORFOCA have been skilfully exploiting various types of local celebrations to support its economic diplomacy and overseas Chinese work. In 1991, the Jinjiang Federation of Returned Overseas Chinese celebrated its fortieth anniversary, and it used the occasion to invite leaders of overseas Jinjiang communities to visit their hometown. Altogether 545 of them returned; and contracts were concluded on thirty-six investment projects and on foreign trade amounting to HK$4.4 million (*Fujian Jingji Nianjian,* 1992:103). In May 1992, Jinjiang changed its status to a county-level city, and a similar exercise was repeated. The Jinjiang authorities sent over ten delegations to Southeast Asia, Hong Kong and Macao to extend invitations to successful businessmen among overseas Jinjiang communities. The celebration activities led to investments of hundreds of million *yuan* (*Fujian Jingji Nianjian,* 1993:456).

This mode of operation reached its peak in 1995 when five major celebrations were held to attract overseas Chinese investments. In November 1994, the Asian Federation of Jinjiang Associations held its third congress of representatives in Singapore, and decided to organize its fifth anniversary celebrations in 1995 in Macao as well as to convene the Second World Jinjiang People's Friendship Conference. When news reached Jinjiang, its leaders decided to link the third anniversary celebration of the establishment of Jinjiang as a county-level city with these overseas activities, and formulated a plan of five major celebrations in Hong Kong, Macao and Jinjiang. In January 1995, the secretary of the Jinjiang Party committee, Shi Yongkang, met the leaders of overseas Jinjiang communities in Shenzhen and secured their endorsement of the plan. Besides the three celebrations mentioned above, the plan also included the tenth anniversary celebration of the Hong Kong Jinjiang Clansmen's Association and the eighth anniversary celebration of the Macao Jinjiang Clansmen's Association. The first celebration was held in Hong Kong on 23 November, and the final celebration took place in Jinjiang where more than 400 overseas business leaders originating from Jinjiang arrived from Southeast Asia, Hong Kong and Macao. They were given detailed briefings of the achievements and future plans of their hometown by the leaders of Jinjiang ('Jinjiang Qiutian de Touzi Yuehui (A Date for Investors in Autumn in Jinjiang)', *Yazhou Zhoukan*, Vol. 9, No. 54, 17 December 1995:46-7).

Jinjiang's performance in overseas Chinese work has often been looked upon as a model. It seems to have been co-ordinating well with the provincial authorities, though most of the problems discussed above also apply to Jinjiang. In particular, the law of diminishing returns begins to be felt. Nevertheless, through its efforts, Jinjiang attracted substantial donations and investments from the overseas Jinjiang communities. Since the 1980s, their annual donations have amounted to tens of millions of *yuan*, sometimes the figure might even reach one hundred million *yuan*. In the first few years of the 1990s, their investments exceeded 300 million *yuan*, about one tenth of Fujian's total foreign investments.

INTERACTIONS BETWEEN *QIAOXIANG* AND OVERSEAS CHINESE

Most overseas Chinese originating from Guangdong and Fujian are now in Southeast Asia, where they have significant economic influence. One estimate in 1997 indicated that the assets of overseas Chinese amounted to US$200 billion, with over 90 per cent in Southeast Asia (before the financial crisis in the region in the latter half of the year) ('Jinjiang Qiutian de Touzi Yuehui (A Date for Investors in Autumn in Jinjiang)', *Yazhou Zhoukan*, Vol. 9, No. 54, 17 December 1995:46-7). Another study in 1995 revealed that there were over 20 overseas Chinese business groups in Singapore each with capital exceeding US$100 million, about 40 overseas Chinese business groups in Malaysia each with capital over US$200 million, and more than 10 such business groups in the Philippines each with capital exceeding US$100 million. Overseas Chinese business groups are similarly very strong in Indonesia and Thailand (Chen Jing, 1996:195). Fujitsu Research in Tokyo studied the listed companies in six Asian countries. It discovered that an overwhelming majority were owned by overseas Chinese: 81 per cent in Thailand, 81 per cent in Singapore, 73 per cent in Indonesia, 61 per cent in Malaysia and 50 per cent in the Philippines. According to Bustanil Ariffin, a former Indonesian minister, small and medium-sized companies employed half of the labour force in most Asian countries, and Chinese owned 90 per cent of these companies (J. Naisbitt, 1996:19-20).

Guangdong and Fujian have always accorded priority to attracting overseas Chinese originating from the respective provinces to participate in their hometowns' economic construction. In the economic reform era since 1978, overseas Chinese work has integrated with economic work, and has been treated as a focal point in the work of the two provincial governments. In the 1980s, the ORFOCA of the two provinces concentrated on the implementation of the new overseas Chinese policy, including the reversal of verdicts concerning unjust cases involving returned overseas Chinese and family members of overseas Chinese. In the 1990s, the focus shifted to the attraction of overseas Chinese investments in the economic construction of their hometowns. To achieve this goal, the ORFOCA in the two provinces conducted considerable research in developing contacts with the overseas Chinese communities.

As indicated earlier, overseas Chinese *qiaoxiang* associations are mainly based on kinship ties (kinship organizations or family name organizations, *zongqinhui*), *qiaoxiang* ties (clansmen's associations or regional associations, *tongxianghui*), as well as business and professional ties (trade associations). *Guangdong Qiaobao* reported in 1995 that there were 111 *zongqinhui* and 99 *tongxianghui* in Singapore; and in Malaysia there were 34 clansmen's associations (*huiguan*) related to Guangdong and 40 related to Fujian (*Guangdong Qiaobao*, 11 April 1995). Since the late 1980s, the ORFOCA's interest in the overseas Chinese *qiaoxiang* associations has generated a new vitality in the latter which feel that they have a new sense of mission. They take pride in being able to contribute to the economic construction of their *qiaoxiang*; and they also have been able to offer honour and business opportunities to reward their leaders and activists through China's ORFOCA. In this way, a symbiotic relationship has been gradually established between the ORFOCA and overseas Chinese *qiaoxiang* associations. This has been reflected by the latter's enhanced activities and increase in membership, as well as the formation of linkages among them and even kinship organizations and clansmen's associations on a global scale.

The ORFOCA in Guangdong and Fujian often describe their mode of operation as inviting them in (*qing jin lai*) and reaching out *(zou chu qu)* in establishing and strengthening their ties with overseas Chinese communities. At the same time, the symbiotic relationship analysed above also provides considerable incentive for overseas Chinese *qiaoxiang* associations to co-operate through sending delegations to their hometowns to visit families and relatives, to seek to identify their roots there, to engage in tourist activities and to establish business ties. They also reciprocate the invitations from China's ORFOCA by inviting the latter to take part in their activities such as inauguration ceremonies and anniversary celebrations as well as involving the latter's assistance in forming their global and regional federations. There is also an increasing trend for the ORFOCA and overseas Chinese *qiaoxiang* associations to involve each other in organizing their activities.

Since 1990, the 'inviting them in' operations of the ORFOCA of Guangdong and Fujian have been expanding in scale. In 1990, Fujian's ORFOCA at various levels received almost 600 overseas Chinese (including Taiwan, Hong Kong and Macao compatriots) delegations totalling 10,000 people. Most of these delegations were from kinship organizations and clansmen's associations. Quanzhou alone in 1990 received 252 delegations from overseas Chinese including the Malaysian Huian Clansmen's Association (*Gonghui*), the Singapore Jinjiang Clansmen's Association (*Huiguan*), the Singapore Nanan Clansmen's Association (*Huiguan*), the Singapore Anxi Clansmen's Association *(Huiguan)*, the Singapore Yongchun Clansmen's Association (*Huiguan*), etc. (*Fujian Jingji Nianjian*, 1991:337). In 1995, Fujian's *qiaoxiang* associations at various levels received 70,000 people, including more than 500 important delegations, including the Malaysian Hakka Culture Root-Seeking Delegation, as well as that of the Philippines Jinjiang Clansmen's General Association, the Malaysian Federation of Fujian Associations, and the Malaysian Jinjiang Clansmen's General Association (*Fujian Nianjian*, 1996:108). In the same year, Guangdong's ORFOCA at various levels altogether received 3,087 groups of overseas Chinese totalling 270,514 people (*Guangdong Nianjian*, 1996:675).

Table V No. of Overseas Chinese (Including Taiwan, Hong Kong and Macao) Received by Fujian's ORFOCA at Various Levels, 1991-5

Year	1990	1991	1992	1993	1994	1995
No. of People (in thousands)	10	30	60	65	80.6	0

Source: Fujian *Jingji Nianjian* Editorial Committee, *Fujian Jingji Nianjian* (Fujian Economic Yearbook) (Fuzhou: Fujian Renmin Chubanshe), 1991-4 issues and Fujian *Nianjian* Editorial Committee, *Fujian Nianjian* (Fujian Yearbook) (Fuzhou: Fujian Renmin Chubanshe), 1995-6 issues.

In view of the strengthening of the global and regional linkages among overseas Chinese *qiaoxiang* associations, organizing related activities on their behalf has become an important part of the 'inviting them in' operations of the ORFOCA in Guangdong and Fujian in the 1990s. In November 1993, the Second World Chinese Entrepreneurs Convention was held in Hong Kong and one of the agenda items was a visit to the Pearl River Delta in Guangdong. The provincial Office of Overseas Chinese Affairs assumed responsibility for receiving the 600 Chinese businessmen, and they were divided into three groups and visited Guangzhou, Shenzhen, Zhuhai, Zhongshan, Dongguan, Shunde, etc. (*Guangdong Qiaobao*, 27 September 1994). In 1994, the Guangdong provincial authorities accepted responsibility for organizing the World Mei Family Name Kinship Conference (*Kenqing Dahui*), the World Panyu Kinship Conference and the Twelfth World *Hakka* Kinship Conference. The latter was held in Meizhou city on 8-10 December, and was attended by leaders of the NPC, CPPCC and the Guangdong provincial Party committee and government. More than 80 delegations from 30 countries and regions attended the conference, and participants exceeded 1,900. The rewards for Meizhou city were substantial: overseas donations for the expenditure of the conference amounted to more than 6 million *yuan*, for local welfare facilities more than 60 million *yuan*, and letters of intent/contracts concluded on investment projects totalled more than 6 billion *yuan* (*Guangdong Nianjian*, 1995:620).

Similarly, Fujian authorities organized two global overseas Chinese *qiaoxiang* association activities in 1994, namely, the Third World Fuzhou Shiyi (ten counties or county-level cities) Clansmen's Association and the Second World Anxi Clansmen's Friendship Conference (*Xiangqing Lianyihui*). The latter was held in Anxi county in October, and was the first of its kind organized in Anxi. It attracted 2,500 representatives from overseas Anxi *qiaoxiang* associations from over 20 countries and regions. During the conference, contracts on 195 investment projects were signed amounting to 1.05 billion *yuan*, involving the use of foreign capital amounting to US$100 million. Donations from the representatives totalled more than 22 million *yuan* (*Fujian Nianjian*, 1995:73). Two other examples were: in October 1993, the World Yongchun Associations Friendship Conference (*Shetuan Lianyihui*) held its inauguaration ceremony in Yongchun in Fujian; and in October 1995, the First World Dabu Clansmen's Friendship Conference (*Tongxiang Lianyihui*) was organized in Dabu in Guangdong.

The 'reaching out' operations of the ORFOCA in Guangdong and Fujian have also been expanding in scale since 1990, and the foci are Southeast Asia, Hong Kong and Macao.[4] In 1995, various levels of ORFOCA in Guangdong dispatched 526 delegations involving 21,966 people to visit overseas Chinese *qiaoxiang* associations in all five continents (*Guangdong Nianjian*, 1996:675). In the same year, the Fujian provincial Office of Overseas Chinese Affairs alone organized or participated in 11 group visits to Hong Kong, Macao and foreign countries (*Fujian Nianjian*, 1996:108). In the 1990s, ORFOCA's involvement in the activities of overseas Chinese *qiaoxiang* associations has become the norm, and it constitutes a very important part of the 'Reaching out' operations of ORFOCA of Guangdong and Fujian.

CONCLUDING REMARKS

Chinese civilization and China's long history have probably contributed to a strong sense of nationhood and common identity among Chinese. Many overseas Chinese residing in foreign countries consider that their roots are in China and they still have strong feelings for China. The mission of the ORFOCA in China is to foster the above sentiments of overseas Chinese communities and to maintain close ties with *qiaoxiang* associations. As the largest *qiaoxiang* in China, the ORFOCA of Guangdong and Fujian, through the 'inviting them in' and 'reaching out' operations, through various activities with *qiaoxiang* characteristics and local attractions, through publications and other channels of communications, etc. have been able to establish and consolidate strong links with the overseas Chinese communities, strengthen their feelings for their motherland, and attract them to invest in the two provinces, thereby contributing to their rapid economic development. The achievement of the ORFOCA in Guangdong and Fujian in mobilizing their overseas Chinese communities to support the economic construction in the two provinces fully demonstrate the ORFOCA's significant role in economic diplomacy.

ORFOCA in China constitute a complex system involving official and semi-official organizations. The Office of Overseas Chinese Affairs at every level of government is the key organization; it is responsible both for policy-making and policy implementation. The Federations of Returned Overseas Chinese at various levels are the mass organizations representing and serving returned overseas Chinese. Since the latter maintain extensive ties with overseas Chinese communities, the federations assume an important role in economic diplomacy and support the Offices of Overseas Chinese Affairs. United front organizations such as the United Front Work Departments of the Party system and the Chinese People's Political Consultative Conference, together with their local counterparts, also play a limited role. Due to their obvious political roles, they tend to avoid high-profile, well-publicized activities. In 1980, the Chinese government clearly stipulated that overseas Chinese did not fall within the domain of united front work. The approach towards foreign nationals of Chinese origin belonged to the realm of friendship with people of foreign countries (Dangdai Zhongguo Bianjiweiyuanwei (ed.), 1996:211). Hence the networks of China Overseas Exchange Association and China Travel Service are also involved in the economic diplomacy targeted at overseas Chinese communities.

The performance of the ORFOCA is mainly dependent on their understanding of overseas Chinese communities. Since the Second World War, the latter have much improved their economic status. Their international economic influence has been growing; and important transnational business groups controlled by overseas Chinese business leaders have emerged. Overseas Chinese have certainly retained their tradition of helping their ancestral hometown through contributions to their economic construction. In view of the overseas Chinese's increase in economic strength and China's open door policy, the former's inclination to invest in China has been rising in the economic reform era. Compared with other foreign investors in China, overseas Chinese investors have distinct advantages because of their retention of the Chinese language and culture. Most overseas Chinese investors have a good grasp of the dialects in their hometowns, and many of them still retain some kinship ties there. They normally find it easier to cultivate the necessary *guanxi* (networks of relationships) to develop their businesses. They obviously believe they have an edge over their competitors, hence they tend to focus their investments in their hometowns (C.S. Fan, 1997). For example, the Lippo Group is one of the major business conglomerates in Indonesia, and the ancestors of its head, Mochtar Riady, came from Fujian. Lippo's investments in China are largely in Putian, Fujian (*Time*, 10 May 1993:28-30).

The Chinese authorities appreciate that their liaison with overseas Chinese communities may arouse the suspicions of the governments of the countries concerned, especially those in Southeast Asia. Hence ORFOCA in China try to camouflage themselves as semi-official. or non-governmental organizations in their activities, which explained the emergence of the China Overseas Chinese Exchange Association affiliated to the State Council Office of Overseas Chinese Affairs and the Guangdong Overseas Friendship Association set up by the provincial people's political consultative conference. The latter, of course, are guided by the official ORFOCA, and their personnel establishments clearly overlap. Take Guangdong as an example: the former head of the provincial Office of Overseas Chinese Affairs, Lu Faquan, served as the honorary president of the provincial Federation of Returned Overseas Chinese, as well as the vice-chairman of the provincial Overseas Exchange Association. Deputy head of the United Front Work Department of the provincial Party Committee, Xie Wenlin, was also a vice-chairman of the provincial Overseas Exchange Association. In the city of Maoming, the president of the city people's political consultative conference, Wu Zhaoqi, was president of the city Federation of Returned Overseas Chinese and chairman of the city Overseas Friendship Association. This said, the *qiaoxiang* provinces of Guangdong and Fujian have, for the most part, been sensitive to the concerns of Southeast Asian states worried about China's strengthening ties with overseas Chinese communities: as is apparent from the pace at which they have been actively establishing 'non-governmental organizations' (to the extent that such bodies can be said to exist in the PRC) to take over 'overseas Chinese work' in the economic reform era.

In view of China's improving relations with Southeast Asia in the same period, this 'softly, softly' approach seemed to have achieved satisfactory results. Eliminating the suspicions of Southeast Asian governments is essential to attracting investments from the overseas Chinese there, and the Chinese ORFOCA adopt a very pragmatic attitude to accommodate the concerns and worries of the Chinese diaspora as well. The Chinese government maintained a very low profile during the riots in Indonesia in spring 1998. It was aware that it could offer little help to the ethnic Chinese under attack. Strong protests would be counter-productive as they might further arouse local antagonism and exacerbate ASEAN suspicions against the existing relationship between PRC authorities and ethnic Chinese abroad.

The recent economic crisis in Southeast Asia may well have altered the situation. In spring 1998, Indonesians of Chinese descent became major targets of attack in the anti-government riots. This will encourage the ethnic Chinese communities in ASEAN to diversify their investments and move their assets to other countries, including China. At the same time, the credit crunch and the currency crises have made ASEAN governments highly sensitive to capital outflows. Attempts by the Chinese authorities to attract overseas Chinese investments are bound to create friction with ASEAN governments in the foreseeable future. Naturally Chinese officials also anticipate a decline in investments from ASEAN.

The scope for economic diplomacy through the exploitation of kinship ties and *qiaoxiang* associations in overseas communities is not limited to attracting their investments. Authorities consider the wealth of overseas Chinese communities as part of the capital of the national bourgeoisie of the countries in which they reside, and investment from overseas Chinese communities constitutes part of China's trade and economic co-operation with the countries concerned (*Guangdong Qiaobao*, 13 January 1994). Further, the Chinese authorities appreciate that overseas Chinese investors, besides *qiaoxiang* considerations, are basically looking for profitable investment opportunities; and they will not limit their investments to their hometowns. The Chinese government understands that it still has to continue to improve the overall investment climate to keep, as well as attract, investors. After making substantial contributions to his hometown in Fujian, the Filipino Chinese billionaire, Chen Yongzai, once commented: 'There isn't any worthwhile investment project in my hometown (in Jinjiang).' (*Guangdong Qiaobao*, 13 January 1994, 'Jinjiang Qiutian de Touzi Yuehui [A Date for Investors in Autumn in Jinjiang]') But this is the fundamental paradox: the problem which results from mixing emotional and cultural ties with profit-oriented business decisions.

BIBLIOGRAPHY

Chen Jing
1996   'Haiwai Huaren Da Caituan Laihua Touzi Dong xiang (Moves of Major Overseas Chinese Business Groups Regarding Investments in China)', in: *Huaren Jingji Nianjian* Editorial Committee (ed.)
Clough, R.N.
1995   'The PRC, Taiwan, and the Overseas Chinese', in: Young C. Kim (ed.) *The Southeast Asian Economic Miracle*. New Brunswick, New Jersey: Transaction Publishers
Dangdai Zhongguo Bianjiweiyuanwei (Contemporary China Editorial Committee)
1996   *Dangdai Zhongguo de Tongyi Zhanxian* (The United Front of Contemporary China), Vol. 2. Beijing: Dangdai Zhongguo Chubanshe
Fan, C.S.
1997   *Overseas Chinese and Foreign Investment in China: An Application*

of the Transaction Cost Approach. Hong Kong: Working Paper Series, No.49, Centre for Asian Pacific Studies, Faculty of Social Sciences, Lingnan College

Fang Xiongpu and Xie Chengjia (eds)
1993   *Huaqiao Huaren Gaikuang* (A Survey of Overseas Chinese). Beijing: Zhongguo Huaqiao Chubanshe

FitzGerald, S.
1972   *China and the Overseas Chinese*. London and New York: Cambridge University Press

Fujian *Jingji Nianjian* Editorial Committee
1991   *Fujian Jingji Nianjian 1991* (Fujian Economic Yearbook 1991). Fuzhou: Fujian Renmin Chubanshe
1992   *Fujian Jingji Nianjian 1992* (Fujian Economic Yearbook 1992). Fuzhou: Fujian Renmin Chubanshe
1993   *Fujian Jingji Nianjian 1993* (Fujian Economic Yearbook 1993). Fuzhou: Fujian Renmin Chubanshe
1994   *Fujian Jingji Nianjian 1994* (Fujian Economic Yearbook 1994). Fuzhou: Fujian Renmin Chubanshe

Fujian *Nianjian* Editorial Committee
1995   *Fujian Nianjian 1995* (Fujian Yearbook 1995). Fuzhou: Fujian Renmin Chubanshe
1996   *Fujian Nianjian 1996* (Fujian Yearbook 1996). Fuzhou: Fujian Renmin Chubanshe

Kong Qingrong and Liang Shan (eds)
1994   *Xinhui Qiaoxiang Yingjuli* (The Cohesive Force of Xinhui Qiaoxiang). Guangzhou: Zhongshan Daxue Chubanshe Guangdong *Nianjian* Editorial Committee
1992   *Guangdong Nianjian 1992* (Guangdong Yearbook 1992), Guangzhou: Guangdong Nianjianshe
1993   *Guangdong Nianjian 1993* (Guangdong Yearbook 1993), Guangzhou: Guangdong Nianjianshe
1994   *Guangdong Nianjian 1994* (Guangdong Yearbook 1994), Guangzhou: Guangdong Nianjianshe
1995   *Guangdong Nianjian 1995* (Guangdong Yearbook 1995), Guangzhou: Guangdong Nianjianshe
1996   *Guangdong Nianjian 1996* (Guangdong Yearbook 1996), Guangzhou: Guangdong Nianjianshe *Huaren Jingji Nianjian* Editorial Committee
1995   *Huaren Jingji Nianjian 1995* (Yearbook of the *Huaren* Economy 1995). Beijing: Zhongguo Shehuikexue Chubanshe
1996   *Huaren Jingji Nianjian 1996* (Yearbook of the *Huaren* Economy 1996). Beijing: Zhongguo Shehuikexue Chubanshe

Lin Tien-wai (ed.)
1991   *Collected Essays on Local History of The Asian-Pacific Region: Contribution of Overseas Chinese.* (in Chinese and English). Hong Kong: Centre of Asian Studies Occasional Papers and Monographs, No.96, University of Hong Kong
Lin Jinzhi (ed.)
1993   *Huaqiao, Huaren yu Zhongguo Gemin he Jianshe* (Overseas Chinese and China's Revolution and Construction), Fuzhou: Fujian Renmin Chubanshe
Lin Jinzhi and Zhuang Weiji
1985   *Jindai Huaqiao Touzi Guonei Qiye Shi Ziliao Xuanji, Fujian Juan* (Selected Materials on the History of Overseas Chinese Investments in China's Enterprises in the Modern Era, Volume on Fujian). Fuzhou: Fujian Renmin Chubanshe
1989   *Jindai Huaqiao Touzi Guonei Qiye Shi Ziliao Xuanji, Guangdong Juan* (Selected Materials on the History of Overseas Chinese Investments in China's Enterprises in the Modern Era, Volume on Guangdong). Fuzhou: Fujian Renmin Chubanshe
Liu Yingjie,
1997   'Haiwai Huaren yu Zhongguo Dalu de Jingji Guanxi (The Economic Relationship Between Overseas Chinese and Mainland China)', *Hong Kong Economic Journal Monthly* (a Chinese monthly magazine in Hong Kong), Vol.21, No.8
Naisbitt, J.
1996   *Megatrends Asia.* New York: Simon & Schuster
Redding, S.G.
1993   *The Spirit of Chinese Capitalism.* Berlin and New York: Walter de Gruyter
Stewart, S.
1995   'Return of the Prodigals: The Overseas Chinese and Southern China's Economic Boom', in: Jane Khanna (ed.) *Southern China, Hong Kong and Taiwan.* Washington, D.C.: The Center for Strategic and International Studies
Wang Gungwu
1991   *China and the Chinese Overseas.* Singapore: Times Academic Press
Zhongguo Qiaolian
1996   *Zhongguo Qiaolian Sishinian 1956-1996* (Forty Years of All-China Federation of Returned Overseas Chinese, 1956-1996). Beijing: Zhongguo Huaqiao Chubanshe

Notes

1. *Guangdong Qiaobao* (Guangdong Overseas Chinese News, a Chinese newspaper published in Guangzhou), 29 December 1994.
2. Two more terms require clarification. Returned overseas Chinese (*guiqiao*) refers to those Chinese who, after residing abroad for some time, have come back to settle in China as PRC citizens. They might or might not have acquired foreign citizenships before. Family members of overseas Chinese (*qiaojuan*), legally speaking, should be family members of Chinese living in foreign countries with PRC citizenship or without foreign citizenship. But it appears that official statistics tend to include family members of foreign citizens of Chinese descent in this category as well. A strict definition of family members should only include spouses, parents, children and siblings; but official statistics appear to include grandparents, grandchildren and close relatives such as uncles, aunts, nephews, nieces and first cousins.
3. In 1994, for example, the ORFOCA in Guangdong organized 25 summer camps and winter camps for 603 overseas Chinese youths from 17 countries and regions. In the same year, Fujian organized 13 summer camps for 288 overseas Chinese youths originating from Fujian from 7 countries and regions. See *Guangdong Nianjian*, 1995, p. 621 and *Fujian Nianjian*, 1995, p. 72.
4. In 1991, various levels of *qiaoxiang* associations in Fujian altogether sent 246 people overseas for liaison with overseas Chinese *qiaoxiang* associations, both in formal capacities and informal using the pretexts of visiting relatives or travelling. In the same year, their counterparts in Guangdong sent 1,967 groups involving 7,037 people to Hong Kong and Macao, and 381 groups involving 2,093 people overseas. See *Fujian Jingji Nianjian*, 1992, p. 98 and *Guangdong Nianjian*, 1992, p. 603.

The Singapore-Anxi Connection: Ancestor Worship as Moral-Cultural Capital

Khun Eng Kuah

Located in the southeastern part of Fujian, Anxi County is a poor, mountainous area not too far from Xiamen.[1] It was an important source of emigrants to Southeast Asia and to Singapore in particular, where an estimated 10 per cent of the inhabitants can claim a connection. Some 40,000 people left in the first half of this century, mostly for that port city. But there was also a significant outflow (as many as 20,000 people) during the Civil War and early communist years which added considerably to the first-generation migrant population. Whilst younger Singaporeans are far less sentimental about their ancestral land, the older, China-born generation still maintains an emotional attachment to the home district. Family relationships were apparently maintained through a long period of political hostility when visits were not permitted and communication was, at times, extremely difficult. But, once establishment of diplomatic relations between the two countries relaxed travel restrictions,[2] increasing numbers have returned to Anxi where they have contributed needed developmental capital. However, a principal reason Singaporeans are visiting today is for purposes of ancestor worship.

INTRODUCTION

Of all the reforms that have taken place in the People's Republic since 1978, one of the most interesting from an anthropological point of view is the revival of ancestor worship. Although some individuals or households had, no doubt, always ignored the official prohibition (Parish and Whyte, 1978:283), overt, communal displays of what was long regarded as a superstitious feudal practice were impossible. Yet, as this chapter will document, formal ceremonies to honour ancestors have not only been revived in Anxi; they are now being used as a means of strengthening ties with overseas Chinese. In Peng Lai district, political authorities now actively encourage activities that would once have been severely punished. Whilst, at an instrumental level, this clearly began as a means of attracting additional investment dollars for business and community infrastructure, far more is now at stake. By permitting the restoration of various socio-religious ceremonies for the benefit of visiting Singaporeans, local cadres have, in the process, helped restore the ancestral hall to its traditional place at the very centre of village life.

This research uses a combination of anthropological fieldwork that provides qualitative data and a standard sociological questionnaire survey that provides a quantitative data. As the research deals with two main groups of people living in two different locations, it is divided into two parts: Singapore and Anxi. In both regions, research was conducted at various levels: (i) participant-observation where collection of these data was unstructured. (ii) in-depth interviews were conducted with selected members (across generational and gender divide). (iii) a questionnaire survey (using two sets of questionnaires) was conducted to a random sample of members. During the survey interviews, the conversations between the researcher and the respondents were recorded. In addition, for the Anxi part, in order to enhance the quality of participant-observation, the researcher usually followed the Singapore Chinese back to Anxi whenever there were some major events apart from the above stages of research.

ETHNOGRAPHY

Ancestors have long occupied a central position in Chinese cosmology, where death was never seen as the ultimate end (De Groot, 1964, vol. 1:4). Rather, it was a separation of *yin* and *yang* energies. After dying, the spirit, *hun* was believed to have merely moved from one realm of existence, the human world (*renjian*), where the physical form was visible, to another: the netherworld (*yinjian*), where it was no longer visible to mortal eyes. Either there, or in the heavenly realm, *yangjian* (Yang, 1961:150-1), the dead continue to interact with the living, keeping a protective watch over their descendants. They were not only fundamental to the traditional family system but also regarded as the transmitters of Chinese culture. Confucius outlined the proper treatment of relatives, both living and dead, in works like the 'Classic of Filial Duty' (*Xiaojing*). Children were instructed to treat parents with piety (*xiao*) and their ancestors with ritual propriety, *li*. In life, elders were to be treated with respect and revered in death. Such acts were said to '[express] gratitude towards the originators and recall the beginning' (Yang, 1961:44).

The resulting cult of ancestor worship (observed from the emperor downwards) involved the maintenance of ancestral halls (*zongtang*) and memorial temples (*citang*) for the preservation of tablets and carrying out the required ritual offerings. Whereas a propitious burial following the rules of *fengshui*, might harness *yangqi* and bring earthly benefits, neglected ancestors - especially those destined to be wandering ghosts (*kuhun*) - could just as easily turn malevolent (Freedman, 1958:81-91, 118-54). Hence, the disposal (*sangli*) of the deceased, like the respect shown to dead ancestors through ancestor worship (*jizu*) took central stage in traditional culture.

Like many of the other practices described in this book, the ritual respect for the dead was transplanted to Southeast Asia. Not only do many Singapore households engage in forms of private and communal ancestor worship today but, with characteristic pragmatism, they sometimes place their ancestral tablets in a leased space in a memorial hall where offerings can be made by monks or nuns to ensure that their ancestors were well cared for (Tong, 1982).

Not only do ancestors need to be looked after materially and spiritually; they also need to connect themselves with their place of origin. Ancestors were seen as important members of the family and the lineage. Thus, with the right political climate, the Singapore Chinese returned to their ancestral village to reconstruct the lineage ancestral houses to enable ancestors, like themselves, to be reconnected with their source.

RECONSTRUCTING LINEAGES

Undoubtedly the most-important activity undertaken by Singaporeans, with the encouragement and assistance of permanent *qiaoxiang* residents, has been the reconstruction of lineage ancestral houses (*zuzai*) either destroyed by the Cultural Revolution or run down after years of neglect. Superficially similar to the *zongci* or *citang* commonly found in Chinese communities overseas, where groups have likewise gathered together in communal worship, the 'new' *zuzai* in home villages also provide the participants with much more than bricks and mortar. Whereas a great number of memorial halls were erected by Chinese migrants throughout the world in the nineteenth century, often carrying out important socio-economic services in alien environments (see Yen, 1986), there can, in contrast, be only one *zuzai*: in the locality where the first ancestors so honoured are believed to have planted their family tree. As a physical place which also occupies socio-religious space,[3] an ancestral lineage house long served as a significant marker which has allowed individuals to lay claim to common ancestry, irrespective of geographical disbursement, and thus come to better terms with both the past and future. It was an important feature of village life before the communist victory. Although a subset of immediate ancestors could, and can still, be worshipped at a number of locations in Anxi, including the old homes (*laojia*) of wealthy families - or when the well-to-do set up an altar table or shrine (occasionally even a private room) in their new homes (*xinjia*) - every lineage, by definition, requires a *zuzai*. A new one would never be established unless a disparate or outcaste group wished to establish an independent ancestry, thereby severing ties with the historically accepted place of origin: something which did happen over the centuries, especially in times of massive internal migration or political disorder.

Following reforms in China, members of the Ke lineage in Singapore, in co-operation with their Anxi relatives, obtained approval for the reconstruction of their lineage ancestral house: the Kway-Tau Zhor Chu (*Kuitou Zuzai*). It was the norm that the male elders from both the Singapore and Anxi villages who suggested and negotiated with the county and village governments to reconstruct their lineage ancestral house. The official cadres often readily gave approval. With considerable enthusiasm on both sides, two branches were reunited after four to five decades of separation in geographical space and historical time. The new *zuzai* would serve 'not only as a memorial to remember ancestors' but also 'a reminder of one's origin'. It was 'also an important visible monument for the future generations if they want to trace their cultural roots'.

Completed in 1988, the building is constructed in a traditional architectural style with curved tiled roof. Its shrine hall, which faces an uncovered courtyard, is divided into three main sections. In the middle, there are the built-in shelves reserved for the ancestral tablets. To the left, an altar is reserved for the village guardian god, *kui-xing-gong* or *kway-sin-gong* in Hokkien, and, to the right, is another altar for the earth god, *tudi gong*. The hall and adjoining courtyard are sufficiently spacious to allow for large congregations of lineage members for ancestor worship and or other events. The facility has obviously become important to both Ke groups as demonstrated by the activities described below.

ELEMENTS OF CONTEMPORARY PRACTICE

Once the ancestral lineage house has been re-established, there are four major features in current practice, which play a critical role in bringing Singaporeans and Anxi villagers together. These are (i) 'the gratification rite for the flow of descendants'; (ii) 'the rite of meritorious deeds'; (iii) reconstruction or relocation of graves; and (iv) the 'opening doors' ceremony whereby the successful thank their *qiaoxiang* ancestors and thus gain local status.

The Gratification Rite

A major event in ancestor worship, as practised by the Ke clan in Anxi, is the 'gratification rite for the flow of descendants.' The term *xiezu* means 'thanking the ancestors' while *juan* suggests a 'continuous flow' and *ding* is 'descendants'. This rite is performed once a year, usually during the Spring Festival - Chinese Lunar New Year. The Singapore visitors, usually numbering 20 or more, apparently time their visit in order to take part. On this important occasion, the doors of the *zuzai* are opened and members are expected to participate in both communal and private worship. The women busy themselves preparing traditional rice cakes, poultry, and vegetables. About mid-morning, the entire family arrives and sets out their dishes, arranged on tables in rows, in front of the ancestral temple. Because of the large number of households participating in this communal ancestor worshipping, they are divided into two groups. One would do the offerings in the morning and the second in the late afternoon.

The ancestral house was packed with lineage members and curious villagers. Buddhist or Daoist priests were engaged to perform important rituals whilst representative members of the lineage, both the Singapore and village male elders, also participate. After this formal service, the remaining men, women and children strolled into the ancestral house to offer their own prayers and incense whilst others burned paper money. When finished, they collected the food and placed it in a basket and returned home (or to where they were staying) where it was consumed as lunch or dinner.

Unlike Confucian China, where ancestor worship was entirely the responsibility of male elders, women have begun to take on important roles. Indeed, female members of the lineage are often the main participants in communal ancestor worship. Women, including married and unmarried daughters, and younger members are now regarded as an integral part of the lineage. A possible reason for their incorporation may be that Singapore women take more interest in genealogy and religion - a pattern consistent with the modern West. They undertake food preparation, give independent offerings and seem to know, even instruct about, the details of ritual performance. Undoubtedly, the breakdown of the traditional social structure under Communist rule and of the rapidly changing environment in Singapore has made it easier to include older women. Likewise, younger people are also taking part. By incorporating them into acts of ancestor worship, it may well be hoped that they, too, will feel part of the lineage and, thus, become interested in the future of Anxi.

The Rite of Inclusion

In traditional Chinese culture, disposing of the dead in a ritually correct manner was the first step in their transformation. The passage from death to becoming an ancestor involves various stages: cleansing the body of the dead, mourning, funerary, merit making (*gongde*), burial and burial grounds (*fengshui-di*), and, ultimately, ancestor worship. These stages allow the dead to move from deceased personhood, to a spirit and, finally, authentic ancestor status: something of a post-mortem 'rite of passage' not unlike those defined by Arnold van Gennep as 'rites which accompany every change of place, state, social position and age' (Van Gennep cited in Turner, 1969:94). These are transitional stages which are 'marked by three phases: separation, margin and aggregation'. Under communist rule, death rituals became highly secularized and simplified with cremation the norm: in part because in-ground burials were seen as taking up valuable space and resources (Whyte, 1988:289-316). After several decades of repeated anti-feudal campaigns, the formal 'ancestor-making' process had, virtually, come to a halt. But, with the liberalization of religious practices, visiting *qiaoqing* and their Anxi kin have now begun to meet the spiritual needs of the departed.

Literally speaking, *gongde* means 'public virtues and morality' though it is commonly translated as 'meritorious deeds'. In Anxi today, it embraces what both Singapore Chinese and local residents are doing for their relatives who died in a time of more radical politics, when formal rituals were not possible. The dead relatives include grandparents, parents, siblings and, at times, have been extended to include parents' siblings. It has also to be performed for those who died in Singapore but continued to regard themselves as part of the home village and might have been buried there had circumstances allowed. The origin of such a ritual can perhaps be traced to a combination of Buddhist and folk religious belief as much as to Confucian tradition. There are various interpretations. However, among the Singapore Chinese, the Buddhist notion of karma has quite clearly influenced the practice.[4] All those interviewed found it hard to provide me with a completely satisfactory explanation. Orthopraxy seems to be more important here than either consistency or orthodoxy (see Watson, 1988:3-19 and the conflicting views of Whyte, 1988:289-316) though this should not be surprising given the long period when religious expression was outlawed.

For my informants, *gongde* is essential for a various reasons. First, it is a ritual which, adapting the Buddhist belief in merit-transfer whereby those with an excess of good deeds, such as a Boddhisattva, can provide the dead with the karmic energy needed to move up from the underworld to higher planes of existence.[5] But in this case, it is more a matter of the living informing the relevant gods of the virtues of the departed. By proclaiming their achievements, it is hoped that dead relatives will finally receive their just rewards. Furthermore, it is also a clear redemptive quality, where the fate of the not so meritorious can still be improved by the intervention of their descendants. I was told that the dead, like the living, have wants and needs in the netherworld. They therefore need various resources to help them live through the required time there. In this sense, the Anxi dead are treated not unlike what was described by Ahern (1981) who found that the Chinese she studied perceive the spirit world as similar to the human world and the needs of the spirits akin to that of the humans. Without help from the living they would become hungry ghosts. *Gongde* allows the dead to cease wandering as a spirit. Secondly, to this group of Anxi-Singapore Chinese at least, *gongde* is a major rite that needs to be performed for the cycle of death and rebirth to be complete. Most importantly in the present context, it is the final rite of inclusion which installs them in their appropriate niche in the ancestral hall: actually inviting them to take an honoured position. Failure to perform this rite excludes the dead from the ancestral entourage.

Gongde involves a series of rituals performed over a period of three to five days. The first is usually the *yinhun* ceremony and the last the placing of the ancestor in his or her permanent home. Each day, two to three or five services are performed for the ancestors. Only the first and last involve the full participation of the lineage, those in between are reserved for monks or priests and the immediate family members. Like the rites of passage through the bridge of no return and the ten hell gates, the ceremony concerns rescuing the 'soul' of the dead from the netherworld. During this rite, the monks or Daoist priests (the Singapore Chinese have a preference for Buddhists) direct the eldest-male descendant to carry the *yinhun* streamer to provide direction to the soul of the ancestor. He is then followed by the rest of the family. This is usually arranged by the monks from the Qing Shui Yuan Temple. The main reason given for the preference for Buddhist monks is that they are better-trained, now full-time religious personnel, with some knowledge of liturgy, who also recite appropriate sutras. Daoist priests, on the other hand, are perceived to have a different type of training and are suited for different religious functions rather than for the care of the dead ancestors. The *gongde* ceremony requires three, five or seven clergy - depending on the amount the family is willing to spend (the fee, not surprisingly, being higher for monks).

At the appropriate moment in the ceremony, a big two or three-storey paper house, the *dawu* or *lingwu* is prepared for the deceased, beautifully decorated with intricate details as it would for the living. Shaped in the traditional style, it now includes the indispensable items required for modern living such as motor car, television, video cassette recorder, together with maids, paper money, chests of gold and silver ingots, incense sticks and other religious paraphernalia. All made of paper. Traditionally, those present would have been required to dress in proper mourning attire made of a coarse hemp material. Today, the Singapore visitors and their *qiaoxiang* kin simply wear ordinary clothing with a thin, symbolic hemp overdress, over it. The grandchildren were required to dress in blue. They all dressed in blue tee shirt and navy blue pants.

The cost of performing a *gongde* ranges from several thousand to over 20,000 *yuan* or more. This includes all the religious paraphernalia and the *dawu*, the services of the monks or priests, service money to participating kin, food, drinks and all meals for the monks and village kin. If the affair is an especially elaborate one, with three to five services a day; the expense for monks goes up considerably. Nonetheless, in my survey, a majority of the households, especially those with Singapore connections, had conducted a *gongde* for their dead ancestors sometime in the 1980s and 1990s. An opera or puppet troupe might also be invited to entertain the guests: both the dead and the living. There is also a large banquet. In this context, feast giving is an important expression of inclusion. Those who are invited are obviously insiders. But, at the same time, the feast givers are incorporated into the lineage structure.

Opening Doors

Several Singapore members have opened the doors of their ancestral house in a ceremony known as *kai zuzai men*. One example was when a member wanted to thank an ancestor when his son attained a doctoral degree. For him, and his village kinfolk, this honour would 'fragrance the name of the ancestor and his family'. 'Opening the doors' is considered an important act of sharing success with the entire lineage. Before one is allowed to 'open the doors of *zuzai*', the Singapore and village elders must agree on the appropriateness of the deed to the occasion. Having decided that the circumstances actually warranted the ceremony, the family (and an academically gifted son in this case) were invited to return. With the date set, they began preparations, helped by locals who supplied the required paraphernalia and arranged a plaque with the name of the new Dr X and his precise university achievement. In contrast to the anti-intellectual years gone by, the production of a scholar-literati is now a positive accomplishment. Likewise, becoming a high official abroad has much more appeal than before.[6] A relevant example is the former Philippine President Corazon Aquino who visited the restored grave of her ancestors in Hongjian Village, Longhai Country, Fujian.

Such recognition can only elevate the status of one's lineage in competition with others. Although the term 'opening doors' has its negative connotation in contemporary China, where political corruption and nepotism are rife, the *kai zuzai men* ceremony is a genuine rite of celebration. It is an important act of sharing whereby the prestige and achievement of the individual, and his family, also bring prestige to the overall lineage. As wealth and success become part of the social fabric of emigrant villages, then other criteria are needed to measure social status and differentiate one *qiaoxiang* from another. In the words of an informant, 'not every emigrant village could produce a *boshi* (doctorate)'.

RESITUATING BURIAL GROUNDS

Because years of disorder or apathy destroyed many graves and cemeteries were routinely converted into agricultural land, there has been an on-going search for physical remains. The few graves that were not destroyed were found buried in hillsides. Consequently, one of the main concerns has been 'finding' and then, 'relocating' burial sites in more propitious locations. Borrowing the term from geomancy, locals call the process 'making *fengshui*'. While some families were able to buy back the original site and thus restore ancestral graves to pre-communist conditions, others have not been so fortunate. Competition for land is keen, pushing the price higher and higher. Usually this means buying uncultivated hillsides from villagers or the district government in a straightforward business transaction. Many have been left dissatisfied. But, nevertheless, graves that had been in ruins for years have been repaired and are now being maintained. Just like the *zuzai*, where the spirits of the dead reside, the ancestral grave has taken on new importance at the end of the twentieth century. The material resting-place can be seen by all (living and dead). Its location and condition is a visible reminder of the lineage and one's obligations to it: proof of the filiality - and therefore, socio-cultural authenticity, of overseas Chinese.

To villagers, the Singaporeans have a responsibility to ensure that the ancestor's grave be protected and restored to its original form, if at all possible, since overseas Chinese wealth is related directly to good *fengshui*. Thus, I was told, having obtained wealth, they should not forget the ancestors as in the saying *fu-gui-bu-li-zu*: 'wealth cannot be divorced from ancestors'. This is also the reason why they should not neglect their home village and their lineage members living in South China. But, in turn, since the overseas Chinese began returning from Southeast Asia, local attitudes have themselves changed. Graves now dot paddy fields and no longer lay hidden in tall grass. In fact, villagers seem proud of the change.

COMMENTARY

Within the ancestral hall stood key players, made up of both the Singapore and village kin. Emanating outward from this centre of power are traditional values of wisdom, compassion and morality. Those within the core group are expected to perform duties befitting the status bestowed upon them. Such values ripple through the various layers of social relationships, moving them to the outermost periphery where all kin would benefit from their association with a rebuilt *zuzai*. Individual wealth or social prestige can only be recognized when they are converted into virtuous deeds that benefit the community as a whole.

ANCESTOR WORSHIP AS A FORM OF MORAL CAPITAL

The revival of ancestor worship has been achieved as a result of collaborative efforts by Singapore Chinese (who gave financial support in order to fulfil a serious family obligation) and Anxi villagers (who provided considerable labour as well as indispensable local knowledge). By helping overseas kinfolk discharge their familial obligations, villagers have clearly achieved material goals. Indeed, something of a cottage industry has grown up to cater for the needs of the dead (see Kuah, 1998). As a direct consequence, additional capital has undeniably come into Anxi for the construction of roads, bridges, schools and hospitals. In Peng Lai district, for example, visiting Singaporeans have also put funds into retailing and small-scale production, undoubtedly helped, in their own pursuit of profit, by *guanxi* relationships reinforced by newly-established kinship. But what are we, as outside observers, to make of this whole, admittedly morbid, business?

Even in this cynical age (in China as well as in the West), it must be admitted that more than money is being exchanged. Although the term 'moral economy' is out of fashion, there may still be something called 'cultural' or even 'moral-cultural' capital.[7] Part of the non-monetary transaction clearly concerns 'identity'. Overseas Chinese are keen to find their 'roots' (*gen*) and genuinely seek 'ancestors' (*zong*) in the same way that the villagers want foreign 'relatives' - whether they are financially successful or not. As one villager put it: 'It is good to have a *zuzai* we can identify with.' Another felt that 'it is good that the Singapore Chinese and we, Anxi people, are able to identify our ancestors again. It makes us feel like one people.' Thus, they welcome visits from blood relations (*xuetong guanxi*) with a special warmth: which is not to say that those who fail to send remittances are not denigrated as 'uncivilized' (*fan*), with no sense of propriety or kinship (*qinqing*). 'They do not behave like the others and do not know our culture and way of life.' The 'good' migrant should always remember where he or she came from.

Perhaps the revival of Confucianism as a state-sponsored ethical system in Singapore may also have played a role in linking ancestor worship with sentiments of moral cultivation. The very idea of performing a *gongde* was brought up by Singaporeans who wanted to complete their mourning process. Most of their dead ancestors had not been given a proper burial during the Communist regime and, worst still, had their graves disturbed. There was a feeling of guilt, perhaps even a sense of having failed to discharge moral duty to their ancestors. Many now find it difficult to ignore pleas for further financial assistance. One common comment is that 'when the elders come to us for contributions for village projects, it is hard for us to turn it down. Somehow, it just does not seem right to say no. We usually gave whatever they asked from us. After all, it is our ancestral village.' But villagers are also expert at moral persuasion: 'they are wealthy and we are poor, so they should help us'. 'They should search for their roots.' Moreover, Singaporeans are 'part of one family'. 'When they drink water, they should remember the source (*yinshui sheyuan*). After all, they are offshoots from this lineage.'

THE ROLE OF CADRES

All of the activities related to ancestor worship have been given support by the district and county cadres, who have often established close relationships with Singapore Chinese. Most attended feasts and some have even taken part in ritual ceremonies. Although higher officials tend to be more restrained, the general attitude is one of pragmatism:

'It depends on how you look at this. If it is purely religious practices, then it is superstition and we would not support it. But this is the ancestral house and they are engaged in ancestor worship. This is our ancestral place and it is very important for the future generations. It is a place to remind us of our ancestors and to remember them. Through it, we will be able to foster closer relationships among our blood relatives, within the villages and with the Chinese overseas. This will also allow them to develop stronger bonds with their home village. An ancestral house is a place where we, the Chinese, search for our roots. It is beneficial to the lineage and provides an opportunity for the Chinese overseas to express their love for their motherland and home village. Because this is a cultural practice and not a superstition, we would support it.'

In my survey, the village cadres are very much central to the Singapore-Anxi connection. To understand better the transformation of ancestor worship from a prohibited superstition to a cherished cultural tradition, we need to see the political leadership from a wider context. When contacts were being re-established after the Cultural Revolution, they actively encouraged traditional cultural practices such as ancestor worship as a means to an end: an obvious trading of favours in order to bring material benefits to their area. Because of the goodwill created, Chinese overseas capital flowed into poor villages, thereby increasing their own status.

At county level, the responses of the cadres can be divided into the following: (i) *sentimental*, where the existence of an ancestral house would help the Chinese overseas in the search for their cultural roots and ancestors. They saw the early emigrants as a group of kinsmen who were forced to emigrate because of poverty in the villages; they should not discriminate against them by not acknowledging their present status and their needs to search for their roots. But they also hoped that such acts would strengthen their sentiments towards the home village; (ii) *moral*, where this is seen as a concession in order to remind the successful and wealthy Chinese overseas not to forget their ancestral home; (iii) *instrumental*, where ancestor worship can build stronger contacts and result in further investments.

CONCLUDING REMARKS

Anxi County has been officially listed as an important emigrant region. Here, local and regional government policies are, quite consciously, aimed at encouraging Southeast Asian Chinese to assist with village reconstruction. So far, these activities have been highly successful and become something of a benchmark for measuring *qiaoxiang* ties. Since the reform movement permitted them, Singaporeans (who maintain a sentimental attachment to the emigrant villages that they, or their ancestors, came from) have been returning - often accompanied by their children or grandchildren. By reinvigorating ancestor worship and its related rituals, the reconstructed *zuzai* has, once again, become an important focal point for two member groups of the same lineage, separated as they have been in time and space. It has allowed them to rekindle their relationship and to reproduce a new socio-religious culture, one that consists of elements drawn from both the past and present.

Not insignificantly, it has given Singaporeans an opportunity for grieving and healing whilst, at the same time reminding them of their moral duty to the dead. And, perhaps more important in the long run, it has also reaffirmed a sense of on-going responsibility to the living. But the process of cultural reproduction described in these pages is not without irony. Whilst political cadres no doubt believed that they were facilitating economic modernization, the reciprocity networks that have resulted may well have unintended social and political consequences. The revival of ancestor worship (the rites of *xiezu juanding* and *gongde,* rebuilding graves and the opening of temple doors) have now allowed the lineage to re-emerge, once again, as an important feature of village life.

BIBLIOGRAPHY

Ahern, E.
1981   *Chinese Rituals and Politics*. Cambridge: Cambridge University Press
Bourdieu, P.
1993   *The Field of Cultural Production*. New York: Columbia University Press
Castells, M.
1976   'Theory and Ideology in Urban Sociology', in: C.G. Pickvance (ed.) *Urban Sociology: Critical Essays*. London: Tavistock
Daye, D.D.
1978   'Cosmology', in: C.S. Prebish (ed.) *Buddhism: A Modern Perspective*. University Park: Pennsylvania State University Press, pp. 123-6
De Groot, J.J.M.
1964   *The Religious Systems of China*. Taipei: Literature House, vol 1:4.
Douw, L.M. and P. Post (eds)
1996   *South China: State, Culture and Social Change During the 20th Century*, Amsterdam: Royal Netherlands Academy of Arts and Sciences
Freedman, M.
1958   *Lineage Organisation in Southeastern China*. London: Athlone Press
Harvey, D.
1985   *Consciousness and the Urban Experience*. Oxford: Basil Blackwell
Holm, D.
1991   *Art and Ideology in Revolutionary China*. Oxford: Clarendon Press
Kuah, K.E.
1998   'Rebuilding Their Ancestral Village: The Moral Economy of the Singapore Chinese', in: G.W. Wang and J. Wong (eds) *China's*

Political Economy. Singapore: Singapore University Press and World Scientific, pp. 249-76

Obeyeskere, G.
1968   'Theodicy, Sin and Salvation in a Sociology of Buddhism', in: E.R. Leach (ed.), *Dialectic in Practical Religion.* Cambridge: Cambridge University Press, pp. 7-40

Parish, W.L. and M.K. Whyte
1978   *Village and Family in Contemporary China.* Chicago: Chicago University Press

Tong, C.K.
1982   *Funerals, Ancestral Halls and Graveyards: Changes and Continuities in Chinese Ancestor Worship in Singapore.* National University of Singapore, Department of Sociology, unpublished MA dissertation

Turner, V.
1969   *The Ritual Process.* Ithaca: Cornell University Press

Watson, J.L.
1988   'The Structure of Chinese Funerary Rites: Elementary Forms, Ritual Sequence, and the Primacy of Performance', in: J.L. Watson and E.S. Rawski (eds), *Death Ritual in Late Imperial and Modern China.* Berkeley: University of California Press, pp. 3-19

Whyte, M.K.
1988   'Death in the People's Republic of China', in: J.L. Watson and E.S. Rawski (eds) *Death Ritual in Late Imperial and Modern China.* Berkeley: University of California Press, pp. 289-316

Wolf, A.P.
1996   'The "New Feudalism": A Problem for Sinologists', in: L.M. Douw and P. Post (eds) 1996, *South China: State, Culture and Social Change During the 20th Century.* Amsterdam: Royal Netherlands Academy of Arts and Sciences, pp. 77-84

Yang, C.K.
1961   *Religion in Chinese Society.* Berkeley: University of California Press

Yen, C.H.
1986   *A Social History of the Chinese in Singapore and Malaya 1800-1911.* Singapore: Oxford University Press

Notes

1. It has 186,000 households and a total population of 916,000 people. Of these, 94 per cent are engaged in agricultural production - paddy and tea cultivation. The region is most famous for Chinese tea branded under the labels Oolong. Since May 1995, when Lung Men Tunnel was completed and opened to traffic, the time taken to travel to Anxi has been halved to two and a half hours. The district occupies an area of 122.4 sq. km. and is divided into thirty-one districts with a total population of 67,800 people (Anxi Xian Zhi, 1994, vol. 2, p. 854).

2. Prior to 1978, all Singapore citizens travelling to China were required to apply for exit permit from the Singapore Immigration Department. It was a policy that only those forty-five years and above were permitted to visit China.

3. For a good discussion of the relationship between space and social structure, including identity, see Castells, 1976, pp. 60-84 and Harvey, 1985.

4. For a detailed treatment of karma and merit, see Obeyeskere, 1968, pp. 7-40.

5. The six layers are Hell, Preta, Animal, Asuras, Human, Heaven. See Daye, 1978, pp. 123-6.

6. In recent years, many other overseas Chinese, who had achieved high public positions in adopted countries, have had their achievements acknowledged by government authorities in the People's Republic.

7. Here I am adapting an argument proposed by Bourdieu (1993, p. 75) who proposed the existence of 'cultural capital' - a specialized knowledge which puts one person or group in a stronger bargaining position *vis-à-vis* others.

GETTING THINGS DONE ACROSS THE HONG KONG BORDER: ECONOMIC CULTURE IN THEORY AND PRACTICE

ALAN SMART[1]

The rapidity with which hegemonic institutions of the capitalist world-economy have been accepted and managed in the People's Republic of China since 1978 is one of the most significant changes of the late twentieth century. In the last militarily-important communist nation, a profusion of rules, laws, practices and even the country's constitution have been modified to try to encourage investment to support rapid modernization. Yet the demand for new changes to facilitate the effective transfer of foreign capital, technology and expertise is equally unrelenting. The financial crises throughout Pacific Asia since 1997 have heightened the intensity of calls for greater 'transparency' in economic dealings, and for institutional reforms which would abandon the belief that there are distinctively 'Asian' ways of being capitalist. While China has so far maintained financial stability and economic growth despite regional chaos, partly due to the lower level of financial integration with the global economy, the pressures are seen there as well. Even in the short two decades that the country has been open to foreign investment, there has been a shift away from reliance on a pioneer form of foreign investment where the foreign counterpart either has to be willing to cope without standard guarantees and protections, or to endure long and unprofitable negotiations and start-up processes. Particularly since the temporary reduction in foreign investment after the Tiananmen Square incidents in 1989, the trend has been toward a higher level of routinization of capitalist business in China, with clearer (if still far from clear and dependable) rules and less necessity to rely on local partners. Although Hong Kong and overseas[2] Chinese are the major source of foreign investment, the adoption of rules compatible with the global capitalist economy may ultimately mean less reliance on social and cultural practices that depend on muddling through the inconsistency of the rules on either side of the capitalist/socialist political economic boundary. But, for the present, at least, many investors still depend on trust as much as clearly specified rules. By relying on shared expectations and practices, the need to build institutions and more-formalized procedures may, in fact, be somewhat reduced or at least delayed.

INTRODUCTION

The success enjoyed by ethnic Chinese outside of the People's Republic of China has led scholars to claim that there are important commonalities in their overall style of enterprise (Gates, 1996:3). For example, Yeung notes that Hong Kong Chinese industrialists 'are known for their entrepreneurship and higher propensity to engage in risky business and overseas ventures' (Yeung, 1994:140). These tendencies are said to be due, in part, to shared experience of repression (reducing local opportunities) in their home territories, the existence of active social networks in other countries, and historical experience of specialization in 'middleman capitalism' (Chirot, 1997). A main theme of his book is that this form of organization is 'peculiarly effective and a significant contributor to the list of causes of the East Asia miracle' (Chirot, 1997). Social networks are also said to be constructed and mobilized to develop particularistic interpersonal forms of trust which encourage 'co-operation, loyalty, obedience, duty, stability, adaptiveness and legitimacy in the short and long term' (Thrift and Olds, 1996:324). Other studies have likewise pointed to the frequency of the family enterprise and the strengths offered by the overlap between household and enterprise (Redding, 1990:143, Hamilton and Biggart, 1992, and Yeung, 1998). According to Redding what is special about Chinese business organization is that: 'it retains many of the characteristics of small scale, such as paternalism, opportunism, flexibility, even to very large scale.' (Redding, 1990:3) Hamilton and Waters also believe that common organizational forms can be identified, and likewise suggest that what has been significant is the migrants' ability to adapt to very different contexts so as to succeed in 'ways as numerous as the institutional and organizational contexts of the societies in which they lived and worked' (Hamilton and Waters, 1997:279).[3] It has been hypothesized that the conditions that now encourage transnational production and distribution, including flexible response to rapidly changing consumer demands, have rewarded the kinds of organizational skills that the overseas Chinese are well known for (Thrift and Olds, 1996). However, there are scholars who, after critically examining the discourse about 'Chinese capitalism', reject many of the 'culturalist claims' which attempt to explain business success in terms of 'essential, exclusive and unchanging Chinese values' (Dirlik, 1997; Ong,

1997; Nonini, 1997; and Greenhalgh, 1994). But merely demonstrating the ideological nature of these narratives does not resolve the question of whether or not there is something fundamentally different about the way Asian societies have accomplished their rapid economic growth. With some reluctance, I have come to accept that there is something called 'economic culture', which has clearly played a significant role in the cross-border relationships to be discussed below and, more generally, in the rapid growth of the South China region.[4]

Culture does not determine success or failure, but my argument is that it can provide a set of interpretive schemas and interactional resources that, if mobilized effectively and with a bit of luck, has often enough served to provide solutions to the challenges faced by globalizing economies.[5] If this seems vague, it is because I think that generalizations about the role of culture in economic interaction and development are necessarily uncertain. Social capital and obligation are not objective, measurable things, but the negotiated (and renegotiable) outcomes of interaction. Rather than determining behaviour, culture needs to be seen as an open-ended set of interpretive and rhetorical devices that permit those who want to co-operate to find ways to do so and to make the compromises necessary to muddle through the constant difficulties that arise from doing business in a non-routine context. Thus, social capital and trust are not fixed entities in any particular context, but are themselves uncertain and open to negotiation. Situations are constantly being assessed and reassessed to decide whether the new demand is an acceptable quid pro quo or represents evidence that you are being taken advantage of.

On the one hand, many Hong Kong entrepreneurs I have interviewed agree that trust and co-operation can be established more easily due to the multi-faceted mutual obligations and accountability between those who share social ties. On the other hand, it is acknowledged that personal connections alone give no guarantee that someone will ally more strongly with one's business interests than those without prior ties. A relative whose productivity and performance are not up to standard cannot easily be fired because such an action may have far reaching repercussions on one's other social relationships. Thireau and Hua (this volume) quote one entrepreneur's apt comment that 'a relative who is okay makes the best assistant; a relative which is not okay makes the worst assistant'. But, having said this at the outset, there is also evidence to suggest that trust can make it easier for Chinese entrepreneurs to do business across the former 'Bamboo Curtain'.

CROSSING BOUNDARIES

Doing business (as opposed to piracy) across borders, or indeed a sharp political boundary of any kind, would seem to require at least minimal consistency and/or compatibility[6] between the rules and practices on both sides. Global hegemonic institutions are currently offering one main mechanism for ensuring consistency. Local societies must adopt the general ground rules and practices of capitalism as practised in the United States, the European Union and, to a lesser extent, Japan, if they are to be successful in attracting foreign investment or in being permitted equal access to world markets. If you want to be able to play, you have to be willing to work on 'levelling' your playing field in accordance with the emerging international norms (Blim, 1997; Jones, 1994; Merry, 1992). Clear examples of this in the Chinese context include the heavy requirements being imposed as prerequisites for accession to the World Trade Organization, the intellectual property rights dispute with the United States, and the common incorporation in joint venture agreements of contractual rights to take disputes to international arbitration courts.

Changing local institutions and practices to fit with global standards is only one way in which co-operation across boundaries of sharp discontinuities can be accomplished, however. Although China has been making substantial changes, it is clear that China's goals were both to absorb and to control foreign investments (Pearson, 1991:14), and particularly to preserve central control over society. Another way in which China has facilitated transnational economic integration has been by relying on groups of foreign economic actors who may hold feelings of patriotism and obligation to China, and who often have economic cultures more similar to or at least compatible with those found in China: ethnic Chinese outside the political boundaries of China.

Chinese business practices developed in contexts where the legal system was distant and often antagonistic to Chinese entrepreneurs. These practices offer new advantages (but also challenges and pitfalls) in a new world economy characterized by the need for flexibility and rapid responses, and are particularly applicable in the difficult but promising terrain of investment in China. Since regulations are often unclear, and their implementation uncertain, reliance on them is a dangerous strategy. Developing relationships based on trust, built through reciprocity and social commonalities, offers a more attractive strategy for entrepreneurs accustomed to operating on such terms. Insecurity of property rights and other rules for Hong Kong investors in China, and widespread distrust of the system, have further encouraged reliance on personal relationships, which have helped produce one of the fastest growing economies in history.

Despite accomplishments, it is essential to avoid romantic evaluations: business relations across the Hong Kong-China political and economic boundary are also fraught with ambiguity, conflict, and misunderstanding. The development, maintenance and instrumental use of *guanxi* requires skilled practice which can negotiate the conflicts between interests, wider risks and competition, maintaining balance between opportunism and social obligations.

THE QUESTION OF TRUST

Getting things done, even in market economies, involves moral evaluations. On purely self-interested grounds, there are good reasons to prove yourself to be trustworthy and to avoid free-riding on the efforts of others who might think of you as part of an us, but are always willing to reconsider that evaluation. The question, of course, is how such trustworthy relationships and communities can be constructed. Being born into groups with a strong sense of solidarity is clearly one solution, but new relationships of trust are also constructed outside of bounded communities. A gradual process of relationship building and testing is often involved, and reciprocity or gift exchange is a central part of this process. Extending trust outside bounded communities can involve risks, but it also opens up new opportunities. As long as transactors do not invest too large a fraction of their resources in any one new relationship, then it is possible to 'test the waters', to see if the counterpart will follow their obligations, and subsequently to slowly build up a relationship which can stand the dangers of larger investments. But the difficulties, potential for misunderstandings, and risks are substantially reduced when those engaged in the building of a trustworthy relationship share common values, beliefs, or idioms of interaction, reducing the potential for misunderstanding (Smart and Smart, 1993).

Trustworthy relationships are strategically critical in situations where there are few acceptable external guarantees for exchanges, or when the system is actively distrusted (Menning, 1997). But it may precisely be in such situations, as where boundaries are being crossed or brokered, that the potential for profit may be greatest. Those who are effective at constructing and managing such relationships may reap considerable rewards as a result. But where they do so, and where the transactors occupy very different roles in different systems, that relationship may involve double-sided representations of its nature to power-holders outside the relationship. It may often involve what Bailey has called 'collusive lying', which occurs when two parties: 'knowing full well that what they are saying or doing is false, collude in ignoring the falsity. They hold it between them as an open secret' (Bailey, 1991:35). Whenever something is presented as one thing to some, and another thing to others, collusive lying would seem to be present (even if people may manage to avoid acknowledging that they know this). Numerous scholars have demonstrated the role of tacit knowledge in social life, but just as important is what is kept inexplicit, since making it explicit would be rude. Tact often involves choice about describing events, but still allows cognoscenti (i.e. those initiated into the nuances of those idioms) to understand what is being alluded to. Tact would seem to be particularly crucial in contexts where there are high levels of distrust for the prevailing institutions (and perhaps symmetrical distrust by agents of the institutions for trusted relations in the society at large), and trustworthy relationships are relied upon instead.

Fukuyama characterizes Chinese societies as 'low-trust' (Fukuyama, 1995), but I suggest that this applies only to trust in the system itself: Chinese interactional culture has a considerable potential for trustworthy relationships. Dealing with people with whom you have a pre-existing social relationship has been part of this, and often this has led to investment in one's native place. Just as common, though, is to invest through, but not in, your native place if certain required features were not available there or because doing so created too many other risks. Below, I explore the way in which the use of *tongxiang* (shared native place) relationships and idioms of interaction are related to the question of trust. One of the important ways in which economic co-operation has been facilitated is by claims made by agents on both sides of the border about the existence of an 'us' carrying implications of obligations and solidarities. Claims about trust, however, take different patterns when they are between employers and employees compared to those in less asymmetrical power relationships. I first look at how small and medium overseas Chinese enterprises are established, involving interactions with local officials and partners, and then turn to employer-subordinate relationships.

ESTABLISHING AN ENTERPRISE

Along with many other analysts, Hsing concluded that Taiwanese investors in China used interpersonal *guanxi* networks to 'bypass bureaucratic demands on foreign-investment projects and maintain and enhance flexibility in production and marketing'. By investing in their ancestral native places, social relationships are built up with officials. These local officials have 'developed the skill of making decisions based on what higher-level officials would not oppose rather than what they would allow' (Hsing, 1997:150). These flexible adjustments of rules and policies were particularly critical in the early years of foreign investment, when in most respects the institutional context was singularly uninviting for capitalist entrepreneurs concerned about the 'bottom line'. For Western corporations, the biggest attraction, which convinced them to overlook the dubious prospects for short-term profits and the heavy transactions cost of negotiating arrangement, was simply the huge potential market. For small and medium overseas Chinese investors, however, profits could hardly be ignored, while the negotiation of detailed contracts was neither feasible nor seen as providing much real security. The attraction for them was more often access to cheaper factors of production (labour and land) to maintain Hong Kong's strategy of labour-intensive manufacturing for the world market (which was being threatened by increased labour costs in Hong Kong), than access to the Chinese market itself.

The standard alternative to prolonged negotiation with central authorities was to reactivate, intensify, or create social connections in the place of investment. These connections were often based on kinship, but due in part to the restrictions on mobility for residents of rural areas, they were often also focused on native places. Emphasizing loyalty to one's native place was also politically more acceptable than emphasizing personal kin ties, particularly since the ambiguity of patriotism and loyalty (whether to a specific place or to China as a whole) could be manipulated in presenting the nature of the co-operation with foreign capitalists) (Smart and Smart, 1998).

Social ties with overseas Chinese has been one of the most important assets for the counties of the Pearl River Delta. According to Fitzgerald, for every 100 native residents of Dongguan municipality, there are 50 Hong Kong residents who trace their descent to the area, and another 25 who live overseas. The number of Hong Kong and overseas descendants per 100 for Zhongshan municipality is 56 and 47 for Shunde (Fitzgerald, 1996:13). On the one hand, the historical connections between these areas and the diaspora Chinese is used to appeal to feelings of obligation and loyalty. On the other hand, the personal connections have helped to provide 'easy and reliable links between investors and their manufacturing partners' (Lin, 1997:174). I have argued elsewhere that these relationships have helped investors resolve the many organizational problems involved in transplanting capitalist production into a socialist society, but have also generated a dynamic where overseas Chinese investors 'push the envelope' of what is allowed, and regulations are subsequently altered to legitimate what was already being done (Smart, 1998).

Despite this, the situation is not one that is wholly beneficial. One investor suggested in an interview that it is not a smart move to build a factory in one's place of origin because 'industrial manufacturing is certain of failure'. To publicly exhibit one's failure in one's home village or ancestral place of origin could bring shame to one's family and lineage. Another common reservation Hong Kong investors have about investing in or near one's place of origin in China is the concern that one's business interests may be overrun by social obligations and other demands from their close kin and distant relatives. Returning to one's ancestral home village or county as an investor automatically raises one's social and economic status in the eyes of the local residents. The investor is a local son or daughter who has made it in the world. The perceived and real differentials in earning potential and quality of life between Hong Kong and mainland China legitimizes the local residents' expectation that a returning investor owes it to his or her kin, no matter how removed, to do them good in the form of employment offers and economic contribution to public and personal causes. Such demands and expectations may result in a net drain on one's economic resources. Should the investor refuse to fulfil such obligations, he or she may lose face and status in the local community.

One response is to establish only a shell company and office in the native place, while using the village cadres' social connections to make arrangements elsewhere, often a place with better transportation and infrastructure. Another response is to try to carefully manage the obligations, providing key jobs without excessively overmanning the operation, and trying to ensure sufficient reciprocity in favours (breaks on taxes, application of official regulations, lax inspections, unpaid overtime work during peak periods, etc.) to maintain the viability of the enterprise. Both sides may make claims about obligations that have not been met, or favours that have not been adequately appreciated. The benefits and costs of investing in one's native place usually involve a precarious balancing act, and effective interactional performance and persuasive application of rhetoric is required if the benefits are to be optimized and the costs reduced. Trust on both sides is an outcome, not a precondition, for co-operation, and where co-operation succeeds, it is because routines and expectations have been developed through give and take on both sides of the relationship. Characteristically, effective partnerships require considerable attention to explaining the demands on either side of the political economic boundary between the way things get done in China and in the global capitalist economy.

When trustworthy relationships with relevant counterparts have been forged, these can be used to help protect the entrepreneur from arbitrary demands for 'fees', or at least ensure that the amount that must be paid is predictable. Local counterparts, particularly knowledgeable or well-connected ones, are crucial in navigating through the uncertain governmental system, and to find ways to 'fix' problems. Labour management provides further examples of the dynamics of these processes, and the ways in which common cultural schemas can be appealed to in trying to manage the inconsistencies between capitalist enterprises and the socialist nation in which they are endeavouring to make profits.

LABOUR RECRUITMENT AND MANAGEMENT

Once an enterprise is established, some of the most demanding problems for investors involve managing labour. Entrepreneurs who had operated previously in the British colony characteristically employ more workers in China than they did in Hong Kong, and the patterns and expectations of labour relations are very different. One of the most important areas in which 'special arrangements' have been made with local officials and partners has been in enhancing managerial autonomy in recruiting and managing workforces. Personalism has been a very common element in these labour regimes, and asserting the benevolence of the employer and the obligations of the workers is part of this process. Narotzky's comments on the situation in the Catalan region of Spain apply remarkably well to Hong Kong run factories in Guangdong province:

'workers tend to interpret "trust" in contractual terms: labour power and goodwill balanced against good piece rates and continuity of employment; whilst employers tend to interpret "trust" in paternalistic terms: doing favours, caring for the local women's well-being (by offering jobs) is balanced by respect, obedience, quasi-filial "love" and is expressed in hard work and good work.' (Narotzky, 1997:203)

Hegemonic words or idioms of interaction like these that are accepted on both sides of the labour hierarchy may receive so much consensus because they mean different things to each side. They may thus produce powerful but fragile ways of getting things done. The fragility comes from the divergent meanings attributed to the term or value by the different actors, even while they agree on its desirability, as I will suggest below.

Emphasis on personal ties in recruitment and management in Chinese businesses involves the use of an available resource which permits the solution of certain problems inherent in labour relations, rather than being a direct outcome of cultural propensities. If employing employees who possess personal ties with the employer reduces the risks and transaction costs of employment, then strategic rationality alone would be sufficient to account for its utilization, where the existing social structure makes its efficient manipulation possible, and where the economic situation makes it advantageous. But such an outcome is far from certain, as a number of articles in this volume make clear, and while benefits might potentially result, the risks may be even higher. Perhaps it is only those who have no choice but to adopt risky tactics that rely on relatives rather than on weaker ties.

Burawoy and Wright argue that domination and coercion are not the only techniques which can be used to extract labour from workers (Burawoy and Wright, 1990:252-3). Of particular relevance here is their account of one of the alternatives, asymmetrical reciprocity, in which 'labour effort is based on consent, on the positive agreement by each of the parties concerned over the mutual, if still unequal, benefits of the exertion of such effort' (Burawoy and Wright, 1990:253). A distinguishing feature of consent-based mechanisms is that coercion is not directly applied to generate labour effort. Cultural commonalities and social ties may provide a degree of trust which makes it easier to construct employment relationships based upon asymmetrical reciprocity. When there are social ties outside the employment relationship, a higher level of trust may be more easily achieved, and the investments, with their delayed returns, required from both parties may be more secure, and more easily monitored. Lee observes that localistic networks organized according to a worker's native village, county or province were a major structuring principle within the factories she studied in Shenzhen. While the management 'used localism as a mode of domination, workers actively manipulated localism to temper managerial despotism' (Lee, 1997:126). While this is clearly true, it does not provide a full picture of the complexities of localism in Hong Kong-invested factories. Firstly, she does not deal with *tongxiang* linkages between Hong Kong managers and local workers. Secondly, the emphasis on localism as a strategy of domination obscures the ways in which reliance on such ties may either improve or undermine managerial control and effectiveness depending on how it is managed. An account of some labour issues related to *tongxiang* in a Hong Kong-invested shoe factory will flesh out these suggestions.[7]

Most of the initial workforce of this small concern (which started with twenty workers and never had more than 100) were hired by the owners based on kinship and *tongxiang* ties. One of the three partners provided most of the initial investment of HK$380,000. While he left the daily management and front line work to the other partners, this senior partner always had the final say in every aspect of the production ranging from the hiring and dismissal of workers to quality control. As a result most of the first workers were young men and women from Kaiping (a county in the western part of the Pearl River Delta), the senior partner's place of origin, hired by himself without consultation with his other partners. Few of these workers had previous experience in shoe manufacturing. When production expanded in subsequent years to involve over 80 workers in 1991, most of the new workers were hired through introduction by existing workers. Most of the initial group of workers who started in 1986 and early 1987 remained. The core of permanent workers has always been dominated by Kaiping people. In July 1991, there was a total of 13 permanent workers. With the exception of two male workers, the rest (six women and five men) were all from Kaiping.

Workers in the shoe factory are organized in three categories. At the bottom are the new workers. They worked for a month as an 'apprentice' at a wage of 60 *yuan* in 1986-8 and 90 *yuan* in 1991. They received their food and lodging free during this trial period. After passing probation, workers were retained as regular workers paid by the piece. During work rushes, overtime was common and workers could earn up to 500-1,000 *yuan* a month depending on productivity. During periods of reduced production, they may earn just enough to cover their room and board cost of 80 *yuan* per month. The majority of the workers in small and medium Hong Kong factories in China are hired under similar arrangements which give the employer enhanced security and flexibility since it is the workers who shoulder the burden of fluctuating production levels. But during periods of low production, under-utilized workers may be tempted to seek better employment in other factories. One of the ways to protect the investors against a significant loss in human resource investment during each period of low production is to develop and maintain a 'good' relationship with workers on an on-going basis.

At the top of the labour hierarchy are permanent workers, paid a flat rate of 400-500 *yuan* per month for 12 months a year, plus free room and board. They receive better living quarters and food. Permanent workers are usually assigned to the most skilled positions and assume supervisory and training responsibility. The senior partner of this shoe factory considered his offer of employment to the children of his close relatives to be a way of 'looking after' them. He maintains close association with his native village in Kaiping through yearly participation in the various local festivals. For instance, he sponsors his village team to participate in the yearly inter-village boat races during the Dragon Boat Festival. His wife and children remained in Kaiping until the early 1980s, which contributed to close social ties with his home village. Before his wife and children came to Hong Kong, he visited them regularly in Kaiping. Both he and his wife were involved in wide-ranging reciprocity with local kin and friends.

The employment of Kaiping workers raises the partner's status and reputation in his home village. It was also a reasonable strategy at the beginning of the venture to use workers bound to him by social ties. These ties obliged them to assist him in overcoming various initial organizational problems. Despite unfavourable working conditions, they would not consider leaving for another factory because doing so would be a betrayal. They felt obliged to do many non-work related chores that were necessary to put the factory into shape - organizing the dormitory, doing shopping and other errands for the Hong Kong managers and investors, working overtime without pay to organize their work stations and material, and so on. Despite these advantages, the Kaiping workers were involved in a long series of labour and management problems that arose in 1990 and 1991. They resisted any kind of managerial authority in the dormitories, disturbing other workers by noisily playing mahjong long into the night, claimed rights not accorded other workers, and in other ways asserted their distinctive status. By early 1991, the junior managing partner was feeling very irritated about his loss of face and authority in the factory after the senior partner repeatedly overruled his decisions to discipline workers who resisted his orders. Economic downturn for the enterprise became a convenient excuse to withdraw from the partnership. Within a year, the factory had been closed because it was no longer generating profits. The senior partner's protectionism towards the Kaiping workers, arising from his sense of social obligation, was at the root of the break-up and widespread discontent within his workforce.

This outcome was not inevitable, but it does indicate the dangers involved in overreliance on *qiaoxiang* and other personal connections. In this case, the use of such ties in labour recruitment and management was not simply intended to increase economic advantage, instead it was related to the investor's feelings of obligation and desire for an enhanced reputation in his native place. This may have exacerbated the tensions involved in the strategy, but I do not believe that the attempt to pursue both goals was doomed from the start. Instead, there is evidence that problems were related to the tact with which the goals were pursued. While tensions might have been inevitable with a divided workforce, effective communication and persuasion could have considerably reduced the negative effects of such tensions. Certainly there are many other cases where such practices have worked effectively, as the litany of reports of success in Chinese family business culture suggests.

TRUST AS SOCIAL CAPITAL

The productivity of cultural idioms lies partly in the ambiguity that makes their mobilization possible in a wide variety of situations. It is in the complexity of interaction that culture as skilled performance comes to the fore. I would argue that it is in contexts of flux and uncertainty, rather than routine activity, that both the strengths and weaknesses of these cultural forms of interaction are most significant and apparent. I will attempt below to illustrate this through an examination of reliance on trust between individuals connected by social ties and exchanges as a basis for business dealings.

Trust has come to be emphasized in many critical arenas of interdisciplinary and public debate (Tyler and Kramer, 1996). For example, in debates about the emergence under post-Fordism of flexible specialization, involving increased levels of integration of production through networks rather than by markets or within firms, trust is critical for effective transition to such patterns. Team-oriented flexible production is also seen as dependent on higher levels of trust within the workforce and between labour and management, as well as between networks of suppliers. Diego Gambetta has defined trust as;

> 'a particular level of the subjective probability with which an agent assesses that another agent or group of agents will perform a particular action, both before he can monitor such action ... and in a context in which it affects his own action.' (Diego Gambetta, 1988:217)

If we say that someone is trustworthy, we mean that the probability that (s)he will perform an action that is beneficial or at least not detrimental to us is high enough for us to consider engaging in some form of co-operation (Diego Gambetta, 1988:217). Granovetter has argued that the sources of enterprise inefficiency can be found in their undersocialization (opportunism) as much as in their oversocialization (excessive socially-based claims), and that overseas Chinese have been particularly successful at generating an effective balance between the two dangers (Granovetter, 1990). In contrast, Francis Fukuyama has recently argued that certain societies, such as Japan and Germany, have high levels of 'social capital' which produce high levels of trust, which in turn make possible the effective exploitation of available economic opportunities. Other societies, such as China and Italy, are characterized as low-trust societies which consequently have experienced 'difficulties in creating large organizations that go beyond the family, and in each, consequently, the state has had to step in to promote durable, globally competitive firms' (Fukuyama, 1995:12).

Other than the specifics of his treatment of Chinese societies, there are at least two major problems with Fukuyama's general account of trust and its contribution to economic efficiency. First of all, he seems to conceive of trust as a characteristic of societies or cultures, rather than as an expectation held by individuals. It is true that if trust was a unidimensional and undifferentiated variable, then theoretically it should be possible to take aggregate measurements of it. However, I do not believe this to be possible. If trust is based on an individual's beliefs about how another person 'will perform on another occasion' (Good, 1988:33), then it would seem that there could be a variety of different kinds of trust: trust in known individuals, trust in strangers who are members of the same collectivity such as a city or nation, and trust in the institutions of the society. Furthermore, these different kinds of trust might not co-vary. For example, a society with a high level of trust in its institutions and in the trustworthiness of strangers' intentions may become less dependent on the support of kin and others with whom pre-existing social ties exist, so that at an extreme it might be seen as preferable to co-operate with strangers rather than closely associated others. On the other pole, high levels of distrust for the institutions of the system may lead to investments committed to social relationships that are carefully cultivated as secure bulwarks in a dangerous world (Menning, 1997). If we were conceivably able to quantify the amounts of trust in these two situations, we might find that they were identical, good enough reason for distinguishing between different varieties of trust.

There is another assumption in Fukuyama's analysis: the more trust there is in a society, the better. This may be so, but it should hardly be simply taken for granted (Gambetta, 1988:214). Accepting that too little trust of the right kinds can cause serious problems, it doesn't necessarily follow that after a certain threshold, more trust is necessarily even better (Woolcock, 1998:158). Some degree of uncertainty about others' expectations can sharpen our perceptions, leading to tensions rather than complacency. Even Japan, taken as an epitome of a high-trust society by Fukuyama, was able to mobilize this trust for continually transforming its economy partially as a result of a high level of distrust for outsiders, against whom Japan must continually improve its competitive position.

I am very concerned about the tendency to romanticize trust, a tendency that is of course common throughout the history of anthropological analysis. Trust is a tool, something that certainly can promote co-operation, but before we can assess it, we need to know what kind of co-operation is being promoted. As Gambetta points out, there are many forms of co-operation based on trust that we would prefer to do without, such as that involved in organized crime or in collusion between government officials and lobbyists (Gambetta, 1988). Thus, I would be inclined to disagree with the assumption in Fukuyama's thesis that 'the more trust, the better'. It really depends on what kind of trust, how it is distributed, and what it is being used to accomplish. Trust is often abused in exploitative labour relations, and may result in the tolerance of offences against environmental regulations.

Woolcock argues that the possibility of having too much of particular kinds of social capital (within which he includes trust) produces distinct developmental dilemmas. At the grass-roots level, when there is too much social capital invested in integrated communities, so that it limits the construction of linkages outside the community, this may produce the equivalent of 'amoral familism'. At the macro level, integration between state and society without bureaucratic integrity can result in corruption and predatory states, while coherent state organizations that lack linkages with society may produce inefficient and ineffective programmes. What provides the best developmental contexts, he suggests, are community level forms of integration that encourage and foster extra-community linkages, and state processes that generate accountable and flexible bureaucratic organizations that have non-corrupt linkages with society for the transmission of information and influence (Woolcock, 1998).

The crucial question, of course, is how these combinations can be accomplished. Woolcock identifies seven conditions that reduce a community's prospects for achieving sustainable and equitable economic development. Interestingly, at least three of these apply strongly to the People's Republic of China, while several other conditions apply to a certain degree. The three that most clearly fit China are: 'poverty is endemic, unchecked by social safety nets, and difficult to escape through stable employment'; 'uniform laws are weak, unjust, flaunted, or indiscriminately enforced'; and 'polities are not freely and fairly elected or voters have few serious electoral choices' (Woolcock, 1998:182). Despite this, China as a whole and particularly areas like the Pearl River Delta have achieved economic growth rates among the highest ever recorded.

I am not suggesting that Woolcock is wrong in identifying these conditions as posing obstacles to development. My argument instead is that there are other ways to accomplish the needed balances between community integration/linkage and state coherence/responsiveness. In the case of China, institutional and legal weaknesses have been compensated through reliance on skilled use of interpersonal relationships. The idioms and practices of social interaction provide a variety of ways in which inappropriate rules and institutions can be side-stepped, and community obligations can be kept from undermining the ability to build outside linkages and take advantage of new opportunities. Both the literature on local corporatism in China (see, for example: Walder, 1995 and Oi, 1989) and that on overseas Chinese invested enterprises provide ample evidence of the ways in which cultural forms and expectations make 'inequality among brothers' (to allude to the important analysis of Rubie Watson in another context) (Watson, 1985) both feasible and apparently sustainable. One of the crucial contributions of economic culture to development, then, is the way in which it can reduce contradictions, and allow people to do one thing while saying another. Such collusive lying seems to be particularly necessary in a context like China's where the contradictions between relying on market and capitalist mechanisms to develop socialism are so stark and apparently unpromising as a route to modernization.[8]

In the case of Hong Kong investment in China, particularly during the first decade after the adoption of the open door policy in 1978, the rules and conventions observed in the British colony were quite starkly different from those prevailing in the People's Republic. Jin and Haynes suggest that China's reforms have operated at the edge of order and chaos, a potentially disastrous situation which has nevertheless managed to produce remarkable results (Jin and Haynes, 1997). When chaotic conditions are managed skilfully, they can be turned from threat to risky opportunity (Smart, 1998). My argument is that elements of culture shared by overseas investors and local counterparts have been crucial resources in making it possible not just to cope with these circumstances, but often to produce rapid increases in local prosperity.

The outcomes of such encounters between different ways of doing things matter a great deal. Brokerage across chaotic border conditions has the potential to expand prosperity, sometimes dramatically as in the ethnic Chinese contribution to China's rapid growth in the last 18 years. But it also can serve to destabilize local situations, and in some circumstances it can produce very broad instabilities, as the history of colonialism indicates. With regard to *qiaoxiang* ties, Johnson and Woon argue that in the western Pearl River Delta, households with close relatives overseas are less committed to local economic development because they expect to leave sooner or later, leading to a variety of unproductive results (Johnson and Woon, 1997:49). Common understanding or interactional practices that allow those on opposite sides of a border to live with distinct interpretations of the situation can smooth out rough edges, and may thus reduce transaction costs, but it can also empower agents to manipulate the local system in detrimental ways.

RETHINKING ECONOMIC CULTURE

The influence of culture on economic practice has been receiving a great deal of attention, more than it has since modernization theory became academically unfashionable in the 1970s. But the newer theories of postmodernity are diverse and internally divided. At one pole, there are theorists like David Harvey, Allen Scott and Manuel Castells who see postmodernism as essentially hypermodernism, a speeding up of some of the tendencies of capitalism which had been tamed by the modes of social and economic regulation constructed in the Fordist regime of accumulation. The emerging post-Fordist regime simply releases the creative destruction of capitalist profit-seeking in new ways that create niches for more flexible ways of producing goods and services. Dirlik notes that changes in the international division of labour seem to favour subcontracting and network-type organizational structures, so that:

'it seems reasonable that Chinese who have been prominent all along in small business in Southeast Asia, and who have retained network-relations of one kind or another over the years, should be particularly well-placed to take advantage of the new division of labour in production.' (Dirlik, 1997:310)

At the other pole, there are more radical postmodernists who take the shift away from a unilineal view of development that leads either to convergence or stagnation farther still. They argue for the feasibility of a wide range of economic possibilities, a strong example of this being found in Gudeman's book *Economics as Cultures* (1986), which argues that almost any kind of economic model can work, as long as the people concerned believe in it.

Older versions of modernization theory, harbouring as they did a 'thinly-veiled disdain for traditional societies', primarily saw culture as representing obstacles to technical rationality which would be superseded as systems converged (Woolcock, 1998:153). It is now more common to acknowledge the multiplicity of organizational outcomes and possibilities. Neo-modernizationists (such as Robert Putnam and Francis Fukuyama) often accept the distinctiveness and viability of some other paths to development (most commonly the Japanese approach). However, while there may be more than one way to become prosperous, there are still some common problems that have to be dealt with: such as encouraging longer-term investment patterns rather than short-term rent-seeking (which generates profits while reducing overall efficiency). Fukuyama accounts for varying degrees of economic success through reference to the quantity of social capital and trust that are found in different societies. David Landes draws extensively on cultural factors to explain why some countries are rich while others are poor. For him, more than for Fukuyama, the values that truly count - such as hard work, thrift, honesty, patience and tenacity - can be cultivated by latecomers if they so desire (Landes, 1997). The key variable in neo-modernizationist analyses is social capital ('the information, trust, and norms of reciprocity inhering in one's social networks'), without which 'seemingly obvious opportunities for mutually beneficial collective action are squandered' (Woolcock, 1998:153). While many traditional practices may hinder effective development, the way in which social capital can foster co-operation in a particular context will, necessarily, be conditioned by cultural values and institutions.

The neo-modernizationist approach to the role of culture in the contemporary world economy, then, is to see it as something that inhibits or facilitates development. If development is to result, certain universal problems have to be resolved, and there are only a limited number of ways in which the solutions can be found. Some apparent successes may simply be piling up problems that will have to be dealt with later. Convergence towards the Euro-American model may not be absolute, but a considerable degree of it seems likely, particularly as business becomes more and more transnational in nature. However, global capitalism itself is thought by many to be taking new paths of development that are leading to more, rather than less, diversity. A very influential type of analysis identifies the economic dimensions of the postmodern era as involving a shift from Fordist to post-Fordist (or flexible) regimes of accumulation (Harvey, 1989). Whereas the Fordist regime combined mass production with increased capacity for consumption by workers within bounded economies, post-Fordism involves heightened capital mobility and increased demands for flexibility among local labour forces and governments if they are to attract and retain capital. Localities and nations increasingly compete among themselves for scarce capital and jobs, or to generate entrepreneurial workforces to create their own economic opportunities.

A common theme in this literature asserts the increased 'importance of *local histories* and specific *cultural contexts* as the key elements behind this new reorganisation of capitalist social relations' (Narotzky, 1997:204; emphasis in original). In studies of the prototypical examples of the Third Italy[9] and Japan, analysts have stressed both the benefits of giving ordinary workers greater control over the work process, and the importance of cultural contexts which provide the basic elements of trust and idioms of co-operation which make such models work.

Recent developments in evolutionary economics provide support for the idea that there may not be a single optimum solution for economic efficiency, and that instead there may be multiple stable equilibria (See Grabher and Stark, 1998). Furthermore path-dependent development (Stark, 1994) means that you might not easily be able to get to another solution from the place you are already at. Which organizational and institutional compromises are feasible and effective in a particular context may depend on social and cultural resources and expectations. We might be tempted to conclude that we can say little more than that we can identify a situation of 'path-dependent development' requiring different solutions building from local conditions, so that:

> 'where you end up depends on where you've been, and whatever optimality properties may be claimed for the equilibria are at most local rather than global.' (Bowles and Gintis, 1993:197)

One possible terminus of such an argument is Gudeman's conclusion that economically 'anything goes', as long as local actors are convinced of the viability of such arrangements. I would argue that we cannot go this far (see Smart, 1998, for details).

In essence, I believe that neo-modernizationist theory and certain approaches to postmodernity are not incompatible. Rather than a qualitative divide between the perspectives, there is often more of an empirical disagreement about the relative strength of convergence and viable difference. Post-Fordist analyses seem to have much more to offer in making sense of transnational development processes, since neo-modernizationists have tended to follow their predecessors in emphasizing the nation-state as the bounded unit of analysis. However, there are limitations here as well, since post-Fordists usually consider globalization of production from the viewpoint of theorizing the transformation of national economies, which retains its analytical primacy (Smart, 1998). The trend towards the study of global commodity chains (Gereffi, 1994) offers some advantages here, since it starts with empirical cases rather than assumptions about the relevant units of analysis. In dealing with issues as complex and incomplete as modernization, and the transition from modernity to postmodernity, there are many benefits accruing to a methodological approach that begins from concrete exchanges and relationships, rather than theoretical positions. Starting with the ethnography of particular transnational processes forces the analyst to consider whether the questions being asked are the right ones, and what might be going on that would not have been expected.

The most-sophisticated contemporary approaches to culture do not emphasize coherent sets of ideas which determine behaviour. Instead, they attend to improvisational bases for action that are 'created on the spot, but regulated because they are guided by previously learned patterns of associations; they are not improvised out of thin air' (Strauss and Quinn, 1994:287). Furthermore, improvisational responses to uncertain and changing conditions are neither linguistic nor purely cognitive; instead they are based on emotional responses to the circumstances and the various responses that are perceived as possibilities. Certain solutions to challenges may provoke visceral reactions that rule them out as 'unthinkable' even

176

after we have thought about them: eating the family dog when there is a shortage of cash to buy groceries, for example (Sahlins, 1976). Such approaches tend, though, to sideline issues of power in constituting what is thinkable.

Entrepreneurs and employees do not simply automatically enact standard routines, but nor do they approach challenges with a clean sheet of paper (Trice and Beyer, 1993:7). When new circumstances demand actions, a complex network of associations, tactics and past solutions present themselves, each in the context of associations with fears, desires and assumptions about how significant others would assess the various possibilities. But stopping at this cognitive level is inadequate. First, dominant ideas and powerful institutions constrain what can be easily thought. Second, the network of associations within the community, rather than inside the head, is often just as important. For example, Hamilton and Waters demonstrate how the Chinese in Thailand did not succeed in only one way: rather they responded to changing political and economic circumstances. Successful entrepreneurs from one period often could not effectively respond to new conditions. Indeed, new success stories emerged while others faded, partly because prior success had generated a set of alliances, networks and practices that made exploitation of the new opportunities more difficult. The result is that the history of the Chinese in Thailand is 'not one of economic or even ethnic continuity. Instead, it is a story of changes, of sudden transformations, of ethnic reconstructions, and of a succession of distinct groups of Chinese entrepreneurs' (Hamilton and Waters, 1997:279). An adequate model of economic culture must, therefore, be one that can help to illuminate these kinds of processes and outcomes.

In summary, I have argued that as long as culture is not reified, treated as homogenous, and seen as a active process related to both individual interests and hegemonic institutions, it can be seen as having had an influence on the developmental process. Its role becomes particularly apparent in situations like economic co-operation across borders, because reliance on institutions and laws is less viable. Instead, emphasis on common idioms and practices of interaction provide alternative ways to generate the understanding and trust that is crucial for effective co-operation. In these situations, though, the profound incongruities require a great deal of skill, tact, and knowledge of relevant etiquette in order to emphasize the commonalities, particularly common interests, and downplay the conflicts. As soon as we recognize the amount of skill involved in any kind of interaction, and magnify that in the light of border-crossing complexities, we realize that culture does indeed play a role in business practices. The question, of course, is how big that role is, and how relevant it is in comparison to, for example, the policies and practices of govern-mental decision-makers, or the dynamics of the capitalist world-economy.

Economic culture does not determine outcomes. Instead, it is important because it can provide resources that allow people to co-operate (among other things) despite stark divergences in the rules and conventions across national and social boundaries. Of course, such resources can also be used for numerous other purposes. Even conflict and violence relies on co-operation at other levels. But I am not dealing in this chapter with a single system within which rules and resources are uniformly measured and evaluated. Instead, cross-border economic relationships involve situations where the rules vary on each side of the border, and getting things done requires developing ways to deal with the incompatibilities. Jin and Haynes' insightful treatment of the process of economic reform in China as producing fruitful responses to a mixture of order and chaos provides an apt image for this situation (Jin and Haynes, 1997). While the way things are done within your own society or context can be seen as reasonably orderly and predictable, the practices across a boundary of radical disjuncture seem chaotic and uncontrollable. As well, the resources that each agent brings to the deal are differentially evaluated in the distinct social and economic systems.

Culture, rather than fixed and determined or determinant, needs to be seen as flexible and indeterminate, always subject to reinterpretation. And this 'fuzziness' has made it invaluable in the uncertainties and contradictions of doing capitalist business in a socialist society. Whether or not those advantages will be preserved as the ground-rules are routinized is uncertain, but there is certainly considerable evidence that even in the most developed heartlands of advanced capitalism, social capital, routines and handshake deals are still important components of getting things done. As Chinese and other capitalists come to co-operate ever more intensively, finding ways to productively co-operate across the edges of chaotic yet ordered cultural differences (within as well as across language groups) should become ever more profitable. What such profits will buy for the world of the future remains to be seen.

Economic culture does not by itself explain much of anything. What does, then, explain Chinese business success? This is obviously a large and complex question. Part of the answer, though, lies in recognizing the extent of individual failure (Nonini, 1997). The structure of the contemporary world economy provides a set of opportunities for groups organized as the Chinese tend to be, and while on average the overseas Chinese have been more successful in capitalizing on these opportunities than many other citizens of lesser developed countries, most individuals still earn wages rather than run companies.

CONCLUDING REMARKS

Boundaries have always simultaneously generated risk and potential profit, and those who can manage the risk effectively have been able to profit handsomely from their brokerage or arbitrage across those borders. But getting things done across borders requires tact, and this is certainly the case in the People's Republic of China. Tact, of course, is embedded in expectations about interactional proprieties and etiquette, which must be accomplished, not just submitted to as cultural determinism[10] would suggest. When tact and agreement are absent or fail, brokerage across borders can have less positive outcomes, including failed endeavours; pariah status for the brokers; corrupt and illegal activities; and reliance on coercion, as in colonialism. Hong Kong entrepreneurs who pioneered foreign investment in China did not always succeed, but they had a variety of symbolic, social and cultural resources that made operating across boundaries somewhat less risky, and helped to legitimize the conduct of capitalist practices within a socialist polity. Hong Kong and Macao residents, for example, were not 'foreigners' but *tong bao* - compatriots - and could thus contribute to national modernization in a way that was less threatening than assistance from capitalists who were also non-Chinese, who were not part of an imagined cultural/racial us (Smart, 1998). A critical point to keep in mind is that economic cultures are not coterminous with national economies, just as cultures generally are not coherent with nation-states (Keesing, 1994:303). With globalization and postmodernity, national economies are becoming more diffused and deterritorialized. The novelty of this tendency should not be exaggerated: for diaspora Chinese (as for some other groups such as South Asians in Africa or Jews in prewar Eastern Europe (see Chirot, 1997)), economic activity has for centuries involved transnational networks that cut across national borders.

The Hong Kong entrepreneurs who set up small and medium factories in China are capitalists, but as capitalists *per se* they have relatively few advantages over large transnational conglomerates. The advantages that they have are a higher willingness to accept the gamble of risky profits, and what and who they know in China. Within China, their advantages are partially access to knowledge about the global marketplace, and the techniques necessary to produce goods that can achieve a share of that market. But as subcontractors, this gives them no advantage over the large corporations that they subcontract for. What makes them easier to deal with is their willingness to rely on what higher officials 'would not oppose rather than what they would allow' (Hsing, 1997:150), and secondly the ability to portray themselves as patriotic Chinese rather than just as capitalists.

In this chapter, I have asked whether economic culture can be said to have made contributions to this surprisingly successful integration of China into the world economy. In doing so, I tried to sharpen the notoriously blunt edge of cultural explanations of economic performance, by drawing on important work by social economists of a variety of disciplines. My basic answer to the question of what role culture plays in overseas Chinese investment in their *qiaoxiang* is that cultural forms of interaction shared by overseas investors and local counterparts have been crucial resources in making it possible not just to cope with the challenges of cross-border economic co-operation, but often to produce rapid increases in local prosperity. Despite the radical differences between the ways things get done on the two sides of the border, entrepreneurs on both sides have found ways to overcome the difficulties and meet the challenges. Rather than simply relying on the transnationalization of business practices through rapidly transforming China's official rules and policies, overseas Chinese have simultaneously utilized social connections and common cultural understandings to deal with the dilemmas and contradictions that have presented themselves.

BIBLIOGRAPHY

Bailey, F.G.
1991   *The Prevalence of Deceit*. Ithaca: Cornell University Press
Blim, M.
1997   'Can NOT-Capitalism Lie at the End of History?', *Critique of Anthropology* 17(4), pp. 351-63
Bowles, S. and H. Gintis
1993   'The Revenge of Homo Economicus: Contested Exchange and the Revival of Political Economy', *Journal of Economic Perspectives* 7(1), pp. 165-222
Burawoy, M. and E.O. Wright
1990   'Coercion and Consent in Contested Exchange', *Politics and Society* 18(2), pp. 251-66
Chirot, D.
1997   'Conflicting Identities and the Dangers of Communalism', in: Daniel Chirot and Anthony Reid (eds) *Essential Outsiders: Chinese and Jews in the Modern Transformation of Southeast Asia and Central Europe*. Seattle: University of Washington Press, pp. 3-32
Dirlik, Arif
1997   'Critical Reflections on "Chinese Capitalism" as Paradigm', *Identities* 3(3), pp. 303-30
Fitzgerald, John

1996   'Autonomy and Growth in China: County Experience in Guangdong Province', *Journal of Contemporary China* 5(11), pp. 7-22

Fukuyama, Francis
1995   *Trust: The Social Virtues and the Creation of Prosperity.* New York: The Free Press

Gambetta, Diego
1988   'Can we Trust Trust?', in: D. Gambetta (ed.) *Trust: Making and Breaking Cooperative Relations.* Oxford: Basil Blackwell, pp. 213-37

Gates, Hill
1996   *China's Motor: A Thousand Years of Petty Capitalism.* Ithaca: Cornell University Press

Gereffi, Gary
1994   'The Organization of Buyer-Driven Global Commodity Chains: How U.S. Retailers Shape Overseas Production Networks', in: G. Gereffi and M. Korzeniewicz (eds) *Commodity Chains and Global Capitalism.* Westport: Greenwood Press, pp. 95-122

Good, David
1988   'Individual, Interpersonal Relations, and Trust', in: Diego Gambetta (ed.) *Trust: Making and Breaking Cooperative Relations.* Oxford: Basil Blackwell, pp. 31-48

Grabher, Gernot and David Stark
1998   Organising Diversity: Evolutionary Theory, Network Analysis and Post-Socialism', in: John Pickles and Adrian Smith (eds) *Theorizing Transition: The Political Economy of Post-Communist Transformations.* London: Routledge, pp. 54-75

Granovetter, Mark
1990   'The Old and the New Economic Sociology', in: R. Friedland and A. Robertson (eds) *Beyond the Marketplace.* New York: Aldine de Gruyter

Greenhalgh, Susan
1994   'De-Orientalizing the Chinese Family Firm', *American Ethnologist* 21(4), pp. 746-75

Gudeman, Stephen
1986   *Economics as Cultures: Models and Metaphors of Livelihood.* London: Routledge and Kegan Paul

Hamilton, Gary G. and Tony Waters
1997   'Ethnicity and Capitalist Development. The Changing Role of the Chinese in Thailand', in: Daniel Chirot and Anthony Reid (eds) *Essential Outsiders: Chinese and Jews in the Modern Transformation of Southeast Asia and Central Europe.* Seattle:

University of Washington Press, pp. 258-84

Hamilton, Gary G. and Nicole W. Biggart
1992   'Market, Culture and Authority: A Comparative Analysis of Management and Organization in the Far East', in: Mark Granovetter and Richard Swedberg (eds) *The Sociology of Economic Life*. Boulder: Westview Press, pp. 181-221

Harvey, David
1989   *The Condition of Postmodernity*. Oxford: Blackwell

Hodder, Rupert
1996   *Merchant Princes of the East: Cultural Delusions, Economic Success and the Overseas Chinese in Southeast Asia*. New York: John Wiley & Sons

Hsing, You-tien
1997   'Building Guanxi Across the Straits: Taiwanese Capital and Local Chinese Bureaucrats', in: Aihwa Ong and Donald Nonini (eds) *Ungrounded Empires: The Cultural Politics of Modern Chinese Transnationalism*. New York: Routledge, pp. 143-64

Huntington, Samuel P.
1993   'The Clash of Civilizations?', *Foreign Affairs* 72(3), pp. 22-49

Jin, Dengjian and Kingsley E. Haynes
1997   'Economic Transition at the Edge of Order and Chaos: China's Dualism and Leading Sectoral Approach', *Journal of Economic Issues* 31(1), pp. 79-101

Johnson, Graham E. and Woon, Yuen-fong
1997   'The Response to Rural Reform in an Overseas Chinese Area: Examples from Two Localities in the Western Pearl River Delta Region, South China', *Modern Asian Studies* 31(1), pp. 31-59

Jones, Carol A.G.
1994   'Capitalism, Globalization and Rule of Law: An Alternative Trajectory of Legal Change in China', *Social and Legal Studies* 3(2), pp. 195-221

Keesing, Roger H.
1994   'Theories of Culture Revisited', in: Robert Borofsky (ed.) *Assessing Cultural Anthropology*. New York: McGraw-Hill, pp. 301-10

Kipnis, Andrew B.
1997   *Producing Guanxi: Sentiment, Self, and Subculture in a North China Village*. Durham: Duke University Press

Landes, David S.
1997   *The Wealth and Poverty of Nations*. New York: W.W. Norton and Company

Lee, Ching Kwan

1997 'Factory Regimes of Chinese Capitalism: Different Cultural Logics in Labor Control', in: Aihwa Ong and Donald Nonini (eds) *Ungrounded Empires:The Cultural Politics of Modern Chinese Transnationalism*. New York: Routledge, pp. 115-42

Lin, George C.S.
1997 *Red Capitalism in South China*. Vancouver: University of British Columbia Press

Menning, Garrett
1997 'Trust, Entrepreneurship and Development in Surat City, India', *Ethnos* 62(1-2), pp. 59-90

Merry, Sally Engle
1992 'Anthropology, Law, and Transnational Processes', *Annual Reviews in Anthropology* 21, pp. 357-79

Narotzky, Susan
1997 *New Directions in Economic Anthropology*. London: Pluto Press

Nonini, Donald M.
1993 'On the Outs on the Rim: An Ethnographic Grounding of the 'Asia Pacific' Imaginary', in: Arif Dirlik (ed.) *What it is a Rim? Critical Perspectives on the Asia Pacific Idea*. Boulder: Westview, pp. 29-50
1997 'Shifting Identities, Positioned Imaginaries: Transnational Traversals and Reversals by Malaysian Chinese', in: Aihwa Ong and Donald Nonini (eds) *Ungrounded Empires: The Cultural Politics of Modern Chinese Transnationalism*. New York: Routledge, pp. 203-27

Oi, Jean
1989 *State and Peasant in Contemporary China*. Berkeley: University of California Press

Ong, Aihwa
1997 'A Momentary Glow of Fraternity: Narratives of Chinese Nationalism and Capitalism', *Identities* 3(3), pp. 331-66

Pasternak, Burton
1983 *Guests in the Dragon*. New York: Columbia University Press

Pearson, Margaret M.
1991 *Joint Ventures in the People's Republic of China*. Princeton: Princeton University Press

Redding, S. Gordon
1990 *The Spirit of Chinese Capitalism*. Berlin: De Gruyter

Sahlins, Marshall
1976 *Culture and Practical Reason*. Chicago: University of Chicago Press

Smart, Alan

1998   'Economic Transformation in China: Property Regimes and Social Relations', in: A. Smith and J. Pickles (eds) *Theorizing Transition in Eastern Europe*. London: Routledge, pp. 428-49

Smart, Alan and Josephine Smart
1998   'Transnational Social Networks and Negotiated Identities in Interactions between Hong Kong and China', in: M.P. Smith and L.E. Guarnizo (eds) *Transnationalism from Below: Comparative Urban and Community Research* V. 6. New Brunswick: Transaction Publishers, pp. 103-29

Smart, Josephine and Alan Smart
1993   'Obligation and Control: Employment of Kin in Capitalist Labour Management in China', *Critique of Anthropology* 13(1), pp. 7-31

Stark, David
1994   'Path Dependence and Privatization Strategies in East Central Europe', in: J. Kovacs (ed.) *Transition to Capitalism?*. New Brunswick: Transaction Publishers, pp. 63-100

Strauss, Claudia and Naomi Quinn
1994   'A Cognitive/Cultural Anthropology', in: Robert Borofsky (ed.) *Assessing Cultural Anthropology*. New York: McGraw-Hill, pp. 284-97

Thrift, Nigel and Kris Olds
1996   'Refiguring the Economic in Economic Geography', *Progress in Human Geography* 20(3), pp. 311-37

Trice, Harrison M. and Janice M. Beyer
1993   *The Cultures of Work Organizations*. Englewood Cliffs: Prentice Hall

Tyler, Tom R. and Roderick Kramer
1996   'Whither Trust?', in: R. Kramer and T. Tyler (eds) *Trust in Organizations*. Thousand Oaks: Sage, pp. 1-15

Walder, Andrew
1995   'Local Governments as Industrial Firms: An Organizational Analysis of China's Transitional Economy', *American Journal of Sociology* 101(2), pp. 263-301

Watson, Rubie S.
1985   *Inequality Among Brothers: Class and Kinship in South China*. Cambridge: Cambridge University Press

Woolcock, Michael
1998   Social Capital and Economic Development: Toward a Theoretical Synthesis and Policy Framework', *Theory and Society* 27, pp. 151-208

Yan, Yunxiang
1996   *The Flow of Gifts: Reciprocity and Social Networks in a Chinese*

Village. Stanford: Stanford University Press

Yeung, Henry W.C.

1994   'Hong Kong Firms in the ASEAN Region: Transnational
        Corporations and Foreign Direct Investment', *Environment and
        Planning* A 26:1931-1956

1998   *Transnational Corporations and Business Networks*. London:
        Routledge

Notes

1. This paper has benefited from the advice and assistance of a large
   number of people. Funding has been received from the University of
   Calgary Research Grants Committee. Ideas contained in this paper have
   been discussed with Michael Blim, Tang Wing-Shing, George Lin,
   Henry Yeung, Don Nonini, Kris Olds, a variety of students, and
   particularly with Josephine Smart. My thanks also for the close editorial
   oversight of Leo Douw, Cen Huang and Michael Godley. But most of
   all, my gratitude goes to those who have put up with my pestering
   questions in the field.
2. The English terms used to refer to Chinese residing outside China are
   politically contested, as discussed in the Introduction. 'Ethnic Chinese
   residing outside the People's Republic of China' is the least objectionable
   of the various possibilities, but is rather awkward for regular usage.
   'Overseas Chinese' is frequently used to include both *huaqiao* (Chinese
   citizens living abroad), *huaren* (ethnic Chinese), and *tongbao*
   (compatriots, generally referring to Chinese residents of Hong Kong,
   Macao and Taiwan). When I refer in this chapter to 'overseas Chinese' I
   am using it in this inclusive sense.
3. While their approach is quite critical of narrow, cultural determinist,
   explanations, it does leave poorly explained the question of why the
   Chinese have shown so much more flexibility than many other ethnic
   groups - a weakness they acknowledge.
4. I was trained in a British-influenced social anthropological tradition in
   which reference to culture was a sign of mental or moral weakness, and
   emphasis on social relations and structure the preferred analytical mode. I
   do not mention this simply because of the postmodern fashion of
   declaring one's position and reflexively analysing its impact on the
   analyses offered. In this case, making my starting point clear helps to
   explain the discomfort with which I have in accepting the idea of cultural
   influence on business practice in South China and elsewhere.
5. It would be foolish to argue that some vague entity such as 'Chinese
   culture' can explain the present situation all by itself. However, it is less

clear that skilled [reinterpretation and] mobilization of Chinese practices of interaction and forms of discourse cannot have played a role in these accomplishments. Dirlik suggests that the widespread interest in Chinese capitalism is 'an integral aspect of the discourse on Global Capitalism' or flexible production, and that this 'Confucian' alternative may be 'little more than an invention of a new post-socialist post-revolutionary discourse on capitalism' (1997:304). From this perspective, 'rather than a cause of Chinese Capitalism, what have come to be identified as Chinese characteristics may be the effect of the development of a capitalism that has its sources elsewhere, in the global economy' (pp. 304).

6. The two are not necessarily the same: inconsistent practices may be compatible, or even complementary. Consistent practices may lead to competition rather than co-operation. Assessing what kind of 'fit' there may be between dissimilar practices across a boundary cannot be reduced to a formula. What fits now may produce conflict later, so interpretation must be provided for particular instances and circumstances.

7. The following section is a condensed and revised version of a longer account in Smart and Smart 1993.

8. For more analysis of how this was accomplished, see Smart and Smart, 1998.

9. The Third Italy is a traditional region of central Italy which has in recent decades prospered greatly through clustering of small enterprises producing similar products.

10. For an elaborate inquisition against cultural determinism in treatments of the overseas Chinese, see Hodder (1996). While I agree with many of his arguments against cultural determinism, he seems a bit too eager to discover it in everyone else but himself. Applied as rigorously as he does, I doubt that he succeeds in avoiding being culturally determinist himself.

OVERSEAS CHINESE ENTREPRENEURS: CULTURAL NORMS AS RESOURCES AND CONSTRAINTS[1]

ISABELLE THIREAU AND HUA LINSHAN

The analysis of the cultivation of *qiaoxiang* ties, including lineage, by overseas-Chinese entrepreneurs, usually mobilizes two contradictory approaches: one that we may call substantivist or culturalist, and the other one instrumentalist. Although many stimulating studies belong to the first category (see, for example, Redding, 1990), they tend to reify culture and describe its influence on economic practices in a more or less deterministic way. Cultural norms and practices are assigned too much homogeneity, while the part played by individuals and groups in the selection and interpretation of the cultural resources available, or in the new usage made of given cultural arrangements for economic purposes, is usually ignored. On the other hand, a variety of authors (e.g. Dirlik, 1996) have convincingly demonstrated the instrumental use made of the various narratives of Chinese capitalism while putting aside the question of how overseas entrepreneurs and their counterparts effectively co-operate and how, in order to do so, they eventually negotiate the common meaning assigned to given principles and forms in order to legitimate their interests and actions. Another approach is developed here, stressing the part played by cultural forms as resources and constraints for social actors. Such a perspective follows the important assertion made by Anthony Giddens, namely that structures simultaneously constrain and enable social agents. But the second classical sociological insight we would like to emphasize here, is that cultural resources are not only reproduced but also transformed in the process of interaction and negotiation between social actors. To look for structural emergence and transformation, we should therefore look at social agents' interaction, and the eventual institutionalization process of its outcome. More pointedly, to analyse the common practices eventually developed by overseas Chinese and their counterparts on the mainland, we should carefully observe the disagreements arising, as well as the agreements, reached by both parties in the process of their co-operation.[2]

INTRODUCTION: THE ISSUE OF 'CULTURAL REVIVAL'

A few remarks may be necessary regarding the study of cultural practices today in China, including the ongoing debate about 'cultural revival' in order to delineate more clearly the broad perspective in which the cultural aspects of present-day transnationalization of ethnic Chinese business activities may be discussed. As a matter of fact, since, during the 1980s, economic reforms were launched in China, attention has been paid by various studies to the meaning of the revival of given traditional practices and norms, a revival coinciding with the reforms (Wolf, 1996; Siu, 1989). The extent of continuities versus discontinuities in the practices performed today, as compared with the pre-1949 period, has often been discussed, as well as the margin of freedom enjoyed by the population in this realm. The analysis of such a cultural revival, or more exactly, the analysis of present continuities and discontinuities in China with different past temporal sequences, should be clearly distinguished from another, related field of enquiry to be touched upon below: the study of what has been qualified as Chinese capitalism, a paradigm which stresses the cultural homogeneity between Chinese business communities all over the world.

The first-mentioned perspective, on cultural revival, envisages to analyse the changes induced by the reforms launched at the end of the 1970s in the People's Republic of China, after decades during which long-standing cultural practices were officially banned and had apparently disappeared. Studies that can be included in this broad category vary of course. Some authors are more inclined to look for and explain current continuities with the past. As far as we are concerned, our objective pursued in a previous project (see below) was to observe the emergence of new norms in the countryside and analyse how society members reinterpret the different historical sequences they went through and make specific uses of the social forms and arrangements stemming from these various pasts. The focus was therefore on the experience of time in a specific territory having undergone successive ruptures, and on the way present social norms emerge out of the new use of arrangements linked to different past temporal sequences.

Moreover, it should be pointed out that the political and social dimensions of the reforms rather than their economic consequences seem to be at the origin of the use of all kinds of former cultural practices and ideologies. In other words, the mobilization of pre-1949 forms in China (institutions, practices, beliefs) is not primarily the result of market liberalization. As a matter of fact, the reforms promoted have had far-reaching social and political consequences in the countryside before their economic effects could be felt. The redistribution of land and other means of production to the household, the disappearance of the People's Communes, and the acknowledgment of private enterprises have indeed contributed to the shared feeling that the authorities acknowledged some of the wrong choices made during the collectivization era. A rather explicit if not official re-evaluation of the 1949 rupture followed, that was further encouraged by official measures amounting to a reversal of past decisions such as the rehabilitation campaign or the movement, aiming, in southern provinces, at giving back to overseas Chinese some of their past properties.[3] The transformations implemented during what Chinese authorities have called economic reforms while they clearly go beyond the economic realm have therefore assigned in China a new legitimacy to pre-1949 cultural resources and social norms, whose mobilization to justify specific behaviours was further supported by the decreasing direct interference of the State in many social and economic exchanges.[4] To state only one example, in many villages, pre-1949 property rights on land, houses, and ancestors' temples were claimed by some inhabitants to have regained some legitimacy just after the reforms, in a situation where collective property still prevailed and the market economy was far from having any local influence. Cultural resources anchored in the pre-1949 period were therefore more explicitly than before used in many localities to answer old needs or to find acceptable solutions for many of the situations arising out of the reforms. But we should add at once that they were in the same process confronted to and often transformed by resources anchored in the three following decades, a period that definitely cannot be qualified as an interregnum. The forms and rules stemming from this later period were for instance accommodated with by necessity if they were still supported by existing institutions. They were sometimes part and parcel of the present creation of new norms, following the consideration that it would be unfair to deprive people of rights assigned to them during a certain period in the past. But they were also sometimes mobilized as legitimate principles governing social relationships.

Finally, the new expression of traditional cultural practices and ideologies was further supported by some of the economic dimensions of the reforms: the rise of new types of economic exchanges between individuals and groups thanks to the development of a more market-oriented economy, a situation for which pre-1949 experience could provide some resources, and the revival in some geographical areas of the links established between overseas Chinese communities and their relatives in China. As a matter of fact, one of the outcomes of the new development of *qiaoxiang* ties has been to provide financial funding for given institutions and rituals whose legitimacy is anchored in the past. More importantly for our present purpose, the establishment of successful economic ties, and among them, of transnational exchanges, relies on the specific and flexible use of given traditional principles and behavioural patterns to assess ethnic identity and to particularize relationships as a way to cope with all kinds of economic and political uncertainties. Nonetheless, it is important to distinguish between the more general process by which past resources are used today in China to understand present situations and elaborate the correct way to behave, and the more specific and somehow limited influence of the increased globalization of ethnic Chinese business on the expression of given cultural practices and ideologies.

The main point concerns the need to distinguish between two different processes: one having a temporal dimension - the process through which individuals and groups having shared the same historical experience work out the new rules deemed necessary to live together and co-operate, and do so by using the resources offered by different temporal sequences - and the second one having a spatial dimension: the confrontation of members of the same ethnic group who have nonetheless been placed in different contexts and may therefore assign different meanings to the same cultural practices. If these two processes are often confused, it is because of the reification and essentialization process of culture. In other words, it is because the historicity of cultural forms tends to be disregarded.

THE HISTORICITY OF CULTURAL PRACTICES

We would like to stress the need to take into account the influence of a specific historical and social context on the transformation of cultural forms. This will be done by showing how given practices, often said to be important components of Chinese economic culture - namely the mobilization of lineage and kinship ties - may be objects of disagreements today between individuals and groups in China. We borrow here some data from a previous research project concerned with observing the expression of disagreements in the Chinese countryside, the eventual reaching of agreements and the consecutive institutionalization process of new norms and practices. The fieldwork was done by the authors in four localities of Anhui (Nanling county) and Guangdong (Taishan, Nanhai and Panyu counties) provinces since 1993.[5]

Lineages such as those found during a certain historical period in Guangdong and Fujian provinces, that is localized patrilineal descent groups characterized by a certain degree of ritual unity in the performance of ancestors' cult, and by the possession of corporate property linked to a given ancestor temple, have been the object of many studies.[6] Lineages, and their internal divisions called lineage segments - which establish distinctions among the members of one single lineage and put them in very different positions as far as competition for local resources and protection from all kinds of uncertainties are concerned - were a very important component of individuals' identity and of social organization before 1949 in southeastern China. However, even in that specific geographical area, the effective use made of lineage institutions and its norms varies according to different periods. This is not to say that the basic principles of the lineage have been altered, such as descendant from a common ancestor or the importance of ritual unity in performing the ancestor's cult. Whatever the period under study, these features contribute to delineate relevant social groups and to legitimate the values regulating them (both social equality and inequality for instance are legitimated by the relationship established within the lineage between ancestors and their living descendants).[7] Nonetheless, behind apparent institutional continuities, an ongoing process of redefinition of the norms governing the lineage and the forms it should adopt can be observed.

The use made of institutions and norms may vary indeed according to different periods.[8] It may also vary according to different individuals. Members of the society who do not enjoy the same social position, who have not gone through the same historical experiences, or who have not faced them at the same stage in their life-course, would interpret and use lineage norms differently. In China, the historical ruptures of the last decades, the banning of lineages, the establishment of other norms and institutions cannot but have affected the type of resource represented today by the lineage norms and obligations for different individuals. According to their past experience and to their present situation, they may even rely today on institutions and norms other than kinship or the lineage to develop social exchanges, thus enlarging their choices and their opportunity for negotiating lineage rules. As a consequence, the recognition of lineage norms and their effective use by social actors are often marred today in China by uncertainty and unpredictability, illustrating the diversity of positions adopted and the need for negotiation to reach a common understanding.

As a matter of fact, during our previous research project, we collected many cases of disputes arising in the countryside out of conflicting perceptions of the importance and of the meaning of lineage and kinship obligations. A few examples will briefly illustrate this point. The first one concerns the present diversity of norms, influencing the definition of 'correct' local practices. In 1986, Hua Linshan came back to Ping'an after twelve years spent abroad. Quickly upon his arrival, the lineage elders asked him to organize a village banquet to announce his return. A long discussion then followed concerning the list of guests, with one group of people advocating to follow the traditional rule and invite all members of his own lineage segment plus one member per household for the other three segments; another group arguing that he should invite all the members of the production team he had belonged to when he had been living in the village, from 1969 to 1974, when lineage segments were ignored, and one member per household for the other team; and a last group voicing the opinion that Hua, having spent such a long time in a Western country, should follow Western principles and simply invite those members he liked most. In this type of case, compromises are usually found in which the closeness of social proximity plays a paramount role. Answers seem once more to differ according to the individuals concerned. For instance, a dispute arose one day between one of Ping'an's inhabitants, Ban Niao, and a member of his lineage segment, A Liu. The latter not only was a local official at the market-town, but had also created his own construction team. When Ban Niao decided to build a new house, he requested the services of a member of another lineage segment, also head of a construction team. Later criticized by A Liu for having given priority to a distant relative rather than to a close one, Ban Niao explained:

'Between a member of the lineage and a non-member, I would not have hesitated. But within the village, it is much more difficult for me to make a choice. You and I are from the same segment, that's true, but I tell you, during my most difficult time, I belonged to the same production team with A Liu, and he helped me whenever I needed him. I actually owe more to him than I owe to you. But you should not be so angry for such a small issue, after all we are all called Mai! ...' (Ping'an, June 1997).

It follows that, instead of speaking about a revival, and analysing continuities and discontinuities using the concept of inheritance from previous periods, it seems more relevant to adopt what the French historian B. Lepetit (1995) qualified as a 'regressive' approach and to try to understand how current needs, and among them the new needs born out of the reforms, are met today by redefining or applying in a new way resources coming from the past, a past which includes the pre-1949 period as well as the following decades. Such a perspective takes the present as its point of departure and looks at what elements of the past are being chosen, and what meaning is assigned to them.

This discussion has another important implication, it seems to us, more closely linked to the analysis of the revival of *qiaoxiang* ties. If disputes arise today in the Chinese countryside, between persons who nonetheless share the same historical experience, regarding the use and the meaning assigned to different cultural practices, then it is even more difficult to posit a high degree of cultural homogeneity between overseas Chinese and their counterparts in China. In other words, if the social and economic context matters, as we tried to show, social exchanges between members of a given overseas Chinese community, between members of spatially distinct overseas communities, and between overseas Chinese and their relatives or partners living in China, should not be assumed to rely on the use of the same rules and principles, that is, on an automatically shared understanding of the institutions - and among them, of the traditional institutions - mobilized. Both consistencies and inconsistencies should be the focus of our attention, and the way eventual differences are overcome in the process of interaction should be further stressed as playing a fundamental part in the emergence of new cultural forms. One example may suffice to illustrate this. An overseas Chinese, Xiegen, also member of the lineage Mai, asked one of his kinsmen, Douwen, to build his new house. A few weeks after having settled a final price according to the use of specific materials, Douwen offered his relative to use a better quality of some of the materials, a proposal that was quickly agreed upon by the future owner. Xiegen at that time made the following comment:

'Douwen wants to show me that he knows how to behave. He does not want to treat me like an ordinary client, like someone who would not be his relative. So he is using better materials, by thus making a smaller profit, to acknowledge the special ties existing between us ...' (Ping'an, October 1997).

A few months later, when the house was built, a row happened between the two men, the price asked by Douwen - who actually followed strict market rules - being much higher than the initial one, on the grounds that the materials used were much better.

As a further consequence, the study of transnational linkages and, among them, of the economic exchanges between China and members of the emigrant community, can be stimulated by, but cannot borrow directly from the theories elaborated to explain specific ethnic and kinship trading networks such as those existing among overseas Chinese residing in the same foreign country. For instance, Janet Tai Landa (1994). in her discussion of ethnic trading networks in Southeast Asia, mentions the Confucian code of ethics shared by overseas Chinese in Malaysia and the important role it plays as a functional equivalent to the law of contracts. A careful analysis of the code of ethics which developed in this context would reveal its specific use of Confucian values, its focus on some of these values and its neglect of others, the new meaning assigned to some Confucian norms in given economic transactions, and the particular distinction drawn between close and distant social bonds. In other words, the analysis of Chinese trading practices among emigrant communities shows how given norms have functioned as resources, partly transformed in the process of their use, to organize economic exchanges in a very specific setting, characterized by the need to find reliable partners in a multi-ethnic society where many uncertainties prevail. The fact that such a Confucian code of ethics came into being and is shared to a certain extent by a group's members is nonetheless the outcome of a complex process, enhanced by the existence of rather effective sanctions to punish eventual breaches of the code.

It is difficult to assess beforehand that the Confucian code of ethics mentioned in those studies is shared today by overseas Chinese and those who never left China. The situation they have been confronted with during the past decades is so different, from the political, economic and social perspectives, that the group they represent cannot be assimilated to the type of club-like arrangement so clearly described by Landa. Other compromises and arrangements are bound to emerge from the negotiations and the exchanges carried on between the members of the two communities. We would, therefore, argue that a careful and systematic comparison of the different types of transnational linkages, of the various uses made by their participants of cultural resources, of the mutual influence the practices and rules elaborated in different settings exercise upon each other, is required to understand the cultural aspects of the current transnationalization of ethnic business enterprises.

By relying on the data collected by discussions with a sample of Hong Kong entrepreneurs, we would like now to go beyond the claim made above regarding the historicity of cultural forms in order to understand how, despite existing differences, given cultural principles and norms are being mobilized, selected or reinterpreted to provide common grounds and rules for co-operation between spatially distinct Chinese communities. In doing so, we will narrow down our concern to economic exchanges, which can be said to be broadly built on the protection of mutual material interests. This situation cannot fail to influence the pace and the nature of the agreements reached on the use of given cultural forms.

THE USE MADE OF GIVEN CULTURAL ARRANGEMENTS BY OVERSEAS CHINESE ENTERPRISES

A group of twelve Hong Kong entrepreneurs were thus interviewed, in January and February 1998, who had made different types of economic investments in China. They were all linked to Taishan county (Guangdong province): six of them had decided to invest in Taishan county although they originated from another place; three of them originated from Taishan and chose to develop an economic activity there; the remaining three, also native from Taishan, established their enterprise in another county in the Pearl River Delta. Some of them were introduced to us by a friend, a member of the People's Consultative Conference of Taishan, and others by Hong Kong residents originating from Taishan. The interviews were done either in Hong Kong (most often in the informants' office), or in Taishan, or during the four hours needed to reach Taishan from Hong Kong by car: some entrepreneurs had stated very clearly that to accompany them during such a trip would provide the only opportunity for discussions with them because of their very tight time schedule.

THE SELECTIVE CHOICE OF CULTURAL PRACTICES: THE CASE OF KINSHIP TIES

The first empirical issue analysed here concerns the use made by the interviewees of kinship ties to develop their economic endeavour, a feature often considered as characteristic of overseas Chinese businesses. This topic was usually raised by asking entrepreneurs to explain the choice for a given locality, and the role assigned to relatives in this choice. It should be noticed, that in such a choice, aside from the existence of kinship relations, many factors come into play. The size of the enterprise matters: for instance, highly industrialized localities such as Dongguan county are perceived by informants as being reluctant nowadays to accommodate small size industries. The type of commodity produced may also create specific constraints. If the product has to be delivered abroad very quickly, as is usually the case, for instance, in the garment industry, proximity to Hong Kong and good quality of transport will be viewed as essential. When approval by the authorities at the national level is required, local officials may or may not be supportive. One informant explained, for instance that he cumulated two defects in the eyes of the Dongguan authorities: his enterprise would hire only about one hundred workers, and an authorization from Beijing was required for the article to be produced. Although he was a native from Dongguan, local officials made no efforts to help him. After more than a year of unsuccessful attempts, he turned to Taishan county whose authorities, looking for investments, sent two persons to Beijing to get the needed authorizations. Three months after the first contacts with the Taishan Government the plant began to produce.

At least since the beginning of the nineties, the degree of industrialization also affects the nature and the extent of the rules governing local economic exchanges, and the perception of a locality by a given entrepreneur as a favourable place for investment. One informant, native from Taishan county, who chose, by contrast, to invest in Dongguan explained, that his choice was partly due to the existence in that county of rather clear guidelines and expectations regarding business activities. According to him, it was because of its lower level of economic development that rules were very unclear and arbitrary in Taishan.

In looking at the influence of *qiaoxiang* and kinship ties on investment decisions, our informants shared one remarkable common point of view: to invest back in the place of origin today brings no specific benefits, but can eventually be harmful to the economic interests pursued. Those who started their economic endeavour just after the beginning of the reforms had indeed no other choice but to go back to their native place.

One entrepreneur explains for instance:

'I came back to Taishan to establish a knitting industry in 1980. I had been living there until I escaped to Hong Kong illegally at the beginning of the seventies. This was the only place I knew in China, and the only place where I was known. It is difficult now to imagine what the situation was at that time. Everything was confused, no one knew what was allowed or not, the local cadres were afraid to be punished if they supported us ... Everything had to be built up from scratch and the risks involved were very high. In such a confused and uncertain situation, there was no other choice than to go back to the place where your family originated from.'[9]

However, the situation appears to be quite different today. The development of all kinds of industries, the elaboration of fundamental formal and informal 'rules of the game' have lifted many uncertainties. Moreover, if reputation and trust are acquired gradually, they can be gained in any locality, because their acquisition is so clearly anchored in the protection of existing material interests. As pointed out by an informant who opened a factory in Zhuhai, in 1987:

'Just after the reforms were launched, it was easier to establish trust back home. But now, other channels exist, there are factories everywhere, and you can be recognized as trustworthy by local officials in other localities. The most important thing is your own behaviour. I have built a good reputation in Zhuhai. Everyone knows for instance that the customs never asked me to pay any fine over the past ten years. Moreover, I know the few cadres who are important, I know how much to give them at Chinese New Year. It is a matter of interest. If you satisfy their material interests, they will not distinguish between a person native from their locality and one who is not.' (Hong Kong, April 1997)

Informants mention various negative consequences stemming from the choice of one's hometown for the development of an economic activity. The first one has to do with the financial contributions asked by officials, particularly in overseas-Chinese counties which have a tradition of requesting emigrants' support for local development. The second one concerns the necessity to answer the demands for financial support of a vast network of relatives. Some feel, as in one case mentioned above, that they cannot afford it; others claim that relatives have become too much dependent on overseas Chinese and that assistance is required for very trivial issues such as the sinking of a well. According to them, the common origin and the discrepancy felt to exist between the fate encountered by the entrepreneurs and their relatives back home encourages the kinsmen's perception that they are entitled to be compensated for the unfairness of their situation. The last and most important concern is related to the difficulties faced when relatives become employees; this is considered as taking a risk. Several informants stressed the fact that they cannot treat their relatives in the same manner as ordinary workers:

'Almost everyone in the locality I come from can claim to be my relative. Relatives will usually ask for higher salaries than *mingong* (migrant workers) but it will be more difficult for me to ask them to work long hours, or to work all night if that would be necessary to deliver the merchandise on time. One of the most difficult things in most plants today is the problem of how to treat the workers. This is already a very delicate issue. It would be just impossible if there were relatives among them.' (Hong Kong, March 1998)

Aside from the occurrence of long working hours and the irregularity of workload, very often Hong Kong entrepreneurs rely, to varying degrees, on the use of coercion, or, at least, on the use of very strict rules to control workers. Entrepreneurs prefer therefore to employ *mingong* (migrant workers) rather than local inhabitants, and non-relatives rather than relatives. Mr Ma says for instance about his employees, all *mingong*:

'How I decide about workers' salaries? I look at what the other factories are offering, and I offer a little bit more. Of course, it is still very low. I find a salary reasonable when the workers can accept it. Of course there are so many people looking for jobs, that workers are forced to accept very low salaries. As far as salaries are concerned, I think the employer's interests should be protected, first of all, but you should not go too far in neglecting workers' interests ... Actually, relationships are quite tense and difficult, and we must be very strict. I cannot trust workers. Every rule is intended to prevent them to create problems, to help me control the situation. If I see a worker who just seems to take himself seriously, or who makes comments, I will fire him the same day to avoid further trouble ... I don't need any excuse, I just tell him the factory does not need him anymore ...' (Taishan, January 1998)

Most interviewees describe the situation in similar terms. Since the moral obligations towards relatives are at odds with such a labour relationship, entrepreneurs avoid as much as possible to hire individuals to whom they are linked by kinship ties. They usually make explicit claims about the need to distinguish between *renqing* and business matters; one of them qualifies kinship ties as belonging to the 'private sphere' (*si*) and his business as being linked to the 'public sphere' (*gong*) and concludes that both should be clearly delineated.

Some of the entrepreneurs who had made the choice to invest in their native place mention the strategies developed to avoid hiring relatives:

'I'd rather help a relative by giving him some money, which I often do, rather than by hiring him. It is one thing to invite a relative for lunch, it is another one to have him work for you. In my plant in Taishan, there are 600 workers. None is a relative. I told the head of the plant to refuse them, even if their technical skill is not bad. At the beginning, I was not aware of the problem. I hired some relatives and then I found out that they stole some of the clothes produced, and that the security guards did not dare to say anything because they were my relatives. Since then, I made it a rule not to hire relatives but to help them through other means.' (Taishan, March 1998)

The same argument applies to the factory management force. Entrepreneurs investing outside their native place are often reluctant to hire relatives to help them run their business. 'A relative who is okay makes the best assistant; a relative which is not okay makes the worst assistant ...'. 'Relatives are easy to hire, difficult to dismiss ...'. 'I would be inclined to hire a relative because he should be more trustworthy than any one else, but the problem is that you know if this is the case in China today only once you hired him ...'. These statements reflect two main difficulties. First, kinsmen are not automatically more reliable than non-kinsmen. Nor are close kinsmen more reliable than distant ones. Once more, the situation is quite different from the one described as prevalent among ethnic trading networks in Southeast Asia: this is not the club-like situation where breaches to the code of ethics will be punished by clear and effective sanctions. The relatives concerned here are anchored into two different communities, where the values promoted during the past decades, and the effectiveness of the social control established within each community as well as between them, do vary. Remarkably, it is also different from the situation in China. A study from 1995 on Chinese private entrepreneurs reveals that 52 per cent of them would hire relatives to help them run their businesses.[10] These appear to be close relatives such as sisters and brothers, while Hong Kong entrepreneurs usually mobilize more distant relatives.

Secondly, relatives cannot be dismissed just like ordinary employees. The margin of freedom of Hong Kong entrepreneurs is thus limited by their own perception of the obligations linked to kinship. One interviewee explains:

'I asked the elder brother of my father-in-law to come to Dongguan and help me take care of the plant in my absence. He was in charge of buying all needed items for the maintenance of the plant. I found out very quickly that he was earning a lot of money. All the receipts were fake... He is a relative, so I thought, okay, no problem if he earns some money. But then I thought that if this money had to be stolen by someone, why not by my father-in-law? I went to see that relative working for me, I told him his brother had no work, no resource, and he should give him this opportunity. Actually, this was the only way to solve the issue without creating too much trouble: to find an even closer relative needing this job. And this closer relative was my father-in-law. He could not refuse. So I hired my father-in-law, and actually he doesn't cheat at all ...' (Hong Kong, April 1998).

These few examples make it clear that the use of kinship ties by Chinese entrepreneurs is not culturally determined, but depends very much on a specific historical, economic and political context. In actual fact, in the present case, the labour system developed in the factories concerned, in combination with the different factors influencing kinship obligations in

China and in Hong Kong, limits the use of kinship ties as a resource in the economic realm.[11]

CHARITABLE DONATIONS AND ECONOMIC PROFIT

Another issue often mentioned by our informants is the importance of their conformity to a specific cultural practice, namely the contribution of donations for all kinds of social initiatives. This topic appeared to be progressively more worthy of analysis than we had thought at the beginning. Donations serve a large variety of purposes, and different types must be distinguished among them. The various motives harboured by individual entrepreneurs for contributing them, and the manners in which they work out in actual practice tell a revealing story about the socio-political fabric in which foreign entrepreneurs work in China. From our interviews it has appeared that gaining prestige among county and lineage fellows in many cases is at least as important as gaining the trust of local officialdom, and that the former is usually intended to serve the latter. Also, there is a process of institutionalization of newly emerged relationships going on, engendered by the economic reforms and the role therein of foreign entrepreneurs. The broader setting of donation behaviour is important here. As mentioned before, the legitimacy assigned to the cultural resources anchored in the pre-1949 period has been further enhanced in Guangdong and Fujian provinces by the new social and economic links established with overseas-Chinese societies. Many returning emigrants expressed a feeling of belonging to a given lineage and to a given locality. Their sojourns, especially the first one after years of separation, are often narrated in local publications; the names of the visitors and the village where they originate from are always clearly stated. The restoration of such social exchanges has promoted the writing of new genealogies to clarify and reassess the complex kinship ties existing within a lineage.

Emigrants contribute to all kinds of activities. Donations may be of a religious character, like the renovation of temples or the performance of given rituals, others are linked to lineage issues such as the support provided to lineage libraries, reviews, and secundary schools. For such occasions, discussions are held, and collections organized, by lineage leaders abroad and in China. Contributions can aim at improving the well-being of social units smaller than the lineage, such as villages, by installing for instance running water or electricity, or broader, such as to support initiatives stemming from the market-town or the county governments. In other words, collections realized at different levels will draw different persons together, and witness the intervention of different types of leaders, some being informal village and lineage leaders, and others, local officials or the representatives of a great variety of institutions. Needless to say, individuals vary also a lot in the amount and the nature of their contributions. Some emigrants are praised for instance for their gift of a water pump to their village and HK$200 to the lineage library (*Jiaolun yuebao*, January 1992:13), while the contributions of another one, also labelled as the 'head of Conglou market-town abroad', will be described as follows:

'When Li Huazhao came back home, after thirty years in Hong Kong without visiting his native place, he gathered the old *fuxiong* and told them: "If our locality is to change, we must develop education; if our people are to remain healthy, we have to develop medical care; we must therefore unite abroad and back home to transform this locality unfit today to the development of human beings." Li Huazhao consequently created the "Hong Kong Association of the four counties" (*XiangGang si yi huisuo*), which has donated more than 20 million *yuan* during the eighties to support all kinds of common affairs ...'[12]

The realms of everyday life chosen to benefit from overseas contributions often exhibit some continuity with the past. Education for instance is privileged as it was before 1949: from 1978 to 1989 for instance, 163 new schools have been created and 295 restored in Taishan county thanks to overseas contributions.[13] Medical care represents another privileged realm. During the same decade, HK$21,577,000 were donated for such purpose, and 22 ambulances were offered, often named after their donator (*Taishan xian huaqiao zhi*, p. 134). But some contributions respond to new social projects launched by local governments, such as the creation of 'houses for the old people' or 'houses for old cadres' in market-towns and villages. The financial support provided is widely publicized either on temples and village walls, or in different kinds of regular journals (a total of 31 local reviews and newsletters aimed at overseas Chinese or *qiaokan* were published in Taishan in 1992, among which 18 are linked to a given locality and the remaining 13 to different lineages) (*Taishan xian huaqiao zhi*, pp. 216-17), but also in specific books or booklets published by institutions such as the Bureau of Overseas Chinese Affairs of the county government, the Overseas Chinese Association, the Overseas Chinese Committee from the Chinese People's Consultative Conference, or the Overseas Chinese Committee of the People's Representatives' Assembly.

Local governments, as is well known, encourage overseas Chinese to invest in China. Unfortunately, when mentioning the number of overseas Chinese engaged in some kind of economic activity in Taishan, the figures provided often do not distinguish between those who are native from the place and those who are not. We know for instance that, by the end of 1990, 87 *sanzi* and 230 *sanlai yibu* entreprises[14] had been established in Taishan, but the geographical origin of the overseas Chinese involved is unknown. Situations actually vary a lot, as in our sample of Hong Kong interviewees: some Chinese entrepreneurs coming from abroad may invest in Taishan without being native of this place, others are native from Taishan but invest in an area of this county other than the one their family and lineage come from, while there are those too among them who do establish their enterprise back in their native locality. Overseas Chinese indirect support to local economic development is also channelled through the establishment of small enterprises owned by dependants of overseas Chinese. According to county estimates, there were for instance about 8,100 such small individual enterprises (*getihu*) in 1993.[15]

Looking, then, at the motives for the contribution of donations, one cannot reject a priori the importance of altruistic attitudes in order to explain the important contributions made by overseas Chinese to various social groups: the lineage segment, the village, the lineage, the hometown. Such an attitude can even be found among overseas entrepreneurs with vested interests in China. An entrepreneur from Hong Kong, whose lineage is located in Taishan county but who decided, in 1984, to establish his enterprise in Dongguan county, explains for instance:

'It makes me happy to help them in Taishan, I cannot contribute much because I do not have that much money, but I like to support education, or old people's care. I give only 6 or 10 thousands HK$ once in a while, but it is really one of the things which makes me feel good. The local governments are so poor... I like also to support non-official activities such as the publication of local literary journals which have no other source of funding than individual contributions. I really prefer to play less mahjong here in Hong Kong and be able to help them ...' (Hong Kong, March 1998).

Of course, to cultivate *qiaoxiang* ties and support various local endeavours may bring important social rewards to the emigrants concerned. First of all, they are being distinguished from other members of the emigrant community, and identified as persons whose origins are known and who have a specific history. Secondly, by contributing to all kinds of religious, social and economic activities, they build up or reinforce their reputation in China. The reputation they gained in the country of residence cannot be easily transferred back home, so that their support to local common endeavours plays a prominent role in the formation of their reputation in

China. Such contributions are also perceived as reflecting their loyalty to China and to their native place, and their commitment to improve and strengthen the locality and the nation. Finally, such financial support exhibits the capacity of the various benefactors to take into consideration other people's interests, and not to act only out of private objectives. Clear identity, high reputation, loyalty, commitment, capacity to put oneself in others' position: those are considered to be major components of the establishment of social prestige but also of interpersonal trust or, more pointedly, of the qualification of an individual as trustworthy.[16]

To assess one's identity and, moreover, to establish a good social reputation in the native place explain the willingness of many emigrants to support lineage and local 'common activities'. As stated by another entrepreneur coming from Taishan:

'Of course I enjoy people back in Conglou to think that I am a good person, that I care for society. Who does not want "face"? Who does not want social prestige (*shehui mingwang*)? It is especially important for me, because my mother left Conglou during the war against Japan and married another man in Guangxi, and my family has been looked down upon for this. But actually it is important for everyone ...' (Taishan, April 1998).

If the obtainment of prestige and a name of trustworthiness are important for any emigrant, it must be so for the establishment of the type of personal bonds and interpersonal trust necessary to succeed in the Chinese economic system... We will follow J.T. Landa in defining this type of cultural practice as belonging to the economics of signalling.[17]

Practices such as the cultivation of lineage ties, the writing of genealogies, the participation in all kinds of collections, have social and religious meanings other than the economic ones just stressed; the latter, in Landa's words, are only 'an additional economic *raison d'être*'. As a matter of fact, most contributors have no material interests at stake, and those who have established business ties may engage in such activities for reasons other than instrumental ones. Nonetheless, as Mr Wong explains:

'In China, if you enjoy social prestige, everything becomes easier, including your economic activities if you have some. And to provide financial support to all kinds of initiatives is a good way to gain prestige. So, how to distinguish between those who contribute for their own interest and the others? You have to look at the initial motive (*chufa dian*), at the intention involved. But actually it is not always easy to distinguish ...'[18]

In other words, in those societies where economic exchanges rely heavily on the social reputation acquired and on the development of personal bonds and mutual trust, the socially approved means to achieve such objectives will benefit economic endeavours and will therefore eventually be mobilized to pursue economic profit. The effectiveness of the economics of signalling relies nonetheless precisely on the difficulty to distinguish clearly between the social and economic objectives of the practices involved.

But let us consider more carefully the type of contributions made by the Hong Kong entrepreneurs interviewed and the form taken by the economics of signalling in their particular case. It appears that they usually differ in one important respect from the economics of signalling among Chinese trading networks in Malaysia: the latter are similar in that they include ancestor worship and the writing of genealogies, and support the identification process of potential trading partners ranging from the more trustworthy ones to the less trustworthy ones, in a hierarchy including near kinsmen, distant kinsmen, clansmen, and fellow-villagers to Hokkien people. However, in our data, in most cases the trading partners, or those who are due to support the business activities of overseas Chinese entrepreneurs, are not members of the same lineage, but local officials. In these cases, the economics of signalling may be used by overseas Chinese entrepreneurs to assess their ethnicity versus non-Chinese entrepreneurs, or to illustrate the fact that they do belong to the Chinese cultural group despite their residence in a foreign country. One of our informants recalls for instance:

'Around 1985, I helped a relative who had left China at the age of ten to go back to Taishan and establish a joint-venture with a local market-town government. He did not want to bother too much with lineage affairs, but I told him that he could not completely ignore the lineage elders. He had to contribute to lineage affairs and participate in all kinds of collections to show to the local cadres whose support was required that he was still Chinese, despite so many years spent abroad, and that he would play by Chinese rules ...' (Hong Kong, April 1998)

The assessment in this manner of one's ethnicity, after decades of residence in a foreign country, in a context where foreigners are looked upon with some suspicion, assigns a new purpose to given cultural forms. For others, contributing to local affairs is an effective method to gain social prestige and to be known by local officials and establish particularized relationships with them. Once more, the question at stake here is not to find a reliable trading partner among kinsmen, but to be recognized as such by the officials concerned.

'You can get to know local cadres through various channels, you can be introduced by a friend who has already some business activity back home, but one of the best ways to achieve this is to participate in all kinds of local affairs, to show your concern and your willingness to help. People will report about you, people will even come to interview you, those in charge of Overseas Affairs, and then it becomes quite easy to know those you need to know, and to establish personal ties with them. Actually, at the beginning, I hadn't intended to open a business in Taishan, I just responded positively to different requests because I liked to do so. Then, progressively, I established such good connections in Taishan that I thought about trying something there ...' (Hong Kong, March 1998)

For many entrepreneurs, if the cultural forms used to cultivate lineage and *qiaoxiang* ties are apparently the same, a certain distinction exists between both. This is so because of the differences existing between lineage members and local officials in the economic realm, at least in those geographical areas where no lineage is dominant enough to include whole administrative units:

'I have a plant in Siju market-town, and so I support some of my relatives' requests to help them for different matters, I also agree to participate in some of the initiatives of local officials. But it is not the same thing. When I discuss lineage affairs, it is with relatives who have no economic power but enjoy prestige among our lineage members abroad. When a local official comes to ask my financial support for a new initiative, I am dealing with someone who can help me eventually in my business activities, and so I feel somehow forced to answer positively. Of course, it is not completely different, because if I do not agree with my relative's request, they will say bad things of me which will damage my reputation ...' (Taishan, April 1998)

Three types of contributions are more or less explicitly distinguished by the informants according to impact on their economic endeavour. The first category concerns those collections directly launched by administrative departments which have the power to intervene directly in business activities, such as customs, tax, environmental or hygiene departments. One informant mentioned that his company in Taishan spends 150,000 to

200,000 *yuan* a year in such donations, while another one summarizes very clearly the positions usually adopted:

> 'I never refuse to make a contribution in such a case, because those are the people who have the power to interfere in your business. They can either give you face and make your life easier if you have established good relationships with them, or find a way to make life very difficult for you, and even force you to close down your business ...' (Hong Kong, April 1998)

The second category includes collections aimed at promoting social benefits and enhancing local living standards, such as the building of schools, hospitals, or old people's houses. Included here are the collections benefiting village or lineage members but linked to broad social issues such as education and health care. A positive response to those requests benefits one's social reputation, and may have some impact on one's economic interests. All informants claim that they often contribute to such initiatives, but they make their own choices and do not hesitate eventually to refuse their co-operation in given instances. It should be added here that the same amount of money contributed to such collections by entrepreneurs native of the locality and by those who are not, have different values. Native entrepreneurs will indeed be accused of 'neglecting their home place' (*bu ai xiang*) if they often refuse their support or contribute amounts of money not in line with their material success. A non-native entrepreneur will on the contrary be praised for participating, even to a small extent, to such initiatives.

Finally, the third realm encompasses the contributions made exclusively to the lineage or to the different groups which compose it, concerning issues where kinship and territoriality play a central part, such as the cult of ancestors or the renovation of a village temple. Such contributions have a rather limited influence on economic performance.

It seems clear, from this breakdown in different types of donations, that the economic rewards from the cultivation of lineage and even *qiaoxiang* ties tend to decrease. This is so, because the two types of contributions bearing an influence on business interests are not linked to a given kinship or territorial network. Since such donations can be contributed efficiently in any locality, entrepreneurs may even obtain higher profits from the same amount of contributions if they invest outside their own native place. But the main point is that different motives and obligations apparently support entrepreneurs' participation in different types of collections. One informant who decided to invest back in his native market-town mentioned:

'If you think that every time when I make a contribution I do it for the sake of economic interests, you are wrong. I like to help my relatives, I feel this is one of my obligations; I like Taishan and I am happy to be in a position today which allows me to do something to improve the situation there a bit. Of course I know that when I give money for a school or whatever, it will enhance my reputation and this will somehow benefit my business. But I don't do it only for this reason. I feel satisfied that people back home think I am a good person. But there are contributions which I make only to protect my business ...' (Hong Kong, April 1998)

In other words, most Hong Kong entrepreneurs and their Chinese counterparts agree that 'to donate money', an established cultural idiom and practice, stands for different actions. On one hand, there are the voluntary donations given to lineage and social endeavours, and on the other hand there are the compulsory contributions to all kinds of local demands made by departments and institutions which can pose a direct threat to the entrepreneurs' economic endeavours. Nonetheless, it should not be taken for granted that all individuals will agree with this polysemic dimension of the cultural practice of charitable donations in order to legitimate one's interests. Mr Wong for instance refused to invest in Taishan to avoid being forced to donate money. Donations, according to him, should be given out of free will.

'You cannot be forced to contribute money. If it is not voluntary, if I cannot say no, then it is no longer a donation... This is why I contribute in Taishan and make profits in Dongguan. I really want to separate both things. I refuse to participate in any business meeting in Taishan. Moreover, contributions should come from individuals' private pockets and not from their company's budget ...' (Hong Kong, February 1998)

On the other hand, the common agreement eventually reached regarding the use of such a cultural practice for the protection of both partners in their economic exchanges, should not be considered as purely instrumental. By using the expression 'to donate money' for the transaction, the two parties are certainly being constrained through the social and moral obligations culturally established between the donator and his beneficiary. For instance, the donator should be given 'face', which includes the necessity to make his life easier, to avoid creating unnecessary difficulties and embarrassing him. To forget such a norm of reciprocity can therefore be sanctioned. Mr Liu, who opened a small cosmetics factory in Taishan narrates for instance that it is on such grounds that he criticized the attitude of the Customs department towards him:

'I am a member of the People's Consultative Conference. Last year, during a meeting, I took the floor to denounce the Customs' behaviour. You know, I am bound to bring in a certain volume of raw materials, and I must prove that I did not sell too much in China by showing what amount of finished products I take back to Hong Kong. There are different ratios of raw materials for finished products for shampoos, creams, and so on ... It is different for every product. I wanted the Customs to make an average estimation and not to bother to calculate for every product. But they kept on looking at the details ... So I said during the meeting "How can we be treated like this, with such suspicion, from the part of the Customs? We not only established our factory here, we donated money for all kinds of projects, even to help retired staff from the Customs department, and this is the way to show your gratitude..." ' (Hong Kong, March 1998)

Similar understandings apply when 'red pockets' are being offered. Hong Kong entrepreneurs rely, for getting things done, on the personalistic ties established with local cadres. 'In China, you better trust individuals and not institutions or official decisions', claims one informant. Most of them consider the *guanxi* developed as their most valuable asset, coming before economic capital, professional experience and a reputation for trust-worthiness, because of the power detained by local officials. They often detail the complex strategies developed in this realm, usually supported by a good knowledge of the existing institutional system. As already mentioned for other practices, cultural forms such as the establishment of *guanxi* and the exchange of 'face' are not performed automatically, but are influenced by the broader context, more pointedly, by the local power structure. One entrepreneur explains for instance:

'You should develop good relationships with the heads of those departments you have to deal with, but also with those who might replace them. You have to consider it as a network and not only focus on a few individuals. Sometimes, I notice a young new official who looks smarter than the others, and I will invite him for dinner, because you never know ... There are different ways to give face to someone according to his position. Sometimes, I don't even need to spend money ... But of course, you have to invest a lot in establishing good ties with the two or three top heads of the district. Some entrepreneurs invest in the wrong persons. I know by experience that if you have very good ties with these heads, because they are very powerful and others have to listen to them, everything becomes easier ...' (Taishan, March 1998)

Cultural practices such as donations for all kinds of social affairs and the distribution of red pocket are used to establish such positive relationships. However, red pockets are used in a large variety of situations. The extent of voluntariness in the offering of red pockets varies a lot, from those given to show gratitude for a specific service to those directly requested by the receiver, to which the entrepreneur must agree if he wants to maintain his economic profit. In this last case, many red pockets are provided not to thank for an action already performed but as a prevention against potential interference and nuisances from the individuals and departments with power in the economic realm:

'First of all, you have to consider red pockets as an insurance ... You should be safe from all kinds of risks due to the absence of clear rules. Secondly, you can save time, money and efforts because people will try to make life easier for you, and they will not abide by the existing rules... I had to change the air system in my factory for instance, and according to the legal dispositions, I should have closed my factory during three days to do so. But I just didn't, and nobody came to say anything ...' (Taishan, February 1998).

Remarkably, a measure of institutionalization is developing regarding the acceptable amount of money, for both parties, to be exchanged through red pockets. One principle is, for instance, that the higher the violation of the existing official dispositions is, the bigger the red pocket should be. A second principle claims that the amount of money paid should be lower than the fees legally required:

'I give a lot of red pockets, but by doing so I spend much less money in many realms that I should. So it may appear as a loss for the budget, but actually it is a gain because for instance I will pay much lower taxes... Imagine for instance that, according to the rules I have to pay 100 *yuan* to the tax department, but I am effectively required to pay 60 *yuan* and I give a 20 *yuan* red pocket to the person in charge. I still save 20 *yuan*. Otherwise, why should I accept such rules of the game.' (Taishan, March 1998)

Once again, we are faced here with a single cultural practice used to assign a meaning to different types of relationships and situations. Moreover, just as in the case of donations, moral obligations play an important part in the exchange performed: most entrepreneurs claim, that a cadre who has received a red pocket from you cannot but help you. Nonetheless, we should notice that the enabling power of the cultural practice represented by the exchange of red pockets seems to be much less than in the case of donations. Red pockets are given to an individual, not to a group. They do not bring social esteem to the donator, and are much closer linked to the protection of particular interests. This may be the reason why one informant mentions another advantage of investing in a locality other than one's hometown: 'It is easier to offer red pockets when you are not too familiar with the person. When there are no other links between you and him, you are not investing in your own native place for instance ...' (Hong Kong, February 1998).

CONCLUDING REMARKS

The second part of this chapter shows that the historicity of cultural practices, underlined in its first part, does not prevent overseas-Chinese entrepreneurs and their counterparts in China to use given cultural forms to co-operate with one another. The uses of kinship ties, and donation behaviour, although these issues as treated above are limited in scope, illustrate first of all the fact that, if the same cultural form is being used by Chinese entrepreneurs involved in different types of ethnic trades, the differences among the economic, social and historical settings influence the choices made among these forms and the meaning assigned to them. For instance, when kinship ties cannot be used to establish the personal relationships with officials required to engage in successful economic activities, a cultural discrepancy emerges, back in the native place or not. In view of such cases, it becomes difficult to encompass forms such as lineage and *qiaoxiang* ties and consider them as being evenly affected by the increased globalization of ethnic Chinese business. In other words, ethnic Chinese entrepreneurs do rely on given cultural practices to develop particularized bonds with their business counterparts and to establish their reputation or demonstrate their trustworthiness. But the practices emphasized and their effectiveness in the economic realm vary with the identity of these counterparts and the existence of particular institutional constraints. Choices are made among the whole range of values or forms offered by a given cultural tradition. And practices considered to be relevant of a given economic culture, such as the use of kinship ties in overseas Chinese businesses, can be ignored in a given context as a useful resource.

Moreover, a cultural practice such as the charitable contribution to public affairs, whose meaning is not established once for all but is open to various interpretations, is here mobilized to designate rather different types of practices. They range from voluntary donations to kinsmen to compulsory fees paid to administrative departments whose power is big and arbitrary enough to force a business to close down. Some Hong Kong entrepreneurs are refusing to put themselves in a position as to be 'forced to donate', in order to preserve what they understand to be the original meaning of donations. Most of them, however, in order to protect their economic interests, accept the new meaning assigned to the practice of donations, while differentiating between the various types of situations occurring when donations are at stake. By assigning new meanings and usages to them, they transform the cultural practices at stake, a process which sometimes leads to the creation of more or less institutionalized forms. Confronted by the variety of situations and relationships resorting under the same cultural practice, the entrepreneurs involved in such an exchange are nonetheless confident that the donations made, although being imposed upon them will, because of the mutual cultural obligations, be reciprocated by the required recognition and support. In the process, despite the existing cultural differences between both groups, given cultural practices are being used to support the social and economic exchanges performed, acting, as stated above, both as resources and constraints for individual action. More pointedly, cultural practices such as those described here are resources *because* they are also constraints.

It is easy to see that the enabling part of a cultural practice lies first of all in the fact that its concrete, observable form is well established and shared, but can be used, at the same time, to support different types of situations and relationships. Thus, they are open to new interpretations. Just as easy to establish is the second enabling characteristic of cultural practices, namely that conformity to them brings social prestige. Charitable donations for instance, are used in the cases observed to assign a positive meaning to a practice which might otherwise be given a much more negative label. They protect the economic interests of both parties but also assign 'face' to the party who is actually on the weak side in the balance of power.[19] The third aspect of cultural practices, however, which contributes to their enabling power is the fact that they also act as constraints: they are usually supported by given social obligations and expectations, thus constraining both parties in the exchange. In this sense, they allow for some degree of predictability of each party's behaviour and encourage the development of the trust needed to co-operate.

BIBLIOGRAPHY

Baker, H.D.R.
1968   *Chinese Lineage Village. Sheung Shui.* Stanford: Stanford University Press
Dasgupta, P.
1988   'Trust as a Commodity', in: Diego Gambetta (ed.) *Trust. Making and Breaking Co-operative Relations.* New York: Basil Blackwell
Dirlik, A.
1996   'Critical Reflections on 'Chinese Capitalism' as a Paradigm', in: L.M. Douw and P. Post (eds) *South China: State, Culture and Social Change during the 20th Century.* Amsterdam, Oxford, New York and Tokyo: Royal Netherlands Acadamy of Arts and Sciences
Gambetta, D.
1988   'Mafia: The Price of Distrust', in: Diego Gambetta (ed.) *Trust. Making and Breaking Co-operative Relations.* New York: Basil Blackwell
Hardin, R.
1996   'Trustworthiness', *Ethics* 107
Kollock, P.
1994   'The Emergence of Exchange Structures: An Experimental Study of Uncertainty, Commitment, and Trust', *American Journal of Sociology* 100:2
Lepetit, B.
1995   'Le présent de l'histoire' (History's Present), in: B. Lepetit (ed.) *Les formes de l'experience. Une autre histoire sociale* (The Forms of Experience. Another Social History). Paris: Albin Michel
Redding, G.S.
1990   *The Spirit of Chinese Capitalism.* Berlin and New York: Walter de Gruyter
Siu, H.
1989   'Recycling Rituals: Politics and Popular Culture in Contemporary Rural China', in: Perry Link, Richard Madsen and Paul Pickowicz (eds) *Unofficial China: Popular Culture and Thought in the People's Republic of China.* Boulder, Colorado: Westview Press
Tai, L.J.
1994   *Trust, Ethnicity, and Identity. Beyond the New Institutional Economics of Ethnic Trading Networks, Contract Law, and Gift-Exchange.* Ann Arbor: University of Michigan Press
Thireau, I. and Hua Linshan
1996   *Enquête sociologique sur la Chine, 1911-1949.* Paris: Presses

Universitaires de France

1998   'Une analyse des disputes dan les villages chinois: aspects historiques et culturels des accords concernant les actions justes et raisonnables', *Revue française de sociologie* 39:3, pp. 535-63

Watson, J.L.

1977   'Hereditary Tenancy and Corporate Landlordism in Traditional China', *Modern Asian Studies* 20:2 , pp. 161-82

Watson, R.

1985   *Inequality among Brothers. Class and Kinship in South China.* Cambridge, London: Cambridge University Press

Wolf, A.P.

1996   'The "New Feudalism": A Problem for Sinologists', in: L.M. Douw and P. Post (eds) *South China, State, Culture and Social Change during the 20th Century.* Amsterdam, Oxford, New York and Tokyo: Royal Netherlands Academy of Arts and Sciences

Woon Yuen-fong,

1984   *Social Organization in South China, 1911-1949, The Case of the Kuan Lineage in K'ai-ping County.* Ann Arbor: University of Michigan Press

Notes

1. Preparation of this paper was assisted by the discussions following its presentation at the conference which gave rise to this volume. We are grateful to the many people who offered commentary and criticism. We are particularly grateful to Leo Douw, Alan Smart and Michael R. Godley for their useful comments on an earlier draft of this paper.

2. Unfortunately, this chapter is not actually based on a careful observation of negotiation processes between entrepreneurs. It relies on data collected by interviewing twelve Hong Kong entrepreneurs having chosen to invest in China. Among the questions discussed with them, two issues only will be analysed here: the extent of the mobilization of kinship ties in their economic endeavour and the links established between donations to all kinds of local initiatives and economic profit. In other words, the present contribution cannot pretend to be a systematic study of any particular aspect of the current transnationalization process of ethnic Chinese business enterprises. Its objective is much more limited: to show, as concretely as possible, how given cultural practices represent resources as well as constraints for social actors but also how individuals and groups are going to modify existing specific cultural arrangements.

3. In May 1984, for instance, the authorities of Taishan county organized a meeting gathering about 400 local officials, and aiming at organizing the

effective reversal of 'wrong decisions taken during political campaigns'. Twenty-five bureaus were opened to return past overseas Chinese properties. To take the lead of such a movement, the authorities gave back to overseas Chinese associations lineage schools that had become public property, such as the secondary school of the lineage Huang, the English secondary school of the lineage Tan, the secondary school previously run by the Lei, Fang and Deng lineages. The movement addressed first the properties belonging to important figures of overseas Chinese societies. In 1991, 97.5 per cent of the cases involving property thus confiscated during Land Reform were said to be settled, as well as most of the cases occurred during the Great Leap Forward or the Cultural Revolution. Moreover, 550 former 'rightists' were rehabilitated. See *Taishan xien Huaqiao zhi*, p. 204.

4. The extent and the use made of this new legitimacy varies among localities, according to the differences existing in the pre-1949 social and cultural practices, the uneven political constraints faced today by localities, as well as the present economic achievements and their degree of reliance on collective means and activities.

5. The five localities under study, four located in Panyu, Nanhai, Taishan and Kaiping counties of Guangdong province, and one in Nanling county of Anhui province, exhibit many situations reflecting the new legitimacy assigned to pre-1949 resources and their interplay with later social and cultural forms. See the article by the authors, 'Une analyse disputes dans les villages chinois: aspects historiques et culturels des accords concernant les actions justes et raisonnables' (An analysis of disputes in Chinese villages: Historical and cultural aspects of local agreements regarding appropriate and reasonable actions), *Revue française de sociologie* 39:3 (July 1998), pp. 535-63.

6. See, for example, R. Watson, 1985, J.L. Watson, 1977, or Baker, 1968. These studies show that, according to the principle of patrilineal descent, any ancestor delineates a group formed by his descendants. Some groups will nonetheless constitute themselves more formally in lineages and lineage segments by erecting a temple named after their common ancestor and providing it with some amount of collective property (land most often, but sometimes shops at the market-town, or other items). This institutionalization process does not amount to the creation of social groups that did not exist before, but assigns a new visibility to some descent groups and increases the capacity of their members for collective action. Anthropologists usually distinguish between clans, which group individuals bearing the same surname, 'higher-order lineages', whose members do not live in a close geographical proximity but are linked by some degree of ritual unity, dispersed lineages' that is lineages whose members are linked by demonstrated patrilinal descent but have no

common ancestor temple, and 'localized lineages', whose formation responds both to the principle of descent from a common ancestor, commemorated by a temple, and to the principle of close physical proximity enabling mutual help.

7. The link between the lineage religious ideologies and the social norms developed in Guangdong villages is stressed in a book published by the authors and entitled *Enquête sociologique sur la Chine, 1911-1949* (A Sociological Study of China, 1911-1949). Paris: Presses Universitaires de France, 1996.

8. A careful analysis of lineage reviews for instance, throughout the twentieh century, reveals the changing part played by the lineage in society, as well as the changing norms governing lineage ties.

9. More specific motives may lay nonetheless behind entrepreneurs' choice. The entrepreneur here mentioned stated for instance that even if he had to choose a locality to invest today, he would choose to go back to the market-town in Taishan he is native from. 'As a landlord son, I went through many struggle meetings. I was a victim of almost all political campaigns until I escaped to Hong Kong at the beginning of the seventies. So I wanted to succeed where I had been discriminated in the past. I wanted those people who despised me yesterday to be forced to respect me today ...' Elements of the personal biographic itinerary of the entrepreneurs concerned can also play a part in their decision-making process. Taishan, March 1998.

10. 'Private Entrepreneurs in China', Chinese Academy of Social Sciences, 1995, unpublished.

11. Actually, even entrepreneurs who made the choice to hire no relatives complain about the negative impact of kinship ties on their economic endeavour. One informant mentions for instance that he avoided having relatives as employees by investing in another county than the one he originated from, but he could not avoid the fact that about 70 per cent of his workers are relatives of local officials. 'It is one of the most important problems we are confronted with. But it is inevitable. Our plant offers good salaries, good working conditions ... I try to limit the harm thus caused by hiring no one if I do not have a vacancy, and by telling the new employees that they will be fired if they make mistakes, whatever their background is ...'

12. *Qingxi louyang*, published by the literary society of Conglou, Taishan, 1993, pp. 1-6.

13. *Taishan xian huaqiao zhi*, edited by the *Taishan qiaowu bangongshi*, 1992, p. 129.

14 *Sanlai yibu* enterprises are enterprises engaged in processing, assembling and manufacturing goods from materials supplied by foreign enterpreneurs. *Sanzi* enterprises are joint-ventures, co-operative

ventures, and foreign-owned ventures.

15. Specific institutions have accordingly been created to encourage overseas Chinese economic investment, such as the 'Taishan Chinese Tourism Agency', which from 1984 to 1989, for example, received 1,828 overseas Chinese of Taishan ancestry out of a total of 33,239 Chinese visitors or the 'Society of investments for the construction of emigrant communities in Taishan county'. *Taishan xian huaqiao zhi*, p. 221.

16. For a discussion of the concept of trust, see: Kollock, 1994; Dasgupta, 1988; Gambetta, 1988 and Hardin, 1996.

17. We extend nonetheless the way J.T. Landa uses this concept to the practices allowing the assessment of one's trustworthiness and not only of one's identity.

18. Hong Kong, March 1997. Such a distinction is also tentatively drawn in many local publications. For instance, the booklet entitled *Qingxi louyang* and published by the 'literature association' of Conglou market-town to describe 'local model figures' who are in majority overseas Chinese, usually adds a sentence such as '(he) or (she) ... has provided an unceasing and unselfish support to common affairs ...' when the person concerned has no business interests in China, while the overseas Chinese entrepreneurs will be praised for their generosity without any mention about their unselfishness. See *Qingxi louyang* edited by the literature association of Conglou (Taishan county), 1993.

19. The analysis of donations practices within a given type of ethnic trade should be considered over a certain period of time because transformations of the existing political and economic constraints may bring about changes in the use of given cultural forms.

THE *QIAOXIANG* IRONY: MIGRANT LABOUR IN OVERSEAS CHINESE ENTERPRISES[1]

CEN HUANG

The ethnic Chinese who live outside of the People's Republic of China's administrative jurisdiction, mainly in Hong Kong, Macao, Taiwan and Southeast Asia, have played a crucial role in the creation of 'the economic miracle' in South China over the past two decades. According to official reports, as much as 80 per cent of total foreign investments in South China have come from 'overseas Chinese' sources,[2] employing an estimated 20 million people (East Asia Analytical Unit 1995:6). What is not as often noted is that many of the workers in these enterprises are migrants workers, who have recently moved into the now-prosperous 'overseas Chinese villages' to take up employment. Although much that has been written on the subject quite rightly assumes that certain common values, referred to in this volume as *qiaoxiang* ties, can provide significant business advantages, these may do little to assist with day-to-day operations on the factory floor. Even shared cultural expectations can easily throw up obstacles, as several contributors to this book document. Whilst readily acknowledging some of the more positive influences traditional ways of doing business have had on China's modernization, including the expansion of socio-economic networks and the encouragement of further investments, this chapter addresses one of the most-common management problems today: the ironic fact that most of the labourers in *qiaoxiang* enterprises today are themselves 'sojourners' albeit in their own country: destined, perhaps, to repeat the experiences of earlier generations, including their present employers, who made their own fortunes in Southeast Asia or North America.

INTRODUCTION

Taking advantage of the obvious linguistic and cultural affinity, the overseas Chinese are widely regarded as bridge builders who, especially after the Tiananmen crackdown, have provided critical capital and know-how for South China's economic takeoff. Some writers believe that this is because of strong feelings for native areas (Huang, 1998:54). Others argue that investments in the People's Republic are made, primarily, for profits, certainly not because of any loyalty to China as a nation-state (Suryadinata, 1995:203). Investors have, in fact, been criticized as opportunists and parvenus eager to enrich themselves while only incidentally benefiting China. Ong, for example, concedes that whilst diaspora Chinese often display an emotional identification with their ancestral homeland, it cannot be assumed that they all have the country's interests at heart (Ong, 1997:175). Realists note that there are any number of sound economic reasons why the overseas Chinese invest in South China. In the first place, rapid development there creates profitable markets. Moreover, many overseas Chinese entrepreneurs readily admit that an abundant supply of cheap labour is an important reason why they set up enterprises there. One Hong Kong investor said that a worker's monthly salary in a manufacturing company in China was one twentieth of what he pays to his Hong Kong workers. There are also good conditions for foreign investment in China, especially in the coastal provinces, where large areas of agricultural land have been transformed into industrial parks, with excellent lease terms, and new commercial housing projects located nearby. It was, for example, reported that the revenue generated from the sale of land in the coastal cities of South China accounts for more than 35 per cent of the total annual revenue of these cities. In Shenzhen and Zhuhai, where special economic zones are located, the figure can be as high as 50 per cent (Hsing, 1997:147). Among the enterprises that were investigated in this study, 57 per cent had leased land from local authorities and in all cases the land lease is for a term of 50 years. All of these enterprises have built their own factory buildings on the leased land. According to a town official from the Pearl River Delta Region, many investors in the region in the 1990s were attracted by favourable land lease contracts.

Be this as it may, a number of writers maintain that there is a correlation between culture, institutions, history, and the direction of transnational capital flows in the fast growth of 'Greater China' and the formation of the Southeast Asia 'growth triangle'. The concentration and the rapid growth of overseas Chinese capital in South China since the late 1980s is said to demonstrate that, although transnational capital does not flow across this space without constraints even if national borders might be threatened in the era of globalization, cultural-institutional maps can still dictate the direction and the way in which transnational capital expands and is accumulated. Based on shared cultural identity and linguistic fluency and shaped by increasing local autonomy in China, overseas Chinese investors are said to have successfully established interpersonal relationships (including ones with state officials) and, as a result, have consolidated their business partnerships. Thus, overseas Chinese enterprises have prospered in South China. Lee Kuan Yew once boasted: 'what ethnic Chinese from Hong Kong, Macao, and Taiwan did was to demonstrate to a skeptical world that *guanxi* connections through the same language and culture can make up for a lack in the rule of law and transparency in rules and regulations.' (Cf. Ong, 1997:181) The statement embraced his vision of a larger reality underlying transnational Chinese co-operation: 'people feel a natural empathy with those who share their physical attributes. This sense of closeness is reinforced when they also share culture and language. It makes for easy rapport and the trust that is the foundation of all business relations' (*International Herald Tribune*, November 23, 1993:4). What this view fails to take into account is the fact that much of the labour involved in *qiaoxiang* enterprises is migrant: a phenomenon which presents a number of practical, even 'cultural', difficulties for all those involved. Although overseas Chinese investors, including those interviewed for this study, will tell you that, when compared to other production sites, China is more attractive for cultural and linguistic reasons, the big question remains: 'How do they apply cultural-based management values in actual practice?'

ISSUES AND PROBLEMS

One of the greatest and most dramatic impacts of foreign investment is the movement of more than ten million migrants from diverse and widely distant parts into southern China. This massive rural labour flow has raised many challenges, not only for the existing labour market mechanism and welfare systems, but also for enterprise management. There were more than eight million migrant workers in Guangdong in 1997; most of them found jobs in the foreign-invested enterprises in the special economic zones and the Pearl River Delta region (*The Guangzhou Daily*, 9 September 1998). In the author's sample of 28,000 workers, 75.6 per cent (21,140) were migrants. In many newly developed industrial towns, migrants made up the majority of the population in the region not only in the labour force but also as residents. The workers were mainly from inner underdeveloped provinces such as Sichuan, Henan, Hunan and Yunnan (Che, 1997), far from the more cosmopolitan, outward-looking, area of South China with its 'overseas Chinese hometowns'.

GENERAL PATTERNS

The role of migrant labour in foreign-funded enterprises in South China has already attracted close academic attention. Lever-Tracy and colleagues studied labour and diaspora capital (Lever-Tacey et al., 1996). Gao focused on labour relations in Taiwanese firms in China (Gao, 1996). Chen wrote about the new trends of migrants in China (Chen, 1997). Scharping and associates conducted a survey on migrant workers in Shenzhen and Foshan cities (Scharping et al., 1997). Schak researched labour problems in Taiwanese-funded firms (Schak, 1997). Huang investigated workers' organizations in overseas Chinese invested enterprises in South China (Huang, 1997 and 1998). Several general points can, therefore, be made.

The purpose of migration

The majority of migrants moved to the *qiaoxiang* region with a clear economic purpose, namely to make a better life for themselves and to earn money to support their families remaining in poorer rural areas. South China provides employment opportunity because of the booming foreign-invested enterprises, which require a large labour force. The large gap in wages, and standard of living between South China and their home villages is clearly the major attraction. However a second reason for migration can be related to a labour surplus in agriculture. According to the Chinese press, China is experiencing a 'tidal wave of rural migration labour'. It was estimated that presently 80 million migrants are making the largest flow of migrant labour in the country's history (Chen, 1997).

Composition of migrant workers

The majority of migrants, at least those surveyed in the studies mentioned above, are young. One report indicated that among 80 million migrants in China, 60 million are under 24 years of age (Chen, 1997). Most are fermales of peasant origin from underdeveloped provinces in the country's hinterland, with little industrial work experience. In my own sample of 28,000 workers in 20 enterprises, 17,780 (63.5 per cent) were female. This gender imbalance reflects the nature of the work, such as sewing and shoe making, which employs mainly female workers. It is also important to note that the majority of these migrant workers had a low education level. However Scharping's study did find that migrants had a higher educational level overall than their non-migrant counterparts in Shenzhen, the special economic zone in China, where strict government policies have controlled unskilled migrant labour (Scharping et al., 1997:41).

Channels of recruitment

A recent study found that information about the opportunities provided by migration came mostly from relatives (48.2 per cent) and friends (41.9 per cent) (Scharping et al., 1997:50). These two groups provided the basic social network not only for the chain migration from the home area but also for finding and changing jobs in South China. Thanks to the help of relatives and friends, most find jobs immediately upon arrival. This emerging social network ensures both emotional and economic assistance and is not unlike those previously established by migrants who left their *qiaoxiang* for overseas destinations in years goneby. I have found that most migrants spent their free time with people of common origin. They also kept close contact with relatives and friends at home through regular visits and remittances (Huang, 1997). Mass migration of labourers into 'overseas Chinese villages' in South China has been an important phenomenon from the early 1980s onward. Although many studies have noted that most of the migrant workers are young, female, and of peasant origin, little attention has been paid to the problems specific to their training and management.

THEORY AND PRACTICE

All the employers interviewed in my case study were from Hong Kong, Taiwan or Southeast Asia. They identified themselves as Chinese in cultural origins and language. They also claimed to practise 'Chinese-style management' in the workplace. But what is this? And how is it applied when dealing with migrant workers?

Cultural roots of management

The management of overseas Chinese invested enterprises is often seen as a model of the Chinese cultural tradition somewhat modified by imported ideology, technology, and technical skills (Huang, 1997 and 1998). Various writers put forward different lists of the key elements, which are likely to have a particular bearing on management. But, undoubtedly, those values which have particular relevance for management in China would include: orientation toward groups; the preservation of 'face'; the respect for age and hierarchy; and the importance of personal relationships (Lockett, 1988:475-96). It is widely accepted that the Confucian tradition stresses order, hierarchy, quality of relationships, and obligations to social groups, especially to the family (Smith, 1974:62-76). This favours organizational hierarchy and centralized decision-making. Much of what has been argued to support the distinctiveness of a 'Chinese' or 'Confucian' approach to management among overseas Chinese firms can be grouped under three headings: (1) paternalism, (2) familism, and (3) trust (Wong, 1996:30; Ng et al., 1997:19). The paternalistic assumption of the employer or owner-manager is that they provide their employees with a net of security and welfare benefits, but this is done at the employer's discretion rather than by being regulated by rules to specify these provisions as his/her contractual obligations. Ng and colleagues found that the practices of Chinese paternalistic management were instrumental in securing the workforce's loyalty and the workers' commitment to work in many Hong Kong firms (Ng et al., 1997).

A strong sense of family orientation lies deep in Chinese culture and, as an extension of the family structure, leaders of social groups are an amplification of the Confucian model of the father as the absolute authority (Pye, 1985:199 and Huang, 1998:64). Just as the father's word is absolute in the family, so the boss can tolerate no challenge. It is said to be difficult for the Chinese to initiate routine family administration without giving it a strong moral or idealistic gloss, suggesting that anyone who fails to comply with the rules is morally deficient. Such is the logic of paternalistic authority; that there must be total conformity. Chinese management, it is argued, exploits fear, an emotion, which is the opposite of hope, as when a leader adopts draconian measures to compel compliance and punish deviance. The mechanics of fear in Chinese family management blends the terror of being out of step, of being singled out in contempt, with the horrors of shame and physical punishment (Pye, 1985:199 and Huang, 1998:64).

A key to the practice of quasi-paternalistic management is said to be the persisting importance of 'trust' as a binding nexus of the employees' loyalty, which in turn gives rise to the continuing 'informality' of Chinese managerial practices that such a 'trust' element sustains (Ng et al., 1997:89). 'Trust' serves as a subtle yet effective managerial instrument in consolidating and inculcating the tacit consent and involvement of the employees in innovations, changes and other exigencies in the workplace. In part, this is because 'trust' represents for the worker a diffuse loyalty to the work enterprise, which, in turn, prompts the individual to accept, as the occasion demands, responsibilities beyond any specific contractual function and stipulations. It is an article of faith binding the individual and the collectivity in mutuality so that to the individual's obligations to the collective are no more precisely specified than the collective's responsibility to the individual. Where high trust prevails at work, the employee is always ready to sacrifice immediate personal interests and conveniences, confident that in the long-run, his dedicated commitment and loyal service will be recognized and rewarded by the employer.

Standard management practices
The following management practices were observed in the overseas Chinese companies studied.

i) Fringe benefits
Many enterprises provided their employees with fringe benefits as part of their management strategies (see Table 2). Managers explain that this paternalistic device was intended to make workers feel comfortable when working in the factory and encourage them to remain longer. They also believed that such incentives would raise workers' productivity and reduce turnover rates in the bargain. All enterprises that were studied gave production bonuses to their employees. Thirteen employers provided workers with subsidized accommodations and seventeen provided free lunches. Work-related injury insurance was adopted by sixteen enterprises, thus meeting the requirements of the labour law. However, fifteen enterprises did not have medical plans and fourteen did not have pension plans for their workers. Some employers explained that due to the temporary nature of employment, they were not willing to provide long-term benefit packages in their factories.

Table 1. Fringe benefit provided in the enterprises*

Type of fringe benefit	yes (# cases)	no (# cases)
production bonus	20	0
subsidized accommodation	13	7
free lunch	17	3
medical plans	5	15
work injury insurance	16	4
pension plans	6	14

* A summary of filed interview notes.

ii) The workplace regime
The workplace regime was commonly practised in the enterprises that were studied. It can be used as a starting point for conceptualizing modes of labour management in these enterprises. Control was found to be overt, visible, and publicly displayed. Some factory grounds were fenced with high concrete walls, and the main entrance gates were watched over by security guards carrying batons. Notice boards tabulated daily and hourly output targets, and the names of the best and worst performing workers were featured on a weekly basis. The visible display of rules and

regulations, plus the amount of fines if violations took place, were posted on the walls along the production lines. Therefore, using publicly displayed policies and punishment to rule workers' consciousness could be seen as manipulative way to create shame and fear and thus to control individuals in the workplace.

iii) Factory handbooks
Other important management tools found were the 'factory handbook' and enterprise regulations. Among twenty enterprises studied, fifteen printed their own workers' manuals, four enterprises had written regulations, and one enterprise had only unwritten rules. The handbooks reflected not only the content but also the style of labour management in these enterprises, containing detailed rules and regulations that the workers had to obey. One handbook contained 143 described rules and fines. The following are the quoted rules collected from several company handbooks: 'Workers must wear a factory identity card on their uniforms. Violators are fined five *yuan.*' 'Workers' punching cards for others are fined three days' wages. Workers who do not line up for punching time cards are fined two *yuan.*' 'Workers who spit or litter are punished to wash the factory toilet for a week.' 'Workers who smoke in the dormitory are fined ten *yuan.*' 'Workers who do not obey the supervisor's orders are given a warning. Workers who do not obey supervisors' orders for the third time are dismissed.' These regulations and rules reflected the traditional Chinese family-business management style, which is authoritarian and punishment-oriented in nature.

The above findings reflect the apparently relevant cultural factor of Confucian mentality about management, that is authority, order, and obligations - a rather familiar theme which has been discussed earlier in this section. The majority of the employers interviewed in the study agreed that strict and punishment-oriented labour policies were an efficient way to manage migrant workers in China. They believed that this type of management would result in high productivity and better performance of the workers. Although no obvious physical abuses against workers were discovered in the enterprises studied, many stories of abuse have been reported elsewhere (Chan, 1998).

SPECIAL CHARACTERISTICS OF MIGRANT WORKERS AND THEIR MANAGERS

Field observations and interviews revealed that there were important attitudinal differences between management and migrant workers in the workplace, some of which can be traced to cultural background and life experiences; they may explain why conflicts often occur.

Table 2. Contrast characteristics of management and migrant workers*

Management	Migrant workers
stable	temporary
loyalty	trust
commitments	alternatives
particularity	ambiguity
collectivism	individualism
disciplines	personal habits

*A summary from field interviews.

A fundamental characteristic of migrant labour is its uncertain and temporary nature. Migrants, who left their country homes and moved into an unfamiliar and not always friendly environment, had many fears and uncertainties. They explained the move to South China mainly in terms of the need to make money. Many of them saw the factory as a short-term situation. Because of their temporary nature and clear purpose, many migrants did not have a desire to stay in one factory for long and instead, frequently moved around looking for better paid employment. Sometimes they move to be with friends who are from the same village. As long as they had reliable information and confidence, the key to their life-style was mobility. In contrast with migrant workers, the employers interviewed emphasized the importance of a stable workplace. They wanted their workers to remain in the workplace for long-term employment and worried about the high turnover in the labour force. This difference in outlook was fundamental to a number of conflicts. Although both the overseas Chinese entrepreneurs and their workers are 'sojourners' in South China, the entrepreneurs seemed to be more committed to the long-term interest of their enterprise than their employees.

The second difference was in the loyalty to the workplace and the personal trust towards the workers. It was clear that all employers interviewed wanted their workers to be loyal. Some of them claimed that they intended to create a family type atmosphere in the workplace in order to build up a base for workers' loyalty. In contrast, the workers interviewed considered that for them trust comes before loyalty due to the uncertainty of their lives. These two expectations conflicted, especially when the labour force was migrant. Although, logically speaking, loyalty and personal trust are connected, in practice they often serve different purposes. This brings about an important management issue, namely, how to establish mutual trust and gain workers' loyalty as well. From observations in the enterprises studied, this conflict played a significant role in workplace management. Both employers and employees complained about the other side for being either disloyal or distrustful.

A third problem revolved around the reluctance of workers to make firm commitments, preferring to keep their options open. Most migrant workers interviewed wanted to have alternative employment available in case things would not work out. This is a result of the temporary and non-contracted status of their employment. The study found that a few enterprises hired migrants on a non-contract basis. In this case, workers did not have fixed employment and could lose their jobs anytime. However, employers would like to have total commitment from their employees in the workplace, but were not convinced that it was necessary to provide migrants with long-term contracts. This feature is also related to the issue of responsibility in the workplace. A common complaint expressed by managers about migrants was that 'very few of them have a sense of belonging to the workplace, therefore, they rarely make commitments to work and they don't take responsibility concerning what they are doing'. In contrast, the migrant workers said that 'how can we have a sense of belonging to the enterprise when we work on a daily contract basis. On the other hand, the employers are too demanding in work and leave no free space in our lives.'

The fourth contrast feature was between management style and workers' life-style: namely, particularity and ambiguity. It was found that many overseas Chinese enterprises studied were family-run businesses. These tended to be particularistic in their management practices (Pang and Liu, 1975:12). The employers interviewed thought that the particularistic type of management ensures that the workers understand every single requirement and step of the production process, and that this would improve the quality and productivity of the workers. However, the workers interviewed complained that there were too many itemized requirements, which made them feel distrusted and made work more difficult. This was not only because there were too many regulations to follow, but also because the regulations were too particularistic to be practised. For example, one workers' handbook contained more than one hundred items of rules and regulations, which the workers were required to memorize. Migrants often complained that because in the country they were used to a life-style that was rather unregulated, they were not comfortable in the new environment, in which situations were precisely defined and structured. It was suggested that to improve mutual communication would be more useful than detailed written regulations.

The fifth characteristic had to do with the position of individual workers within the collective structure of the workplace. In traditional Chinese culture, collective or group consciousness occupied an important position. Individuals were not identified by independent status as such, but by dependent relations within a hierarchical system (Wang, et al., 1998:22). The productivity of a factory today requires constant collaboration with others. Therefore, collectivity is an important quality of successful enterprises. However, the migrant workers interviewed demonstrated a strong inclination towards individualism. They tended to be independent and self reliant; many of them felt remote from the workplace. One of the workers said 'I don't have a sense of being part of the factory because I am always being myself, at work, and after work. Many others feel the same as I do.' Switching in and out of jobs to take advantage of changing situations was evidence of this. Many employers reported that it was very difficult to train migrant workers to work together as a team within the hierarchical structure of the enterprise.

The sixth contradiction observed was between workplace disciplines and workers' personal habits. Many overseas Chinese employers complained that migrant employees lacked discipline in their work as a result of poor personal habits. Empirical data demonstrated that socio-economic status was an important determinant of the amount of human capital investment and subsequent economic success (Wang, et al., 1998:4). Migrants from the countryside lacked market contacts and information. This had an impact not only on the world-view of the individual, but also on his/her respect for work values and habits. Work attitudes were also related to one's personal habits and educational level. It was found that many enterprises under study practised workplace discipline as a fundamental step to train migrant workers. However, this practice was recorded to be trivial and rigid in nature, and sometimes it was military and punishment oriented.

In summary, observations of migrant workers and workplace management in a sample of overseas Chinese invested enterprises indicated that the contrast characteristics between these two social groups were derived from their different cultural, economic, social and psychological backgrounds. In this study, the management represented the nature of overseas Chinese firms, which was, more or less, particularistic, rigid, less personal rapport and punishment oriented. In contrast, the culture of migrant workers was related to the nature of migrants and their personal goals, which was temporary, ambiguous, individualistic and pragmatic.

OTHER DIFFICULTIES

Many among the interviewed overseas Chinese employers shared common experiences in managing workers in their South China operations. The most common complaint was that migrant workers had poor work habits and lacked a sense of responsibility. They often failed to follow instructions and were unwilling to co-operate. A common example given by the employers was 'after ten times you told the workers how to do the work, you will find that they are still working in their own ways'. Many managers were concerned with the quality of their workforce and tried to find ways to improve it.

While much of the literature stresses the importance of socio-economic networks to business success, the informal social networks now being constructed by the migrant workers can pose considerable problems for management. The most important feature of these groups is hometown solidarity. Workers who were part of these informal networks gather together in groups privately after work. On the one hand these networks meet a positive need for sharing and belonging and can produce more-satisfied employees. But, on the other hand, they encourage organized criticism of the authoritarianism of the workplace. Many employers expressed concern and feared strikes or mass walkouts. Therefore, informal networks were strictly forbidden on company property. Some of the enterprises made clear regulations on the prohibition of hometown solidarity groups. One workers' handbook included the following statements: 'Workers who express strong feelings of hometown solidarity are fined or dismissed depending on the degree of violation of the rules.' Another indicated that 'Supervisors who are nepotistic to their village workers are fined 50 *yuan* or demoted.' It was reported that a mass run-away involving enterprises in Shenzhen and Dongguan, which occurred in June 1997, was made worse by rumours spread among informal hometown networks (Huang, 1998).

Cases have been reported in recent years of how badly Chinese workers are treated by foreign managers. Anita Chan found that there were often disgraceful working conditions in the export-oriented foreign-funded sector in South China, including long working hours, low wages, and physical abuse (Chan, 1997). It was found that labour militancy concentrated in foreign invested enterprises and involved mostly migrant workers. In Guangdong, spontaneous walkouts and strikes in foreign invested factories protesting maltreatment by foreign capitalists have been widely reported in the press (*Xiandai qiye bao* (Modern Enterprise Daily) 18 August 1996; *Yangcheng wanbao*, 22 March 1995; *Ming Pao*, 4 December 1996 and 18 September 1996). In Shenzhen between 1993-4, there were 1,100 labour disputes, of which 90 per cent occurred in foreign invested firms (Liu, 1996:127). Mistreatment of workers in foreign-funded enterprises has drawn attention from both inside and outside China.

There are other difficulties in managing migrant workers, such as a lack of respect towards authorities, poor hygiene habits, and stealing, etc. Although the employers interviewed acknowledged problems in managing migrant workers, they nevertheless admitted that most of the workers were bright and had good hearts. (This was also found by David Schak. See his chapter in this book.) Their problems were blamed on the failure of the rural educational system, which lacked moral education (such as honesty, respect, and hard work) and basic vocational skill training in the curriculum. However many of the differences between management and labour can also be explained by a 'cultural gap' between owners and/or managers who have lived in more-sophisticated foreign-influenced locations in China, Hong Kong, or abroad. As Scharping and associates found, wanting to be rich and wealthy, to be successful, and to be self-fulfilled were top personal values of migrants: which they obviously shared with managers (Scharping et al., 1997:83). But some other values often observed among migrant workers - such as avoiding risks, personal conflicts and responsibilities - seemed be an important cause of conflict.

THE NEED FOR TRAINING

To help solve some of the difficulties mentioned above, the government has begun to push for pre-employment training. For example, in Guangzhou, one of the places in South China most densely populated with migrants, the city government issued a labour permit policy in 1994 stipulating that all migrants who wanted to work needed to obtain a work permit through attending an approved training programme. As a result, several schools for migrants have been established in the city. The 'Jinyan (Golden Wild Goose) Training School' was first established for this purpose (Fu, 1995). It offers courses in a variety of subjects including an introduction to urban living, law and regulations of the city, basic industrial skills and moral principles, workers' rights and obligations, welfare and insurance, as well as occupational health and safety practices. Migrants received a work permit only if they passed examinations. Although the migrants who had attended this kind of training school were limited in numbers, the plans for pre-employment training have been praised both by enterprises and migrants. In September 1998, the Labour Department of the Guangzhou city government further strengthened its policy by stipulating that 4,000 occupations require certificates to work (*The Guangzhou Daily*, 18

September 1998).

The bold initiative taken by the 'Jinyan Training School' has already had a significant impact on the nature and flow of migrant labour into the city. It also made the governments of both receiving and sending places realize the importance of quality control and their responsibility to provide suitable training programmes for potential workers. On the other hand, it drew attention to the need for pre-employment training in the general school curriculum. Studies revealed that, for employers, cognitive skills developed by the school system were not always as important as qualities such as patience, discipline, obedience, acceptance of authority, and adaptability to new situations (Pang and Liu, 1975:4). Therefore, moral education, life and vocational skill training must be strengthened (in school and adult education), especially in the rural areas which produce most of the migrant workers. My research found that many township and city governments have now begun to take action to improve pre-employment training.

All employers in the study realized that the lack of relevant training had become a key constraint in the ability of a majority of the migrant workers to participate in high-productive work. Quite a few placed an emphasis on education in their management plans, even though they commented, that it will be difficult to see results in the short term. The study found that training activities provided for the migrants were variously organized. Some factories selected a few 'high' qualified workers to be trained, then let them be examples and tutors for the rest of the workers; while some held monthly training sessions for newly-recruited workers; and a few sponsored selected workers to attend structured programmes in external training and educational institutions. An important quality that was strongly stressed in the training was workers' discipline habits. A manager told us that he expected workers to learn work-related skills and to change their value attitudes towards work and life in general through the training.

Other educative approaches included regimented paramilitary training of workers. Some factories had their workers line up in formation before and after work. Morning exercise was commonly practised. The employers believed that these exercises would help stimulate workers' spirits towards work, therefore, it would raise their productivity. Slogans on the walls were used to urge workers to work hard, do good work, be careful, put quality first - put the customer first. Many enterprises carried out punishment-oriented policies in the workplace. These methods were thought to be educational, but in reality played a negative role in the process of educating migrant workers. The workers felt they were being mistreated rather than improved through these means. The approach should emphasize mutual respect, be less punishment-oriented, and have better communication channels, and provide rational explanations for strict rules.

Many peasants lack self-esteem because of their poor education. 'In-house training' provided by the employers can help migrants learn required skills and get to know the regulations of the work environment. In addition, migrants can attend the pre-employment classes to be qualified to work in certain areas. However, these formal channels can lead to success only if the migrants themselves understand the importance of adapting to modern industrial life and its values. Therefore, it is important to provide migrants with self-esteem education, starting with self-respect, self-discipline, and then self-motivation. This education should be included in the moral education of the school curriculum. For the majority of migrant workers, education in (and for) the workplace would ultimately provide more opportunities, a chance to meet people from different backgrounds, to experience new things, whilst learning additional employment-related skills. Moreover, migrants can improve themselves through informal social networks. Many have already used hometown connections to find work and share job information.

FUTURE PROSPECTS

The trends in migration observed in South China cannot be explained by changes in the labour market alone but can also be explained by other economic and social factors. From an economic perspective, remittances sent to country families greatly benefit both migrants' families and their communities. They help solve pressing financial difficulties and improve daily lives. Remittances also play an important role in the development of migrant 'hometowns' throughout the country. For some sending places, migration for employment has even become part of a medium-term development strategy. For example, five million emigrant workers from Sichuan province sent home remittances of RMB20.2 billion in 1996, which equalled the total financial revenue of the province in the same year (Chen, 1997). Mass labour migration into the overseas Chinese invested enterprises in South China was not a one-way flow, but also created flows of capital and knowledge back to the countryside. If each emigrant labourer brings (or sends) 2,000 *yuan* home per year, the total income remitted by eight million migrant workers in Guangdong will reach 16 billion *yuan* and the total income remitted by the 80 million migrants in the whole country would reach 160 billion *yuan*. This amount would make out 79.7 per cent of the total expenditures on fixed assets for production purposes and housing which rural households invested, and 3.7 times as much as the total expenditures on agricultural production and administration from the state budget (Cai, 1998). Moreover, when migrants return home they bring not just money and the skills which they learnt on the job, but also a more-modern outlook consistent with the requirements of village development. It is difficult to say, at this stage, whether the accumulated savings will be used to raise the consumption levels or be invested in more productive agriculture or perhaps actually used to set up small industrial ventures on models learnt in South China. However, the experience of migration and work skills developed in the enterprise could be invaluable not only for one's personal development, but also for the benefit of society as a whole (Cai, 1998).

The history of labour migration in other countries suggests that at least some of the migrants are likely to remain permanently and that if they do they will likely demand a greater share of the value of their products as well as decent working conditions and more secure employment (Lever-Tracy, et al., 1996:279). Therefore, the emerging migrant working class may well move rapidly from a passive and victimized status to higher levels of class consciousness and take a more active role in both the workplace and surrounding communities. One important feature of this trend, as has already been observed, is the expansion of 'hometown' based social networks, which may well result in the creation of 'sojourner' associations of all kinds as happened before in North America and Southeast Asia.

CONCLUDING REMARKS

When overseas Chinese investors claimed that they shared the same cultural values with the mainland Chinese, and could therefore take advantages of cheap labour and favourable investment conditions in South China, none of them would have expected to encounter a 'cultural shock' in their hometown business operations. Although both overseas Chinese managers and migrant workers represent 'sojourner' populations with a similar purpose, namely to make money, the conflicts between them reflect more than just labour-management disagreement; they also reflect differing backgrounds and experiences. The most obvious differences between the two groups revolve around loyalty vs. trust; commitment vs. alternatives; particularity vs. ambiguity; and collectivism vs. individualism. This study argues that the so-called 'shared cultural values' among Chinese including mainland, Hong Kong, Taiwan, and Southeast Asian Chinese, might not necessarily provide overseas Chinese entrepreneurs with as many business advantages as some writers have suggested, especially when they have to deal with migrant workers.

However, mutual trust and understanding between migrant workers and employers can be built based on the implicit 'psychological contract' in the workplace, which is exemplified by the welfare 'paternalism' of the Chinese enterprises as reflected in their managerial ethos. The resulting expectations are hoped to not only cover the contractual exchange of how much work is to be performed for how much pay, but also involve the whole pattern of rights, privileges and obligations. Hence, the psychological contract is a moral embodiment of that diffusive bond of trust and affective commitment between the parties to an employment relationship. Despite what the scholarly literature says about 'trust' as a factor in the management of Chinese enterprises, it is clear from my study, that many employers need to work more on this dimension by providing more benefits, and by displaying more respect and a more friendly work environment. They also need to acknowledge the rural, 'cultural', background of their workers.

A last important observation from the study concludes this chapter. An overseas Chinese employer believed that good management was based on proper moral standards set up in the factory, and that to respect workers is the best way of educating them. He adopted moral teachings, mainly from Confucianism, with some from Christianity, and practised them in his management. In this factory, posters on the walls told workers how to become good human beings, with such qualities as sharing, modesty, tolerance, and generosity being strongly encouraged. Rules and regulations were written in a format, which was thought to make workers feel more comfortable in accepting them. Meetings with workers were arranged regularly to discuss problems and share decisions made between managers and workers. It was related by a local labour official that the turnover of workers in this factory was the lowest in the district, although its wage level was rather low compared with most other foreign-funded enterprises. The reason for workers staying was attributed directly to the atmosphere of the factory and the way in which the workers were treated. Although there are very few cases like this in the study, it was found that many employers expressed their interest in learning new ideas and methods of management in China. It is hoped that through the study of different characteristics of migrant labour and management, a better understanding of the relationship between these two social groups will be reached. Thus employers will gradually find a better approach for the management of migrant workers.[3]

BIBLIOGRAPHY

Cai, Fang
1998   'Pattern of Migration in China's Reform Period', paper presented at the International Conference: Labour Mobility and Migration in China and Asia, organized by the Institute of Asian-Pacific Studies

of the Chinese Academy of Social Sciences (Beijing), the International Institute for Asian Studies (Leiden), and the Institute of Social Studies (The Hague), Beijing, 17-18 April

Chan, Anita
1997   'Workers' Rights and Human Rights: The Plight of Chinese Workers Must Be on the International Agenda', *Journal of Human Rights in China*, summer 1997, pp. 4-7
1998   (ed.) The Conditions of Chinese Workers in East Asian-Funded Enterprises, a special issue of the *Journal of Chinese Sociology & Anthropology* 30(4)

Che, Xiaohui
1997   'Hong Kong Invested Enterprises Opened Up Channels for Employment in Guangdong', *The People's Daily* (European Edition), 25 August

Chen, Qiang and Shiaowei Hu
1997   'An Analysis on China's Utilization of Foreign Investment', *The Study of Overseas Chinese Affairs* 72(2)

Chen, Yaoming
1997   'The New Choices of Migrant Labour', *China News Digest (CND)*, 16 January

East Asia Analytical Unit
1995   *Overseas Chinese Business Networks in Asia*, Department of Foreign Affairs and Trade, Australia

Fu, Weili
1995   *Laodong li shichang yu jiaoyu de zizhu tiaojie wenti* (Labour Markets and Educational Self-adjustment). Changsha: Hunan Educational Press

Gao, Charng
1996   *Industrial and Labour Relations of Taiwanese Enterprises in Mainland China*. Chung-Hua Institute for Economic Research, Taipei

The Guangzhou Daily, Guangzhou

Hsing, You-tien
1997   'Building Guanxi Across the Straits: Taiwanese Capital and Local Chinese Bureaucrats', in: Ong, Aihwa and Donald M. Nonini (eds) *Ungrounded Empires, The Cultural Politics of Modern Chinese Transnationalism*. New York, London: Routledge

Huang, Cen
1997   '*Haiwai huaren he nanbu zhongguo de huazi kuaguo qiye* (Overseas Chinese and Transnational Enterprises in South China)', *The Journal of Overseas Chinese History of Bagui* 4(36)
1998   'The Organization and Management of Chinese Transnational

Enterprises in South China', *Issues & Studies* 34(4), pp. 51-70

International Herald Tribune, 1993

Kerr, Clark; John T. Dunlop; Frederick Harbison, and C.A. Myers
1973   *Industrialism and Industrial Man*, Harmondsworth: Penguin, 2nd edition

Lever-Tracy, Constance; David Ipid; and Noel Tracy
1996   *The Chinese Diaspora and Mainland China: An Emerging Economic Synergy*. New York: St. Martin's Press Inc.

Liu, Alan
1996   *Mass Politics in the People's Republic*. Boulder, CO: Westview

Lockett, Martin
1988   'Culture and the Problems of Chinese Management', *Organizational Studies* 9

Ming Pao, Hong Kong

Modern Enterprise Daily (Xiandai zhiye bao), Guangzhou

Ng Sek-Hong; Sally Steward; and Chan Fun-ting
1997   *Current Issues of Workplace Relations & Management in Hong Kong*. Center of Asian Studies, The University of Hong Kong

Ong, Aihwa
1997   'Chinese Modernity: Narratives of Nation and of Capitalism', in: Ong Aihwa and Donald M. Nonini (eds) *Ungrounded Empires, The Cultural Politics of Modern Chinese Transnationalism*. New York, London: Routledge

Pang Eng Fong and Liu Pak Wai
1975   *Education, Socioeconomic Status and Labour Market Success: A Case Study of Manufacturing Workers in Singapore*, Working Papers. International Labour Office, Geneva

Pye, Lucian W.
1985   *Power and Politics: The Cultural Dimension of Authority*. Cambridge, Mass. and London: The Belknap Press of Harvard University

Schak, David
1997   'Taiwanese Enterprises in the Pearl River Delta Region: Problems and Prospects'. Paper presented at the International Seminar: International Social Organizations in East and Southeast Asia, Leiden, the Netherlands, 28-9 August

Scharping, Thomas; Walter Schulze; Huaiyang Sun; Tongjin Jia; and Runtian Chen (eds)
1997   *Migration in China's Guangdong Province*, Mitteilungen, Des Instituts fur Asienkunde, Hamburg

Smith, David Howard
1974   *Confucius*. London: Paladin

Suryadinata, Leo
1995   'China's Economic Modernization and the Ethnic Chinese in ASEAN: A Preliminary Study', in: Leo Suryadinata (ed.) *Southeast Asian Chinese and China, the Political-Economic Dimension*. Singapore: Times Academic Press
Wang, Yuan; Zhang, Xin Sheng; and Rob Goodfellow
1998   *Business Culture in China*. Butterworth-Heinemann Asia
Wong, Siu-lun
1996   'Chinese Entrepreneurship and Economic Development', in: Leo Douw and Peter Post (eds) *South China: State, Culture and Social Change during the 20th Century*. Amsterdam: KNAW
Yangcheng wanbao, Guangzhou

Notes

1. This chapter is based on the author's field study in Guangdong and Fujian provinces in April and December 1997. Interviews were conducted with overseas Chinese investors, managers, and migrant workers in twenty overseas Chinese enterprises. This study is a preliminary research into the management of migrant labour in overseas Chinese invested enterprises, and has several limitations. First of all, the data were collected through short field study trips to South China, and thus the enterprises and migrant workers studied might not represent other enterprises and migrant workers in the region. Secondly, the study was limited to general discussions on management issues of migrant labour. A comparative analysis between female and male, and between unskilled and skilled migrant workers on the research topic would be needed to further develop the study. Therefore, the purpose of this paper is to 'cast a brick to attract jade'; in other words, to offer a few remarks by way of introduction so that others may contribute deeper and more valuable opinions.

2. The majority of the approximately 270,000 foreign-funded firms in 1997 were located in southeastern coastal China. Given that foreign investment in China was estimated at US$45 billion for 1997, this brought the total for the six years from 1992 to more than US$190 billion. Overall, foreign-funded enterprises account for nearly 50 per cent of China's total foreign trade and contribute nearly a quarter of total industrial production. See: Chen and Hu, 1997, p. 21; and Huang, 1998.

3. Kerr, et al., 1973, p. 181, believe that: 'Human resources may be upgraded for industrial employment in three ways: workers may advance themselves; they may be provided with education by the community or by the state; and, they may be trained by enterprise managers. In most cases, advancement is the result of all three processes.'

CULTURE AS A MANAGEMENT ISSUE: THE CASE OF TAIWANESE ENTREPRENEURS IN THE PEARL RIVER DELTA[1]

DAVID C. SCHAK

Like other overseas investors, Taiwanese look for plentiful supplies of cheap labour and for other reductions in factory costs. Countries in Southeast Asia initially provided the desired workers, though some entrepreneurs complained that Malaysia, for example, was already losing its competitive advantage. When movement to China became possible, many firms jumped at the opportunity, not only because labour there was cheaper and more plentiful, but also because of the attraction of the domestic market and, very important for the owners of small and medium enterprises (SME), the belief that, since Chinese on both sides of the Taiwan Straits could speak Mandarin and shared so many cultural traits, it would be far easier to operate there. As this chapter demonstrates, however, they soon discovered that the separate development paths followed since the retreat of the Kuomintang (*Guomindang*) government in 1949 had led to significant differences in values, outlook, work habits, goals and, perhaps most-importantly, the *modus operandi* of officials. Although 'cultural difference' was only one of the problems Taiwanese entrepreneurs encountered when they began relocating some or all of their production to mainland China in the late 1980s, it was probably the one that was least expected.

INTRODUCTION

Taiwanese entrepreneurs were forced overseas for a number of reasons: labour shortages, rising wages, indirect labour costs and land prices, restrictions on overtime work, an appreciating local currency against the US dollar, and stricter environmental protection, as well as a growing rejection of 'dirty' factory work in favour of white-collar jobs among young workers (see Schak, 1994). Initially, the People's Republic of China was off limits because of the formal state of war, so factories relocated or set up labour-intensive subsidiaries in Southeast Asia, Malaysia at first, then Indonesia, Thailand, and the Philippines, and more recently Vietnam. That these countries were second choice is demonstrated by the rapidity with which Taiwanese went to Mainland China as soon as they were permitted to do so. Once contacts were permitted, there was a flood of investment: from US$100 million in 1988 to US$1.4 billion in 1991 and US$3.4 billion by 1992. Hsing believes that Taiwanese direct investments in China totalled US$10 billion between 1978 and 1994, with probably an equal amount from Taiwanese capital registered in Hong Kong (Hsing, 1998:3). In yearly figures, investment grew from US$10 million in 1988 to US$340 million in 1992 (Hsu, 1993). Indeed, The Mainland Affairs Committee reported investments of US$4,634 billion in the first five months of 1996 alone (MAC, 1996). Official statistics report that some 37,000 Taiwanese firms presently operate in China, a figure thought by many to be a gross underestimate. Hsing notes that indirect China-Taiwan trade through Hong Kong totalled over US$15 billion by 1992, and between 1979 and 1992, Hong Kong and Taiwan together accounted for 72 per cent of the direct contracted foreign investment in China (Hsing, 1998:15-18). Much of the growth was at the expense of investments in Southeast Asian countries, though Taiwan remained a leading investor in Vietnam (Schak, 1998).

This preference for the People's Republic, over other possible locations, has often been explained in terms of language (Mandarin, spoken by the Taiwanese and the workers, who come from poorer inland provinces) as well as by shared patterns of social interaction, including an understanding of *guanxi*, face and gifts. Be this as it may, as the following pages will illustrate, many investors have discovered that they cannot so readily transfer their worker management methods from Taiwan to China:

'Our company came to the mainland in 1986. We lost NT$100 million in the first three years. When the company first moved here, I couldn't come because Taiwanese were not allowed to so I invested through a relative with an American passport. He managed it for three years and lost NT$100 million. I came here to be greeted by a strike. Now a strike, quite naturally, is bad. I said to our Director, my wife's elder brother, "How can you manage a company like this. They're on strike!" I was very unhappy. I said he hadn't been very attentive. He pulled out a book, [Company Name]: Taiwan Management System. Nothing was changed! "Come on", I said. "How can you use a system designed for Taiwan to manage in China?" There's no way that you can. They are different cultures!'[2]

As the above quotation from a Taiwanese factory owner shows, Taiwan and China had become, similar to what is sometimes said of the English and the Americans: 'two countries separated by the same language'. The following pages will explore these difficulties: all of which, according to Taiwanese informants,[3] can at least in part be traced to the cultural gulf which has grown up between the 'two Chinas'.

PROBLEMS CONFRONTING TAIWANESE ENTREPRENEURS

Investors have found that the skills, work habits and attitudes of workers are quite different from what they had become used to in Taiwan. Although labour costs are cheaper per worker, productivity levels were far below those of Taiwan workers; moreover, there were additional costs from pilferage. They found other cost pressures as well, which made it more difficult to make a healthy profit than they had first imagined. But an even more-critical problem has been corruption: described as even worse than experienced earlier on in the Republic of China, where corruption had been very serious in the 1950s and 1960s, but had been cleaned up considerably, especially as the political system opened up, a strong opposition party emerged, the reigns were taken off the press, and more alternative and critical voices were heard which applied pressure to clean up the system.[4] In field research carried out in the Pearl River Delta Region (PRDR) of Guangdong Province, the main problems informants spoke of were capricious charges and fees along with corrupt officials, increased competition and difficulties in making reasonable profits, barriers to entry into the mainland market and difficulties with workers. Not all faced the same problems, or to the same degree, but no informant felt that everything was running smoothly. They all acknowledged the adjustments necessary to operate successfully there, also admitting that it was not the same as operating in Taiwan.

CORRUPTION AND CAPRICIOUS FEES

Corruption is endemic to many Asian countries. According to Levi (Levi, 1997:4), China ranks high in corruption in published surveys of foreign business persons, and Chinese themselves rank its seriousness second only to inflation.[5] Rocca states that in 1988, an amount equal to the national education budget, 25-30 billion *yuan*, was spent on banquets alone, and another two and one-half times that amount on trips, food, drink and gifts (Rocca, 1992:412). A recent news account stating that even the Communist

Party, where much of the corruption lies and which has control over both press and police, sees its legitimacy undermined by the level of corruption (Lawrence, 1998a).

Much of the literature attempts to account for the high level of corruption. Rocca argues that its being seen as a problem is a product of changing times and changing expectations of official behaviour, especially their separation of public and private interests (Rocca, 1992). Lu states that a major portion of corruption occurs during the reorganization of units as cadres simply help themselves to valuable property (Lu, 1998:4-5). He also points to two sets of workers as being particularly prone to corruption because of the uncertainties they face, those in mid-career who feel they are stuck at their level and fear they will be the first to go; and the younger, better educated cadres who see the competition for promotion as tough and who wonder when will be a good time to 'take the plunge', as competition there is tough as well. The result is that these groups are in a sense just marking time (Lu, 1998:6-8).

Frank Ching has pointed to the initial distrust by the Communist Party of government by law (seen as a tool used by one class to oppress another), the poor training and pay of the judiciary, the fact that they are hired locally thus must give hometown decisions (Ching, 1998). Ke Lin blames the transitional period China is now experiencing with its multiple systems of markets and procedures, the lack of openness in the political and administrative systems, and 'some negative and obsolete traditional Chinese concepts and values' such as the unquestionable authority holders of government offices are assumed to possess, the notion of officials as a privileged class, and the idea that leaders can arbitrarily override law (Ke Lin, 1997:50).

Schottenhammer suggests a number of possible causes - Chinese tradition, the moral depravity of Communist Party members, the lack of democracy, bourgeois ideology - but rejects these, arguing that it is caused by a contradiction in the call to 'enrich oneself' as it affected post-reform industrial enterprise managers. The state wants them to make a profit, but they cannot do that if they do not disengage the enterprise from the relationship with the state according to regulations still in effect. But in making a profit they will enrich themselves, which could lead to their being regarded as corrupt. This kind of corruption is based on a contradiction, 'a reform program which economically requires the use of the functions of private property, although the private means of ownership of the means of production, which can be used to promote the state economy, has not (yet) be (sic) installed in Chinese society'. The contradiction is linked to the need to access credit, rather than merely rely on the ploughing back of much smaller amounts in profit, in order to make future profits. 'For the party leadership most of such business transactions had of necessity to appear to be a kind of unfair business, of corruption' (Schottenhammer, 1995:66-8).

I would argue that another factor is a psychological one: with the reforms, the cadres, who formerly sat atop Chinese society in class and status as well as power, saw their positions deteriorate as their salaries, thus the desirability of their positions, fell behind not only of those who entered the private business sector but even of persons such as taxi drivers and hawkers, people previously far beneath them in society. Moreover, to the extent that they sincerely believed in the communist ideology, their positions fell victim to the least legitimate of persons, free market capitalists. The solution was to commodify the one thing they had which was worth money or influence, their authority. Any authority which involved granting permission could be commodified. As to whether this failure to live up to the Communist Party's image of public servants as persons who unselfishly 'serve the people' might have brought forth pangs of conscience, I offer the following anecdote. A Chinese friend, now a law lecturer in Australia, related his return after doing his law degree (in China) to visit the area of rural Fujian where he had spent his time as a 'sent-down' youth. He found, much to his sorrow, that the forests had been denuded, and making enquiries, he found that the cadre in charge of the area had had this done to sell the wood to a lumber mill. He enquired of the cadre, who admitted that this was a bad thing to do, rationalized that 'if I don't do this, my successor will'. My friend said this was a very common attitude in China today.[6] Indeed, Rocca distinguishes between *tanwu*, corruption, when an official misappropriates state property, and *shouhui*, bribery, when a public servant uses hers/his position to demand or receive bribes (Rocca, 1992:405).

Taiwanese entrepreneurs in China are most directly affected by the latter. Despite frequent complaints from my informants about bribes they had to pay, the literature on corruption pays little attention to the extent of the demand for bribes from Taiwanese or other outside entrepreneurs. My introduction to this topic occurred one day at lunch in my host factory not long after I began my field study. Two fellows arrived about twenty minutes late, very angry. They had just been at the local customs trying to get a shipment of polyester yarn from Taiwan, the main raw material used in making zippers, released. The 'problem' was in the customs declaration. The person who shipped the goods in Taiwan had used the English word plus the Taiwanese translation of polyester, *duoyuan zhi*, instead of the Chinese translation, *juzhi*. The customs official accused them of making a false declaration. 'We explained that the word used was simply the Taiwan translation,' one said, 'but the officer retorted "This is mainland China, not

Taiwan!" He just used that as an excuse to demand money from us.' Had the shipment contained only the English word, there would not have been a problem. The general manager of a wire and cable factory related a similar incident; his Hong Kong office had used the Hong Kong translation of solder wire, *xixian* (lead string), rather than *xisi* (lead silk), the mainland China term, and he, too, had to pay a fine. Other informants complained about having to pay as much as 5,000 *yuan* to get shipments out of customs even when mistakes on the declaration form were very minor, e.g. getting the wrong sum for a column of figures even though the column was there for the inspector to read. To be questioned or even reprimanded was one thing, but to be fined such large amounts was another.

Had the two managers pursued these matters through channels, they would probably have won the day, but it would have cost them their own time and could have shut their factories down. Taiwanese and other foreign business operators and managers value their time very highly, moreover those in export manufacture know the importance of meeting delivery dates on orders.[7] Local officials know this and take advantage of it. A Hong Kong manufacturer said that whenever he is stopped by traffic police in China, he simply hands a one-hundred Hong Kong dollar bill over with his licence. 'That is what they want,' he said. 'If I don't give it to them, knowing that I am an outsider, they will demand that I accompany them to the station, and that will delay me for several hours.'

Interviewees also complained about other exactions from local authorities. It was not that they did not expect to pay levies on such things as water, fire protection, and so on. They did, although some complained that they had to pay for services that were not rendered, that when they wanted those services provided they had to pay again. Moreover, they pointed to a number of irregularities. For example, one informant said that in his area, after paying a police levy, officers came around to the factories in the district to collect donations for the provision of new uniforms for the local force. Another, while looking over office furniture in a shop, laid down his handbag and mobile phone on a table and turned around for a moment to measure the dimensions of a desk. When he turned back around, his phone and bag were gone. He went to the police, who told him that it would cost 4,000 *yuan* to retrieve them. He bargained but still ended up paying 3,000 *yuan*.

Informants also complained that whenever the head of a local township or industrial district (*gongye qu*) changed, the successor brought in a host of new charges in order not to have to wait for the next billing period to get on the gravy train. A sweater manufacturer was dunned for payment of an 'animal and plant inspection fee'. Somewhat baffled, he asked the official why he should have to pay since he did not use animals or plants in his factory, that he made sweaters. 'Sweaters,' exclaimed the official. 'Sweaters are made from wool. Wool comes from animals. You must pay!' In fact, the yarn used was from man-made fibres, but that distinction was lost on the collector.

Yet another tactic is the 'invitation'. A female entrepreneur said that every so often the Labour Bureau, Public Security (police) or Customs will 'invite' her to dinner at a particular restaurant for a banquet consisting of specified dishes, to be followed by singing at a particular karaoke. Although she was the one invited, it was understood that she would pick up the bill. 'Do I dare not go?' she said. 'They can always find problems in what you do. So you go and you pay. You must budget for these events in your expense projections. Fortunately they don't often do this to me because my company is small and I don't make all that much.'

It is *de rigeur* to invite Customs officials to banquets on the three major festivals (Chinese New Year, *Duanwu*, and Mid-Autumn). At one such banquet I attended with my host factory General Manager, the three Customs officials made a brief show of maintaining sobriety, but within half an hour they were drinking toasts to anything they could think of and by the end of the meal they were very drunk.[8] As we left, they invited us to a banquet to be held in three days, however, the General Manager said after we had parted company that he didn't have time to go and would send a red envelop, i.e. a gift of cash, instead. Just before a recent Chinese New Year, he spent over 60,000 *yuan* on dinners and red envelopes for Customs and local industrial district officials.

The cost of extricating oneself from an awkward situation with Customs or an occasional banquet for officials is small compared to the possible consequences; some informants even said that if one did not go along with expected behaviour the Public Security Bureau would suddenly drop in and search their entire premises under the pretext of looking for drugs, or the Labour Bureau could make trouble for one's workers. Such intrusions were costly in that they held up production and local officials used that as a weapon against them. To Taiwanese and other outside manufacturers it is not only the cost of these fines, fees and imposts but also their unpredictability and their resentment at being stood over by local authorities.[9] They complained over and over that China was ruled by individuals (*renzhi*), not by law (*fazhi*). They readily admitted that there was corruption in Taiwan as well, but they claimed that even at its most serious, it had never been as blatant as in China. They noted the relative opulence of the local industrial district headquarters and the fact that the officials drive luxury automobiles (Mercedes-Benz, BMW, Lexus). Moreover, their disdain toward the mainland Chinese, whom they regarded as very backward and incompetent,[10] increased their difficulty in accepting the power the Mainlanders had over them. Yet, few felt the situation was so intolerable that it would affect their viability or their willingness to stay.

PROFITABILITY

Informants found difficulties beyond their original expectations in earning profits. A popular stereotype is that because labour costs are so much cheaper in China than in Taiwan - on a per unit basis, one-eight to one-tenth the cost - that Taiwanese companies are earning super profits. However, that is not the case. First, Taiwan labour is more efficient, so fewer workers are needed to do the same work than in China (labour problems will be discussed in more detail below). Second, there are non-wage costs in China such as lodging, meals and higher administration costs owing to higher turnover rates that employers in Taiwan do not have to pay. Third, while labour costs are lower overall, other costs are higher. Power is dearer and is less reliable unless factories have their own generating equipment (many do). Raw materials are more costly because most come from Taiwan or another outside location. Informants said locally sourced raw materials were unreliable; they were too uneven in quality, moreover, some had been told by local suppliers, even after purchasing from them several times, that they had no surplus to sell them. Taiwanese suppliers, informants said, would always ensure that steady customers obtained what they needed.

Administration is higher because rather than having one location, as was the case in Taiwan, companies with mainland facilities have three: the Taiwan home office where orders are processed and other business taken care of; a Hong Kong office to take care of shipping, foreign exchange, finance, remittances, etc.; and the mainland factory. This also increases communications costs - faxes and long-distance telephone calls rather than local calls or conversations in the office. The mainland factory location also increases wages costs for Taiwanese cadres. They earn twice as much as they would in Taiwan, in addition to which they have free room and board, several round trip airfares between work and home in Taiwan, and a good deal of free entertainment - when the company has guests, the Taiwanese cadres participate in banquets, drinking and other entertainment. Thus, some expenses are considerably higher than they would have been in Taiwan. It should be understood, however, that companies such as those I visited do not have a choice between continuing to operate in Taiwan or transferring manufacturing to China or another overseas location; their only choice is between moving offshore or closing down. Aside from environmental protection problems and exchange rates, the stark fact is that they cannot get workers in Taiwan. Workers there eschew factory work for service industry jobs, 'dirty' work for clean. Taiwan now imports foreign labour not just to do very arduous work such as construction but even for assembly line workers in very clean jobs such as semiconductor factories.

There are other elements in the difficulty in making expected profit levels. One manager found that before she, herself, went to manage her mainland factory her cadres were using company money to cover entertainment expenses which largely benefited themselves and were even embezzling funds. However, that was rare. A more general set of related problems is the truncated production networks and increased production capacity. One of the factors which produced Taiwan's industrial dynamism is the small size of the island and the very high density of factories and service companies. For example, in the area between Taibei and Xinzhu, the location of Taiwan's two top science and technology universities and its high-tech industry park, there are tens of thousands of enterprises, which means that 'just in time' inventorying is very easy. In most cases, whatever one needs can be delivered within a few hours.

The number of enterprises and their density are results of Taiwan's satellite industrial system. Taiwan's export sector is largely made up of SMEs, many of which were established by men who started with few resources. As they grew and prospered, the demonstration effect of their success was not lost on many of their employees, who left to start up their own companies, often making or processing something that had been made in the company they left. A boss sometimes even encouraged this as it allowed him to 1) retain the skills of good employees as they were in essence still working for him; 2) reduce his risks by using the capacity of a satellite factory as his spare capacity, thus making it unnecessary for him to invest in more factory space or capital equipment; and 3) off-load relatively peripheral aspects of his operation in order to concentrate on his core business.[11] This led to a very fine division of labour in industry, with companies often carrying out only one step or making only one component in the manufacture of a product. It also led to the phenomenon of a 'mother factory' (*muchang*) itself manufacturing less than half of its production, the rest being manufactured by satellite factories.[12]

Neither the factory density nor the network of mother and satellite factories exist in China. Regarding density, even in a concentrated area such as the Pearl River Delta Region, distances are greater, as are travel times, because the road system is inferior. This, in combination with the relatively long shipping times from locations abroad to the mainland location and the possibilities of delays at Customs, reduces the capital efficiencies of factories because it means that factories must keep larger inventories. As for factory networks, while they still exist, they are far more limited than they were in Taiwan, though there is still some subcontracting. For example, nylon zipper manufacturing is broken down into three main processes. 'Primary processing' (*qian jiagong*) consists of spinning the tape and making the teeth from polyester yarn. In 'secondary processing' (*hou jiagong*) the stoppers and the slider are inserted. The third process is dyeing. In Taiwan, it was quite common for factories to carry out only one of the processes, but in China, it is more common to do at least both initial and secondary processing. Some companies do all three, but many as dyeing requires considerable skill and not all factories have a skilled dyer, companies often subcontract that process. However, the mother-satellite factory system has not been replicated on the mainland.

Taiwanese who go to the People's Republic have enough capital and orders to establish a fully-fledged business. As for locals, some informants said they were prohibited by law from sub-contracting to local *getihu* (household enterprises), though others did so anyway. A bigger problem appeared to be the question of trust. Most Taiwanese did not trust locals to manufacture quality products or, if prepaid, to fulfil their end of the contract. Some said that while Taiwanese had heavy investments in China (many had long-term leases on land and had built factories complete with dormitories and other employee facilities), many small local factories consisted only of a rented room and a few machines: 'They don't need to earn as much as we do, so if they get a 5,000 *yuan* or so advance on an order, they can take it and run. So I don't do business with them. I would only do business with well-established locals and then on a strictly cash basis'.[13]

The absence of a satellite system and the desire, since one is setting up a business in China, to go for something larger means that it is common for companies established there to have a larger capacity than they had in Taiwan. Some even wound up a manufacturing in Taiwan then invested the money in a more high-profit product. Hence, productive capacity in many industries has expanded more rapidly than has demand, resulting in falling levels of profit. One informant had manufactured plastic window blinds for a decade, but he gave it up about three years ago because, he said, within one year profits fell by 50 per cent making the industry no longer viable. His experience is extreme, but several informants complained that it was much harder to maintain profits than they had expected, and they looked very hard for ways to cut production expenses and to expand their customer base.

DIFFICULTIES IN SELLING INTO CHINA

Many Taiwanese industries have moved production to mainland China with the hope of selling into the domestic market. Hsing cites 1992 CIER figures showing that domestic market entry was a key factor for moving to China for 46.34 per cent of electronics manufacturers, 70.58 per cent of textile manufacturers, and 67.74 per cent of processed food manufacturers; this factor placed third in importance, abundant supply of cheap labour and low-cost land ahead of it (Hsing, 1998:19; CIER, 1994:160). Most informants did not go to China with the primary aim of domestic marketing. Instead, they went there to service customers they had been servicing in Taiwan. In some cases these were foreign customers, e.g. blanket and suit bag, shoe and handbag manufacturers. Others were upstream suppliers of other manufacturers. Zippers, for example, were mostly sold to handbag, luggage or plastic bag manufacturers, and zipper manufacturers themselves were supplied by makers of sliders, pullers, stoppers and a polyester thread incorporated into the teeth which acts as a spine and gives strength to polyester or nylon zippers. Although these upstream products were sold to neighbouring factories, the end product was exported, so they were regarded as export products themselves. Nevertheless, informants were well aware of the enormous potential of the mainland market and hoped someday to exploit it.

What prevented them from doing so at the time of my research was the tax regime. The Chinese government levies a 17 per cent tax on all imported goods that are not re-exported, and since Taiwanese import most of their raw materials, this impost makes their goods uncompetitive with those from Mainland companies. Only a small number of informant factories sold on the domestic market, by complying with the local content rules and buying raw materials from Chinese suppliers. Interestingly, in contrast to many others, this seems to be a relatively 'unbreakable' regulation, i.e. one that is at least very difficult, if not impossible, to circumvent through bribes or other means, as no informant described any method of ways to get around it.[14]

Another way to be able to sell domestically was to create a joint venture with a local company.[15] However, smaller Taiwanese companies, such as most of those I studied, were loathe to share control of their companies with persons with whom they had not built up a relationship of trust. Many Hong Kong entrepreneurs had entered into joint ventures, but they were more likely to have close kin living in the Pearl River Delta Region (PRDR), people who could be regarded as more trustworthy, whom they could involve in the agreement. The Taiwanese did not. They were not opposed on principle to co-operation and partnerships - indeed many informant companies were partnerships or limited share companies, some of which moved away from family ownership when they decided to invest in China - but, as pointed out above, especially the smaller ones were unwilling at the time of the research to trust Mainland partners. Their inability to sell domestically was not so serious a problem as the others as it did not affect the core business of most informants. But many did see it as a missed opportunity and an eventual goal, and some were looking into establishing mainland registered companies so they could tap into it.[16]

LABOUR PROBLEMS

When I embarked on this research in the PRDR, although I was interested in the relationships between workers and managers, i.e. what is referred to as *guanxi*, I had not planned to gather extensive data on industrial relationships itself. However, after a few interviews and casual conversations with Taiwanese managers, it was obvious that this was a topic much on their minds, and they volunteered information on it. Much of the work on workers and industry in China and elsewhere in East and Southeast Asia has taken the perspective of view of the workers and sees employers, to one degree or another, as exploiters (See, for example: Ong and Nonini, 1997; Hsing, 1998). Although I lived in a factory and stayed overnight in two others, I had little opportunity to interview workers themselves, though I did interview Chinese cadres in several. Thus, what appears below is based on information largely from managers.

It was labour problems that informants complained about most, even more frequently than corruption and *ad hoc* fees, probably because such problems were unexpected and because Taiwanese felt that the quality of Mainland workers differed so greatly from that of Taiwanese workers. The quality of Taiwanese workers has gone through a great metamorphosis in the past four decades. It the 1950s and 1960s, Taiwanese workers had low skill levels and scant understanding of the importance of quality standards or meeting deadlines. That changed, however, as SME exporters came increasingly under the discipline of the international market, and the quality of the labour force improved as average education levels rose from primary school to senior middle school. By the 1980s, Taiwan had a reputation for quality products and prompt delivery, made possible in part by an efficient, productive, committed and enthusiastic workforce.

When Taiwanese entrepreneurs began moving offshore in the 1980s they would have preferred to invest in China, as is indicated by the speed with which investment fell in Southeast Asia and rose in China as soon as the Taiwan government lifted restrictions. The reasons for this are the perceptions of similarity in language and cultural practice,[17] very important to the typical SME operator, who mostly have a junior college or lower level of education and are not proficient in foreign languages. Aside from some minor differences in word usage and a bit of getting used to regional accents rarely heard in Taiwan for the past twenty years, Taiwanese found no problems with the language. While some may have expected minor differences in the skill levels and attitudes of Mainland and Taiwanese workers, they were unprepared for the extent of those differences, and Taiwanese bosses and managers were generally unprepared for what they found, and they had to make major adjustments in how to manage workers. One informant said, 'I moved to Hong Kong in 1990 and took the opportunity to open this factory. I had a partner, but two years later we failed. The reason is because he applied the same management methods he had used in Taiwan to our operations here.' His sentiments were echoed by many others.

The most common complaint made was that Mainland workers are slow and do not work hard. Informants gave estimates of a single Taiwanese worker being able to achieve the productivity of three to ten Mainland workers.[18] Many said that the workers had to be supervised constantly or they would malinger. Other complaints included workers failing to follow instructions, not co-operating, and either not understanding the importance of making products to a particular standard of quality or not caring. One informant manufactured plastic garment and blanket bags which had to be sewn. 'There is a two millimetre tolerance for the seam, but if you don't watch the workers carefully, in a couple of days it will be a full centimetre.' Several said that workers did not understand the importance of their doing quality work so that the company could make money and they could be paid.

Another very common complaint was the way workers regarded their jobs. Most Mainland workers come to the coastal areas to work for a few years and earn some money, then go back home, marry, build a house, and settle down. In contrast to Taiwanese workers, they do not see their work there as a way to learn skills or begin a career. Many jumped from one job to another in order to earn a bit more money. Thus, employers saw them as lacking loyalty toward or identification with the company. In addition, most showed no interest in advancing themselves, preferring to earn less but have less responsibility. They were quite content to do the one part of the overall process that they had been taught and not have to learn anything else. They thus lacked an overall perspective of the work, making work management more problematic. One informant said that in Taiwan, one had to manage people (*guan ren*), to make sure that employees were getting along with each other, but in China, one had to manage the work (*guan shi*), to break the processing of a product down into as many individual steps as possible then assign workers to one of those steps because if one requires too much of them, they cannot cope and forget to do things. He echoed the sentiments of many who said that if you give a Taiwanese worker a general instruction, s/he can carry out the whole job because s/he understands it in the context of production as a whole and is committed to getting it done. If some Taiwanese workers finish before others, they will go help out their work mates who have not yet finished. However, Mainland workers understand and care about only the job to which they have been assigned and complete only that particular task; they do not help others.

Informants explained the differences between Taiwanese and Chinese workers as results of work practices either fostered by the Communists or not changed by them. Most commonly mentioned was the 'big rice bowl' mentality, that in the socialist system companies were not driven by the bottom line and there was little pressure on workers to be productive or to be careful to produce quality products. They also brought up the socialist practice of making work, thus giving workers a very limited task to do so that more workers would be employed, and the Chinese practice of guarding one's job knowledge and not sharing it with others so that one cannot be replaced.[19] When asked whether it was not easier, after a factory was well-established and had a trained workforce, for new workers to learn the work, many said that this made no difference because old workers would not willingly teach new ones. Aside from these system-level problems, some informants also felt that a lot of workers were simply lazy and did not care.

Informants frequently cited as evidence the high worker turnover rates. This was not so great a problem in factories that had been in operation for four to five years, but in newer ones rates of ten per cent per month were commonplace, and in the initial start-up period they could be even higher. One factory I visited had been in operation for just six months; the General Manager said that of the 180 production workers he had started with, only three were left. Many had stayed only a week or two before leaving. Things settled down after the first couple of months, and retention rates of those who had stayed for three months were quite acceptable; moreover, most who left after staying that long did so because of an emergency back home rather than for work related reasons. The informant felt that part of the explanation was that workers coming to new jobs decide fairly soon whether they are willing to do that sort of work, so over time enough people came who found the work there acceptable that he could build up a more stable workforce. However, he was still shocked by this experience.

Aside from the inconvenience and cost of turnover, what irked many Taiwanese managers were the frivolous reasons many gave for leaving.[20] Whereas they accepted as legitimate an emergency at home such as a sick father or the death of a grandmother, a genuinely better job offer, or the fact that an employee had already worked and lived away from home for several years and felt it was time to return and start a family, many complained that workers too often left for what they regarded as an inconsequential amount of extra money, as little as 10-20 *yuan* per month. Informants, recalling their own early work years, felt that for a young worker learning a trade was far more important than a little extra money, and one did that primarily by staying with a job for several years until able to handle all the processes on one's own and putting oneself in a position to manage a factory or even to start one's own enterprise. One can thus understand the dumbfounded reaction of a manager to the following exchange with some workers:

'The other day two workers resigned. I asked them why they were leaving. At first they hemmed and hawed, not saying anything precise. I pressed them and one finally said, "the other day I visited a neighbouring factory. There are fifteen of us Henan people there but only two here". "Well," I asked, "how much do they pay over there?" "I don't know". "How many days off do you get per month?" "I don't know". "How is the food over there?" "I don't know." "What about the dormitories?" "I don't know." "Then why are you going?" "Because there are fifteen Henan people there and only two of us here".'

This is by no means an isolated example; many other informants told similar stories.[21]

'Hometowner' feelings (*laoxiang guannian*), such as those expressed by the worker in the above exchange, were another source of problems for Taiwanese bosses. These particularistic feelings toward people from one's own area of origin[22] carry a potential for hostility toward others and are kept prominent in people's minds because of linguistic and dietary variations that workers encounter several times each day. For example, food in worker dining halls is almost always prepared in common, and dishes spiced with enough chilli to satisfy workers from Hunan and Sichuan will be too hot for those from Guangxi or Henan. Because of this consciousness minor disputes between two workers, e.g. over queue-jumping or taking too long in the shower, have the potential to escalate and even to involve whole groups. Some informants said that stealing in the dormitories frequently involves a worker from one locale taking the belongings of a worker from another. Such conflicts can lead to fights, and these can easily involve not only the parties to the conflict but their hometowner mates as well; one informant said there had been an out and out gang war between different groups involving hundreds of persons in the industrial district where he was operating.[23] That such fights are almost always between males strengthens managers' preference for female over male workers.

Even if fighting does not become widespread, it can still be disruptive of large numbers of workers. At my host factory two workers, one from Guizhou, the other from Shandong, became involved in a fight one evening. The General Manager very calmly interviewed both, asking what had happened and why. However the fate of both was sealed: he, like other informants, would not accept fighting among workers under any circumstances, and both were fired. Two days later, when the fellow from Guizhou left, some of his hometowners left with him; the others, ten or so, stopped work for about three hours that morning to say goodbye. The company receptionist complained that their actions were inappropriate and unacceptable in a company but added that this often happened when someone was being fired. One manager said that leaders often emerge in hometowner groups, and that one has to be very careful about firing them because they may take a whole group of workers with them. Another said that at one time, in order to reduce the potential for friction between workers from different hometowner groups, he assigned new workers to jobs with other hometowners. This backfired, however, as hometowner groups each performed different tasks in the factory, and his production was crippled after one group left *en masse*, leaving him with no workers experienced in that particular task.

Hometowner loyalties also affect the ability of cadres to do their work properly. To please the employer, a cadre must act even-handedly toward all those in her/his charge (See Hsing, 1998:104-6). But by so doing, her/his own hometowners may take offence for not favouring them. A manager said that on the instances of fighting outside his factory which had warranted calling the police, all were groups of workers beating up a hometowner cadre who had not favoured one of her/his own.

As mentioned above, fighting was one offence which was ground for automatic dismissal. The other was stealing. Several informants were nonplussed by the level of stealing. 'Mainland workers will steal *anything*,' said one. 'Taiwanese workers would not dare steal like this because if they were caught word would spread and they would be blackballed. No one would hire them. But the Mainland is too big. A worker can always go elsewhere, and her/his past will not follow. Or, if they steal something big, they can always escape back to their home province. Who would go to look for them there? It's too big, and it's too far away.'[24] Theft of company products was most common. Some were directly useful to employees, e.g. purses or shoes, but others, such as zippers, were simply sold to other factories. Only one employer said he had no problem with employees stealing things; he manufactured polyester thread, which was rolled only large spools weighing over twenty kilograms. Their size and weight, in combination with the guard post at the gate to the industrial district, prevented employees from taking them.[25]

Theft by white collar workers was also a problem. One informant suspected that his purchasing officer was dipping into the petty cash. Another said that an office employee was discovered by the gate guards trying to take out photocopies of product specifications and customer lists which she had intended to sell to a Chinese company from her home province. Most common, however, was using company resources for private gain (*jiagong jisi*). One boss complained that his Customs agent frequently ran her own errands while out on company business, using company time, the company vehicle, and the company driver to do so.[26] In my host factory, a driver found himself in serious trouble when he arrived forty-five minutes late to pick up some cadres from a restaurant, his girl friend sitting in the front seat with him. An angry cadre did not accept his claim that his lateness was caused by heavy traffic.

Finally, Taiwanese managers were dissatisfied with the personal habits of Mainland workers. Most often mentioned were spitting and littering or not tidying up their area in their dormitories. Taiwanese bosses regard the appearance of a factory and its employees as very important. First there are considerations of health, hygiene and sanitation. Rooms in factory dormitories varied in size, but generally eight to twelve workers slept in a room on parallel rows of bunk beds along two walls. Obviously poor sanitation under such conditions could spread disease rapidly. Moreover, workers not keeping their belongings put away or who littered the floors or did not clean up after themselves in the shower, toilet, etc., were not only an inconvenience for other workers but a potential source of conflict. Thus it is not surprising that they viewed these habits not only as unsavoury but also unsanitary. Second, they believe that a tidy factory signals to customers and potential customers a management team that is proud of what they produce and which will produce quality products. Third, they believe that workers will have a stronger identity with a tidy factory the workers of which have some sort of uniform with a company logo. Finally, many of the factories I visited were designed and built by the Taiwanese themselves, and there was certainly an element of being 'house-proud' in their attitudes. Some managers, in fact, gave bonuses to workers who kept their dormitories clean.

Despite the level of dissatisfaction displayed by most informants and the seeming inability or unwillingness of workers to learn to work the way their employers wanted them to, no Taiwanese regarded them as stupid. In fact, almost all informants prefaced their complaints with remarks to the effect that the workers were bright, had good minds, etc. However, they regarded them as very much lacking in both practical and moral education (the latter being that which teaches honesty, loyalty, hard work, etc.), and they blamed this on the Cultural Revolution, its attacks on family ties, traditional virtues, and the destruction of the education system and the curriculum in the 1960s and 1970s. This view is increasingly shared by Chinese on the mainland as well. They say that the lack of a widely accepted moral system is a serious problem.

Thus, one very frequently mentioned method of solving such problems is education. In many factories, Taiwanese cadres and managers held classes, usually for cadres but in some cases for workers as well. These classes were aimed at both work related skills and at changing their outlooks, especially toward work but also toward life in general. During one interview, the boss called several of his young cadres in and said, 'This researcher and I are going to be talking about management. I want you to hear us.' After the interview we all went to dinner together. There is a good deal of emphasis on training of good workers to become cadres and of lower cadres to become higher ones. Naturally, when a factory is first established cadres must be hired from elsewhere, but all informants said they preferred to train their own, and within a few years of a factory being established, all cadres are home trained.

Other educative approaches are slogans and aphorisms (*biaoyu*) and daily talks to the employees by the management. Many factories have slogans on the walls urging workers to work hard, do good work, be careful, put quality first - put the customer first, orders are the life-blood of the company, etc. Sceptical about the usefulness of slogans because of the tendency of both the Kuomintang government in Taiwan and the Communist government in China not to spare in their use, I asked a manager I knew fairly well and who also made liberal use of them if he thought they were effective. He chuckled: 'I'll tell you, the Kuomintang in Taiwan comes from the same origins as the Communists in China, and socialist countries love this way of doing things. But I did not write these. I had the workers themselves write them then had the cadres choose the best of them. Writers of those we chose to post received a reward of 10 *yuan* for each one. I did not put up any of the slogans I use for my own inspiration.'[27]

Some Taiwanese managers have workers line up in formation before work in the mornings where they lead them in some stretching exercises and address them. The topics range from praising or chiding one or another section of the factory for their work performance, instructions for work on a new order, or words of concern such as 'the weather is getting a bit chilly. You should wear another layer of clothing and drink lots of warm water'; a message about being careful or doing a good job; or general words of wisdom about work. One manager liked to remind his workers, 'Although I am the boss and you are the workers, you and I have much in common. We all come from far away to make money. You came across the mountains, and I came across the ocean, but we are both here to make money. You help me make money, and I'll help you make money.'

As mentioned above, Taiwanese are concerned with the appearance of the factory and employees, and many feel that Mainland workers lack discipline in their personal habits, their work, their dress and the way they carry themselves. To achieve their aims, some adopted a quasi-military approach. In Taiwan, all males have to do military service, usually for two or more years, and many felt that one reason for the laxness in China was the lack of such an experience. One measure they took was to provide uniforms, usually a smock, apron, shirt or jacket, because workers looked more presentable when in uniform and it also gave them a sense of identity with the factory.[28] Gate guards[29] had a more complete uniform, often even down to the shoes they wore, and to make them appear disciplined and give them a more official bearing, Taiwanese cadres in many factories gave them close order drills. The extent of militarization varied. In no case did I see or hear about cadres acting as sergeants barking orders to workers, however, some were quite enamoured with a military style. One day I lunched with a General Manager and several Mainland cadres after an interview. Struck by the silence during the meal, very different from the atmosphere at my host factory and other places I had visited, I enquired of the General Manager about it. 'I was in the Army in Taiwan,' he replied. 'This is more disciplined. I think it is better this way.'[30]

Another approach was to stress the sentiment in the slogan, 'Regard the factory as home'. Although this is not part of Taiwanese management in Taiwan, where most employees went home to their families everyday, it reflects a Taiwanese management philosophy that an employer should take good care of the employees. Several said they realized that their workers were far from home and family and in very new surroundings (as, indeed, they themselves were), and they hoped that some paternalistic treatment and concern from them would settle the workers and give them a sense of security, reducing turnover rates in the bargain. These positive instrumental outcomes should not detract from the genuine concern bosses had for the workers and some, despite being critical of poor work habits, also expressed their gratitude toward them. One said:

> 'I tell them, "At home, you are your parents' treasure.[31] Here you are
> my treasure. Regard me as your elder brother and I'll regard you as my
> younger brother or sister. You are helping me to earn money. That

makes you the best, the greatest. You workers all help me to earn money. How can I not treat you well." So I have to take care of them. If they have a problem, my door is open to them, especially after the day's work is done. I am quite willing to help them in appropriate ways. I feel better after having done so.'

Finally, Taiwanese try to improve performance through 'carrot and stick' measures. This means using piece rates whenever work done can be credited to an individual or team and where the danger of rewarding for quantity does not negatively affect quality, giving performance related prizes and bonuses, sometimes linked to daily quotas. Piece rates were seen as the most direct antidote to slow work, something the workers could easily understand. This lesson was amplified in that piece workers averaged higher earnings than wage workers in the same factories, and good piece workers made much more than slow ones did. However, not all tasks can be easily remunerated through piece rates. Much of the work in my host factory was automated, with workers essentially simply feeding and watching machines. Workers there all earned wages. But in other zipper factories more tasks were done by hand, so the productivity of individuals could be counted, and they were paid piece rates. In some other industries, managers eschewed piece rates because they feared that, despite the presence of quality control personnel, workers would emphasize speed over good work in order to earn more money. A metal products manufacturer found a way to resolve that problem in his factory. Facing a problem of slow workmanship he switched to piece rates. That raised output greatly but it also increased rejects to an unacceptable level. So he combined the two, paying those working the pressing machines piece rates for parts which passed quality control checks, and paying his quality control workers a bonus if customers did not return goods for failing to meet specifications. The other side of bonuses, of course, is fines, and, aside from fining workers for breaches of certain stipulated company rules, some also fined for poor performance, especially for repeatedly making the same mistake.

Some informants said they did not like to employ such measures, preferring instead what they called a humanist (*rendao*) approach, i.e. treating workers with respect and expecting them to reciprocate that respect by working hard for the company. They claimed that one can do this in Taiwan because workers there understand that what they do affects the company's ability to make money, which in turn affects its ability to pay them and also the size of their bonus. However, their efforts to employ humanistic management techniques in China failed because workers did not reciprocate, so they turned to strict disciplinary regimes with bonuses for very good work, fines for breaking company rules, and sacking for failure to perform. They felt Mainland workers responded much better to that approach. Although most managers remained displeased with levels of productivity, turnover and other aspects of worker performance, a small number are satisfied. These have adopted very manifest systems of material rewards for good work, they keep a close eye on the management of workers, and they have been able to demonstrate to the workers their concern for them. Some have also put extra resources into training so that workers are shifted around the factory to various jobs, giving them a better overall understanding of the work and increasing the flexibility with which they can be deployed.

CONCLUDING REMARKS

When Taiwan lifted foreign exchange controls in 1988, Taiwanese rushed to set up companies in Hong Kong from which they could invest in China. Investment itself was legalized in 1990, though many had already gone to reconnoitre; factories were established soon afterward. After the government relaxed its stance toward travel by its citizens to The People's Republic of China, entrepreneurs, pressed by rising business costs at home, leapt at the chance to re-establish their firms in China, where, they surmised, they would not have to negotiate language and cultural differences as those who had gone to Southeast Asia had had to do. They found language differences minimal, though they could be vexing as this chapter has noted. However they also discovered a more sizeable cultural gap in dealing with persons whose outlooks, norms and values they thought they knew but, as it turned out, differed in a number or significant ways. Most of the Taiwanese employers interviewed respect the intelligence of their employees: 'They have very good minds. They are very bright.' Beyond that they also found a number of shortcomings, and though they blamed the social and labour systems under which employees were socialized more than the workers themselves, these nonetheless created problems for management.

It is clear that Taiwanese entrepreneurs remain less than completely satisfied with mainland conditions, however it would be a mistake to suggest that these are insurmountable or crippling problems or that those who invest do not make money, as some Taiwan government reports claim. Clearly, investors would be very happy if bribery could be curtailed, if they could sell on the domestic market without having to pay punitive taxes to do so, if their costs could be reduced, and if labour were more efficient and committed. While the management in my host factory was putting a good deal of effort into expanding its marketing network, and the President said that it would take them a year or two longer to recoup their investment than they had originally hoped it would, the management of that company, like that of others, had solved their problems to the extent that they regarded their performance acceptable. The Taiwanese Government from time to time claims that many Taiwanese companies in China are failing and not making a profit. However, a Chung-hua Institute of Economic Research[32] economist interviewed doubted these claims, putting them down to government efforts to discourage other Taiwanese from investing in the Chinese mainland. Only one informant regretted her investment in China, but she did so not for the reasons given above but because she found her Taiwanese cadres to have been untrustworthy in her absence and realized that she would have to remain there to oversee things. The others are satisfied enough with their decision to invest there and had found ways to cope with the most pressing of their problems.

BIBLIOGRAPHY

Bosco, J.
1995   'Better the Head of a Chicken than the Tail of an Ox: On Cultural Explanations for the Development of Family Factories in Taiwan', *Fairbank Center Working Papers*, Number 12, Harvard University
Ch'en, Chieh-hsüan
1994   *Xieli Wangluo yu Shenghuo Jiegou: Taiwan Zhongxiao Qiye de Shehui Jingji Fenxi* (Co-operative Networks and the Structure of Life: A Social and Economic Analysis of Taiwan's Small and Medium Enterprises). Taibei: Lianjing
Ching, Frank
1998   'Rough Justice,' *Far Eastern Economic Review* 161(34) August 20, pp. 13-14
CIER
1994   *Taiwan-China Economic Statistics Yearbook* (*Liang'an jingji nianbao*). Taipei: Chunghwa Institute of Economic Research
Hsing, You-tien
1996   'Traders, Managers, and Flexibility of Enterprise Networks: Taiwan Fashion Shoe Industry in China', a paper presented at the Economic Governance and Flexible Production in East Asia Conference, Hsinchu, Taiwan, 3-6 October
1998   *Making Capitalism in China: The Taiwan Connection*. New York and Oxford: Oxford University Press
Hsu, Song-ken
1993   *Taishang yu Liang-an Jingmao Fazhan* (Taiwanese Entrepreneurs and the Development of Cross-Straits Trade). Discussion Paper

8208, Economics Institute, Academia Sinica

Ka, Chih-ming
1993   *Taiwan Dushi Xiaoxing Zhizaoye de Chuangye, Jingying yu Shengchan Zuzhi: Yi Wufenpu Chengyi Zhizaoye wei Anli de Fenxi* (Market, Social Networks, and the Production Organization of Small-Scale Industry in Taiwan: The Garment Industries in Wufenpu). Nangang: Institute of Ethnology, Academia Sinica

Ke, Lin
1997   'On China's Corruption Problem', *China Strategic Review* II(5), pp. 47-53

Lawrence, Susan V.
1998a   'Erasing the Cancer', *Far Eastern Economic Review* 161(34) August 20, pp. 10-13
1998b   'Crooked Cops,' *Far Eastern Economic Review* 161(34) August 20, p. 12

Levi, Michael
1997   'Stealing from the People', *China Review* 8 (Autumn-Winter), pp. 4-9

Lu, Jui-ling, (ed.)
1998   *Inside Mainland China*, 20(9)

MAC
1996   Website, 12/9/96, Mainland Affairs Committee, Executive *Yuan*, Republic of China

Ong, Aihwa and Donald Nonini (eds)
1997   *Ungrounded Empires: The Cultural Politics of Modern Chinese Transnationalism*. New York: Routledge

Purves, B.
1991   *Barefoot in the Boardroom: Venture and Misadventure in the People's Republic of China*. North Sydney: Allen & Unwin

Rocca, Jean-Louis
1992   'Corruption and its Shadow: An Anthropological View of Corruption in China', *China Quarterly* 130, pp. 402-16

Schak, David C.
1988   *Begging in Chinese Society: Poverty and Mobility in an Underclass Community*. Pittsburgh: University of Pittsburgh Press
1994   '*Dalu Re* and *Liugen*: Investment Decisions of Taiwanese Entrepreneurs' in D. Schak (ed.) *Entrepreneurship, Economic Growth and Social Change: The Transformation of Southern China*. Australia-Asia Papers no. 71, Griffith University Centre for the Study of Australia-Asian Relations
1997   'Taiwanese Labour Management in China', *Employee Relations* 19, p. 4
1998   'Taiwanese-PRC Trade and Investment', in: C. Mackerras, D. McMillen and A. Watson (eds) *Dictionary of the Politics of the*

People's Republic of China. London & New York: Routledge
Schottenhammer, Angela
1995   'On the Necessity of Corruption amongst the Members of the
        Chinese Communist Party', in: P. van der Velde (ed.) *IIAS
        Yearbook*. Leiden: International Institute for Asian Studies, pp. 61-
        72
Shieh, G.S.
1992   *Boss Island: The Subcontracting Network and Micro-
        Entrepreneurship in Taiwan's Development*. New York: Peter Lang
Wolf, Arthur
1972   'Gods, Ghosts, and Ancestors' in: Arthur Wolf (ed.) *Religion in
        Chinese Society*. Stanford: Stanford University Press

Notes

1. I wish to acknowledge and express gratitude for a grant from the School of Modern Asian Studies, Griffith University. I also thank informants who gave their time and their hospitality, especially my host factory. Finally, I thank the Taiwan-Australia Business Association, especially Mr. Benjamin Huang, for their assistance in introducing me to many business migrants who served as preliminary interviewees to help me in preparing for this research, and colleagues at Griffith University, especially Larry Crump and Greg Trotman. I also wish to thank the International Institute of Asian Studies for sponsoring the conference at which this paper was presented.
2. Informant interviewed in Zhuhai, 22 November 1996.
3. Research for this paper was carried out in the course of a project on Taiwanese management culture and practice. I chose to carry it out in China rather than in Taiwan as the result of a visit to a factory there owned by a business migrant I had met in Brisbane. Whereas I had found visiting factories in Taiwan difficult to arrange in terms of both a suitable time to meet and transport to and from, the day I visited the factory in China I met and chatted with about a dozen other factory owners who dropped by in the afternoon for a chat and a cup of tea or whom we met in the evening at dinner or in the karaoke bar. The next day, as I was being driven to the train station, I was offered lodging at the factory I visited, an offer I gladly took up. I returned the following year and spent ten weeks between late August and early December 1996, not in the factory I originally visited but a new zipper factory in which the owners had shares and in which one brother was the general manager. My hosts decided that, as it was a new factory, management was much more active socially getting their business established, and

that would facilitate my research. They provided me with introductions to their friends and customers, some of whom provided me with further introductions. I met others through a Taiwanese manager whose acquaintance I made on a ferry trip to Hong Kong and also through a British friend of a postgraduate student who was at the time working for a German company. I interviewed a total of thirty-six Taiwanese factory owners or managers, thirty of which were complete interviews, the others being disrupted and less complete. I also toured the factories in about two-thirds of the cases. I also interviewed management personnel in a German, a South Korean, and two local Chinese enterprises. Thirty-four of the companies visited were SMEs (small and medium-size enterprises), and two were larger. They ranged in size from 40 to 3,300 workers, most being in the 200-600 range. All save two were low-tech, labour-intensive industries with most processes requiring much manual processing (*shougong*). Products manufactured included zippers or products related to them, shoes (athletic and ladies), handbags, wire and cable, pottery, bicycle parts, plastic bags and metal parts for handbags. One of the two exceptions manufactured packing tape, the other polyester yarn. Line supervisor to department head positions were usually filled by Mainlanders with the top cadres being Taiwanese. Interviews, conducted in Mandarin, ranged from forty-five minutes to over two hours. They were recorded and later transcribed and translated.

4. From conversations with friends in Taiwan in late November 1998, the progress made toward cleaning up Taiwanese society in the past two years has been remarkable. The trigger was the kidnapping and brutal murder of Bai Xiaoyan, the daughter of well-known TV personality, Bai Bingbing in March 1997. This was at the time simply the latest in a series of horrific crimes, including the rape and murder of a prominent opposition party politician (not politically motivated) and the execution of the Taoyuan County Magistrate and several members of his household. Because of what the public perceived as business as usual type inaction on the part of government, citizens in Taibei mounted large overnight demonstrations on three weekends, which brought about the resignation of the Premier. The following December saw unexpected gains by the opposition party in county and mayoral elections. According to friends in Taiwan, the civil threat from organized crime has been greatly reduced in the past year.

5. The following incident demonstrates that corruption among those in authority is common knowledge. I was returning to my host factory after an interview in a taxi. The driver, on learning that I was studying

Taiwanese entrepreneurs, remarked, 'Taiwanese businessmen certainly like to go to karaoke and get women there.' 'Yes,' I said, 'and so do the Hong Kong entrepreneurs.' He nodded, and I continued, 'And so do the Gong'an (local police).' 'Oh yes,' he replied, 'but they don't have to pay!'

6. Another acquaintance and her husband both lecture in history in a university in a coastal city in China. Her husband had a project which involved Master's degree students research the history of the local Customs office. Upon graduation, his students qualified for good, middle level jobs at the customs office. But they turned these jobs down in favour of jobs as customs inspectors. That was where opportunities to transform their authority into money lay.

7. Taiwanese entrepreneurs value their reputation for reliability very highly. They have a formula for being good business persons: the cost must be competitive, the quality good, the delivery on time, and after sales service prompt and to the customer's satisfaction. As shipment time draws nigh, management teams go all out to meet the deadline, working day and night if necessary.

8. For example, the men were all Hakka, and it just so happened that the General Manager's family business, when he first came to China, was located in Mei County, a Hakka area. He learned to speak Hakka, and his brother had married a Hakka woman. So we had several toasts to Hakka-ness. Then they asked me how old I was, and it turned out that two were born the same year as I was, the other a year earlier. Toasts to each of *tongnian* (same year) and another to our 'elder brother'.

9. The actions of police and officials are reminiscent of Arthur Wolf's noting that Taiwanese see a great similarity between local hoodlums (*liumang*) and beggars; what they want is usually not a lot, and in both cases people pay them off just to get rid of them (1972; see also Schak, 1988).

10. As an illustration, an informant related the following incident. A friend came to visit and brought his golf clubs. My informant went to Taiping, the local hydrofoil port, to pick him up. He waited and waited. Finally an hour after all the others had come out, he enquired what had happened, and he was let inside. A Customs official was insisting on holding up the friend's golf bag and clubs on the suspicion that the visitor was going to sell them in China. 'What is he doing with so many clubs? One or two should be enough.' My informant, who is a Taiwan Business Association Vice-President, told the Customs official's superior that such stupidity was making China look foolish in the eyes of the world.

11. Much has been written on Taiwan's satellite system. See, for example: Bosco, 1995; Ch'en, 1994; Ka, 1993; Shieh, 1992; and Hsing, 1996.

12. Mother factories receive the orders and then sub-contract that which they do not manufacture themselves to their satellites, retaining a percentage of the profit and taking responsibility to the customer for ensuring that the product meets quality standards and is delivered on time. The obvious question is what prevents the satellite factory owner from bypassing the mother factory. The answer is that they do not have the links with the customer or trading company necessary to get the order; moreover, they often manufacture only one part of a product or carry out one process, and they often do not have the skills or the equipment needed to take responsibility for the whole product.

13. I visited one such factory with a manufacturer of plastic bags (for suits, blankets, etc.); he had taken bags there to have zippers sewn into them. But he said using this company was a trial basis only. One of his friends in the same industry had used them, and he did so on his friend's recommendation. But he was not about to risk giving the local factory a large quantity of goods to process, at least not yet.

14. A high level manager in a mainland enterprise said that mainland firms were under complementary restrictions, having to pay the same level of duties, and that this caused them difficulties similar to those paid by outside entrepreneurs.

15. The share owned by the domestic company does not have to be large. While attending a seminar of MBA students at National Sun Yat-sen University who had interviewed some Taiwanese firms in the Shanghai area I learned of a joint venture company the ownership of which was divided as follows: 55 per cent Taiwanese, 40 per cent Japanese and 5 per cent local capital. One of the students, who worked for the Taiwanese company, said the local company had actually paid contributed capital, that the other two had given them the shares in order to use their status as a way to sell into the domestic market.

16. The family company of my host factory General Manager made plastic blanket and garment bags, and he and his brothers had plans eventually to manufacture rain gear for domestic consumption in a city in the interior. The political uncertainty between Taiwan and China over the past few years had made them take a more cautious approach.

17. The idea that overseas Chinese return to their home counties to invest, despite some well publicized and spectacular cases (e.g. Liem Sioe Liong), has, I believe, been overstated, especially with regard to the Taiwanese. First, by contrast to many Hong Kong investors, many of whom are first generation away from their native places, there has been

little migration from the Fijian home counties of most Taiwanese for a century. Second, there are far more Taiwanese investors in the Pearl River Delta Region than in the Xiamen region.

18. Hsing estimates that in the shoe industry, Chinese workers were about half as productive as Taiwanese workers were, though at one-tenth the salary, there were still great savings in production costs. Labour costs per pair were 30-40 per cent of the total in Taiwan while in China they were 8-12 per cent. However, it is unclear whether this includes the higher wage costs of Taiwanese cadres.

19. Taiwanese managers mentioned this, but I have independent confirmation from other sources. In 1995, I was a member of a delegation from a body in the Australian Department of Education and Employment Training sent to China to look into adult and technical education in order that the educational qualifications of intending migrants could be assessed. Several of those who guided our tours of technical education schools mentioned this to us.

20. Most managers come from a blue-collar of technical school background, and in their eyes, it is most important for young people to get *yi ji zhi chang*, a skill that will take them through life. Hopping from one job to another was a very short-sighted thing to do. There may be small immediate rewards, but one will then get to the time in life when it is important to be able to support a family, and one will be without the skills needed to get a stable and decently paying job.

21. Frequent changes of workplace were actually quite common among female workers in Taiwan during the 1960s and 1970s, though males were more likely to stay with a line of work for several years in order to learn a skill.

22. The actual unit or size of the area varies from a sub-county unit (*xiang*) to a province, depending on the context. In the Pearl River Delta Region, it was province, but within one's province it could be much smaller, perhaps a dialect area.

23. At least Shenzhen and Dongguan were divided into industrial districts (*gongye qu*), areas for administering foreign investments. They vary in their size and complexity. Where my host factory was located, they seemed merely to collect land rents, but in other places, they built factory buildings or even complexes which they then rented to foreign investors. In the district referred to in the text there was a compound with a number of factories and several thousand workers. Dormitories, dining halls, and recreation facilities were centrally located rather than near the individual factory, as was usually the case. Moreover, the district administrators did all the hiring of workers, and it received a

percentage of their monthly pay; some workers told me that they paid 100 *yuan* per month out of a salary of around 500 *yuan*. This impost was much higher than I saw elsewhere.

24. In a discussion with a Mainland Chinese assistant hotel manager about the differential pay scale for local Cantonese workers and those from the interior, I asking why one would hire locals when one can get someone from the interior with equivalent or better qualifications for about half the wage. He said that he would, quite expectedly, hire the outsider for all work except that involving money, but if the employee was to be hired as an accountant or some other such position, he would hire a local. He explained, 'If a Cantonese steals money from you, your chances of finding her/him are fairly good, but if an outsider does so, not only are your chances of apprehending the person very slim, even if you do it won't be worth your while.'

25. Purves (1991, pp. 13-14) describes employees taking company stocks and using them in private ventures - which were carried out on company time.

26. This employee is a local Cantonese woman. Cantonese are generally paid much better than others. I brought up this case as well as similar ones with my wife's cousin, a local woman in her forties who lives near Guangzhou and who has run her own clothing factory. 'How much did she make?' she asked. 'If she didn't get 2,000 *yuan* per month in salary, she will take the equivalent of that to make up for it. She will regard it as her due, not as stealing.'

27. Actually, the use of slogans or aphorisms in factories and other workplaces is associated by many in Taiwan with Japan. Japanese work practices have most certainly influenced Taiwanese manufacturers. Especially in the early days of small-scale industrialization in Taiwan, many satellites of Japanese factories were established, and many learned their trades as workers in Japanese factories. However, as mentioned in the text, the Kuomintang government was not at all sparing in the use of patriotic or moralistic slogans, even on such things as wrappings of packs of toilet paper and on match boxes.

28. Whether it did is open to question; several who had abandoned the practice did so because turnover rates were too high, and they saw the uniform as an unrecovered cost.

29. In Chinese, *bao'an*, they open the gate for visitors, check visitors as they come in and have them sign in if that is required, and take identity badges from employees when they leave. Although their name makes them sound official, they are solely employees of the company and are not part of the Chinese military of police force.

265

30. Hsing (1998, Chapter 4) relates a very different set of observations than mine, and to discuss these in detail will require another paper. However, the incident in the text relates only to the cadres in the factory, not to the workers' cafeteria. I saw nothing that would indicate workers not being allowed to speak during meals or being punished for dropping a grain of rice on the floor. In fact, in many Taiwanese-built factories, the cafeterias had TV sets for the workers to watch while they ate.

31. Western readers may regard this phrase as excessive, making the speaker sound disingenuous, but Chinese readers will recognize it as *baobei* which literally means 'a treasured object' and is a very common way to refer to a child.

32. CIER is a large government supported institute with three branches, one of which deals exclusively with Taiwan-Mainland economic relationships. Some scholars there are among the best in their fields in Taiwan.

THE MORAL ECONOMY OF PROFIT:
DIASPORA CAPITALISM
AND THE FUTURE OF CHINA

MICHAEL R. GODLEY

This book is primarily concerned with the relationship between culture and economic development and, more particularly, with how recently-reconstructed linkages between the ethnic Chinese diaspora and their home villages (referred to as '*Qiaoxiang* Ties') affect the operation of enterprises in South China. Although the concepts involved have a long pedigree, 'Cultural Capitalism' is a new (and entirely artificial) term, coined by the editors in order to focus attention on the ways that the Chinese are said to conduct business: relying heavily on personal connections (*guanxi*), patrimonial management techniques, and certain (allegedly-shared) expectations about the greater political economy around them. Readers will already be familiar with 'social capital' as a way to profit from social status or relationships,[1] or 'cultural capital', as used by Bourdieu, who postulated the existence of specialized knowledge which might put one person or group in a stronger bargaining position *vis-à-vis* others. Uneasy with the 'ethnic essentialism' behind some of the recent literature, Philip Kuhn (1997) has preferred to use 'historical capital', by which he means the skills and outlooks learnt in the 'Ancestral Land', which assisted survival in foreign environments. Others advocate 'economic culture'. But whatever terminology is employed, a new generation of 'economic sociologists', building upon Schumpeter's earlier interest in the 'sociology of capitalism', has begun to take a special interest in migrant entrepreneurship. While the contributors to this volume are not necessarily cultural determinists, they all agree that 'culture' needs to be taken into consideration in any study of contemporary developments - if only because the Chinese themselves appear to believe that it is important. Although there have been some judicious warnings about the sometimes exaggerated nature of the contemporary discourse on 'Chinese capitalism' (see, for example, Berger, 1996; Dernberger, 1997; Dirlik, 1996b; Nonini, and Ong, 1997),[2] all the more problematic is the increasingly-popular belief that China, *simply because she is China*, can follow her own, unique, path to development.

SUMMARY OF KEY ISSUES

Rightly or wrongly, 'culture' has long been used to explain economic success and lies at the heart of much of the existing 'modernization' literature: with its built-in Western bias. For the great historical sociologists, culture not only explained the rise of capitalism in northern Europe but also its failure to develop in Asia.[3] Even economic determinists, most notably Marxists, debated whether or not there was a distinctly 'Asiatic' mode of production (Brook, 1989). Adapting Weber, Gordon Redding has written (1996) about 'the distinct nature of Chinese capitalism' and Francis Fukuyama (1995:69) likewise believes that it is possible 'to speak of a relatively homogenous Chinese economic culture'. For the former, 'the Overseas Chinese make up one of the world's most effective *economic cultures* [my emphasis]'. They have also been described as 'the new power in Asia' and 'the world's most-dynamic capitalists' (Kraar, 1994). More to the point of this volume, a number of writers (Lever-Tracey, et al., 1996; Bolt, 1996) have proposed that culturally-influenced traits can help explain the ease with which members of the Chinese diaspora have established successful enterprises in China. As Wong Siu-lun (1996:29) put it: 'the economic miracle occurring in the PRC is the product of the dynamic blending of two patterns of Chinese entreprenurship', the external and the mainland. It was actually fashionable in some quarters to think that the Chinese diaspora represented some sort of 'invisible empire', to use Sterling Seagrave's unnecessarily provocative language (1995:4): an economic powerhouse built around 'ethnic solidarity, underground networks, political pragmatism, and exceptional information'. Nothing, however, offends the student of economic history like the unsupported generalizations of those who regularly confuse culture with structure.

Leading the attack, Rupert Hodder (1996:xi) has maintained that: 'Their material success is an outcome, not of "Chineseness", but of multi-dimensional values, institutions and actions which have been consciously manipulated and "tuned" toward the extension and internationalization of trade.' Raj Brown (1995:10) argues that 'a culturally induced propensity for business may be a "necessary" but it is not a "sufficient" explanation for business success' perhaps providing a competitive edge by reducing transaction costs, but she still favours structural or institutional explanations. Others (Nonini and Ong, 1997 or Dirlik, 1996b) take the view that 'transnational' networks of 'overseas Chinese' businessmen are really only part of a global capitalist expansion increasingly characterized by 'flexible production' and 'capital mobility'. Traditional ways of doing business have proven successful, not because they are inherently superior, but because they fit the requirements of an international market place which handsomely rewards the organization of cheap labour and needs the services of a new-generation of 'comprador' middlemen to deal with China's authoritarian state structure and more easily penetrate the countryside. Indeed, family firms make perfect subcontractors.

My own view is that whilst great sums of money can obviously be made through the use of personal contacts (including political connections), sustained development requires a firmer foundation. 'Culture-based capitalism', that is to say an economic system founded largely on personal ties, is distinctly different from 'institutional-based capitalism', even when person-to-person relationships remain important. At least until contract law and the expectation of incorruptible public servants becomes the accepted cultural norm itself. Although Mario Rutten (1994) was quite correct to take on those who would argue that contemporary forms of Asian capitalism are inherently inferior, simply because they may have followed different, even their own characteristic, patterns of development, using alternative means to modern ends as it were, it is a mistake to believe that traditional ways of doing business are, in and of themselves, enough to ensure integration into the new world economic order on equal terms. To the extent that 'cultural capitalism' (to reintroduce that artifice) can be said to exist in China, it may have significant limitations. At best it needs to be viewed as an intermediary stage between a 'corporate' mercantile economy and an 'incorporated' modern one.

It was, in fact, once thought that the 'overseas Chinese' were unlikely entrepreneurs. Allegedly held back by the absence of an accumulation ideology akin to the Protestant ethnic, and restrained by the small size, if not also by the limited imagination of the traditional family firm, they were said to be slow to grasp the benefits of corporate structure and modern management techniques.[4] Even remarkable exceptions, such as the Oei Tiong Ham's Kian Guan conglomerate in the Netherlands East Indies (Panglaykim and Palmer, 1970; Onghokham, 1989; Yoshihara, 1989) or the Khaw Concern in Penang (Cushman, 1990), only served to prove the general rule. But how perceptions changed to keep up with the success enjoyed by ethnic Chinese in Southeast Asia[5] and elsewhere around the world.[6] Turning Max Weber on his head, a number of writers began to praise aspects of Confucian culture: especially the importance assigned to patrimonial institutions as well as intangibles such as the value placed on duty, education, diligence and thrift (Crissman, 1977; Wong, 1985; Wu, 1983; Tai, 1989; Redding, 1990; Menkhoff, 1990, Hamilton, 1996).

Several even went so far as to suggest that ethnicity and commercial ability were somehow related (Lim Mah Hui, 1981; Jesudason, 1989; Raymond Yao, 1991). Others argued that various forms of socio-economic 'networking' provided significant business advantages by facilitating access to labour, markets, and credit information.[7] Furthermore, renewed interest was shown not only in the survival, but also the apparent modern efficiency, of the traditional family firm (Wong Siu-lun 1985 and 1988; Redding 1990; Whitely, 1990). Whilst a few sociologists did recall the diaspora's position as a 'middleman' (or pariah) minority,[8] most political economists continued to stress the on-going importance of government patronage.[9] If there was serious controversy in the 1980s, it was over whether they could, as yet, really be considered 'entrepreneurial' in the classical meaning of the word (Yoshihara, 1988). However Ruth McVey clearly felt confident enough to begin the introduction to her edited, 1992, book with the now ironic line: 'the spectre of capitalism is haunting Southeast Asia'. Given the recent economic meltdown, future scholars might yet set out to explain the reasons for business failure. Although this chapter cannot begin to canvass all that has been written on the subject, it will still be possible to highlight a few of the issues which need to be considered in any discussion of the relationship between culture and capitalism, before addressing the role of the diaspora in the future of China.

The very notion that 'overseas Chinese' capital can help jump-start development goes back to the late-Qing period, as I have demonstrated elsewhere.[10] Far more debatable is the claim, also made from the earliest days of the reform and revolutionary moments, that the new - largely Western and bourgeois - ideas gathered through residence abroad (or even by living in the treaty ports along the coastline) could dramatically alter basic attributes of the Chinese state and society. Although it was once fashionable to think that the communists might have managed to introduce fundamental socio-economic change themselves, most scholars now admit that many of the basic features of the country's traditional political culture - including official corruption and the exploitation of labour - appear to have gone largely unaltered (Godley, 1989b; Jenner, 1992). Indeed observers have been struck by the emergence of various forms of 'neo-traditionalism' (Walder, 1986; Pearson, 1996) and, especially, the way that personal ties survived an otherwise rigid authoritarianism. Even if encouraging signs have emerged as a result of the post-1992 reforms, China's new business élite is still 'Janus-faced' (Pearson, 1996) wanting bureaucratic protection even whilst struggling to be free of state control. The resulting 'clientism' or 'corporatism' - it may, or may not, make sense to argue that there is a uniquely 'socialist mode of corruption' (Kwong, 1997:51-75) - raises serious questions about what may lie ahead.

The character for profit (li[4]), with its 'knife' radical, has long had multiple meanings implying not just monetary gain (including interest earned on money and, presumably, the cut taken by bureaucrats) or competitive advantage (including a slicing wit) but also a special sharpness at doing business. No one who really knows anything about China's economic history - which was so mercantile by Han times that Sima Qian included biographies of 'the moneymakers' in his *Shiji* (first century BC) doubts that the profit motive has always been central to the Chinese way of life, the Confucian bias against commerce notwithstanding. What is really at issue is the extent to which traditional practices still influence the way business is conducted today and, perhaps more importantly, what their persistence might mean for the country's future. Using a language that would not be unfamiliar to *laissez faire* economists today, the Grand Historian once advised: 'By noting surpluses and shortages, you can tell what will be expensive and what cheap. When prices rise too high they must fall again; when prices fall too low, they will rise again. When things are expensive, sell them off as if they were dirt, and buy cheap goods as if they were jewels.' 'Money should circulate like flowing water.' Very much the 'economic rationalist', he also observed that 'The laws governing poverty and wealth are immutable; and the shrewd have plenty while the stupid go short.' As something all men desired instinctively, they spared no effort in their quest for wealth. 'How quickly after gain the whole world races! How madly after gain, the whole world chases!' Worried about the reintroduction of Qin-style monopolies on iron and salt, Sima Qian even warned Emperor Han Wudi that: 'The highest type of ruler accepts the nature of people; the next best leads the people to what is beneficial; the next gives them moral instruction; the next forces them to be orderly, and the worst kind enters into competition with them.'[11] Thus concern over the market economy and how the state should relate to it is hardly new in China. What is novel, at least since the country was first opened to the West in the nineteenth century, is the need to harness individual enterprise to advance the economic goals of the nation.[12]

It is not my intention to critique the 'moral economy' construct as it was once applied to China (but do see Chen and Benton, 1986), although it would probably be hard to find a scholar in the 1990s who would still argue that peasants were, by their very nature, anti-capitalist radicals. The old axiom 'scratch a peasant and find a capitalist' probably comes closer to the mark for there was always a very strong sense of peasant household individualism, which is not to say that forms of village co-operation, even communalism, never existed. Quite to the contrary, the family (or extended clan in south coastal provinces) clearly maintained its own version of a 'value-based economy' where, as Milton Singer (1972:290-7) first argued for South Asia, traditional society embraced management strategies (albeit sometimes only at a subsistence level) that can rightly be regarded as a form of 'entrepreneurship' today. This is certainly the position taken by a number of current writers on Chinese family enterprise and its contemporary relevance. The difficulty, as Hill Gates (1996) observed, is that there has also been a contradiction, when one looks more closely at actual practice, between the Confucian virtues of loyalty, trust, harmony and, ultimately, filial piety, and the calculating, even ruthless, way in which family members (not to mention outsiders) have been (and are still being) exploited in the name of family-style enterprise.[13] The continuing problem with contemporary Chinese 'role ethics' is the extent to which the 'unethical seeking of advantage by use of human relationships' (Chan, 1997:47) remains so critical to business success.[14]

What needs careful reconsideration is the belief that, because the family unit (nuclear or extended) remains so important, the Chinese can maintain modern businesses based, not upon society-transcending legal institutions, but upon an antiquated moral order. Students of Chinese economic history are well aware that it was the lack of trust, not its fulfillment, when small family-centred businesses first expanded beyond the home village, that led to the rise of guilds, native-place associations and the institution of guarantorship, which remained critical to employment prospects well into this century (see McElderry, 1997). For *guanxi* to work effectively it must be genuinely reciprocal, not the product of uneven power relationships: either within small groups, the workplace, or within the larger community and, most certainly, not when dealing with political authorities. State sanctioned capitalism of the sort we have seen in Southeast Asia and, now, South China, is not likely to promote new moralities that challenge the status quo. Greed may not be good but it definitely makes China, if not also the world, go round and is likely to remain a feature of Chinese life for a number of years to come. One does not need to view the 'free market' as a gift from God to accept that there are important cultural (also philosophical and, yes, even religious) principles behind Western capitalism that have not always been easily transplanted to Asia: even though Meiji Japan, and more recently the Taiwan and South Korean experiences, clearly established that rapid industrialization is, indeed, possible without them. After all, modernization is partly a matter of ideological change and this inevitably involves both politics and culture.

ECONOMICS WITH 'CHINESE' CHARACTERISTICS

Until quite recently, debate over capitalism on the mainland was conventionally couched in a counter-factual manner: why, when the Song period (960-1279) seemed so pre-modern, for example, did the economy fail to develop along European lines?[15] Whereas neo-Weberians continued with this line of argument, observing the many ways merchants remained under the thumbs of officials, late twentieth-century scholarship has gone on to discover thriving commercial quarters and a business subculture which, despite frequent lip-service to Confucian ideals (see, for example, R.J. Lufrano, 1997) seems to have been every bit as calculating as that found in the West (Gardella, 1992). Whilst experts on Adam Smith still argue over how he really viewed unfettered competition, Marx quickly came, early on, to the conclusion that the invisible hand was nothing more than 'super-structure': a philosophical justification for the class exploitation which modern 'economic rationalists' now see as saving the poor. Where European Marxists had generally viewed the capitalist stage of economic development as progressive, especially when compared to the traditional situation in Asia (causing some awkward moments for later Chinese thinkers; Brook, 1989), its unpleasant association with foreign imperialism left most writers to reject capitalism as reactionary.[16] Although Mao admitted that international trade had permitted expansion of the 'commodity economy' he blamed foreigners for the destruction of the traditional handicraft industry and, ultimately, for restricting development of Chinese capitalism: a point of view widely accepted by Leftist writers in the West.[17] As he argued in 1939, 'National capitalism has developed to a certain extent and played a considerable part in China's political and cultural life, but it has not become the principal socio-economic form in China: quite feeble in strength, it is mostly tied in varying degrees to both foreign imperialism and domestic feudalism.'[18] When the second united front was in its infancy, Mao Zedong observed that 'China's feudal society ... carried within itself the embryo of capitalism' and how 'China would of herself have developed into a capitalist society, even if there had been no influence of foreign capitalism.'[19] The resulting search for capitalist roots keep Chinese economic historians occupied into the 1990s.

Readers may be familiar with what Mao wrote in his 1945 work *On Coalition Government*: 'Some people fail to understand why, so far from fearing capitalism, Communists should advocate its development in certain conditions...' By then, however, he undoubtedly looked not to the emerging bourgeoisie but to the peasantry, implying at times during the Cultural Revolution that China was the world's most-developed society precisely because it was so economically backward. In the final analysis, as Maurice

Meisner observed some years ago, Mao completely rejected the basic Marxist proposition that socialism requires capitalism,[20] leaving the door open for the critical reassessment of both capitalism and socialism that is taking place today. But the suggestion that China had created its own economic system has in no way been limited to Red Guards. The seeds can be found in the writing of Sun Yat-sen.

While Sun may have been willing, at least for a time, to equate the socio-economic vision he called 'the principal of people's livelihood' (*minsheng zhuyi*) with 'communism', his uneasiness over class conflict and awareness of some of the problems Lenin was experiencing with the 'New Economic Policy' in the Soviet Union, convinced him that it was better to equate the concept with 'socialism'. Clearly rejecting the argument that material issues were central force in history, but determined in his own way to solve the land problem, he once advised a younger generation already drifting toward Marxism, that China was suffering more from poverty than unequal distribution of wealth (Sun 1924:182). What he proposed was a system which could 'check the growth of large private capital and prevent the social disease of extreme inequality'. The state was to play a role in regulating capital and establishing a national economic infrastructure but he was never specific about the proper public-private mix. Although it is very difficult to find much consistency in Sun's writings, A. James Gregor (1995:194) has nevertheless maintained that 'Throughout his life, Sun continued to maintain that market-governed international economic relations were not, in and of themselves, exploitative.' Be this as it may, it is clear that Sun did not fear capitalism; he once hatched a grandiose scheme to use international capital to develop China (Godley, 1993) and was, as political circumstances dictated, quite willing to identify his ideas with socialism, if not also communism. Virtually from the beginning, his disciples argued that he deliberately chose the term 'people's livelihood' as a 'middle path' or 'third way'. As the always controversial *minsheng* lecture number two ends: 'When the people share everything in the state, then will we truly reach the goal of the *minsheng* principal, which was Confucius' hope of a "great commonwealth".' Not surprisingly, his ideas have been enjoying something of a revival in the People's Republic of China.

The argument that China could follow her own, uniquely 'Chinese' economic principles was further developed by Tao Xisheng, ghost writer for Chiang Kai-shek's *Chinese Economic Theory*, published in 1947: 'Most so-called scientific thinkers tend to disparage things of their own country and to esteem highly everything foreign.' The country needed to combine Chinese and Western economic theories in order 'to find the right path for our own economic development' in accord with Sun's 'people's livelihood concept'. Their theory defined economics as 'the study of managing men and adjusting things', in simple terms, 'how to make the nation strong and rich' - which was, in essence, 'the study of national development'. Citing classical texts like the 'Book of History' (*Shujing*), Chiang advised how 'the relations between men and things should therefore be studied and controlled from the standpoint of the whole'. 'Chinese economists regard goods as the products of manpower and the land, and money simply as a medium of exchange.' Unlike Western theory, 'Chinese economic theory is not confined to private enterprise or market transactions, but is a combination of the people's livelihood and national defence'. Its goal: to administer the relationship between men and goods so that man's rational nature will, consequently, improve his livelihood.[21]

In work published under his own name, Tao Xisheng (who had, ironically, been profoundly influenced by orthodox Marxist writings) argued that China had been 'proto-capitalist' since Sima Qian's time but that the 'commercial capital', which should have transformed the country, had been squandered because of the survival of 'feudal' ideas. These had allowed the landed gentry, in league with imperial institutions (and, then, militarists from the end of the Han Dynasty) to appropriate the profits so that merchants, as a group, never really had an opportunity to develop until after the arrival of the West (Dirlik, 1978). Because so much was at stake, communist writers quickly entered the debate. If, as Mao would eventually add, unequal treaties and foreign competition, had arrested the country's independent development along capitalist lines, should not ways be found to protect China's indigenous capitalists? Just why had the country remained feudal and so backward? One Kuomintang (*Guomindang*) theorist, who incidentally advocated the eventual absorption of all private capital by the state, concluded that the government needed to 'protect Chinese capitalism because of China's unique society' (cited by Bedeski, 1971:323).

Without much in the way of acknowledgment to Sun Yat-sen, his ideas began to reappear on the mainland in the mid-1980s.[22] The People's Republic of China was said to be 'developing a socialist planned commodity economy which is fundamentally different from the capitalist commodity economy'. Why? Because it was based on the *minsheng* ideal based on 'public ownership of the means of production as the national economy's foundation' and a 'solely foreign-owned economy' together with a private sector. 'Since socialism and capitalism have inhabited the same planet for so long, why should they not be able to operate side by side in the same country' (*Beijing Review*, 3 February 1986:16-17, 20). The first wave of reforms (see Sun Yan, 1995) had, of course, begun in 1979 with the first draft law on 'joint ventures'. Initially it was argued that foreign capital was only 'supplementary'. Then, the Special Economic Zones were described as 'state capitalism within a socialist system' or 'a composite capitalist economic form in which China's society is coupled with foreign capital' (*China Constructs*, June 1985). Even the second wave of reforms beginning in 1992, were not intended to lead to mass privatization but rather to reduce state subsidies to losing enterprises in what Dorothy Solinger (1993:128) called 'saving the state budget by capitalist means'. In October 1992, the party still believed that a market economy could somehow be grafted on to the struggling state sector. But from then onwards, more and more Chinese economists openly praised the efficiency of the market and the need to further encourage the development of private enterprise.[23] Whether this is called 'capitalist measures with Chinese characteristics' (Solinger, 1993), or we accept that we are now discussing 'socialism with capitalist characteristics', as Zhao Ziyang initially described developments to the 13th Party Congress, there are many unresolved issues. Among these are: the pressing need for legal reform, the plight of migrant workers and the unemployed, the role which will be played by the state, and the connection between capitalism and the emergence of democratic institutions.

The official position is that, even though China continues to take the socialist road and opposes 'wholesale Westernization', capitalist methods can still be utilized and, in any case, should not be rejected out of hand. Whether this is labelled 'socialism with Chinese characteristics' or 'capitalism with Chinese characteristics', a 'market-oriented commodity economy' or some yet to be named hybrid (one which merely reinforces the present bureaucratic corporatism, where power itself is bought and sold, or permits a more-individualistic, American-style, entrepreneurship), this will surely be characterized by a resurgent nationalism and require the construction of a new value system consistent with the country's continuing search for wealth and power in the international arena. What remains to be seen is whether the present transitional system, which Frank N. Pieke (1995) has labelled with the oxymoronic, yet highly appropriate term, 'capital socialism', can maintain the pace of growth without ultimate resource to the 'alternative moralities' feared by the central leadership.

No one would deny that the 'God of Wealth' has returned to South China (Ikels, 1996). It is much more difficult to say what this might mean for the future. Although Rupert Hodder (1993) could well be right to suggest that important 'wealth values' will need to be still further institutionalized, and thereby legitimized, if the country is to continue to prosper, a number of thoughtful commentators have warned that the People's Republic will eventually need to create a more-stable ideological foundation: something to replace the present 'make money' ethos, however beneficial the 'to get rich is glorious' attitude may have proven to be in the short run, with a more public-spirited outlook. Perhaps this will come in the form of a resurrected 'Confucianism' as in Lew Kwan Yew's Singapore, or even a return to a collectivist mentality. It is just as likely that China's new value system will come in the form of a new 'Victorianism' - not entirely unlike what evolved in nineteenth-century England and Meiji Japan - where the 'self-made man' served, simultaneously, as both a moral model and a cog in the machine: pushing along economic development whilst strengthening the political power of the state. In only the former case did the 'profit motive' lead to greater personal freedom. Now that writers of the 'dependency school' have faded from scene, replaced by the globalists of the present decade, it has once again become popular to believe that, as state controls over the economy are weakened, 'free enterprise' will produce 'free association' and, eventually, democratic institutions:[24] as is said to have already happened on Taiwan. Until this occurs on the mainland, however, the debate about the relationship between capitalism and democracy, like the arguments over cultural influence on economic development, will undoubtedly continue and involve the so-called 'overseas Chinese'.[25] Just what they can bring to their ancestral homeland today - other than capital and business expertise - is still subject to debate. Whereas individuals from Europe, North America and Australasia might well serve as democratic role models, the extensive use of 'backdoor' relationships with party cadres by many would-be entrepreneurs, especially from Southeast Asia, clearly points the country in the wrong direction.

REFLECTIONS ON THE NANYANG CONNECTION

Transnational business is certainly not new to the Chinese. From the time of the Han dynasty, thriving communities of merchants have tied the Middle Kingdom to her neighbours and, through them, to the wider world. There were colonies along the Silk Road, in Korea and Vietnam. Sixteenth century Europeans encountered them in Nagasaki, on Taiwan, and at Bangkok and Malacca, as well as in the far reaches of the Nanyang (the 'Southern Ocean' or maritime Southeast Asia). However it was not until the second half of the nineteenth century that large-scale migration took place, with coolies, independent businessmen, and students venturing still further to Europe, Africa, the Americas and Australasia. Eventually, small islands in the Pacific and distant Caribbean gained sizeable populations, prompting China's first attempt to formulate a policy to protect, but more often to exploit the expatriate community. Still the most numerous (and historically) important diaspora population remains the twenty odd million residing in Southeast Asia. Since the earliest days of the junk trade to their present dominance of ASEAN commerce, they have helped create a sense of regional identity by constructing extensive business networks. Today, when these are being expanded to include not only South China but also Europe, North America and Australia, it is obviously important to appreciate something about their origins. But, as several other chapters have demonstrated, we must move beyond ethnic stereotyping to understand how enterprises actually operate. What has too often been missing from the analysis (especially that based entirely on social science theory or contemporary field research, not to mention the worst of the journalistic hyperbole) is a historical perspective.

There is no question that traditional Chinese practice, with its emphasis on kinship and other social relationships, was transplanted to Southeast Asia where it continues to influence commercial activities: especially in the case of the family firm. More work clearly needs to be done on China which, from early times, enjoyed great wealth and booming trade without the blessings of a modern economy. Conventional explanations that the Middle Kingdom fell behind because it lacked a profit-oriented religion and authentic business outlook, or that merchants were forever under the thumbs of mandarins, seem to have lost most of their analytical conviction. Recent studies of the Ming-Qing period show a cash economy, complex markets, sophisticated credit arrangements and thriving merchant quarters, which were tied to the surrounding countryside by rational, and undeniably proto-capitalist, institutions. We know that business networks could be highly intricate and involve not just trade, clan, and place-of-origin associations but also professional brokers. Some guilds actually multiplied after the country's opening to the West: at first, to protect monopolies but then to make their industries more competitive. Old-style banks proved quite adaptable, lending money to new treaty-port enterprises. Other bodies proved equally capable of adaptation, continuing to adjudicate disputes and regulate commerce well into the republican era. They maintained connections with inland locations (sometimes in league with compradors for Western firms) and, like the infamous secret societies or various benevolent associations, also expanded overseas, right along with modern banks and chambers of commerce: building upon, but never entirely replacing previous forms of co-operation. Indeed, Maurice Freedman (1959) proposed some forty-years ago that the Nanyang Chinese penchant for collective action was a clear indication of their sophistication when it came to handling money.

Ties to Southeast Asia can easily be traced in the case of clan organizations, but other 'pseudo-lineages' of convenience had been absolutely essential to the Nanyang trade well before Europeans arrived on the scene in any numbers. Financing the long and dangerous voyages often required the construction of 'extra-parochial' relationships forced merchants to join together in co-operatives (*hang*), collectives (*hui*) and credit pools (*yinhui*). Some of these may have been sworn brotherhoods, as were private gangs. Successful networking through occupational or niche specialization is most frequently attributed to traditional Chinese organization which is assumed to have tied migrants from a similar sub-ethnic or dialect background together from the earliest days (see, for example, Cheng 1985). Most research on network-building has naturally concentrated on *huiguan* (associations), especially the *bang*, mutual aid groups based on dialect or place of origin in China (Freedman, 1960; Suyama, 1962; Yen, 1986:35-109; Ng, 1992). Closely related were the secret societies. Originally benign brotherhoods, at least in the Nanyang context, they soon became involved in warfare, the discipline of coolie labourers, and the marshalling of urban merchant funds for hinterland ventures. It is impossible to study nineteenth-century business without finding links to both secret societies and revenue farms, most notably opium (see Butcher and Dick, 1993). We know that secret society and *bang* leadership became closely related to economic leadership in the nineteenth century - though just which came first is sometimes hard to establish. In either case, the overall trend is clear enough: although *huiguan* control generated wealth in the nineteenth century, twentieth-century community leaders were more likely to be selected from amongst businessmen who were already economically successful. In part, this was because such individuals had consequently gained recognition from political authorities in Southeast Asia (and/or China) but also because they were in a better position to protect common interests. Lacking a scholar-gentry class *per se*, overseas merchants quite naturally took over community leadership, adding the veneer of purchased degrees or titles just for status and, perhaps, insurance when it came time to return to China (Yen, 1970). Moreover, it was not at all unusual for important business deals to be cemented by marriage alliances: vertically with official families in China (and the indigenous élite in Southeast Asia, most notably in Thailand; see the excellent study by Ian Brown, 1988) as well as horizontally with important trading partners.

Philip Kuhn has suggested that, from at least the sixteenth century, China was a gigantic 'school for emigrants' teaching - despite literati prejudice and government discrimination - the very skills they needed to prosper abroad. These included a cash economy and commercialized crops, a market-oriented handicraft industry and tradition of internal migration in the face of land shortages and natural disasters but also in search of employment or generally better prospects. And, perhaps most important of all, they had experience dealing with political authorities. Similarly, Wang Gungwu (1981) has postulated that because Confucianism and the imperial governments behind it had generally been unfriendly to commerce, traditional merchants became incredibly 'flexible' and, given their uncertain status, quite skilled at turning quick profits. Once free from bureaucratic control, the Chinese living overseas were able to build upon their mercantile (*huashang*) subculture, ironically bolstered by filial piety. 'Being peripheral to Confucian scholars and mandarins was advantageous to the trading classes' offering, as it did, a degree of freedom from official control (Wang, 1989). But he and a number of other perceptive scholars have also acknowledged that the Nanyang Chinese were, precisely because of their experience in China, perfectly suited as bureaucratic capitalists in Southeast Asia since merchants had so long been accustomed to seeking special favours, including licensed monopolies, from government officials.[26] Even today, when Chinese success can, in large measure, be traced to the liberalization of ASEAN economies and the corresponding growth of regional trade, political patronage has remained extremely important, perhaps more so than opportunity, management or structure: at least for the bigger players.[27] Yoshihara (1988 and 1995) has long regarded 'overseas Chinese' capitalism as somehow 'ersatz' for just this reason.

Writing of the Chinese on Java early this century, Clive Day remarked how 'they seem to lack the breadth and boldness of conception that would enable them to enter large enterprises as rivals of Europeans but between the two races they have an assured position.'[28] Reflecting emerging stereotypes, he noted their role as tax farmers and middleman position but, like so many other European writers, Day failed to acknowledge the part that the colonial state was already playing in restricting the scope and scale of ethnic Chinese enterprises, even as it was providing new opportunities in the intermediary trade. A more-complicated answer would include the fact that European colonial governments (the trend takes longer to develop in Siam where a Sino-Thai accommodation extended into the highest political strata) had begun to move away from the earlier *laissez faire* policies which permitted large Chinese enterprises to thrive in the first place. The so-called 'Ethical policy' in the Netherlands Indies, openly anti-Chinese legislation in the American Philippines and manifest favouritism toward Westerners in crucial government or development contracts all had an immediate impact. Those that survived later encountered the world depression, Japanese occupation and the emergence of new, independent but extremely nationalistic, regimes. When the political climate allowed, and new opportunities appeared in the ASEAN setting, the Chinese have resumed their earlier position. In the final analysis, circumstances (and especially political conditions) have probably been far more important than culture. At least, to the extent that culture *is* relevant, it can only be appreciated in a broader historical context.

Much that has been written about the ethnic Chinese could just as easily have been said about the Scots, whose economic pre-eminence in the colonial period was itself legendary. Building at first upon small family firms or partnerships with limited capital or technological edge, the great overseas-Scottish entrepreneurs initially traded with friends and relatives, often serving as agents for longer-established concerns, until they were able to use government connections and their knowledge of the home market to consolidate their business dominance of British Asia. Even the most-cursory study of how pioneering Western firms began their enterprises, quite often in co-operation with Chinese companies (or, time after time, in their footsteps), and then thrived under government patronage, immediately reveals more convergence than ethno-cultural uniqueness. In fact, there were some striking parallels with the ways that business continues to be done in the region. It can also be quite misleading to write only about 'Chinese' business networks since many of the most-successful merchant families developed, very early on, symbiotic relationships with indigenous élites and/or Europeans (then, later, with the Japanese) collecting native produce for export whilst using their own extensive ties with the hinterland to distribute Western manufactured goods. Hence the critical importance of the agent or comprador. There is no need to go on and document how complex the East-West partnership has now become throughout the Southeast Asian region: all the more so with the involvement of Malay politicians, Thai and Indonesian military officers, and modern multi-nationals.

The assumption that Chinese success is *sui generis* not only offends indigenous sensitivities but it also masks the extent to which practices so often labelled 'Chinese' are, in actual fact, only a natural response to changing political or economic conditions. Good illustrations are: the Western-inspired chamber of commerce; the interlocking board of directors; and the business group. All three can be traced back to the turn-of-the twentieth century when capital shortages, foreign competition, and a changing political environment forced a conscious modernization of the way business was being conducted. We must never be tempted into thinking that the functions being performed by business networks are 'Chinese' by definition. Linda Lim (1983) has rightly cautioned that social organization is neither a 'necessary' nor 'sufficient' explanation of continuing economic dominance since so many successful Chinese businessmen now appear to have much in common with other business élites, in Asia or the West. In an economic, as distinct from a sociological sense, even antiquated *bang* linkages are still being maintained today because they perform necessary modern functions. Although the Nanyang Chinese may even find it useful to grade relationships according to kinship, clan, and other parochial ties, they still desire an 'optimal mix' of trading partners depending upon the 'transaction costs' of including outsiders and the 'opportunity costs' of excluding them, as Landa's (1983) study showed some years ago. Menkhoff and Labig (1996) have also shown that quality, price and the reliability of supply can be just as important as personal connections. Indeed: the utility of Chinese business networks can be easily overstated. They certainly do not, *ipso facto*, guarantee success. Even if certain features of 'traditional' commercial life are being maintained to the present, the ethnic Chinese living in Southeast Asia have, as a general rule, become quite 'cosmopolitan' in outlook: with many now having relatives in Europe, North America or Australasia and displaying a penchant not only for a bourgeois lifestyle, but also for complicated business arrangements (interlocking directorates and even 'conglomerate' structures) which, while superficially similar in some ways to much older commercial arrangements, now boast (even in the case of some of the smaller import/export firms) conspicuous connections to multi-national corporations. The Rotary Club (or similar service organization with extensive international membership) has already begun to displace the Chinese Chamber of Commerce as the meeting place of choice in major business centres. At the dedication ceremony for the new American School in Singapore, Lee Hsien Loong, son of the long-serving prime minister Lee Kwan Yew, was heard to remark how Americans overseas invariably organized themselves in business associations and social groups, and urged Singaporeans cultivate the same quality of self-help *(The Sunday Times* [Singapore], 3 November 1996).

The reasons for business success (or failure) are undoubtedly complex everywhere in the world and, in the case of Southeast Asia, also politically sensitive. All the 'speculations about Chinese networks, often without the support of empirical evidence' have, as Menkhoff and Labig (1996:129) complained, only 'helped perpetuate prejudices about the social exclusiveness of ethnic Chinese in Southeast Asia'. Who really knows why Chinese work so hard (but do see Harrell, 1985) or seem so adept at handling money? Even scholars who have devoted their careers to the problem are unsure how to balance their own account books: how much credit should be given to culture, structural, political and class considerations or just plain luck. As Robert Cribb (1996) observed: 'In some respects, Chinese business dominance in Southeast Asia is *unremarkable* [my emphasis].' The region had vast frontier areas and great natural resources which were ripe for development in the nineteenth century, just as they are today. It is far better to ask more meaningful questions about the boom and bust nature of Chinese enterprise and the apparently critical role played first by colonial authorities and, more recently, by independent national governments.

It was not until the final decades of the nineteenth century that Europeans first began to overtake Chinese in important areas: mining, inter-island shipping, sugar planting and numerous aspects of general commerce. In the Netherlands East Indies, for example, the Chinese were well-entrenched in batik, lumber and agriculture and would continue to play a critical role in the development of Sumatra (and other outer islands) well after Governor General Van Heutz began to pursue a more paternalistic attitude toward the 'native' population on Java. Even then, the Chinese continued to contribute capital, labour and organization which remained quite critical to economic development during the period of, at least-superficial, Western supremacy (Cator, 1936). No less an authority than Frank Swettenham admitted that 'up to the year 1900 it may be fairly said that the prosperity of the Malay States was due to the enterprise and labour of the Chinese' (cited by Allen and Donnithorn, 1956:39). Using capital raised in their mercantile pursuits, as well as through tax-farming, they had already diversified into land speculation, mining and plantation agriculture, and were expanding into value-added milling and steamer shipping. Yet, at the end of the colonial era, Allen and Donnithorn (1956:6) nonetheless felt certain that 'it was Western enterprise alone which enabled the vast resources of the region to be tapped, thus creating a new source of income in which Asians and Westerners have both shared. For Boeke (1953), developing the plural economy thesis for the Indies, only large-scale enterprises along Western lines could neutralize risks on the world market. Another popular explanation was that the Europeans triumphed because of their advanced technology, easier access to capital and, most importantly, their superior organizational and entrepreneurial ability: pretty much the same reasons given to explain ethnic Chinese dominance in the region today.[29] In the final analysis it is surely opportunity, *not* ethnicity which is the key to success.[30]

THE PROBLEM WITH *QIAOXIANG* TIES

Concerned as they were with overseas trade, early Chinese merchants undoubtedly possessed an outward-looking mentality, though not necessarily any more so than the Arabs or indigenous Southeast Asians who called at ports such as Malacca. No doubt the pursuit of riches demanded a certain mobility. Even after sinking local roots, market considerations required traders to keep one eye on what was happening elsewhere and, ultimately, to maintain on-going business contacts. Since by definition, traders traded, it is not surprising that the Chinese established widespread networks. In time, these tied the far corners of Southeast Asia together, linking them to

China and the wider world. Virtually all 'overseas Chinese', even poor labourers, had a part to play in the introduction of modern values. Their very preoccupation with material success already marked the sojourners as agents of change. I have argued elsewhere (1981b and 1996) that earlier generations of diaspora Chinese provided China with an innovative and open-minded outlook, one backed by foreign experience and also shored up, as it were, by far-flung connections. Part of an emerging bourgeois, 'treaty port', environment such individuals invariably brought new ideas to China and could, thus, rightly be considered entrepreneurs (the famous Wing On Department Store or Nanyang Brothers Tobacco Company, for example). Some years ago, I thought (1981a) that rather than concern oneself with the differences between revolutionaries, reformists and monarchists in the early years of the century, the 'overseas Chinese' in Southeast Asia needed to be appreciated for the values they shared. By the nineteenth century, they were already part of a movement larger than China (see also Duara, 1997).

Because of the basically commercial nature of the European expansion into Asia, the pioneer mediators between East and West, whether in Singapore, Hong Kong or Shanghai, were much alike. It is true, that merchants who dealt largely in commodities at one end or the other of the trade may have enjoyed less European competition and felt less pressure to adapt. But most were quickly affected by changes in the global market and, as suggested earlier in this chapter, were forced to make adjustments to business practices: although, superficially, networks still seemed to be networks. Old-style banks and the chamber of commerce are probably the best-studied examples. Astride two cultures, the comprador-type naturally enough developed cross loyalties. Qing honours foreign-language education for children, Christian faith sometimes wed to Confucian wisdom and an early recognition of the necessity for China to be strong despite a personal debt to imperialism were endemic to port cities throughout the East. And there were other similarities since, first 'John Comprador' and, then, independent Chinese businessmen, became established fixtures along the coast and throughout Southeast Asia.

According to Rhoads Murphey's controversial argument (1977), the Westernizing cities and their 'apostles of progress' did not really transform the countryside in a non-colonized China. Modern urban centres were more of an 'irritant' than real agent of change. If anything, the obvious foreign influence in the littoral environment may only have stimulated resistance in the interior. Through minimal adjustments introduced through the sieve of intermediaries acceptable to traditional leaders, the hinterland was able to withstand major reforms well into the twentieth century. In some important ways, of course, capitalism did change China. Cigarettes and kerosene lamps managed to reach remote villages to introduce the beginnings of a consumer society. Once the 'pursuit of profit' became an accepted, and open, goal for merchants in the late nineteenth century, the traditional culture and its guardian state were both put on the defensive (Hao, 1986). Not only did innovative enterprises emerge, often under the nose of warlords and imperialists (as Chinese economic historians have rediscovered for themselves; see Wright, 1992 and 1993), there really was a 'Golden Age of the Bourgeoisie' (Bergère, 1989) in major port cities. The fundamental question is not why the country failed to develop capitalism but why China adopted socialism!

If 'entrepreneurship' is nothing more than 'arbitrage', the discovery and exploitation of price spreads, then Chinese have been entrepreneurs since the early days of the empire. Likewise, if 'innovation' is central to your definition. By the Sung period, blast furnaces were running twenty-four hours a day while imaginative land reclamation schemes introduced new pumps and rice strains. Certainly no student of the Chinese in Southeast Asia would disagree with the proposition that entrepreneurship is a form of 'speculative intermediation', with the entrepreneur defined as someone who makes judgemental decisions about the co-ordination of scarce resources. Manifestly, the Chinese were already 'market entrepreneurs' in Sima Qian's day. Schumpeter, who saw a clear connection between entrepreneurial activity and capital accumulation, did not, however, believe that all capitalists were entrepreneurs. What was required was the 'carrying out of new combinations' in a way that produced not only profits but genuine economic development. Although he was right to criticize traditional Marxists for their failure to give adequate notice to the role of human perception, even imagination, as opposed to the determinism of capital and technological change, Schumpeter was just as much captivated by the 'qualitative leap', that transformative moment which re-established economic equilibrium on a different plane if not also a higher level. Ironically feeling that Marx had given far too much credit to capital, Schumpeter correspondingly disregarded the importance of investment. While the successful entrepreneur might surely be a capitalist, he believed that not all capitalists were innovators. The critical issue for me is not whether forms of capitalism and/or entrepreneurship are present in any given society at a given moment, but whether they produce fundamental cultural, as well as economic, change.

I have written before about earlier campaigns to exploit the wealth and talent of the Nanyang Chinese. Through the activities of the Singapore and, after 1893, Penang consulates, and a number of special agents, brevet Qing ranks or other honours were sold and vast sums raised for relief. There were also the first large capital investments in China. Remittances dramatically increased this century to keep pace with the growing number of Chinese in the region, with the bulk of this money continuing to pass through clan and place of origin organizations until the establishment of modern Chinese banks. These, too, were initially set up along *bang* lines, largely to speed remittances to China though they soon began to play an important role in commercial exchange. But, unquestionably, the development most responsible for expanding business linkages was the establishment of the new chambers of commerce. While Southeast Asia may have been divided into European colonial possessions, just as it is now partitioned into nation-states, Chinese businessmen regularly ignored international borders, to move their capital and capability as opportunity dictated. The British, in particular, feared subversion. Indeed, our own academic discourse about *guanxi*, networks, and intricate business connections with the People's Republic (all the more so when packaged as ethnic triumphalism) still raises eyebrows in Southeast Asia.

Not all that many years ago, writers influenced more by Cold War language than visionary APEC talk about the promise of unlimited free trade warned that the diaspora constituted a 'fifth column' marching to Beijing's tune. In those days, the Chinese overseas were often caught between a militantly-revolutionary (Elegant, 1959; Alexander, 1973) China and an anti-communist United States. Later, a number of scholars still portrayed ethnic Chinese as a potentially troublesome minority because of a strong sense of communal allegiance and an almost irksome penchant to make money. There was actually some concern expressed over the extent of remittances to the People's Republic (Wu, 1967). Considerable difficulties occurred in Indonesia, especially over the 'nationality' question. Not only has the Chinese population been large in places like Malaysia and Thailand but, because of earlier colonial policies as well as their own abilities, the Chinese have also held an economic pre-eminence elsewhere in the region. As study after study has confirmed, the Kuomintang's conscious efforts to export China-oriented nationalism through Chinese-language schools, newspapers and other party activities, only enhanced racial tensions during the first half of this century. And privileged economic position, even 'alien' identity, continued to haunt sections of the community in the post-war period. Whilst there has been discrimination and a degree of ethno-cultural aloofness, as well as points of friction and the potential for violence, the vast majority of ethnic Chinese in Southeast Asia must now be considered politically loyal. Where assimilation has not taken place, there is every indication that a new (modern or, for that matter, global) culture has been emerging amongst the middle and upper-classes, one that already crosses ethnic lines and tends to override more-parochial concerns.

Beijing's policy toward ethnic Chinese living outside of China, including the large population in Southeast Asia, was in shambles when the political radicals began to fade from the scene in late 1976. Condemned as reactionaries or bourgeois-capitalists in one Cultural Revolution bombast after another, yet paradoxically and unsuccessfully urged to rebel against their new homelands, the 'overseas Chinese' were, in actual fact, largely ignored by the People's Republic of China for ten years: one of the best things that could have happened in my opinion. Official attitudes began to change in late 1977, when the first serious efforts at damage control began and, with the four modernizations just underway, the anti-Sinitic outburst in Vietnam further underscored the need for a dramatic reassessment. Although China promised 'to protect the interests of the Overseas Chinese and help those who return' (as many as 300,000 as it turned out, quite likely including some refugees from Cambodia), the episode only served to demonstrate the practical limitations to such rhetoric (see Godley, 1980). The first refugees began to arrive just as more-moderate authorities were uncovering the full folly of the previous decade. Not only had Chinese with 'foreign connections' (*haiwai guanxi*) - either of overseas origins themselves or merely with relatives abroad - experienced terrible persecution losing positions, property and self respect (Godley, 1989a), their mistreatment threatened other reforms: most notably, the need to attract foreign investment and support.

Early in 1978, the Overseas Chinese Affairs Office was given broad powers to investigate abuses, more fully integrate the 'domestic overseas Chinese' including 'returnees' (*guiguo huaqiao*) while mending bridges to the many permanently residing abroad: individuals who had been puzzled, if not alienated, by recent events. Closer to home, the 'expatriate' communities in Macao, Hong Kong and Taiwan also needed reassurance. In direct contrast to the radical years of the Cultural Revolution, anyone and anything from abroad began to offer an almost irresistible attraction. Communication with overseas relatives was suddenly encouraged, as was tourism, to stimulate both necessary contacts and the flow of needed foreign currency remittances. Universities in South China which specifically catered to Southeast-Asians were reopened together with other academic institutions with expertise on either the Nanyang region or 'overseas Chinese' affairs. Thus, the opening of China to the world quite naturally began with a concerted effort to rebuild bridges to the Chinese diaspora, whose wealth and talent were needed. Indeed, Deng Xiaoping spoke, unashamedly, of attracting a billion US$ worth of investments, a modest sum as things turned out. On 1 June 1974, well before China's reopening to the world, *The Economist* described the 'overseas Chinese' - including those in Hong Kong, Taiwan and Singapore - as 'the most formidable economic power in Asia outside Japan'.

I cannot, however, help but feel that there is a discrepancy between China's long-standing faith that the Chinese overseas can be readily mobilized for political or economic campaigns in their ancestral homeland and the quite understandable anxiety displayed by Asian neighbours about the threat of external interference and, of more immediate concern, capital drain. As long as there is a considerable flow of 'overseas Chinese' funds to the mainland and crucial points to be scored by indigenous Southeast-Asian politicians frequently on the look-out for scapegoats, the position of the diaspora is likely to remain vulnerable. All the more so, to the extent that communities may become 're-sinicized' or display conspicuous pride in their cultural heritage. The basic paradox is that while all the member states of ASEAN (except Singapore with its large majority) wish to reduce the comparative power of the ethnic Chinese in their domestic economies, to do so risks a further slowdown and the weakening of critical trade connections in the greater Nanyang region, including important business links to South China.

The problem for the People's Republic, as the conclusion to the Cheng and Ngok chapter reminded us, is that the more openly it courts Southeast Asian Chinese for their talent and wealth (to tug at heart as well as purse strings), the more dangerous the situation might become. Although the independent nations in the Asia-Pacific region rightly fear any form of great power hegemony, it again becomes fashionable to speak of a 'Greater East Asia' (for example, Hofheinz and Calder, 1982) and, more recently, of a 'Greater China' (*Da Zhonghua*), including Taiwan, and the 'overseas Chinese' (Harding, 1993; Shambaugh, 1993). As wiser minds, especially Wang Gungwu (1993:926), have already cautioned, the term is unfortunate . If anything, the Chinese in Southeast Asia do not want to appear too 'Chinese' in a cultural - and certainly not in a political - sense. Nonetheless, like the often misused phase 'overseas Chinese', the 'Greater China' construct has become part of popular speech and is hard to avoid. It is now almost as uncomfortable to read of a 'transnational Chinese economy' (Harding, 1993; Lever-Tracey, et al., 1996; Nonini and Ong, 1997). Alas, the diaspora was even absurdly described as China's 'secret weapon' (Branegan, 1993). Both the ethnic Chinese and ASEAN have much to lose if the integration of Hong Kong fails to go smoothly or, because of a miscalculation, the Beijing government renews historical fears about its intentions in the region. As Shambaugh (1993:655) speculated: 'Intra-Greater China interactions also create a variety of social, cultural, economic and political issues - which could as easily accelerate disintegrative processes as vice versa'.

CONCLUDING REMARKS

The reconstruction of *qiaoxiang* ties so ably described by the contributors to this volume begs a number of questions about the role of culture in the development process. Although many scholars have noted the 'modernity of tradition', or commented upon the prominent role played by family-style institutions and various forms of socio-economic networking in contemporary business practice, it is just as important to ask where China's political economy may be headed. For the most part, discourse over the country's rapidly accelerating modernization has been closely tied to a re-evaluation of Western-style capitalism and the essentially-bourgeois values behind it. At stake is not just the fate of the totalitarian state, and its efforts to maintain political power through the introduction of market reforms, but also the need to find an alternative morality capable of sustaining economic growth whilst facilitating the construction of a new sense of commonwealth which, one may hope, will be conducive to the emergence of a civil society. Although diaspora investments are undoubtedly welcome, the continued reliance on personal connections invites forms of 'crony capitalism' which, as has been the case in neighbouring Southeast Asia, may actually slow the pace of financial and legal reform whilst also retarding the introduction of democracy. Whereas status was once said to generate wealth in traditional cultures, whilst wealth led to status in modern societies, China's leadership seems trapped in a no man's ground unwilling to accept the institutional changes required for modernization. In the process, they have lost their own moral authority. Borrowing the approach first used by historical sociologists, this final chapter has traced the origins of China's present wealth-creating value system: from its roots in merchant culture, and within the Southeast Asian diaspora, to the current 'greed is good' era where, as Liu Binyan caustically noted: 'money is more powerful than authority' (1990:27).

BIBLIOGRAPHY

Alexander, G.
1973   *Silent Invasion: The Chinese in Southeast Asia.* London: Macdonald & Company
Allen, G.C. and A. Donnithorn
1956   *Western Enterprise in Indonesia and Malaya.* London: Macmillan
Barton, C.G.

1983   'Trust and Credit: Some Observations Regarding Business Strategies of Overseas Chinese Traders in South Vietnam', in: Lim and Gosling (eds), pp. 46-64

Baum, R.
1994   *Burying Mao: Chinese Politics in the Age of Deng Xiaoping.* Princeton: Princeton University Press

Bedeski, R.E.
1971   'The Tutelary State and National Revolution in Kuomintang Ideology, 1928-31', *China Quarterly* 46, pp. 308-30

Berger, M.
1996   'Yellow Mythologies: The East Asian Miracle and Post-Cold War Capitalism', *Positions: East Asia Cultures Critique* 4:1

Bergère, M.C.
1989   *The Golden Age of the Chinese Bourgeoisie 1911- 1937.* Translated by Janet Lloyd. Cambridge, England: Cambrigde University Press

Boeke, J.H.
1953   *Economics and Economic Policy of Dual Societies as Exemplified by Indonesia.* New York: Institute of Pacific Relations

Bolt, P.J.
1996   'Looking to the Diaspora: the Overseas Chinese and China's Economic Development, 1978-1994', *Diaspora: A Journal of International Studies* 5:3, pp. 467-96

Bonacich, E.
1973   'A Theory of Middleman Minorities', *American Sociological Review* 38, pp. 583-94

Branegan, J.
1993   'The Diaspora: The Secret Weapon', *Time Australia* (May)

Brook, T.
1989   *The Asiatic Mode of Production in China.* Armonk, New York: M.E. Sharpe
1997   'Profit and Righteousness in Chinese Economic Culture', in: T. Brook and Hy V. Luong (eds) *Culture and Economy: The Shaping of Capitalism in Eastern Asia.* Ann Arbor: University of Michigan Press

Brown, I.
1988   *The Élite and the Economy in Siam c 1890-1920.* Singapore: Oxford University Press

Brown, R.A.
1995   'Introduction: Chinese Business in an Institutional and Historical Perspective', in: R.A. Brown (ed.) *Chinese Business Enterprises in Asia.* London: Routledge, pp. 1-26

Butcher, J.G. and H. Dick (eds)

1993   *The Rise and Fall of Revenue Farming: Business Élites and the Emergence of the Modern State in Southeast Asia*. Sydney: Macmillan

Cator, W.J.
1936   *The Economic Position of the Chinese in Indonesia*. Chicago: University of Chicago Press

Chan, Sin Yee
1997   'Confucian Role Ethics and China's Economic Modernization', in: Lieberthal, et al. (eds), pp. 35-56

Chen, Yungfa and G. Benton
1986   *Moral Economy and the Chinese Revolution: A Critique*. Amsterdam: Antropologisch-sociologisch Centrum, Universiteit van Amsterdam

Cheng, Lim-keak
1985   *Social Change and the Chinese in Singapore*. Singapore: Singapore University Press

Chiang, Kai-shek
1947   *Chinese Economic Theory*. [ghost written by Tao Xisheng] English version with notes and commentary by Philip Jaffe. London: Dennis Dobson Ltd.

Chirot, D. and A. Reid (eds)
1998   *Essential Outsiders: Chinese and Jews in the Modern Transformation of Southeast Asia and Central Europe*. Seattle: University of Washington Press

Chun, A.
1987   'Toward a Political Economy of the Sojourning Experience: the Chinese in 19th Century Malaya'. Working Paper, Department of Sociology, National University of Singapore
1989   'Pariah Capitalism and the Overseas Chinese in Southeast Asia', *Ethnic and Racial Studies* 12:2, pp. 233-56

Cribb, R.
1996   'Political Structures and Chinese Business Connections in Maritime Southeast Asia (Especially Indonesia) in Historical Perspective'. An unpublished paper presented at the International Academic Workshop: Chinese Business Connections in Global and Comparative Perspective (Chinese Academy of Social Science and Nordic Institute of Asian Studies) Beijing 10-12 September

Crissman, L.W.
1977   'A Discussion of Ethnicity and its Relation to Commerce', *Southeast Asian Journal of Social Science* 5:1-2, pp. 96-110

Cushman, J.W.

1990   Family and State: The Formation of a Sino-Thai Tin-Mining
        Dynasty 1797-1932. Kuala Lumpur: Oxford University Press
Day, Clive
1904   *The Policy and Administration of the Dutch in Java.* New York:
        Macmillan
Dernberger, R.F.
1975   'The Role of the Foreigner in China's Economic Development,
        1840-1949', in: D.H. Perkins (ed.) *China's Modern Economy in
        Historical Perspective.* Palo Alto: Stanford University Press, pp.
        19-47
1997   'The Interaction of Culture and Economics: Does Culture Count?',
        in: K.G. Lieberthal, et al. (eds)
Deyo, F.C. (ed.)
1988   *The Political Economy of the New Asian Industrialism.* Ithaca, New
        York: Cornell University Press
Dirlik, A.
1978   *Revolution and History: Origins of Marxist Historiography in
        China, 1919-1937.* Berkeley: University of California Press
1989   'Post Socialism? Reflections on 'Socialism . with Chinese
        Characteristics', in: Peter P. Cheng (ed.) *Marxism and Capitalism
        in the People's Republic of China.* Lanham, Maryland: University
        Press of America
1996a   'Reversals, Ironies, Hegemonies: Notes on the Contemporary
        Historiography of Modern China', *Modern China* 22: 3
1996b   'Critical Reflections on "Chinese Capitalism as a Paradigm"', in:
        L.M. Douw and Peter Post (eds) *South China: State, Culture and
        Social Change during the Twentieth Century.* Amsterdam, Oxford,
        New York and Tokyo: Royal Netherlands Academy of Arts and
        Sciences
Duara, P.
1997   'Nationalism Among Transnationals: Overseas Chinese and the
        Idea of China, 1900-11', in: Aihwa Ong and Donald M. Nonini
        (eds), 39-60
East Asia Analytical Unit
1995   *Business Networks in Asia.* Canberra: The Unit
Elegant, R.S.
1959   *The Dragon's Seed: Peking and the Overseas Chinese.* New York:
        St. Martin's Press
Freedman, M.
1959   'The Handling of Money: A Note on the Background to the
        Economic Sophistication of Overseas Chinese', *Man* 59, pp. 64-5

1960   'Immigrants and Associations: Chinese in Nineteenth Century Singapore', *Comparative Studies in Society and History*. 3:1, pp. 25-48

Fukuyama, F.

1995   *Trust: the Social Virtues and Creation of Prosperity*. New York: The Free Press

Gardella, R.

1992   'Squaring Accounts: Commercial Bookkeeping Methods and Capitalist Rationalism in Late Qing and Republican China', *Journal of Asian Studies* 51:2, pp. 317-29

Gates, Hill

1996   *China's Motor: A Thousand Years of Petty Capitalism*. Ithaca, New York: Cornell University Press

Glassman, R.M.

1991   *China in Transition: Communism, Capitalism and Democracy*. New York: Praeger

Godley, M.R.

1973   'Chang Pi-shih and Nanyang Chinese Involvement in South China's Railroads, 1896-1911', *Journal of Southeast Asian Studies* 4:1, pp. 16-30

1975   'The Late Ch'ing Courtship of the Chinese in Southeast Asia', Journal of Asian Studies 34:2, pp. 361-85

1976   'Overseas Chinese Entrepreneurs as Reformers', in: Paul Cohen and John Schrecker (eds) *Reform in Nineteenth Century China*. Cambridge, Massachusetts: Harvard University Press

1980   'A Summer Cruise to Nowhere: China and the Vietnamese Chinese in Perspective', *The Australian Journal of Chinese Affairs* (July), pp. 35-59

1981a   'The Treaty Port Connection: An Essay', *Journal of Southeast Asian Studies* 12:2, pp. 248-59

1981b   *The Mandarin-Capitalists from Nanyang: Overseas-Chinese Enterprise in the Modernization of China, 1893-1911*. Cambridge, England: Cambridge University Press

1989a   'The Sojourners: Returned Overseas Chinese in the People's Republic of China', *Pacific Affairs* 62:3, pp. 330-52

1989b   'Issues in Contemporary Chinese History', *ASAA Review* 13:2, pp. 37-46

1993   'Socialism with Chinese Characteristics: Sun Yatsen and the International Development of China', in: J. Unger (ed.) *Using The Past To Serve the Present: Historiography and Politics in Contemporary China*. London, England and Armonk, New York: M.E. Sharpe, pp. 239-59

1996   '*Nanyang* Connections: Overseas Chinese Enterprise in the Economic Development of South China, 1900-1937', in: Douw and Post (eds), pp. 113-18

Godley, M. and I. Copland

1993   'Reflections on Taxation, Social Structure and Development in the Early Modern Period', in: J. Butcher and H. Dick (eds) *The Rise and Fall of Revenue Farming: Business Élites and the Emergence of the Modern State in Southeast Asia.* London: Macmillan, pp. 45-68

Goldberg, M.A.

1985   *The Chinese Connection: Getting Plugged in to Pacific Rim Real Estate, Trade and Capital Markets.* Vancouver: University of British Columbia Press

Goodman, D.S.G. and B. Hooper (eds)

1994   *China's Quiet Revolution: New Interactions Between State and Society.* New York: St. Martin's Press

Gregor, A.J.

1981   *Ideology and Development: Sun Yatsen and the Economic History of Taiwan.* Berkeley: Center for Chinese Studies, University of California

1995   *Marxism, China and Development: Reflections on Theory and Reality.* New York: Transaction Publishers

Hao Yen-p'ing

1986   *The Commercial Revolution in Nineteenth-Century China: The Rise of Sino-Western Mercantile Capitalism.* Berkeley: University of California Press

Hamilton, G.

1988   'Why No Capitalism in China? Negative Questions in Historical, Comparative, Research', in: A.E. Buss (ed.) *Max Weber in Asian Studies.* Leiden: E.J. Brill

1991   'The Organizational Foundations of Western and Chinese Commerce', in: G. Hamilton (ed.) *Business Networks and Economic Development in East and Southeast Asia.* Hong Kong: Centre for Asian Studies, University of Hong Kong, pp. 48-65

1996   'Overseas Chinese Capitalism', in: Tu Wei-ming (ed.) *Confucian Traditions in East Asian Modernity.* Cambridge, Massachusetts: Harvard University Press, pp. 328-42

Hamilton, G. and T. Waters

1997   'Ethnicity and Capitalist Development: The Changing Role of the Chinese in Thailand', in: D. Chirot and A. Reid (eds), pp. 258-84

Harding, H.

1993   'The Concept of Greater China', *China Quarterly* 136, pp. 660-86

Harrell, S.
1985   'Why do the Chinese Work so Hard? Reflections on an Entre-
        preneurial Ethic', *Modern China* 11: 2, pp. 203-26
Heng Pak Koon
1992   'The Chinese Business Élite of Malaysia', in: R. McVey (ed.), pp.
        127-44
Hewison, K.
1989   *Bankers and Bureaucrats: Capital and the Role of the State in
        Thailand*. New Haven: Yale University Press
Hodder, R.
1993   *The Creation of Wealth in China*. New York: Belhaven Press
1996   *Merchant Princes of the East: Cultural Delusions, Economic
        Success and the Overseas Chinese in Southeast Asia*. New York:
        John Wiley and Sons
Hofheinz, R. jr. and K.E. Calder
1982   *The East Asia Edge*. New York: Basic Books
Hou Chi-ming
1965   *Foreign Investment and Economic Development in China 1840-
        1937*. Cambridge: Massachusetts: Harvard University Press
Ikels, C.
1996   *The Return of the God of Wealth: the Transition to a Market
        Economy in Urban China*. Palo Alto: Stanford University Press
Jenner, W.J.F.
1992   *The Tyranny of History: The Roots of China's Crisis*. London:
        Allen Lane Penguin Books
Jesudason, J.V.
1989   *Ethnicity and the Economy: The State, Chinese Business and
        Multinationals in Malaysia*. Singapore: Oxford University Press
Jomo, K.S.
1986   *A Question of Class: Capital, the State, and Uneven Development
        in Malaya*. Singapore: Oxford University Press
1997   'A Specific Idiom of Chinese Capitalism in Southeast Asia: Sino-
        Malaysian Capital Accumulation in the Face of State Hostility', in:
        Daniel Chirot and Anthony Reid (eds) *Essential Outsiders: Chinese
        and Jews in the Modern Transformation of Southeast Asia and
        Central Europe*. Seattle: University of Washington Press, pp. 237-
        57
Kao, J.
1993   'The World-Wide Web of Chinese Business', *Harvard Business
        Review*, March-April
Kim, Young C.

1995   *The Southeast Asian Economic Miracle.* New Brunswick, New Jersey: Transaction Publishers

Kraar, L.
1994   'The Overseas Chinese', *Fortune Magazine* (14 November)

Kuhn, Philip
1997   'Thinking about the History of the Chinese Overseas'. The Morrison Lecture, Australian National University, Canberra

Kuo, Eddie C.Y.
1990   *Ethnicity, Polity and Economy: A Case Study of the Mandarin Trade and the Chinese Connection.* Singapore: National University of Singapore Working Paper

Kwong, J.
1997   *The Political Economy of Corruption in China.* Armonk, New York: M.E. Sharpe

Landa, J.
1983   'The Political Economy of the Ethnically Homogeneous Chinese Middleman Group in Southeast Asia: Ethnicity and Entrepreneurship in a Plural Society', in: Lim and Gosling (eds), pp. 86-116

Lever-Tracy, C., D. Ip and N. Tracy
1996   *The Chinese Diaspora and Mainland China: An Emerging Economic Synergy.* New York: St. Martin's Press

Levy, M.J. and Shih Kuo-heng
1949   *The Rise of the Modern Chinese Business Class.* New York: Institute of Pacific Relations

Lieberthal, K.G., Shen-fu Lin and E.P. Young (eds)
1997   *Constructing China: The Interaction of Culture and Economics.* Ann Arbor: Center for Chinese Studies, the University of Michigan

Lim, L.
1983   'Chinese Economic Activity in Southeast Asia: An Introductory Review', in: Lim and Gosling (eds), pp. 1-29
1992   'The Emergence of a Chinese Economic Zone in Southeast Asia', *Journal of Southeast Asian Business* 8:1, pp. 41-6

Lim, L. and P. Gosling (eds)
1983   *The Chinese in Southeast Asia, Volume 1: Ethnicity and Economic Activity.* Singapore: Maruzen Asia

Lim Mah Hui
1981   *Ownership and Control of the One Hundred Largest Corporations in Malaysia.* Kuala Lumpur: Oxford University Press

Limlingan, V.S.

1986   *The Overseas Chinese in Asean: Business Strategies and Management Practices*. Manila: Vita Development Corporation

Lippit, V.D.
1979   'The Development of Underdevelopment in China', *Modern China* 4:3, pp. 251-328

Liu Binyan
1990   *China's Crisis, China's Hope*. Translated by Howard Goldblatt. Cambridge, Massachusetts: Harvard University Press

Lufrano, R.J.
1997   *Honorable Merchants: Commerce and Self-Cultivation in Late Imperial China*. Honolulu: University of Hawaii Press

Mackie, J.A.C.
1989   'Chinese Businessmen and the Rise of Southeast Asian Capitalism', *Solidarity* 123, pp. 96-107
1992   'Overseas Chinese Entrepreneurship', *Asian-Pacific Economic Literature* 6:1, pp. 41-64
1995   'Economic System of Southeast Asian Chinese', in: Suryadinata (ed.), pp. 33-65
1996   'The Economic Roles of Southeast Asian Chinese: Information Gaps and Research Priorities'. An unpublished paper presented at the International Academic Workshop: Chinese Business Connections in Global and Comparative Perspective (Chinese Academy of Social Science and Nordic Institute of Asian Studies) Beijing 10-12 September

McElderry, A.
1997   'Doing Business with Strangers: Guarantors as an Extension of Personal Ties in Chinese Business', in: K.G. Lieberthal, et al. (eds), pp. 147-70

McVey, R. (ed.)
1992   *Southeast Asian Capitalism*. Ithaca: Cornell University Press

Mah Feng-hwa
1979   'External Influence and Chinese Economic Development: A Re-Examination', in: Chi-ming Hou and Tzong-shian Yu (eds) *Proceedings of the Conference on* Modern Chinese Economic History. Taipei: Academica Sinica, pp. 273-98

Meisner, M.
1982   *Marxism, Maoism and Utopianism: Eight Essays*. Madison: The University of Wisconsin Press

Menkhoff, T.
1990   *Toward and Understanding of Chinese Entrepreneurship in Southeast Asia: Small Trading Firms in Singapore*. Bielefeld: Universität Bielefeld

Menkhoff, T. and C.E. Labig
1996   'Trading Networks of Chinese Entrepreneurs in Singapore',
        Sojourn: Journal of Social Issues in Southeast Asia 11:1, pp. 128-
        51

Murphey, R.
1977   *The Outsiders: The Western Experience in India and China.* Ann
        Arbor: University of Michigan Press

Myers, R.H.
1995   'Chinese Debate on Economic Reforms: Can China Create a
        Socialist Market Economy', *Asian Pacific Economic Literature*
        9:2, pp. 55-68

Ng Wing Chung
1992   'Urban Chinese Social Organization: Some Unexplored Aspects in
        'Huiguan' Development in Singapore, 1900-1941', *Modern Asian
        Studies* 26:3, pp. 469-94

Nonini, D.M. and Ong Aihwa
1997   'Chinese Transnationalism as an Alternative Modernity', in: Ong
        Aihwa and D.M. Nonini (eds) *Ungrounded Empires: the Cultural
        Politics of Modern Chinese Transnationalism.* London and New
        York: Routledge, pp. 3-33

Omohundro, J.T.
1981   *Chinese Merchant Families in Iloilo: Commerce and Kin in a
        Central Philippine City.* Athens, Ohio: Ohio University Press
1983   'Social Networks and Business Success for Philippine Chinese', in:
        Lim and Gosling (eds), pp. 65-85

Ong Aihwa
1996   'Chinese Modernities: Narratives of Nation and Capitalism', in:
        Nonini and Ong (eds)

Ong Aihwa and Nonini, D.
1997   'Afterword: Toward a Cultural Politics of Diaspora and
        Transnationalism', in: Nonini and Ong (eds), pp. 323-32

Onghokham
1989   'Chinese Capitalism in Dutch Java', *Southeast Asian Studies*
        (Kyoto) 27:2, pp. 156-76

Panglaykim
1979   *Emerging Enterprises in the Asia-Pacific Region.* Jakarta: Centre
        for Strategic and International Studies

Panglaykim and F. Palmer
1970   'Study of Entrepreneurship in Developing Countries: The
        Development of One Chinese Concern in Indonesia,' *Journal of
        Southeast Asian Studies* 1:1, pp. 85-95

Pearson, M.M.

1996   *China's New Business Élite: The Political Consequences of Reform.*
        Berkeley: University of California Press
Pieke, F.N.
1995   'Bureaucracy, Friends, and Money: the Growth of Capital
        Socialism in China', *Comparative Studies in Society and History*
        37, pp. 494-518
Portes, A.
1995   'Economic Sociology and the Sociology of Immigration: A
        Conceptual Overview', in: A. Portes (ed.) *The Economic Sociology
        of Immigration: Essays on Networks, Ethnicity, and Entrepreneur-
        ship.* New York: Russell Sage Foundation, pp. 1-41
Potter, J.M.
1968   *Capitalism and the Chinese Peasant: Social and Economic Change
        in a Hong Kong Village.* Berkeley: University of California Press
Redding, Gordon S.
1988   'The Role of the Entrepreneur in the New Asian Capitalism', in:
        P.L. Berger and Michael Hsiao Hsin-huang (eds) *In Search of an
        East Asian Development Model.* New Brunswick, New Jersey:
        Transaction Books, pp. 99-111
1990   *The Spirit of Chinese Capitalism.* Berlin: Walter de Gruyter
1996   'The Distinct Nature of Chinese Capitalism', *The Pacific Review*
        9:3
Reid, A.
1998   'Entrepreneurial Minorities, Nationalism and the State', in: D.
        Chirot and A. Reid (eds) *Essential Outsiders: Chinese and Jews in
        the Modern Transformation of Southeast Asia and Central Europe.*
        Seattle: University of Washington Press, pp. 33-80
Robison, R.
1986   *Indonesia: The Rise of Capital.* Sydney: Allen and Unwin
Rodan, G.
1989   *The Political Economy of Singapore's Industrialization: Nation,
        State and International Capital.* London: Macmillan, 1989
Rutten, M.
1994   *Asian Capitalists in the European Mirror.* Amsterdam: VU
        University Press
Seagrave, S.
1995   *Lords of the Rim: The Invisible Empire of the Overseas Chinese.*
        London: Bantam Press
Shambaugh, D.
1993   'The Emergence of Greater China', *China Quarterly* 136, pp. 653-
        86
Shin, Yoon Hwan,

1989   'Demystifying the Capitalist State: Political Patronage, Bureaucratic Interests, and Capitalists-in-formation in Soeharto's Indonesia'. Unpublished Ph.D. dissertation, Yale University

Singer, M.
1972   *When a Great Tradition Modernizes: An Anthropological Approach to Indian Civilization*. New York: Praeger

Solinger, D.J.
1993   *China's Transition from Socialism: Statist Legacies and Market Reforms 1980-1990*. Armonk, New York: M.E. Sharpe

Suehiro, Akira
1989   *Capital Accumulation in Thailand. 1855-1985*. Tokyo: Centre for East Asian Cultural Studies

Sun Yan
1995   *The Chinese Reassessment of Socialism, 1976-1992*. Princeton: Princeton University Press

Sun Yat-sen
1922   *The International Development of China*. Taipei: China Cultural Service, 1953 edition
1924   *San Min Chu I: The Three Principles of the People*. Translated by Frank Price. Taipei: China Cultural Service, 1953. [part III *The Principle of Livelihood*]

Suryadinata, Leo (ed.)
1995   *Southeast Asian Chinese and China: The Politico-Economic Dimension*. Singapore: Times Academic Press

Suyama, Taku
1962   'Pang Society: the Economy of Chinese Immigrants', in: K.G. Tregonning (ed.) *Papers on Malayan History. Singapore University Press*, pp. 193-210

Tai Hung-chao (ed.)
1989   *Confucianism and Economic Development: An Oriental Alternative?* Washington, DC: Washington Institute Press

Tong Chee Kong
1989   *Centripetal Authority, Differentiated Networks: the Social Organization of Chinese Firms in Singapore*. Department of Sociology, National University of Singapore

Turner, J.H. and E. Bonacich
1980   'Toward a Composite Theory of Middleman Minorities', *Ethnicity* 7, pp. 14-58

Walder, A.
1986   *Chinese Neo-traditionalism: Work and Authority in Chinese Industry*. Berkeley: University of California Press

Wang Gungwu
1981   'The Culture of Chinese Merchants' reprinted in: *China and the Overseas Chinese*. Singapore: Times Academic Press, 1991, pp. 181-97
1989   'Little Dragons on the Confucian Periphery' reprinted in *China and the Overseas Chinese,* Singapore: Times Academic Press, 1991, pp. 258-72
1993   'Greater China and the Overseas Chinese', *China Quarterly* 136, pp. 926-48
1994   'The Chinese Entrepreneur and his Cultural Strategies', *Asian Culture* 18
1995   'The Southeast Asian Chinese and the Development of China', in: Suryadinata (ed.), pp. 12-34
Weidenbaum, M. and S. Hughes,
1996   *The Bamboo Network: How Expatriate Chinese Entrepreneurs are Creating a New Economic Superpower in Asia.* New York: The Free Press - Martin Kessler Books
Wertheim, W.F.
1964   'The Trading Minorities in Southeast Asia', in: W.F. Wertheim, *East-West Parallels*. The Hague: Van Hoeve, Ltd., pp. 39-82
White, G., J. Howell and Shang Xiaoyuan
1996   *In Search of Civil Society: Market Reform and Social Change in Contemporary China*. Oxford: Clarendon Press
Whitely, R.D.
1990   'The Comparative Analysis of Forms of Business Organization', *Organization Studies* 11, pp. 47-74
Williams, L.E.
1952   'Chinese Entrepreneurs in Indonesia', *Explorations in Entrepreneurial History* 5:1, pp. 34-60
Wong Siu-lun
1985   'The Chinese Family Firm: A Model', *The British Journal of Sociology* 36:1, pp. 58-72
1988   'The Applicability of Asian Family Values to Other Sociocultural Settings', in: P.L. Berger and Michael Hsin-huang Hsiao (eds) *In Search of an East Asian Development Model*. New Brunswick, New Jersey: Transaction Books, 134-52
1996   'Chinese Entrepreneurs and Economic Development', in: Douw and Post (eds)
Wright, T.
1992   'Introduction: Modern Chinese Economic History in a Period of Change', in: T. Wright (ed.) *The Chinese Economy in the Early Twentieth Century: Recent Studies*. London: Macmillan, pp. 1-28

1993   ' "The Spiritual Heritage of Chinese Capitalism": Recent Trends in the Historiography of Chinese Enterprise ·Management', in: J. Unger (ed.) *Using The Past To Serve the Present: Historiography and Politics in Contemporary China.* London, England and Armonk, New York: M.E. Sharpe, pp. 205-38

Wu Chun-hsi
1967   *Dollars, Dependents and Dogma: Overseas Chinese Remittances to Communist China.* Stanford: Hoover Institute

Wu Yuan-li
1983   'Chinese Entrepreneurs in Southeast Asia', *The American Economic Review* 73:2, pp. 112-17

Wu Yuan-li and Wu Chun-hsi
1980   *Economic Development in Southeast Asia: The Chinese Dimension.* Stanford: Hoover Institution

Yao, Raymond W.Y.
1991   'Chinese Entrepreneurial Cultural Issues', in: *World Chinese Entrepreneurs Convention.* Singapore

Yao Souchou
1987   'The Fetish of Relationships: Chinese Business Transactions in Singapore', *Sojourn* 2:1, pp. 89-111

Yen Ch'ing-hwang
1970   'Ch'ing Sale of Honours and the Chinese Leadership in Singapore and Malaya 1877-1912', *Journal of Southeast Asian Studies* 1, pp. 20-32
1982   'The Overseas Chinese and Late Ch'ing Economic Modernization', *Modern Asian Studies* 16:2 , pp. 217-32
1986   *A Social History of the Chinese in Singapore and Malaya 1800-1911.* Singapore: Oxford University Press

Yoshihara Kunio
1988   *The Rise of Ersatz Capitalism in Southeast Asia.* Singapore: Oxford University Press, pp. 66-86
1989   *Oei Tiong Ham Concern: The First Business Empire of Southeast Asia.* Kyoto: Center for Southeast Asian Studies
1995 'The Ethnic Chinese and Ersatz Capitalism in Southeast Asia', in: Suryadinata (ed.)

Yu Chung-hsun
1971   'Capitalist Development and the Overseas Chinese Economy: Thailand', *Developing Economies* (September), pp. 246-67
1995   *Kaikyo keizai no kenkyo* (Study of overseas Chinese economy). Tokyo: Aijiya keizai kenkyo

Notes

1. Francis Fukuyama, 1995, has done much to popularize the concept, along with the 'power of culture in the making of economic society' but there are much better sources. According to James S. Coleman, 'social capital refers to the capacity of individuals to command scarce resources by virtue of their networks or broader social structure' (cited by A. Portes, p. 12).

2. I accept Arif Dirlik's caution that 'any representation of China's present historical path as capitalist or socialist is not just descriptive but also prescriptive'(1989, p. 1).

3. For a good treatment of the issues involved, see: Hamilton, 1988.

4. Williams, 1952, which is based, in part, on the conclusions of J.L. Vleming, *Het Chineesche Zakenleven in Nederlandsch-Indië* [Chinese business life in the Netherlands Indies] (Weltevreden, 1926). Note that key chapters of this important work are now available in M.R. Fernando and D. Bulbeck (eds), *Chinese Economic Activity in Netherlands India: Selected Translations from the Dutch* (Singapore: Institute of Southeast Asian Studies, 1992), pp. 90-259. See also the classic work by Levy and Shih, 1949. This line of argument can also be found in Robison, 1986.

5. In chronological order: Lim, 1981; Wu Yuan-li,1983; Limlingan,1986; Redding, 1988; Wu, 1983; Mackie, 1989; McVey, 1992; Kraar; 1994; Mackie, 1995; Kim, 1995; East Asia Analytical Unit, 1995. For an excellent summary of the pre-'postmodernist' line of argument, see Mackie, 1992.

6. For example: Goldberg, 1985; Kao, 1993; Seagrave, 1995; Weidenbaum and Hughes, 1996.

7. Omohundro, 1981 and 1983; Barton, 1983; Landa, 1983; Lim, 1983; Yao, 1987; Tong, 1989; Kuo, 1990; Lim, 1992; East Asia Analytical Unit, 1995. For Gary Hamilton, 1991, p. 53, this was largely because their business organization rested upon inviolate social relationships.

8. Beginning the list with Wertheim, 1964, and adding: Bonacich, 1973; Turner and Bonacich, 1980; and Chun, 1987 and 1989. But see also the comparative essays in Chirot and Reid, 1998.

9. Deyo, 1988 and McVey, 1992. For more on individual countries, see also: Yu Chung-hsun, 1971; Jomo, 1986; Robison, 1986; Shin, 1989; Suehiro, 1989; Hewison, 1989; Rodan, 1989; Heng, 1992.

10. Godley, 1973, 1975, 1976, 1981b; 1996. See also Yen, 1982 and Duara, 1997

11. *Selections from Records of the Grand Historian, Yang Hsien-yi and Gladys Yang* (trans.). Peking: Foreign Languages Press, 1979, pp. 410-

28. Not surprisingly, modern Chinese businessmen have given remarkably similar answers when asked the secrets to their business success. See Redding, 1990.

12. As Zheng Guanying observed, the country had to wage 'commercial war' if it was to survive in a Darwinian world.

13. Whether readers accept the dialectical materialism behind her recognition of the historical existence of a 'petty capitalist mode of production' in China, there is still much to be said for the conceptualization of the family unit as a 'patricorporation': usefully demonstrating, in the process, the negative as well as positive qualities of household-based enterprise, especially for the individuals involved.

14. The family was always central to Chinese business in pre-communist times simply because the state recognized the *jia* (and extended clan) as a basic unit of property.

15. Besides Weber's well-thumbed study of the 'Religion of China', see: Levy and Shih, 1949; Lippit 1979; Harrell, 1985; Hamilton, 1988.

16. See Meisner, 1982, for an excellent treatment of the complexities involved.

17. The shortcomings of this line of argument were pointed out by Hou (1965) and Mah (1979). Even as the 'Great Proletarian Cultural Revolution' was gaining momentum, Jack Potter (1968) likewise questioned how inimical Western trade had really been to the rural economy. Indeed, Robert Dernberger (1975) went on to show that China 'enjoyed significant absolute gains from trade and a gross transfer of productive capital and technology' over the period from 1840 to 1949. There is even the question of who benefited more from Sino-Western commercial capitalism that developed in late nineteenth-century China (Hao, 1986). When the country was finally reopened to the West, Chinese scholars pretty much conceded the point (see Wright, ed., 1992). By 15 October 1985, a Renmin Ribao ('People's Daily') editorialist was writing: 'There simply cannot be a country stupid enough to refuse knowledge and technology from the outside and to do everything from scratch'.

18. *The Chinese Revolution and the Chinese Communist Party*. Peking: Foreign languages Press, 1954, p. 22.

19. Ibid., p. 13.

20. Meisner, 1982. Mao once remarked that 'If socialism doesn't occupy the battlefront, capitalism surely will' (cited Baum, 1994, p. 23).

21. Chiang Kai-shek, 1947, pp. 241-2, 245, 248, 251-63.

22. It was then being praised on Taiwan as the secret to that island's economic miracle.
23. *Beijing Review* 23 March 1992, 1 June 1992. Also consult the many relevant articles in *Jingji Yanjiu* ('Economic Studies') or the useful survey by Myers, 1995.
24. See, for example, Glassman, 1991; Goodman, 'The Political Economy of Change' in Goodman and Hooper (eds.), 1994, and also White, et al., 1996, who also discuss the 'market hypothesis' although not without a degree of scepticism.
25. I strongly endorse Professor Wang Gungwu's belief that the term *huaqiao* (meaning a 'sojourner') is dangerously obsolete today, reflecting outdated nationalist sentiments in an era when the great majority of the ethnic Chinese residing in Southeast Asia have taken foreign citizenship.
26. Max Weber certainly believed that the prebendal nature of traditional Oriental society made mandarins 'tax farmers' by definition. See Godley and Godley and Copland, 1993.
27. Panglaykim, 1979, p. 90, described the successful combination of the 'five sides of power': (1) management; (2) capital (3) technology; (4) international marketing and information; and (5) government support. He was one of the first scholars to look seriously at Chinese entrepreneurship in Southeast Asia and to challenge Weberian stereotypes. See Panglaykim and Palmer, 1970.
28. *The Policy and Administration of the Dutch in Java* (New York: Macmillan, 1904, p. 361).
29. The Malayan tin and rubber industries are often given as examples where, though they were early pioneers, the Chinese faded into insignificance once the economic might of the British Empire was brought to bear.
30. I am very much indebted to Jamie Mackie for the many insights he has provided over the years we have worked together on this topic. See his 1996 thoughts on these questions.

APPENDIX CHAPTER:

A NOTE ON THE STUDY OF *QIAOXIANG* TIES

CEN HUANG AND *MICHAEL R. GODLEY*

From the beginning of the Open Door Policy in 1978, ethnic Chinese living abroad have made an important contribution to the growth of South China's economy, whilst also facilitating rapid social change. As the major source of migrants, this southern region, embracing Guangdong and Fujian provinces, can claim the home villages for the vast majority of 'overseas Chinese'. As the preceding chapters have already shown, '*qiaoxiang* ties' now concern not just the local communities and government bodies at all levels, but also universities, academic institutes and hundreds of individual scholars. This 'appendix' wishes to acknowledge the work that has been done in the People's Republic of China, whilst also pointing out to those readers who have access to Chinese-language materials some of the more-significant publications. Like all academic areas, our field of study is not free of controversy or bias (exacerbated in the case of the PRC by an active state interest in promoting links with ethnic Chinese living overseas). Although the following account of people, works and institutions cannot claim to be comprehensive, it is hoped that the inclusion of the appendix chapter at the end of this book will help encourage 'transnational' scholarship and further co-operation.

RESEARCH INSTITUTIONS

The Chinese diaspora has drawn attention from both academics and government decision-makers since the Open Door Policy began. The four research organizations specializing in overseas Chinese studies in China in 1998 were: the Institute of Overseas Chinese Studies at Jinan University (Guangzhou), the Institute of Overseas Chinese at the Overseas Chinese University (Quanzhou), the Institute of Overseas Chinese History at the National Office of the Overseas Chinese Association (Beijing), and the Institute of Overseas Chinese Studies at Fujian Academy of Social Sciences (Fuzhou). There are also six major research institutions devoted to Southeast Asian or related studies, which include, the Institute of Southeast

Asian Studies at the Jinan University, the Research School of Southeast Asian Studies at Xiamen University, the Institute of Southeast Asian Studies at Beijing University, the Institute of Southeast Asian Studies at Zhongshan University (Guangzhou), the Institute of Indo-China Studies at Guangxi Academy of Social Sciences (Nanning), and the Institute of Southeast Asian Studies at the Yunnan Academy of Social Sciences. These carry out work related to Chinese diaspora studies in various ways, but each has its own unique orientation. It should be observed that the subject has been closely linked to, and therefore was influenced by changing government policies and priorities.

Both overseas Chinese and Southeast Asian studies have generally had a historical focus and projects or works undertaken from the 1950s through the 1980s carefully avoided sensitive political issues and, especially, the inconsistency of government directives. Contemporary affairs (and the larger developmental questions involved) have really only been pursued in the past ten years as investments have dramatically increased. A number of valuable research projects have been carried out by various institutes and individuals. For example, an important study of Jinjiang *qiaoxiang* has been conducted by the Research School of Southeast Asian Studies at Xiamen University since 1996. The Institute of Overseas Chinese Studies of Jinan University also undertook a survey of current developments of Guangdong *qiaoxiang* in Meixian, Shantou, and the Pearl River Delta Region during 1996 and 1997. These endeavours paid particularly close attention to on-going socio-economic changes. The major institutes have also produced periodicals such as *Issues in Southeast Asian Studies* (Xiamen University), *The Journal of Southeast Asian Studies* (Zhongshan University), and *Materials on Overseas Chinese Studies* (the Institute of the National Office of the Overseas Chinese Association) and *Southeast Asia* (the Yunnan Academy of Social Sciences) (see Appendix I: Chinese Research Institutes of Overseas Chinese and Southeast Asian Studies).

There are a number of local research societies on overseas Chinese studies, such as the Historical Association of Overseas Chinese History in Guangdong, and the Historical Society of Overseas Chinese in Guangxi. These help academics network with other interested researchers and can help establish all-important connections with government officials. Some produce journals of their own. The Historical Society of Overseas Chinese in Guangxi, for example, publishes the quarterly, *Overseas Chinese History of Bagui,* and the Historical Society of Overseas Chinese in Quanzhou publishes a journal called *Overseas Chinese History* (see Appendix II: Major Chinese Journals on Overseas Chinese Studies). Interest has also been shown by the Chinese Heritage Centre in Singapore, which recently published its comprehensive *Encyclopedia of the Chinese Overseas* (1999) under the general editorship of Lynn Pan. But readers should also be aware of what is being done by the 'Shao You Bao Overseas Chinese Documentation and Research Center' at Ohio University. Further research on transnational linkages may also be undertaken by the Australian National University's new Centre for the Study of the Chinese Southern Diaspora.

THE *QIAOXIANG* TIES PROJECT

Established in 1995 by Dr Leo Douw and Dr Frank Pieke, at the International Institute for Asian Studies, Leiden, the Netherlands, the '*qiaoxiang* ties' project produced the volume that you are now reading. It was an outgrowth of an international workshop in May 1995 on the topic of 'South China: State, Culture and Social Change during the 20th Century' sponsored by the Royal Netherlands Academy of Arts and Sciences, which resulted in an edited volume with the same title (Douw and Post, 1995). The project gained momentum in November 1996 when its first research fellow, Dr Cen Huang, was hired. It is concerned, in particular, with international social and business organization in East and Southeast Asia with an eye to how *qiaoxiang* ties work and continue to influence the development of Chinese transnational enterprises in the course of the twentieth century. The aim is: to establish a comprehensive academic research network in the field of '*qiaoxiang* studies'; to provide facilities for international research exchanges and conferences; to conduct joint international field investigations in *qiaoxiang* regions, and to produce quality publications. Dr David Schak, Professor Dai Yifeng, Dr Michale R. Godley and Dr David Ip have been visiting fellows.

In the past two years, scholars have conducted extensive field research in South China, mainly in Guangdong and Fujian provinces. They have established close contacts with research institutes and individual scholars in the field of *qiaoxiang* studies in China (including Hong Kong and Taiwan), Southeast Asia, Australia, North America and Europe. Two international workshop panels were held by the programme in August 1997 and June 1998 respectively. The first one was on 'International Social Organization in East and Southeast Asia: *Qiaoxiang* Ties during the Twentieth Century' in Leiden followed by an international panel on 'Chinese Transnationalism: Cultural and Economic Dimensions' held in Noordwijkerhout, the Netherlands, which ultimately led to the production of this book. A workshop entitled 'Chinese Transnational Enterprises and Entrepreneurship in Prosperity and Adversity: South China and Southeast Asia During the Twentieth Century' is to be held jointly with the Centre of Asian Studies, the University of Hong Kong on 26-27 August 1999 in Hong Kong.

An international joint research project was launched by Dr Cen Huang (IIAS) and Professor Zhuang Guotu (Xiamen University, China) in 1997 to investigate 'The Social and Economic Development of An Overseas Chinese Hometown County: Jinjiang'. The project has carried out comprehensive field surveys with a random sample of 500 families and 150 enterprises in the Jinjiang County of South Fujian. The survey research covered topics of the composition of *qiaoxiang* households, income structures, relationships with overseas relatives, overseas remittances, donations and investments, as well as foreign-funded and local enterprises. An international conference on *Qiaoxiang* Studies was organized by the Research School of Southeast Asian Studies of Xiamen University to evaluate the joint research findings in Jinjiang on 27-31 October 1998. A set of three volumes based on the Jinjiang research data and the conference papers is in the process of being edited, and will be published as an outcome of this joint effort by the Fujian People's Press.

SECONDARY SOURCE MATERIALS

Considerable notice has already been given to the history (and economic success) enjoyed by ethnic Chinese around the world: but especially in Southeast Asia. This is not the place for a detailed documentation of the critical importance of their enterprise to the economic history of that region (though readers new to the topic might want to begin their study with one or more of the standard English-language works: Cator, 1936; Callis, 1941; Purcell 1965; Nevadomsky, 1970; Wang, 1981, 1985, 1991; Suryadinata, 1989; Mackie, 1992; or the chapter by M.R. Godley in this volume, which makes reference to more-recent scholarship). Of broader interest is the extensive literature on Sino-Southeast Asian relations that concerned China long before Westerners became interested in the topic. The many English-language works on the subject by Professor Wang Gungwu are required reading but there are also several good bibliographies (begin with Shu, 1968, for Chinese-language works this century, or Iwasaki, 1983, for the Japanese perspective). Additional research certainly needs to be done on overseas Chinese involvement in modernization during the late-Qing and early-republican periods. Following up earlier work by foreign academics (especially, Godley, 1981; and Yen 1981), China-based scholars have once again been leading the way (Zhuang, 1989). Until recently, no work had equalled Chen Ta's (1940) study of the influence of overseas migration on standards of living and social change. Nor has all that much been written about Kuomintang (*Guomindang*) policy (start with Akashi, 1970; Yong and McKenna, 1990; or Hicks' 1993 reproduction of valuable Japanese figures on remittances ca. 1910-40), although Beijing's own on-again off-again relationship with the diaspora did receive quite a bit of attention by English-language authors (see, for example: Wu, 1967, on remittances; Fitzgerald, 1972, on government policy; or Godley, 1989 for the treatment of returned overseas Chinese) and, not surprisingly, on Taiwan in the 1960s and 1970s as does the on-going, post-1992, wave of investment documented elsewhere in this book.

Systematic academic study of the Chinese diaspora in the People's Republic of China did not begin until the 1980s, when a number of significant bibliographies of relevant works on the 'overseas Chinese' - published mostly in the 1950s and 1970s - appeared. These historical accounts represent an important stage in the study of the Chinese diaspora. The scholars paid close attention to the motives, causes, channels and scale of emigration - preparing the first studies of particular emigrant villages and counties: mainly in Guangdong and Fujian provinces, with an emphasis on what happened before the 1949 revolution. Remittance studies also concentrated on the earlier period. Representative works include Lin Jiajin, et al., 1993; Lin Jinzhi, 1996; and Feng Yuan, 1987. It is interesting to note that among 18 bibliographical publications on overseas Chinese studies in China, half have a historical focus (see Appendix III: Major Chinese Index to the Works Relating to Overseas Chinese Studies). According to the *Index to Periodical Articles Relating to Overseas Chinese Studies, 1980-1990* (Zeng and Chen 1993), the publications are categorized as follows: general overseas Chinese studies, overseas Chinese and politics, overseas Chinese business and economy, overseas Chinese culture and society, history of overseas Chinese, and famous overseas Chinese figures. The history section occupied close to one-third of the total number of articles. The strong historical orientation may reflect the fact that the majority of the scholars then working in the field of overseas Chinese studies were historians by training. But it would also be fair to say that the pre-communist era was a safer, and certainly less controversial, period to study until official policy had been firmly established. The study of *qiaoxiang* really only began when China's Open Door Policy led to an accelerated pace of economic reform. Then, scholars began to look more closely into the relationship between overseas Chinese investments and *qiaoxiang* development (writers such as Feng, 1987; Lin, 1983, 1988, 1989 and 1994; Lin and Zhang, 1985; Lin et al., 1993; and Huang, 1998.) Others, following in the footsteps of Chen Ta (1940), focused attention on social and cultural influences, including the welfare donations made by overseas Chinese in home villages (Song, 1996; Huang, 1997).

It is worth mentioning that two volumes of *qiaoxiang* field reports have now appeared as special issues of Chinese scholarly journals. The first, based on surveys conducted in Guangdong *qiaoxiang*, came out in *Qiaoshi xuebao* (Journal of Overseas Chinese History) in 1995. That issue contained six investigative reports covering Shunde, Panyu, Heshan, Jiangmen, Taishan and Chaoyang. The research had been undertaken by scholars from Jinnan University after the era of Economic Reforms began. The second volume was published as a special edition of *Nanyang wenti yanjiu* (Issues of Southeast Asian Studies) by the Research School at Xiamen University in spring 1999. It included 12 essays with a special focus on social and economic developments in Jinjiang *qiaoxiang*. The significance of this study is its in-depth investigations into 500 households and 150 enterprises. Topics investigated include overseas connections and the restructuring of local economies, the role of remittances in the current economic situation, *qiaoxiang* entrepreneurs, returned overseas Chinese enterprises, family institutions and local-run businesses, foreign direct investment in Jinjiang, and labour relations under the Jinjiang economic development model. This research is among the most-comprehensive and systematic yet undertaken. The two volumes represent the positive trend in *qiaoxiang* studies toward empirical research and non-political analysis.

PRIMARY SOURCE MATERIALS

Mention is made of the Nanyang Chinese in many historical documents, particularly in the late-Qing period when interest in their numbers, wealth, and enterprise first came to the attention of officials, including the first diplomats to visit the region. Numerous reports and other documents survive but of special interest will be the many local 'gazetteers': a number of which are now being brought up to date. However scholars who can read Chinese, should also consult 'overseas Chinese' newspapers which have existed in numerous localities since before the turn of the century. These periodicals tell the story from the 'migrant' end and often contain valuable material now missing on the mainland. There are particularly good collections in Singapore (see Chen, 1967; or Feng, 1976) and Australia (see Australian National Library, 1987). But scholars can also benefit from Hong Kong's *Huazi Ribao* (The China Mail), which provides a good record of the way *qiaoxiang* ties were established and strengthened in the late-Qing and early-republican periods. Also valuable in this regard are clan and *huiguan* records as several contributors to this volume illustrate. Most useful for contemporary developments are, undoubtedly, official, government, publications and the *qiaokan* (hometown publications) - the assorted magazines and newsletters, presently proliferating as a means of strengthening *qiaoxiang* ties. However, as we go on to show, these to be used with caution.

Government Documents
Both national and provincial governments maintained their own, official, publications which gave extensive coverage to overseas Chinese affairs in the Qing and Republican periods. Especially useful for the former is the *Shangwu Guanbao* (Commercial Gazette) which documented important diaspora investments as well as Beijing's role in the establishment of

Chinese chambers of commerce around the world. But, not surprisingly, official (or government-sponsored) publications remain just as important today. The south-eastern provinces still produce official newspapers on overseas Chinese affairs. Some cities with high-returned overseas Chinese populations also publish their own literature. Two types of publications are worth discussing at length: newspapers (including newsletters/directives) and the very helpful annals (or yearbooks) now being produced.

According to the incomplete list compiled below, there were at least 25 major government periodicals related to overseas Chinese affairs published in 1998 (see Appendix IV: Government Publications on Overseas Chinese Affairs). Some deal with sensitive issues and have a restricted circulation. 'The News of Guangdong Overseas Chinese Affairs' is, for example, mainly for government officials and includes material on: (1) overseas political conditions as well as the latest government policies and regulations; (2) matters relating to *qiaoxiang* development; (3) overseas Chinese donations; and investments; and (4) local news from the relevant countries. It is similar to *News of the Overseas Chinese*, a government publication of the 1950s and 1960s, which was intended for the high-ranking government officials and, fortunately, found its way into Western research collections. Clearly, the existence of similar newspapers, especially during the early years of the People's Republic up to the Cultural Revolution when these and other related periodicals stopped publication, made it possible to recreate the shifts in official policy and, now, to compare earlier attitudes and activities with what is happening today. Although such government documents are not, by definition, *qiaoxiang* publications, they often contain reports and news taken directly from these localities and can, of course, be seen as a window into the official policy and the general direction of village developments.

Some of the most-important counties (and some cities) in Guangdong and Fujian have already compiled local annals (see Appendix V: Selected *Annals of Overseas Chinese*) which contain a great deal of information (including statistics). Normally, they are compiled jointly by local officials and academics from nearby universities leading us to categorize them as government publications although a degree of local pride and initiative can, quite obviously, be seen. Indeed, some regions have been updating their annals on regular basis.

The following is a table of contents taken from the Annals of Overseas Chinese in Anxi (Chen, 1994):

Annals of Overseas Chinese in Anxi

General Introduction
Major Historical Events
Chapter One: Overseas Emigration and Geographic Distribution
Chapter Two: Activities in Residing Countries
Chapter Three: *Qiaoxiang* Society
Chapter Four: Contributions made by Overseas Anxi People
Chapter Five: Overseas Chinese Affairs
Chapter Six: Important Overseas Chinese Figures
Appendix 1: A Name List of Famous Overseas Anxi People
Appendix 2: Anxi People in Hong Kong and Macao

Hometown Publications

The *qiaokan* include, in a broad sense, newsletters, newspapers and magazines published by individuals, clans, schools, villages and the government offices in the so-called 'overseas Chinese villages'. It was reported that there were more than 140 *qiaokan* published in Guangdong in 1998[1] and 27 in Fujian in 1998.[2] The following section will discuss: (1) the development of hometown publications; (2) the role that these works currently play in the internationalization process; and (3) how, with a bit of caution, they can be used as primary-source material for the study of on-going social and economic developments, with particular reference to Guangdong province, which has so far produced the bulk of this sort of material.[3] These *qiaokan* are (and were) an outgrowth of that province's special historical experience and remain very important today. Although there have been many studies of cultural and economic developments based on field research (or Hong Kong interviews), little use has, up to now, been made of *qiaokan*.

The history of Guangdong *qiaokan* can be divided into four general periods, largely characterized by the overall political environment.

The Early Stage, 1900s-early 1930s

The first such publication, *Xinning Zhazhi* (Xinning Magazine), began in Taishan (it was called Xinning at the time) in January 1909. This periodical was created to meet the mutual interest and needs of overseas emigrants and their families and communities. On the one hand, overseas residents wanted to re-establish contacts with emigrant communities, especially for the first generation of migrants who had close emotional ties with the families they left behind and found it difficult to sustain contacts when abroad. On the other hand, this magazine represented the wishes of the emigrant families and communities, which wanted to have information about their overseas relatives and the circumstances in which they lived. It is important to mention that this pioneering *qiaokan* also reflected the efforts of local authorities to attract overseas financial support to improve local social and economic conditions. The *Xinning Magazine* contained three main themes: (1) Current problems of Taishan; (2) News of Taishan and other parts of China; and (3) Local history, customs and traditions (*Xinning Magazine*, 1909). The main audience of this *qiaokan* was the overseas emigrants from Taishan. The appearance of this magazine indicates that a collective *qiaoxiang* society was formed in the region at the time.

From 1910 until the early 1930s, Guangdong *qiaokan* reached their peak of the publications. This may be due to the official recognition of the *huaqiao* status of overseas Chinese by both the Qing and the Kuomintang governments, so that the channels of communication between overseas Chinese and their hometown communities could be established easily. Many *qiaoxiang* clans and districts in Guangdong, especially in the Pearl River Delta Region, published hometown publications during this period. For example, the Tan clan issued its first clan publication *Guangyu Yuekan* (monthly magazine) in 1910. Kaiping published *Wenlou Xiangyin* (Local Accents) and Xinhui its *Yagang Yuekan,* both in 1919 (Chen, 1990). Zhongshan (it was the Xiangshan county at the time) published *Dahuan Yuebao* (a monthly newspaper) in 1919 and Taishan followed with *Zuxiu Yueka*n in 1920 (The Taishan County Overseas Chinese Office, 1986). By 1936, according to unreliable figures, there was a total of 63 *qiaokan* published in the Taishan County alone (Chen, 1990).

It was interesting to note that many of the *qiaokan* were run by clans, villages, and schools during this period. For example, the *Guangda Jikan* (a quarterly, 1921) was published by a local elementary school. The *Mao Zukan* (1922) by the Mao clan; and the *Shuinan Qiaokan* (1935) by a village committee in Taishan. In the same period, *qiaokan* also multiplied in Zhongshan County where nine towns published hometown newspapers and/or magazines. Many smaller villages and less-influential clans also had their own, privately-published, periodicals. There was obvious competition and it seems fair to conclude that the proliferation of *qiaokan* reflected the special characteristics of this period. Although a few were sponsored by the government offices, there seems to have been little official interference in the content. They were mainly run by clans, communities, schools and, from time to time, according to the whim of individual editors.

The War Time Stage, late 1930s-1949
During the anti-Japanese war period, many Guangdong *qiaoxiang* districts stopped publishing *qiaokan* due to the Japanese invasion. However, new

ones were specifically created for the anti-war movements, such as *Huaqiao Zhanshi* ('Overseas Chinese Soldiers', 1938), *Huanqiao Zhanxian* (Overseas Chinese Alliance, 1938) in Guangzhou or *Santai Qingnian* (The Santai Youth) and *Zhanshi Taishan* (Wartime Taishan) in 1937. These new *qiaokan* were established with the clear purposes of rallying overseas Chinese behind the anti-Japanese war movement by donating to Chinese national defence funds, and by organizing worldwide anti-Japanese boycotts, etc. For this reason, Guangdong *qiaokan* became a window on what was happening at a national political level as well as a source of local news. Not surprisingly, wartime *qiaokan* delivered strong emotional and patriotic messages and, no doubt, attracted further donations. Many *qiaokan* articles during this period deal with the relationship between the overseas Chinese and China in general, and the role of the overseas Chinese in the anti-war movement in particular (see Tables of Contents of Selected *Qiaokan*: Overseas Chinese Alliances). This was, understandably, a period of great sentiment and patriotism.

After the anti-Japanese war, most *qiaokan* resumed publication - although they were eventually affected, one way or the other, by the civil war between the Kuomintang and the Chinese Communist Party. Taishan County, for example, was publishing a total of 115 different *qiaokan* by 1949: 15 were published by the *xian* government, 16 by the town, 61 by clans, and 23 by schools. By way of comparison, 42 *qiaokan* are believed to have been published in Zhongshan County (Chen, 1990).

The Revolutionary Stage, 1949-1977

The founding of the People's Republic made Guangdong *qiaokan* far more politically oriented. Some old *qiaokan* survived the Communist revolution, and others did not. It was reported that there were only 60 *qiaokan* published in Guangdong, among them 49 were published in Taishan in 1955 (Chen, 1990). Only a few new *qiaokan* appeared: for example, *Huijiao Xiangxun* (news from a particular suburb) in Guangzhou (1957), *Huancheng Qiaokan* in Zhongshan (1958), and *Heshan Xiangyin* (Local Accents) in Heshan (1962) were exceptions to the rule. The slow development of *qiaokan* reflected the constant political movements which occurred in China at that time. Indeed, contact with people living overseas (*haiwai guanxi*) often raised suspicion, and was considered criminal during the Cultural Revolution. Moveover, government policy was frequently inconsistent or contradictory (Godley, 1989). Although *qiaokan*, as a link between overseas Chinese and their hometowns, were criticized and ultimately forbidden by the government, they did play a role in attracting needed food and material as well as foreign currency remittances in the 1950s and early 1960s. Much of the content can easily be described as propaganda but a close reading also reveals the special treatment returned-overseas Chinese received and, ultimately, the hostility this provoked. All *qiaokan* were closed down in Guangdong during the Cultural Revolution (1966-76).

The Open Door Era to the Present

After China's Open Door Policy and Economic Reforms began, *qiaokan* have sprung up like mushrooms. The *Xinning Magazine* of Taishan was the first to resume publication in 1978 quickly followed by others in Guangdong province. There were said to be 42 *qiaokan* in Guangdong in 1983, 69 in 1984, 90 in 1995, 95 in 1986, and 103 by 1987 (Chen, 1990). From 1979 to 1987, more than 8.48 million copies of Guangdong *qiaokan* were printed and circulated (Chen, 1990, AOCG, 1996). From 1987 and onwards, the number of copies of Guangdong *qiaokan* in circulation reached two million per year (Chen, 1990). In 1996 alone, there were more than 140 *qiaokan* published in the province, and 2.3 million copies were printed and circulated to overseas Chinese in more than one hundred countries and areas in the world. It is important to mention that, although *qiaokan* were mainly distributed abroad (including what was until recently British Hong Kong), they also proved popular with *qiaoxiang* relatives and returned overseas Chinese. During this period, Guangdong *qiaokan* set out not only to rebuild the emotional ties between overseas Chinese and their hometowns which had, in many cases, been damaged in the previous years but also to re-establish economic connections. In the 1980s, the main emphasis was put on charitable projects but, by the 1990s, this had switched to attracting capital investments. Thus, the strong hand of government can clearly be seen.

Whereas *qiaokan* produced earlier in the century may well have served greater political and developmental ends, there was still an element of spontaneity and even an amateur quality to many of the publications. Now with so much at stake, most of the *qiaokan* in *qiaoxiang* counties in Guangdong are produced by specialized personnel working for, or in close liaison with, the various organs responsible for overseas Chinese affairs. In fact, many county government offices publish their own *qiaokan*. For example, in 1990 alone, more than 40 per cent of the total *qiaokan* were published by the city or county government offices in Guangdong. This effort seemed to have worked well since Guangdong has become the largest recipient of foreign investment in China. However the strong government involvement in *qiaokan* obviously makes them an important, indeed very useful, channel for the distribution of propaganda, which now includes frequent calls for investment, but could, under the right (or wrong) circumstances also tempt the authorities to make more-overtly patriotic appeals or meddle in the domestic politics of nearby counties. Hometown publications are already an important element in government policy, most significantly in Guangdong province though their numbers are increasing in Fujian and elsewhere.

The *qiaokan* have been called 'the collective letters from hometown' by overseas Cantonese. So far, they seem to have been effective. Part of their present appeal is the highly localized content which, thus far, generally eschews political nationalism in favour of parochial, even familial, sentimentality. Common features include: (1) news and messages of one's hometown; (2) the history and current development of one's hometown; (3) tradition and customs of one's hometown; and (4) articles on Chinese culture and language. The obvious intention is to make the readers feel connected with a particular ancestral place, to strengthen existing emotional ties between overseas Chinese and their hometown communities, and to expand economic connections. However, it must also be appreciated that *qiaokan* are, by definition, transnational publications which cross borders and may well be viewed as interventionist by other states: especially to the extent that capital is being drained away by remittances and investments or when they appear to be testing the political loyalty of their citizens of Chinese ancestry.

USING HOMETOWN PUBLICATIONS

The hometown concept has, of course, been strongly emphasized since the early years of this century and, whilst the Beijing government has now recognized that the vast majority of ethnic Chinese overseas are no longer citizens of the People's Republic and tends to avoid the term *huaqiao* at a diplomatic level, local and provincial authorities do not always appear to have received the message. The destabilizing potential of *qiaokan*, particularly in the Nanyang region, is therefore quite real. But, this said, the content of *qiaokan* is, nevertheless, an important source for the understanding of *qiaoxiang* ties.

Pioneering publications - produced at a time when the *huaqiao* construct and 'sojourner discourse' behind it was more valid (see the opening chapter by Leo Douw) - mainly focused on hometown news and information, initially to help restore communication with overseas relatives, who had lost contact (refer to the table of contents of *Xinning Magazine*, 1909). However, the *qiaokan* rapidly shifted their orientation as the political and economic situation changed: to make emotive calls to the overseas Chinese, who were told to feel proud of being Chinese and to take an active part in political movements and the defence as well as economic development of China. 'Come on, our fellow countrymen! This is the time to save the country!' (*The Overseas Chinese Reciprocity Association*, 1936); 'Every man has a share of responsibility for the fate of his country,' (*Overseas*

Chinese Alliances, 1938); and, rather more disturbingly, 'Dear overseas fellows, let's work together to build a new China!' (*The Voices of Overseas Chinese*, 1988).

Starting from the 1930s, the content of *qiaokan* quickly expanded from its focus of the interest in one's hometown to the interest in one's home country, i.e. China. In the first half of the 1930s, the periodicals began to deliver reports on the government's policies towards overseas Chinese and major news about China (see the table of contents of *The Kiu Siang Semimonthly*, 1936). This immediately changed them from mass publications to 'semi-official' ones. Many *qiaokan* called for donations to the anti-Japanese war effort, and for the establishment of an international Chinese alliance. Even when there was no direct governmental control, the *qiaokan* were strongly patriot (see the table of contents of *Overseas Chinese Alliances*, 1938). Sentimental and political links to the diaspora were further reinforced after the end of the war. The new focus of the *qiaokan* moved from the anti-war movements to the rebuilding of *qiaoxiang*. With the economic problems in China at the time, more space was devoted not only to remittances and welfare donations, but also with the overseas Chinese investment in the economic development of hometown districts. A strong emphasis of the *qiaokan* then, as today, was to advertise favourable government policies toward investments (see the attached table of contents of *Great China and Overseas Chinese Monthly*, 1948).

Also problematic in Southeast Asia were the Kuomintang's cultural and educational activities, which can be seen in various *qiaokan*. Supporting overseas Chinese schools and sponsoring *qiaoxiang* educational activities have been another major task of Guangdong *qiaokan* since the 1920s. It was reported that all schools in *qiaoxiang* areas have more or less benefited from overseas donations (Huang, 1997). It was found that in almost every issue of Guangdong *qiaokan* there were columns on culture and education. *The Voices of Overseas Chinese*, for example, set aside a column to publish names of donors and the amounts of their school donations in every issue of the publication. Some *qiaokan* even published special issues on *qiaoxiang* education. Although the *qiaokan* have had no direct influence on overseas Chinese donations in cultural and educational developments of *qiaoxiang*, they laid the groundwork for the recognition of the value of education and the importance of the maintenance of the Chinese culture, language, and traditions among overseas Chinese and their hometown communities.

The *Xinning Magazine* claimed that Taishan County alone received school donations amounting HK$180 million in 1985. These donations helped to establish 24 new high schools and to reconstruct school buildings of more than 9,000 square metres in the county (Li, 1986). Moreover, the stress placed on history, traditions, and cultural events has, no doubt, provided overseas Chinese and their children with knowledge of Chinese culture, history and language. But it is difficult to assess exactly how the publications are used abroad. Even today, *qiaokan* are apparently utilized (certainly intended to be used) as cultural resources and language texts. Since the 1980s, some *qiaokan* have also included English-language columns to attract young generations who cannot read Chinese.

Most *qiaokan* set out to provide special services to overseas Chinese: most commonly to help locate lost relatives or, perhaps more to the point, to contact relevant government offices over property rights and other concerns, and to make connections for school and other social welfare donations. Most significantly, they promote investment opportunities and explain the rules: sometimes even taking on the role of brokers (Wang and Liang, 1988). A concrete example can be found in *The Voices of Overseas Chinese* (see the sample table of contents from *Qiaosheng*, no. 34, 1998). There were 68 items of news reports in the issue; 18 items were related to overseas donations and investments in the Meixian County; 13 articles news were about hometown industrial and economic developments, and nine items were reports of Overseas Chinese visitors related to potential contributions. It can be seen that the entire issue was, in one way or the other, related to money.

Hometown publications have always played a somewhat contradictory role since first established in the early twentieth century. They were intended to be (and have been called 'mass publications' in Communist terminology) but many of them were, very early on, sponsored and run partially by local governments. This fact has long influenced both their purpose and content and prompts the following note of caution. *Qiaokan* were, from the beginning, designed to deliver news and information in order to make emotional and economic connections between overseas Chinese and their hometown districts. For this reason, they are an absolutely indispensable source for the study of *qiaoxiang* ties but, by and large, they have also been mouthpieces for government propaganda. And this is, undoubtedly, their major role today. They *cannot* and *must not* be used as the sole measure of the success of either the activities they promote (at present, investment opportunities) or the true feelings of the majority of ethnic Chinese living outside of China at the end of the twentieth century. If *qiaokan* are mistakenly taken at face value: all overseas Chinese are emotionally tied to their hometowns and home country; all overseas Chinese are proud of China and its political leadership; all overseas Chinese wish to embrace its culture and language; and all overseas Chinese want to support education, economic development, etc. If taken to its logical conclusion, we would return to the old *ius sanguinis* argument that *all* Chinese are, by the nature of race, ancestry and ethnicity, politically loyal to China. This would invite disaster.

BIBLIOGRAPHY

Akashi Yoji
1970   *The Nanyang National Salvation Movement, 1937-1941.* Lawrence, Kansas: Center for East Asian Studies, University of Kansas
Australian National Library
1987   *Chinese Language Newspapers in the National Library of Australia.* Canberra
Callis, H.
1941   *Foreign Capital in Southeast Asia.* New York: Institute of Pacific Relations
Cator, W.J.
1936   *The Economic Position of the Chinese in the Netherlands Indies.* Oxford: Blackwell
Chen, Kezhen, ed.
1994   *Anxi huaqiao zhi* (The Annals of Overseas Chinese in Anxi). Xiamen: Xiamen University
Chen Mong Hock
1967   *The Early Chinese Newspapers of Singapore, 1881-1912.* Singapore: University of Malaya Press
Chen Shanying
1990   '*Guangdong qiaokan xiangxun gaikuang jiqi zai haiwai de gongneng* (The Current State of Guangdong *Qiaokan* and Functions in Overseas)', *Qiaoshi xuebao* (The Journal of Overseas Chinese History), Guangzhou: Guangdong Huaqiao History Society 3, pp. 40-6
Chen Ta
1940   *Emigrant Communities in South China: A Study of Overseas Migration and its Influence on Standards of Living and Social Change.* New York: Institute of Pacific Relations
Douw, Leo and Peter Post (eds)
1995   *South China: State, Culture and Social Change during the 20th Century,* Amsterdam: Royal Netherlands Academy of Arts and Sciences
Feng Aiqun
1976   *Huaqiao baoye shi* (History of Chinese newspapers [in Asia]). Taibei: Taiwan xuesheng shuzhu
Feng, Yuan
1987   *Jianguo chuqi Guangdong qiaohui qianxi* (An Analysis of Guangdong Overseas Remittances during the Early Years of the People's Republic of China), *Dongnanya xuekan* (The Journal of Southeast Asian Studies) Guangzhou: Zhongshan University 4, pp. 21-9

Fitzgerald, S.
1972   *China and the Overseas Chinese: A Study of Peking's Changing Policy, 1949-1970*. Cambridge: Cambridge University Press
Godley, M.
1981   *The Mandarin-Capitalists from Nanyang: Overseas Chinese Enterprise in the Modernization of China, 1893-1911*. Cambridge: Cambridge University Press
1989   'The Sojourners: returned Overseas Chinese in the People's Republic of China', *Pacific Affairs* 62:3
Guangdong Shengzhi, Huaqiaozhi (The Annals of Overseas Chinese in Guangdong, AOCG, 1996), Guangdong People's Press
Hicks, G.L.
1993   *Overseas Chinese Remittances from Southeast Asia 1910-1940*. Singapore: Select Books
Huang, Cen
1997   'Overseas Chinese and China's Economic Modernization', in: Paul van der Velde and Alex Mckay (eds) *New Developments in Asian Studies*. London: Kegan Paul International, 123-39
1998   'The Organisation and Management of Chinese Transnational Enterprises in South China', *Issues and Studies* 34(3), pp. 51-70
Iwasaki Ikuo
1983   *Japan and Southeast Asia: A Bibliography of Historical, Economic and Political Relations*. Tokyo: Library Institute of Developing Economics
Li, Lianping
1986   '*Guangdong sheng qiaokan xiangxun de jiben qingkuang ji jinyibu zuohao jinhou gongzuo de yijian*' (The Basic Conditions and Further Suggestions of Guangdong *Qiaokan*), *Qiaokan xiangxun yianjiu* (Qiaokan Studies), Guangzhou 1, pp. 4-9
Lin, Jiajin; Luo, Lucai; Chen, Shusen; Pan, Yining; and He, Anju
1993   '*Jindai guangdong qiaohui yianjiu*' (The Study of Guangdong Remittance in Modern Times), *Dongnanya xuekan* (The Journal of Southeast Asian Studies), Guangzhou: Zhongshan University 9, pp. 9-16
Lin, Jizhi
1983   *Jindai Huaqiao touzi guonei qiyeshi yan jiu* (Research on recent overseas Chinese investments in Chinese enterprises), Fuzhou: Fujian renmin chubanshe
1988   *Jindai Huaqiao touzi guonei qiye gailun* (Overseas Chinese Investment in Domestic Industries in Modern China), Xiamen: Xiamen Daxue
1989   '*Qianlun jin shinian lai haiwai huaren zai zhongguo dalu de touzi*' (A Discussion of Overseas Chinese Investments in Mainland China

in the Past Ten Years), *Nanyang* yanjiu (Issues of Southeast Asian Studies), Xiamen: Xiamen Daxue 2, pp. 47-55

1994   '*Haiwai huaren he gangao tongbao zai Fujian de touzi*' (Overseas Chinese, and Hong Kong and Aomen Compatriots' Investments in Fujian), *Huaqiao huaren yu* qiaowu (Overseas Chinese and Overseas Chinese Affairs), Beijing, pp. 50-5

1996   '*Xi huaqiao huikuan jiqi zuoyong*' (An Analysis of Overseas Remittances and their Fanctuions), *Bagui qiaoshi* (The Journal of Overseas Chinese History of Bagui), Nanning, 31(3), pp. 26-31

Lin Jinzhi and Zhang Weiji

1985   *Jindai Huaqiao touzi guoneir qiyeshi ziliao xuanji* (Selected materials on recent overseas Chinese investment in internal enterprises) Fuzhou: Fujian renmin chubanshe

Mackie, J.A.C.

1992   'Overseas Chinese entrepreneurship', *Asian-Pacific Economic Literature* 6:1

Nevadomsky, J.J.

1970   *Publications in Western Languages, 1960-1970*. Berkeley: Center for South and Southeast Asian Studies

Purcell, V.

1965   *The Chinese in Southeast Asia*. Oxford: Oxford University Press

Selected *Guangdong Qiaokan*, 1928-1997

Shu, A.C.W.

1968   *Twentieth Century Chinese Works on Southeast Asia: A Bibliography*. Honolulu: East-West Center

Song, Ping

1996   'An Analysis of Models: How Schools are Run by Overseas Chinese in Southeast Fujian', in: L.M. Douw and P. Post (eds), *South China: State, Culture and Social Change during the 20th Century*. Amsterdam: Royal Netherlands Academy of Arts and Sciences, pp. 197-204

Suryadinata, L. (ed.)

1989   *The Ethnic Chinese in Asean States: Bibliographical Essays*. Singapore: Institute of Southeast Asian Studies

The Taishan County Overseas Chinese Office

1986   '*Women shi zheyang dui qiaokan jinxing lingdao de*' (This Is How We Lead the *Qiaokan*), *Qiaokan xiangxun* yanjiu (The Qiaokan Studies), Guangzhou 2, pp. 15-17

Wang, Peilin and Liang, Shihong

1988   '*Qiaoxiang shehui jiaowang de bianqian*' (Changes in Social Interaction of Qiaoxiang), *Huaqiao yu huaren* (The Overseas Chinese), Guangzhou 1, pp. 14-20

Wang Gungwu

1981   'Southeast Asian Huaqiao in Chinese history writing', *Journal of Southeast Asian Studies* 12:1

1985   'South China perspectives on overseas Chinese', *The Australian Journal of Chinese Affairs* 13

1991   *China and the Chinese Overseas*, Singapore: Times Academic Press

Wu Chun-his

1967   *Dollars, Dependents and Dogma: Overseas Chinese Remittances to Communist China*. Stanford, California: Hoover Institution

Yen Ch'ing-hwang

1981   'The overseas Chinese and late-Ch'ing Economic Modernization', *Modern Asian Studies* 16:2

Yong, C.F. and R.B. McKenna

1990   *The Kuomintang Movement in British Malaya 1912-1949*. Singapore: Oxford University Press

Zeng, Yiping and Chen, Liju (eds)

1993   *Huaqiao huaren yanjiu wenxian yin, 1980-1990* (Index to Periodical Articles Relating to Overseas Chinese, 1980-1990), Xiamen: Xiamen Daxue

Zhuang Guotu

1989   *Zhong guo fengjiajn zhengfude Huaqiao zhengce* (The policy of China's feudal government toward the overseas Chinese). Xiamen: Xiamen Daxue

Tables of Contents of Selected *Qiaokan*

The Xinning Magazine 《新寧雜誌》
January 1909, Taishan
- Discussions of current problems of Taishan
- News of the Taishan county, and other parts of China
- Local history, customs and traditions

The Over-sea Chinese Guidance 《華僑之路》
November 1928, Guangzhou
- Overseas remittances and the overseas Chinese
- Who are 'huaqiao'?
- From the establishment of the Overseas Chinese Affairs Office to the close of the Office
- How should huaqiao comrades prepare for the third People's Congress?
- Huaqiao should participate in the movements of abolishing contract labour
- News from hometown

The Kiu Siang Semimonthly 《僑聲半月刊》
May 1936, Guangzhou
- Mourn for Mr. Hu Han Min (胡漢民先生)
- A murder case of huaqiao in Guangzhou
- A necessary understanding of helping huaqiao
- What is called "Zhu zai"? (piglets, 豬仔)
- The ban of overseas Chinese schools in Vietnam
- New government regulations about overseas Chinese affairs: luggage checks
- News from overseas Chinese: Huaqiao in Vietnam, Chinese associations in Singapore

Overseas Chinese Alliances 《華僑戰線》
March (1st issue), 1938, The committee of the overseas Chinese anti-war movement,
- How can the overseas Chinese support the motherland against Japanese?
- The movement of the overseas Chinese anti-war donations
- To establish an international overseas Chinese anti-war alliance
- To join the anti-Japanese war is an ultimate goal of overseas Chinese
- A report of overseas Chinese war donations in Guangdong province
- To carry forward the revolutionary nature of Overseas Chinese
- To establish the war time education of overseas Chinese

Great China and Overseas Chinese Monthly 《大漢華僑月刊》
September, 1948, Guangzhou
- Introduction to the Guangdong overseas Chinese affairs office
- The current economic reform in China
- Introduction to the new currency (jin yuan quan 金圓券)
- The government regulations on the permit to go overseas
- The must know regulations for returning overseas Chinese
- News from hometown (Taishan, Kaiping, Enping, Xinhui, Zhongshan)
- Mail box for overseas Chinese

* Unfortunately, the archive studies did not find any Guangdong *qiaokan* collections between 1960s and the 1970s

The Voices of Overseas Chinese 《僑聲》
September 1988, Meixian
　　Special Editorial:
　　The warmest welcome to overseas folks' investments in Meixian
　　News from Meixian
- Kejia Thai Chinese delegates spent the Mid Autumn Festival at hometown
- Current industrial developments of Meixian
　　Qiaoxiang's new face
- Two new overseas Chinese companies
- The new overseas Chinese housing projects
　　Education in Meixian: School and overseas donations
　　Special interviews
　　From the heart of overseas Chinese,
- A name list of donations and investments
　　News of overseas Chinese
- Meixian Kejia customs and traditions

Appendix I: Chinese Research Institutes of Overseas Chinese and Southeast Asian Studies (學術研究機構):

華僑大學華僑研究所
Institute of Overseas Chinese Studies, Huaqiao University, Quanzhou

暨南大學華僑華人研究所
Institute of Overseas Chinese Studies, Jinan University, Guangzhou

福建省社會科學院華僑華人研究所
Institute of Overseas Chinese Studies, Academy of Social Sciences, Fuzhou

全國僑聯華僑華人歷史研究所
Institute of Overseas Chinese History, the China's Overseas Chinese Affairs Association, Beijing

廈門大學南洋研究院
Research School of Southeast Asian Studies, Xiamen University, Xiamen

北京大學東南亞研究所
Institute of Southeast Asian Studies, Beijing University, Beijing

中山大學東南亞研究所
Institute of Southeast Asian Studies, Zhongshan University, Guangzhou

暨南大學東南亞研究所
Institute of Southeast Asian Studies, Jinan University, Guangzhou

廣西社會科學院東南亞研究所
Institute of Indo-China Studies, Guangxi Academy of Social Sciences, Nanning

雲南社會科學院東南亞研究所
Institute of Southeast Asian Studies, Yunnan Academy of Social Sciences, Kunming

Appendix II: Major Chinese Journals on Overseas Chinese Studies:
（學術期刊雜誌）：

《八桂僑史》，廣西省華僑歷史學會
《東南亞》，雲南省社會科學院東南亞研究所
《東南亞學刊》，廣州中山大學東南亞研究所
《東南亞縱橫》，廣西省社會科學院東南亞研究所
《廣東華僑歷史學會通訊》，廣東省華僑歷史學會
《廣州華僑研究》，廣東省廣州華僑歷史學會
《廣州僑史》，廣東省廣州華僑歷史學會
《海外華人研究》，中華民國海外華人研究學會，臺北
《華僑與華人》，廣州市華僑歷史學會
《華僑華人歷史研究》，中國華僑歷史學會
《華僑歷史論叢》，福建省華僑歷史學會
《華僑華人資料》，中國華僑華人歷史研究所
《華僑史》，福建省泉州華僑歷史學會
《嘉應僑史》，廣東省梅州華僑歷史學會
《南洋問題研究》，福建省廈門大學南洋研究院
《泉州華僑史料》，福建省泉州僑辦僑聯
《僑史學報》，廣東省華僑歷史學會
《僑務工作研究》，中國國務院僑辦編委會
《汕頭僑史》，廣東省汕頭華僑歷史學會

Appendix III: Major Chinese Index to the Works Relating to Overseas Chinese Studies:

Index to Theses on Overseas Chinese History in Southeast Asia
《南洋華僑史專題論文索引》
廈門大學南洋研究所資料室編，1957

Index to Book Publications on Overseas Chinese Studies
《華僑問題圖書總目》
廈門大學南洋研究所資料室編，1959

Index to Research Papers on Overseas Chinese Studies
《中文華僑問題文獻目錄，1904-66》
張祥義編，東京亞洲經濟研究，1971

Index to Periodical Essays on Overseas Chinese History, 1895-1980
《華僑史論文資料索引，1895-1980》
中山大學東南亞歷史研究所圖書館編，1981

A Collection of Essays on Overseas Chinese History
《華僑史論文集》，陳喬之，周韶仁，余以平
廣東暨南大學出版社，1981

A Collection of Papers on Overseas Chinese History
《華僑史研究論集》，吳澤主編
上海華東師範大學出版社，1984

Index to Major Works on Overseas Chinese History
《華僑華人史書刊目錄》，鄭民等編
中國展望出版社，1984

Proceedings of the International Conference on Overseas Chinese Studies
《華僑華人歷史國際研討會論文集》，1985

A Collection of Essays on Overseas Chinese History
《華僑史研究論文集》，林少川編
泉州華僑大學華僑研究所，1986

A Bibliography of Book on Overseas Chinese Studies
《華僑問題書目索引》，宋健冶編
日本逢甲大學經濟研究所，1988

A Collection of Research Papers on Overseas Chinese History
《華僑華人史研究集》，海洋出版社，1989

Proceedings of the Change of Overseas Chinese after the WW II
《戰後海外華人變化國際研討會論文集》，郭梁主編
中國華僑出版公司，1989

Index to the Works on Overseas Chinese Studies, 1976-89
《華僑華人研究著作題錄，1976-89》
香港新世紀出版社，1992

Index to Periodical Articles Relating to Overseas Chinese, 1980-90
《華僑華人研究文獻索引，1980-90》，曾伊平，陳麗娘編
廈門大學出版社，1993

Selected Bibliography of Articles on Southeast Asian Overseas Chinese in
Chinese Periodicals, 1980-94
《中文期刊有關東南亞華僑的文章目錄，1980-94》
International institute for Asian Studies, Leiden, 1994

Dictionary of Overseas Chinese and Overseas Chinese Affairs
《華僑華人僑務大辭典》，山東友誼出版社，1997

A Guide to Periodical Publications on the Chinese Overseas, 1991-95
《華僑華人研究文獻索引，1991-95》，廈門大學出版社，1998

Ethnic Chinese at the Turn of the Century
《世紀之交的海外華人》，上冊
(A Collection of Essays on Overseas Chinese Studies, 1996-97, V: I)
庄國土，黃猷，方雄普主編，福建人民出版社，1998

Ethnic Chinese at the Turn of the Century
《世紀之交的海外華人》，下冊
(A Collection of Essays on Overseas Chinese Studies, 1996-97, V: II)
庄國土主編，福建人民出版社，1998

Appendix IV: Government Publications on Overseas Chinese Affairs
中國政府僑報一覽表：

Name 報名	Government office 政府機構	Year/Month 出版年月
福建僑鄉報	福建省僑辦	1951-66, 1981 weekly
廣西僑報	廣西省僑辦	1956-66, 1982 weekly
鷺風報	福建廈門僑辦	1956-66, 1981 bi-weekly
廣東僑報	廣東省僑辦	1956-66, 1979 bi-weekly
華聲報	國務院僑辦	1983-1994 weekly
江門僑報	廣東江門市	1984 bi-weekly
佛山僑報	廣東佛山市僑辦	1985 monthly
嘉應鄉情報	廣東梅州市僑辦	1985 quarterly
茂名僑報	廣東茂名市僑辦	1985 monthly
浙江僑報	浙江省僑辦	1985 weekly
雲南僑報	雲南省僑辦	1985 weekly
溫州僑鄉報	浙江溫州市僑辦	1987 weekly
寧波僑鄉報	浙江寧波僑辦僑聯	1988 weekly
惠州鄉情報	廣東惠州市僑辦	1988 weekly
海南僑報	海南省僑辦	1989 bi-weekly
陽江僑報	廣東陽江市僑辦	1989 bi-weekly
柳州鄉情報	廣西柳州市	1991 monthly
北海鄉情報	廣西北海市	1991 weekly
上海僑報	上海市僑辦	1992 weekly
桂東鄉情報	廣西梧州市僑辦	1992 bi-weekly
僑聲時報	陝西省僑辦	1992 weekly
桂林鄉情報	廣西桂林市僑辦	1992 monthly
華僑時報	湖南省僑辦	1993 weekly
深圳僑報	廣東深圳市僑辦	1994 weekly
廣州僑商報	廣州市僑聯	1995 quarterly

Appendix V: Selected *Annals of Overseas Chinese*, 華僑誌

《廣東省華僑誌》，廣東省地方誌編纂委員會，廣東人民出版社
《廣州市華僑誌》，廣州市地方誌編纂委員會，廣東人民出版社
《台山華僑誌》，廣東省台山市地方史誌編纂委員會
《梅縣華僑誌》，廣東省梅縣華僑誌編委會
《福建省華僑誌》，福建省地方誌編纂委員會
《廈門華僑誌》，廈門華僑誌編委會，鷺江出版社
《安溪華僑誌》，陳克振主編，廈門大學出版社
《晉江華僑誌》，吳泰主編，上海人民出版社

Appendix VI: A List of Guangdong and Fujian Hometown Publications
(1) 廣東省僑刊鄉訊一覽表 (Guangdong Qiaokan):

Name 刊名	Place 出版地	Year/ 創刊年
Xinning zazhi 新寧雜誌	Taishan 台山	1909，1
Guangyu yuekan 光裕月刊	Taishan 台山	1910
Wenlou xiangyin 文樓鄉音	Xinhui 新會	1918
Maogang yuebao 茅岡月報	Kaiping 開平	1919
Zhuxiu yuekan 竹秀月刊	Taishan 台山	1919
Dahuan yuebao 大環月報	Taishan 台山	1919
Tunmu xiangkan 敦睦鄉刊	Taishan 台山	1920
Meige qiaokan 梅閣僑刊	Xinhui 新會	1920
Guangda jikan 光大季刊	Taishan 台山	1921
Lougang yuekan 樓岡月刊	Kaiping 開平	1921
Maoshi zukan 毛氏族刊	Taishan 台山	1922
Kanghe yuekan 康和月刊	Taishan 台山	1922
Cuicun zukan 萃村族刊	Taishan 台山	1922
Enping gongbao 恩平公報	Enping 恩平	1922
Shadui qiaokan 沙堆僑刊	Xinhui 新會	1922
Xinmin yuebao 新民月報	Kaiping 開平	1922
Sansheng zuankan 三省專刊	Taishan 台山	1923
Baisha qiaokan 白沙僑刊	Taishan 台山	1924
Jiaolun yuekan 教倫月刊	Kaiping 開平	1924
Wubao yuebao 五堡月報	Kaiping 開平	1925
Guangyu yuebao 光裕月報	Kaiping 開平	1925
Fengcai yuekan 風采月刊	Taishan 台山	1925
Xushan yuekan 胥山月刊	Taishan 台山	1925
Niyuan yuekan 溯源月刊	Taishan 台山	1925
Dulian qiaokan 獨聯僑刊	Xinhui 新會	1925
Dahui qiaokan 大匯僑刊	Taishan 台山	1926
Dajiang qiaokan 大江僑刊	Taishan 台山	1926

Juzhen yuebao 居正月報	Taishan 台山	1926
Tiling yuebao 提領月報	Taishan 台山	1926
Chengxi yuebao 澄溪月報	Kaiping 開平	1927
Liou yuekan 里謳月刊	Kaiping 開平	1927
Guzai yuekan 古宅月刊	Kaiping 開平	1928
Jingxiu yuebao 敬修月報	Taishan 台山	1928
Huaqiao zhilu 華僑之路	Guangzhou 廣州	1928
Runan zhihua 汝南之花	Taishan 台山	1929
Dongzhong xiaokan 東中校刊	Meixian 梅縣	1930
Yuhuan shuangyuebao 玉環雙月報	Taishan 台山	1931
Xialu qiaokan 霞路僑刊	Xinhui 新會	1932
Ziyang yuekan 紫陽月刊	Taishan 台山	1933
Caofeng qiaokan 曹峰僑刊	Taishan 台山	1934
Haiyan qiaokan 海宴僑刊	Taishan 台山	1935
Shuinan qiaokan 水南僑刊	Taishan 台山	1935
Fushan yuebao 浮山月報	Taishan 台山	1935
Xiaohai yuebao 小海月報	Kaiping 開平	1935
Shagang yuebao 沙岡月報	Kaiping 開平	1935
Qiaosheng banyuekan 僑聲半月刊	Guangzhou 廣州	1936
Kaiping mingbao 開平明報	Kaiping 開平	1937
Siyi qiaokan 思義僑刊	Kaiping 開平	1937
Zhanshi Taishan 戰時台山	Taishan 台山	1937
Santai qingnian 三台青年	Taishan 台山	1937
Huaqiao zhanxian 華僑戰線	Guangzhou 廣州	1938
Huaqiao zhanshi 華僑戰士	Guangzhou 廣州	1938
Michong tongxun 密沖通訊	Taishan 台山	1940
Changtang yuekan 長塘月刊	Kaiping 開平	1941
Sanxiang qiaoshengkan 三鄉僑生刊	Zhongshan 中山	1945

Lingfeng 嶺風	Taishan 台山	1945
Hulong yuekan 護龍月刊	Kaiping 開平	1947
Dahan huaqiao yuekan 大漢華僑月刊	Guangzhou 廣州	1948
Gangzhong xiaoyoutongxun 岡中校友通訊	Xinhui 新會	1948
Kaiqiao xiaoyou tongxun 開僑校友通訊	Kaiping 開平	1948
Chonglou qiaokan 沖蔞僑刊	Taishan 台山	1948
Qiaosheng 僑聲	Meixian 梅縣	1951
Gujing qiaokan 古井僑刊	Xinhui 新會	1955
Huijiao qiaoxun 穗郊僑訊	Guangzhou 廣州	1957
Guanghai tongxun 廣海通訊	Taishan 台山	1957
Xinhui qiaokan 新會僑刊	Xinhui 新會	1958
Huancheng qiaokan 環城僑刊	Zhongshan 中山	1958
Heshan xiangxun 鶴山鄉訊	Heshan 鶴山	1962

(Interruption by the Cultural Revolution and other political movements)

Doumen xiangyin 斗門鄉音	Doumen 斗門	1980，1
Zhongshan qiaokan 中山僑刊	Zhongshan 中山	1980，12
Shenzhen xiangyin 深圳鄉音	Shenzhen 深圳	1981，1
Baihe qiaokan 百合僑刊	Kaiping 開平	1981，2
Huaxian xiangyin 花縣鄉音	Huaxian 花縣	1982，11
Jiangmen qiaokan 江門僑刊	Jiangmen 江門	1983，10
Foshan qiaoxun 佛山僑訊	Foshan 佛山	1984，2
Longdu shaxi qiaokan 隆都沙溪僑刊	Zhongshan 中山	1984，2
Shunde xiangyin 順德鄉音	Shunde 順德	1984，7
Shanshui xiangxun 三水鄉訊	Shanshui 三水	1984，7
Dongzhen qiaokan 東鎮僑刊	Zhongshan 中山	1984，9
Gaoming xiangxun 高明鄉訊	Gaoming 高明	1984，9

Yandu qiaoqing 宴都僑情	Taishan 台山	1984，9
Maoming xiangqing 茂名鄉情	Maoming 茂名	1984，11
Xinhui huakan 新會畫刊	Xinhui 新會	1984，11
Songkou xiangqing 松口鄉情	Meixian 梅縣	1984，11
Zhuhai xiangyin 珠海鄉音	Zhuhai 珠海	1984，11
Lixiangqing 荔鄉情	Zengcheng 增城	1984，12
Jiaying xiangqing 嘉應鄉情	Meixian 梅縣	1984
Zhanjiang xiangqing 湛江鄉情	Zhanjiang 湛江	1984
Nanhai xiangyin 南海鄉音	Foshan 佛山	1984
Jianglian xiangyin 江聯鄉音	Taishan 台山	1985，2
Guangzhou huasheng 廣州華聲	Guangzhou 廣州	1985，5
Xijiang xiangqing 西江鄉情	Zhaoqing 肇慶	1985，5
Longtang qiaokan 龍塘僑刊	Kaiping 開平	1985，5
Dongwan xiangqing 東莞鄉情	Dongwan 東莞	1985，5
Xiazhe qiaokan 下澤僑刊	Zhongshan 中山	1985，5
Jieyang xiangyin 揭陽縣音	Jieyang 揭陽	1985，5
Chaoshan xiangyin 潮汕鄉音	Chaoyang 潮陽	1985，8
Huaiji xiangqing 懷集鄉情	Huaiji 懷集	1985，8
Shuibu qiaokan 水步僑刊	Taishan 台山	1985，9
Zuxiuyuan xiaokan 竹秀園校刊	Zhongshan 中山	1985，9
Chaoren 潮人	Shantou 汕頭	1985，10
Chaozhou xiangyin 潮州鄉音	Chaozhou 潮州	1985，12
Dapu xiangxun 大埔鄉訊	Dapu 大埔	1985，12
Puning xiangxun 普寧鄉訊	Puning 普寧	1985
Polu qiaokan 波羅僑刊	Kaiping 開平	1986，3
Jiujiang qiaokan 九江僑刊	Nanhai 南海	1986，3
Jiexi xiangqing 揭西鄉情	Jiexi 揭西	1986
Luokeng qiaokan 羅坑僑刊	Xinhui 新會	1987，3
Tangxia qiaokan 棠下僑刊	Xinhui 新會	1987，3
Jiangmen huabao 江門畫報	Jiangmen 江門	1987，12

Panyu qiaoxun 番禺僑訊	Panyu 番禺	1987，12
Sancun xiangyin 三村鄉音	Xinhui 新會	1987，12
Mianqieshu 緬茄樹	Gaozhou 高州	1987，12
Qingyuan xiangyin 清遠鄉音	Qingyuan 清遠	1987，12
Oucun zhiyin 區村之音	Enping 恩平	1987，12
Xiema qiaokan 歇馬僑刊	Enping 恩平	1987，12
Nanlang xiangyin 南朗鄉音	Zhongshan 中山	1987，12
Huidong xiangqing 惠東鄉情	Huidong 惠東	1987，12
Yuebei xiangqing 粵北鄉情	Shaoguan 韶關	1988，4
Kuicheng xiangyin 葵城鄉音	Xinhui 新會	1988，6
Gaoyao qiaosheng 高要僑聲	Zhaoqing 肇慶	1988，7
Zhenping xiangyin 鎮平鄉音	Jiaoling 蕉嶺	1988，7
Heyuan xiangqing 河源鄉情	Heyuan 河源	1988，8
Beijiang qing 北江情	Qingyuan 清遠	1988，11
Qiaokan wenzhai 僑刊文摘	Taishan 台山	1988，11
Yangchun qiaokan 陽春僑刊	Yangchun 陽春	1989，3
Wuyi xiangqing 五邑鄉情	Jiangmen 江門	1989，5
Junan qiaokan 均安僑刊	Enping 恩平	1989，6
Sanjiang qiaokan 三江僑刊	Xinhui 新會	1989，7
Duhu qiaokan 都斛僑刊	Taishan 台山	1989，11
Kejia ren 客家人	Meizhou 梅州	1989，11
Zhishan xiangqing 址山鄉情	Heshan 鶴山	1989，12
Haifeng xiangyin 海豐鄉音	Haifeng 海豐	1990，5
Tangjiawan qiaokan 唐家灣僑刊	Zhuhai 珠海	1990，5

(2) 福建省僑刊鄉訊一覽表 (Fujian Hometown Publications):

Name 刊名	Place 出版地	Year/創刊年
Jimei xiaoxiao 集美校友	Xiamen 廈門	1942
Luoyang xangxun 螺陽鄉訊	Luoyang 螺陽	1950，12
Yongding xiangxun 永定鄉訊	Yongding 永定	1956
Lufeng 鷺風	Xiamen 廈門	1956
Putian xiangyin 莆田鄉音	Putian 莆田	1957
Anxi xiangxun 安溪鄉訊	Anxi 安溪	1957
Taoyuan xiangxun 桃源鄉訊	Taoyuan 桃源	1958
Minhai 閩海	Fuzhou 福州	1958
Minxi xiangyin 閩西鄉訊	Longyan 龍岩	1958
Qingang qiaosheng 琴崗僑聲	Shanghang 上杭	1960
Wenling 溫陵	Quanzhou 泉州	1962，1
Xiamen caifengbao 廈門采風報	Xiamen 廈門	1981
Songtao 松濤	Zhenpu 震浦	1982，12
Yurong xiangyin 玉融鄉音	Fuqing 福清	1983，10
Xiangjiang 薌江	Zhangzhou 漳州	1984，1
Qingzhi xiangxun 青芝鄉訊	Lianjiang 連江	1984，2
Nanan xiangxun 南安鄉訊	Nanan 南安	1984，6
Fujian xiangtu 福建鄉土	Fuzhou 福州	1985，2
Xianxi xiangxun 仙溪鄉訊	Xianxi 仙溪	1985，8
Shizhai guli 石齋故里	Dongshan 東山	1986，10
Sanmin qiaoxun 三明僑訊	Sanmin 三明	1987，1
Guangxian xiangxun 光賢鄉訊	Fuqing 福清	1987，2
Mindong xiangxun 閩東鄉訊	Ningde 寧德	1987，3
Jinmen xiangyi 金門鄉誼	Xianmen jinyi 廈門金誼	1987，3
Yutian xiangyin 玉田鄉音	Gutian 古田	1988，2
Danshao xiangxun 丹招鄉訊	Shaoan 招安	1988，12
Jinjiang xiangun 晉江鄉訊	Jinjiang 晉江	1989

Notes

1. The statistics came from the co-author, Cen Huang's, fieldwork in Guangdong in August 1998.
2. The statistics were provided by Professor Zhuang Guotu at the Research School of Southeast Asian Studies of Xiamen University.
3. Cen Huang carried out archival research at the Zhongshan Archive of Guangzhou, the Materials Centre of the Institute of Overseas Chinese Studies at Jinan University in Guangzhou, and the Centre of the Research School of Southeast Asian Studies at Xiamen University, Fujian Province, in December 1997 and January and August 1998. In addition, interviews were conducted with scholars and officials who were involved in the development of *qiaokan* publications in Guangdong. The data were collected mainly from the 1910s to 1940s and from the 1980s to the 1990s. There was little *qiaokan* material produced from the 1950s to 1970s.

GLOSSARY

Anxi, 安溪

Baoan, 寶安

boshi, 博士

bu aixiang, 不愛鄉

Changle, 長樂

Chaoyang, 潮陽

Chaozhou, 潮州

Chaozhou gongshang lianyihui
　　潮州工會聯誼會

Chenghai, 澄海

Chen Jiageng, 陳嘉庚
　　(Tan Kah kee)

chun jie, 春節

citang, 祠堂

Dapu, 大埔

Dongshan, 東山

Dongwan, 東莞

duanwu, 端午

Enping, 恩平

fan, 番

fanke, 番客

fenghui, 風水

fengshui di, 風水地

Fengshun, 豐順

Foshan, 佛山

Fujian, 福建

Fuqing, 福清

Fuzhou, 福州

Gangzhou huiguan, 岡州會館

Gaoyao, 高要

gen, 根

getihu, 個體戶

gongde, 功德

gongye qu, 工業區

guhun, 孤魂

Gutian, 古田

guanxi, 觀系

Guangdong, 廣東

Guomindang, 國民黨

haiwai lianyihui, 海外聯誼會

Hanwudi, 漢武帝

Heshan, 鶴山

Hu Wenhu, 胡文虎
　　(Aw Boon Haw)

huagong, 華工

huamin, 華民

huaqiao weiyuanhui, 華僑委員會

huaqiao xuexiao, 華僑學校

huaren, 華人

huashang, 華商

Huaxian, 花縣

Huian, 惠安

Huidong, 惠東

huiguan, 會館

Huiyang, 惠陽

Huizhou, 惠州

hun, 魂

Jiangmen, 江門

Jiaoling, 蕉嶺

Jiedong, 揭東

Jieyang, 揭陽

Jinjiang, 晉江

jizu, 祭祖

junzi, 君子

Kaiping, 開平

kai zuzhaimen, 開祖宅門

kejia, 客家

kenqin dahui, 懇親大會

kuixinggong (M), 魁星公

kway sin gong (H), 魁星公

laojia, 老家

li, 禮

Lianjiang, 連江

ling, 靈

lingwu, 靈屋

Longhai, 龍海

Longyan, 龍岩

luoye guigen, 落葉歸根

Meizhou, 梅州

Meixian, 梅縣

min, 閩

mingong, 民工

Nanhai, 南海

Nanjin, 南靖

neijiu, 內疚

Panyu, 番禺

Pinnan, 屏南

po, 魄

Puning, 普寧

Putian, 蒲田

qiaojuan, 僑眷

qiaoqin, 僑親

qiaoqing, 僑情

qiaowubu, 僑務部

qiaoxiang, 僑鄉

qing jinlai, 請進來

Qingyuan, 清遠

Quanzhou, 泉州

ren, 仁

renjian, 人間

sangli, 喪禮

sanlai yibu, 三來一補

Sanshui, 三水

Sanyi huiguan, 三邑會館

sanzi, 三資

sanzi qiye, 三資企業

shanghui, 商會

Shantou, 汕頭

Shaoan, 詔安

shehui mingwang, 社會名望

shetuan lianyihui, 社團聯誼會

Shiji, 《史記》

Shishi, 石獅

Shouhui, 受賄

shunde, 順德

Sima qian, 司馬遷

Sishui, 四水

Siyi, 四邑

Siyi huiguan, 四邑會館

Siyi shanggong zonghui,
　　四邑商工總處

Taishan, 台山

tanwu, 貪污

tianchao qimin, 天朝棄民

tieguanyin, 鐵觀音

Tongan, 同安

tongbao, 同胞

tongxiang hui, 同鄉會

tongxiang zonghui, 同鄉總會

tudigong, 土地公

wulong, 烏龍

Wuyi, 五邑

Wuyi gonghang zonghui
　　五邑工商總會

yinshui siyuan, 飲水思源

Yongding, 永定

Yuanxiaojie, 元宵節

xiahai, 下海

Xiamen, 廈門

xiang, 鄉

xiangqin lianyihui, 鄉親聯誼會

Xiangshan, 香山

Xianyou, 仙游

xiao, 孝

xiaojing, 孝經

xiezu, 謝祖

xiezu juanding yishi
　　謝祖涓丁儀式

Xinhui, 新會

Xinning, 新寧

xisi, 細絲

xixian, 細線

xuetong guanxi, 血統關係

yang, 陽

yangjian, 陽間

yangqi, 陽氣

yin, 陰

yinjian, 陰間

Yongchun, 永春

youhun, 游魂

Zengcheng, 增城

Zhangzhou, 漳州

Zhanjiang, 湛江

Zhaoqing, 肇慶

Zhonghua dahuitang lianhehui
　　中華大會堂聯合會

zhongqiujie, 中秋節

Zhongshan, 中山

Zhuhai, 珠海

zong, 宗

zongli yamen, 總理衙門

zongqin hui, 宗親會

zongtang, 宗堂

zou chuqu, 走出去

zuo fengshui, 做風水

zuzhai, 祖宅

LIST OF CONTRIBUTORS

JOSEPH YU-SHEK CHENG is chair holder of Political Science and Director of Contemporary China Research Centre, City University of Hong Kong. He is the founding editor of the *Hong Kong Journal of Social Sciences*. His research interests comprise political development in China and Hong Kong, Chinese foreign policy and local government in southern China. His recent publications include *The Other Hong Kong Report 1997*, *China in the Post-Deng Era* and *China Review 1998*.

STEPHANIE PO-YIN CHUNG was born and educated in Hong Kong. She obtained her doctoral degree from the University of Oxford in 1995. She is now assistant professor of the Department of History at the Hong Kong Baptist University. Her major interest is focused on the social and economic development of South China. Her doctoral thesis, entitled *Chinese Business Groups in Hong Kong and Political Changes in South China* was published by Macmillan (London) and St. Martin (New York) in early 1998.

LEO DOUW is a lecturer in Modern Asian History at the University of Amsterdam and the Free University Amsterdam. His research is concerned with the twentieth century intellectual history of China, on which he wrote his Ph.D. (1991), and with the impact of ethnic Chinese transnational investment on the society and politics of South China. He is a director of the IIAS research programme on International Social Organization in East and Southeast Asia: *Qiaoxiang* Ties during the Twentieth Century.

MICHAEL R. GODLEY, who recently retired from Monash University, Australia, was trained in Chinese politics and Asian history. His publications include *The Mandarin-Capitalists from Nanyang: Overseas Chinese Enterprise in the Modernization of China* (Cambridge University Press, 1981) and several dozen chapters, articles and essays. He has been a visiting fellow at the Contemporary China Centre at the Australian National University, the Center for Chinese Studies, Berkeley, the East Asian Program at Cornell University and the International Institute for Asian Studies, Leiden. At present, Dr Godley is a visiting fellow in the Centre for the Study of the Chinese Southern Diaspora at the ANU.

HUA LINSHAN is a historian associated with the Center for Studies on Modern and Contemporary China in Paris (CNRS/EHESS). He is the author of *Les annees rouges* (The Red Years) Paris, Seuil, 1987, an account of the Cultural Revolution in Guangxi province. His specialized fields also include social change in the Chinese countryside and he has co-authored *Enquête socioloque sur la Chine, 1911-1949* (A Sociological Study of China, 1911-1949) with Isabelle Thireau, a study of his own lineage located in Taishan county (Guangdong province), one of the main points of departure of overseas Chinese.

CEN HUANG is currently a research fellow at the International Institute for Asian Studies, Leiden. Her research project is concerned with the structure and social organization of overseas Chinese invested enterprises in South China with a special focus on cultural aspects of transnational managers and migrant workers. She has done extensive fieldwork in South China in the past two years and has published widely on the research topic. Dr Huang has also been a research consultant and lecturer in comparative education, cross-cultural studies, and Chinese studies in Canada and the Netherlands.

KHUN ENG KUAH is currently teaching Anthropology at the Department of Sociology, University of Hong Kong. Her main research areas include: Overseas Chinese and Emigrant Village (*Qiaoxiang*) connections. She has recently completed a manuscript on this topic: *Religion and the State*, in which she has published numerous articles on the topic and she is also currently working on a book-length manuscript on this topic; Women and Politics comparing Hong Kong, Taiwan, and Singapore; and Dialect Associations and Chinese Chambers of Commerce: Globalizing Roles.

HONG LIU (Ph.D. 1995) is assistant professor at the Department of Chinese Studies and assistant director, Center for Research in Chinese Studies, National University of Singapore. His research interests include the Chinese Diaspora in Southeast Asia and the Sino-Indonesian relationship in the post-1945 era. He has done research in China, Southeast Asia, Japan, the Netherlands, and the United States and is the author of more than twenty articles and book chapters, which appear in journals such as *World Politics*, *The China Quarterly*, *Journal of Southeast Asian Studies*, and *Indonesia*. He is currently directing a research project on Chinese business and socio-political change in post-1945 Singapore.

KING-LUN NGOK is currently a demonstrator at the Department of Public and Social Administration, City University of Hong Kong where he just obtained his Ph.D. He received his BA and MA from Renmin University,

Beijing. His major research areas are labour relations, labour system reform, and social policy in China. His Ph.D. thesis is on the formulation process of China's labour legislation.

DAVID SCHAK (Ph.D. Anthropology, California-Berkeley, 1973) is a senior lecturer in Modern Asian Studies and Head of the Taiwanese Studies Unit at Griffith University, Australia. He first went to Taiwan in 1959 and has since spent nine years there, mostly as a field researcher. He has published on dating as a new method of mate selection, poverty and welfare recipients, beggars, and general social change. For the past six years his research has focused on Taiwanese/Chinese business culture and practice, and he has carried out field research on Taiwanese entrepreneurs in both Taiwan and China.

ELIZABETH SINN is Associate Professor and Deputy Director of the Centre of Asian Studies at the University of Hong Kong. Her area of research is Modern China with a focus on Hong Kong history, and the migration of Chinese overseas. She is the the the author of *Power and Charity: The Early History of the Tung Wah Hospital*, Hong Kong (1989) and *Growing with Hong Kong: The Bank of East Asia 1919-1994* (1994). Her recent volumes include *Between East and West: Aspects of Social and Political Development in Hong Kong* (1990), *Hong Kong Culture and Society* (1995) and *The Last Half Century of Chinese Overseas* (1998). Articles she has published include 'Xin Xi guxiang: A Study of Regional Associations as a Bonding Mechanism in the Chinese Diaspora, *Modern Asian Studies* 31:2 (1997) 375-98, 'Fugitive in Paradise: Wang Tao and Cultural Transformation in Late 19th Century Hong Kong', *Late Imperial China* 19:1 (June 1998) 56-81.

ALAN SMART (Ph.D. University of Toronto) has conducted research in Hong Kong since 1982 and in China since 1987. His research has concerned the clearance of squatter areas in Hong Kong, the history of housing and development in Hong Kong, and the operation and impact of Hong Kong-run enterprises in Guangdong province, China. Publications include *Making Room: Squatter Clearance in Hong Kong* (Hong Kong: Centre of Asian Studies, 1992) and articles in a variety of journals including *International Journal of Urban and Regional Research*, *Cultural Anthropology*, *Critique of Anthropology*, *Society and Space*, *City & Society*, and the *International Journal of the Sociology of Law*, plus contributions to a variety of edited volumes.

ISABELLE THIREAU is a sociologist of the French National Centre for Scientific Research (CNRS), presently teaching at the Department of Sociology of the Chinese University of Hong Kong. Her area of research and interest is the emergence of new forms of agreements and social norms in China after the economic reforms. Her publications include *Enquête socioloque sur la Chine, 1911-1949* (A Sociological Study of China, 1911-1949), French University Publishers, 1996, a study of the evolution of a lineage located in Guangdong province during the first half of the century which received the Drouin de Lhuys award from the French Academy of Moral and Political Sciences in 1997.